D0097926

Social Support and Health

Social Support and Health

Edited by

SHELDON COHEN

DEPARTMENT OF PSYCHOLOGY
CARNEGIE-MELLON UNIVERSITY
PITTSBURGH, PENNSYLVANIA

S. LEONARD SYME

SCHOOL OF PUBLIC HEALTH
UNIVERSITY OF CALIFORNIA
BERKELEY, CALIFORNIA

1985

ACADEMIC PRESS, INC.
Harcourt Brace Jovanovich, Publishers

Orlando   San Diego   New York
Austin   Boston   London   Sydney
Tokyo   Toronto

ACADEMIC PRESS, INC.
Orlando, Florida 32887

United Kingdom Edition published by
ACADEMIC PRESS INC. (LONDON) LTD.
24–28 Oval Road, London NW1 7DX

Library of Congress Cataloging in Publication Data

Main entry under title:

Social support and health.

    Includes indexes.
    1. Social medicine. 2. Health. 3. Social interac-
tion. I. Cohen, Sheldon, Date   . II. Syme, S.
Leonard (Sherman Leonard), Date   . [DNLM: 1. Health.
2. Mental Health. 3. Social Environment. WM 31
S6787]
RA418.S649   1984   362.1'042   84-14586
ISBN 0-12-178820-2 (alk. paper)

PRINTED IN THE UNITED STATES OF AMERICA

      87 88   9 8 7 6 5 4 3 2

To
Harry and Ruth Cohen
and
to Marilyn

Contents

4 Supportive Functions of Interpersonal Relationships
Thomas Ashby Wills

5 Measures and Concepts of Social Support
James S. House and Robert L. Kahn

6 Causal Inference in the Study of Social Support
David Dooley

Part II Social Support through the Life Cycle

7 Social Support through the Life Course
Richard Schulz and Marie T. Rau

8 Social Support, Family Relations, and Children

W. Thomas Boyce

9 Social Support and Health in the Middle Years: Work and the Family

Stanislav V. Kasl and James A. Wells

10 Social Support and Health of the Elderly

Meredith Minkler

Part III Social Support and Disease Etiology

11 Social Support and Mental Health in Community Samples

Ronald C. Kessler and Jane D. McLeod

12 The Relationship of Social Networks and Social Support to Morbidity and Mortality
Lisa F. Berkman

13 Social Support and Styles of Coping with Stress
Susan Gore

Part IV Social Support Interventions and Health Policy

14 The Role of Social Support in Adaptation and Recovery from Physical Illness
Camille B. Wortman and Terry L. Conway

Contributors

Numbers in parentheses indicate the pages on which the authors' contributions begin.

ANDREW BAUM (327), Department of Medical Psychology, Uniformed Services University of the Health Sciences, School of Medicine, Bethesda, Maryland 20814

LISA F. BERKMAN (241), Department of Epidemiology and Public Health, Yale University School of Medicine, New Haven, Connecticut 06520

W. THOMAS BOYCE (151), Department of Pediatrics, Health Sciences Center, University of Arizona, Tucson, Arizona 85724

SHELDON COHEN (3), Department of Psychology, Carnegie-Mellon University, Pittsburgh, Pennsylvania 15213

TERRY L. CONWAY (281), Naval Health Research Center, San Diego, California 92138

DAVID DOOLEY (109), Program in Social Ecology, University of California, Irvine, California 92717

RAYMOND FLEMING (327), Department of Medical Psychology, Uniformed Services University of the Health Sciences, School of Medicine, Bethesda, Maryland 20814

SUSAN GORE (263), Department of Sociology, University of Massachusetts–Boston, Harbor Campus, Boston, Massachusetts 02125

BENJAMIN H. GOTTLIEB (303), Department of Psychology, University of Guelph, Guelph, Ontario, Canada N1G 2W1

ALAN HALL (23), Centre for Urban and Community Studies, University of Toronto, Toronto, Ontario, Canada M5S 2G8

JAMES S. HOUSE (83), Survey Research Center and Department of Sociology, University of Michigan, Ann Arbor, Michigan 48106

ROBERT L. KAHN (83), Institute for Social Research, University of Michigan, Ann Arbor, Michigan 48106

STANISLAV V. KASL (175), Department of Epidemiology and Public Health, Yale University School of Medicine, New Haven, Connecticut 06510

RONALD C. KESSLER (219), Department of Sociology, University of Michigan, Ann Arbor, Michigan 48106

CHARLES A. KIESLER (347), College of Humanities and Social Sciences, Carnegie-Mellon University, Pittsburgh, Pennsylvania 15213

JANE D. McLEOD (219), Department of Sociology, University of Michigan, Ann Arbor, Michigan 48106

MEREDITH MINKLER (199), Department of Social and Administrative Health Sciences, School of Public Health, University of California, Berkeley, California 94720

LEONARD I. PEARLIN (43), Human Development and Aging Program, University of California, San Francisco, California 94143

MARIE T. RAU (129), Institute on Aging, Portland State University, Portland, Oregon 97207; and Veterans Administration Medical Center, Portland, Oregon 97201

RICHARD SCHULZ[1] (129), Institute on Aging, Portland State University, Portland, Oregon 97207

JEROME E. SINGER (327), Department of Medical Psychology, Uniformed Services University of the Health Sciences, School of Medicine, Bethesda, Maryland 20814

S. LEONARD SYME (3), Program in Epidemiology, School of Public Health, University of California, Berkeley, California 94720

BARRY WELLMAN (23), Centre for Urban and Community Studies, University of Toronto, Toronto, Ontario, Canada M5S 2G8

JAMES A. WELLS (175), Department of Sociology, Washington University, St. Louis, Missouri 63130

THOMAS ASHBY WILLS (61), Department of Public Health, Cornell University Medical College, The New York Hospital–Cornell Medical Center, New York, New York 10021

CAMILLE B. WORTMAN (281), Institute for Social Research, University of Michigan, Ann Arbor, Michigan 48106

[1]Present address: Department of Psychiatry, Western Psychiatric Institute, University of Pittsburgh, Pittsburgh, Pennsylvania 15260.

Preface

The possible influence of social supports on health and health behavior has attracted the interest of psychologists, sociologists, anthropologists, epidemiologists, and other public health professionals. Seldom has such a diverse group of social and health scientists agreed on the importance of a single factor in promoting health and well-being. Unfortunately, this multidisciplinary interest has not resulted in a unified conceptualization of the meaning of social support, its role in health and health behavior, or even how to measure it. The purpose of this book is to address these issues, to organize and integrate the voluminous literature on social support and health, and to provide an interdisciplinary overview of this area of research.

This volume is intended as a guide for doing social support research, as a compendium of state-of-the-art work in this field, and as a source of information on the implications of existing work for social policy. We define social support as resources provided by others. Although this definition encompasses support provided by professional helpers, professional helping is not covered in this volume. Instead, we focus on nonprofessional (informal) social support provided by friends, relatives, and acquaintances.

The volume contains four parts. Chapters in the first part, "Issues in the Study of Social Support," provide a broad definition of social support, discuss major theoretical, methodological, and practical issues, and show the relationship of social support to research and theory in the areas of social networks and interpersonal relationships. There are separate chapters on measurement issues and statistical issues in support research, with an emphasis on research methods that allow causal inferences.

Chapters in the second part, "Social Support through the Life Cycle," provide special attention to the meanings and functions of social support at different times in life. Chapters in this part illustrate the varied nature and significance of such supports in infancy, childhood, adolescence, and adulthood and review the changing importance of family, friends, spouses, and children at different periods throughout the life cycle. Chapters in the third part, "Social Support and Disease Etiology," provide critical reviews and analyses of empirical and theoretical work on the relationship between support and the etiology, prevention, and treatment of disease. There are separate chapters dealing with the role of support in coping with stress and with the association between support and physical and mental illness. Chapters in the final part, "Social Support Interventions and Health Policy," examine the effectiveness of support interventions, discuss the role of the physical environment in support development and maintenance, and discuss the implications of the existing literature on social support for health policy.

This book is of special interest to the large interdisciplinary group of research professionals concerned with the role of psychosocial factors in both physical and mental health. It is also of special interest to practitioners involved in the increasing number of programs designed to support or establish natural helping networks. It is appropriate for use in upper division and graduate courses in psychology, sociology, epidemiology, and public health and could also be used in courses in education, social work, and other helping professions.

The interdisciplinary appeal of the book is strengthened by the choice of editors (a social-health psychologist and a social epidemiologist) and contributors from a variety of social and health science fields. Special emphasis was placed on selecting contributors whose analyses and reviews will be appreciated and understood across disciplines.

Existing books on social support primarily focus on community mental health, with a great deal of emphasis on community health interventions. Although community mental health is dealt with in the present volume, our emphasis is much broader. This volume is built around an interdisciplinary approach to studying the relationship between social support and both physical and mental health. There is an emphasis on mechanisms responsible for the link between support and health, issues and techniques in research methodology, and the role of social support for different age populations, as well as the implications of the present literature for health policy. Some recent and forthcoming edited volumes provide descriptions of specific research projects; the chapters in our book, however, consist of overviews and analyses of existing data and issues. That is, it is a handbook of social support rather than a collection of individual research projects and is thus intended to provide a description of current developments in this research area.

We did not instruct contributors to limit or focus the approach taken in the different chapters. The resulting diversity of perspective provides a special richness and allows the reader to identify findings and conclusions that emerge in spite of differences in definition of terms, measurement methods, populations studied, and disciplinary focus. Indeed, it could be argued that since such consistencies appear despite the diversity of approach, stronger support is provided for the conclusions reached than if these conclusions had followed a more unified research approach.

Contributors were, however, encouraged to write chapters in a form that would be appreciated and understood across disciplines; they were told to discuss the major issues in their topic area, the methodological and conceptual problems that arise in addressing these issues, and the state of our present knowledge. In most cases, we requested selective and representative reviews of the literature, with critical and analytic comment and, when appropriate, an overview of alternative theoretical approaches. We also asked that gaps in empirical and theoretical work be pointed out. If a strong theoretical position was taken, the author was asked to identify alternative points of view. These instructions were all given within the context of a fairly severe limit on chapter length.

We express our gratitude to the contributors to this volume, who persevered in the face of editorial onslaught and produced creative and well-written products in a relatively constrained time frame. The editors are indebted to Sharon Oddo for her aid in preparing the manuscript, to Esther Pryor for helping with typing, and to the staff of Academic Press for their support and professionalism.

PART I

Issues in the Study of Social Support

CHAPTER 1

Issues in the Study and Application of Social Support[*]

Sheldon Cohen and S. Leonard Syme

Introduction

Since the 1970s, there has been a dramatic increase of interest in the concept of social support as it affects health and well-being. This interest is reflected in an explosion of research as well as an increase in the number of treatment and intervention programs that use social support for therapeutic assistance. The phenomenon is especially remarkable because of the breadth of disciplines concerned with the concept—including anthropology, architecture, environmental design, epidemiology, gerontology, health education and planning, psychology, social work, and sociology.

This book provides a systematic and critical assessment of this outpouring of work, a guide for doing further research on social support and health, and a source of information on the implications of existing work for clinical practice and public policy. Our goal is to facilitate evaluation of what has been done, to identify gaps in knowledge, and to see more clearly what work yet needs to be done.

[*]The authors are indebted to Ron Kessler, Chuck Kiesler, Michael Scheier, Richard Schulz, and Teresa Seeman for comments on earlier drafts. Preparation of this chapter was in part supported by grants from the National Heart, Lung and Blood Institute (HL 29547 and HL 7365) and the National Science Foundation (BNS 7923453).

3

In an attempt to integrate a body of literature that includes multiple perspectives, definitions, and outcomes, we have adopted broad definitions of both social support and health. *Social support* is defined as the resources provided by other persons. By viewing social support in terms of resources—potentially useful information or things—we allow for the possibility that support may have negative as well as positive effects on health and well-being. In the same spirit of breadth, we have accepted the World Health Organization's definition of health as including physical, mental, and social well-being.

Since the meaning and significance of social support may vary throughout the life cycle, we have made an explicit effort to address the different types and functions of social support at different periods in life. Thus, we have paid special attention to the varying nature and importance of social supports during childhood and adulthood as well as to the changing roles of family, friends, spouses, and children at different points in the life cycle.

The purpose of this chapter is to place the book within a conceptual and historical context. We discuss the potential importance of support research, disciplinary differences in perspective, alternative mechanisms by which support may affect health, and focus on selected issues central to the study of social support and health.

Importance of Support Research

The increasing interest in the concept of social support among those concerned with health and well-being can be attributed to several factors. One is its possible role in the etiology of disease and illness. This is an especially important issue because of the difficulties we continue to have in understanding the causes both of noninfectious diseases (including coronary heart disease, stroke, cancer of various sites, mental illness, and arthritis) and infectious diseases where variations in host susceptibility are of critical etiological significance.

Another reason for the increasing attention being paid to social support is the role it may play in treatment and rehabilitation programs instituted following the onset of illness. The benefits of altering behavioral and emotional characteristics in such programs have been increasingly recognized. These changes often require that people stop doing things they previously have done and begin doing things they have not done before. Often, it is important that people accept new self-perceptions. While the value of supportive social relationships in promoting these changes has been assumed, it now needs to be assessed critically. This is of special importance as interest in self-help programs becomes more widespread.

A third reason for increased interest in the concept of social support is its potential for aiding in the conceptual integration of the diverse literature on psychosocial factors and disease. Since the 1950s, behavioral scientists have attempted to identify psychosocial factors that affect health and well-being. From this work has emerged a long list of factors that seem to be of importance. The length of this list is both encouraging and distressing. It is encouraging because it suggests that "something" about psychosocial functioning is of possible importance for disease etiology. It is distressing because of the seeming lack of a central theme in the diversity of findings. The concept of social support is attractive because it may provide an integrative explanation of these findings. Thus, many of these psychosocial factors may affect health and well-being primarily through their disruptive impact on social networks. For example, a considerable body of research has demonstrated a higher rate of disease among persons who have experienced job changes, job loss, residential moves, migration, and the death of a loved one. All of these events involve the disruption of existing social relations. The disruption of interpersonal relationships may also explain why those who are married have lower rates of disease than those who are single, widowed, or divorced and why those exhibiting type A behavior (and who tend not to invest the energy required to maintain close relationships with others) have higher rates of coronary heart disease. Conversely, the lower rates of disease often observed among members of religious groups (such as Mormons and Seventh-Day Adventists) and among women may also be seen as a reflection of enhanced social support in those groups.

Clearly, social support provides a parsimonious conceptual model for the diversity of psychosocial findings related to health. It is important, however, to recognize that with sufficient ingenuity and motivation, it is relatively easy to find consistent patterns of results using virtually any hypothesis. Such consistency, therefore, should be viewed with appropriate caution and skepticism. Nevertheless, a concept that can provide a meaningful and parsimonious integration of seemingly diverse findings is clearly worth careful study.

Models of Social Support as a Causal Factor in Illness and Health

Support has been implicated in the etiology of and recovery from both physical illness and psychological distress. Although there has been a tremendous amount of work attempting to establish the beneficial effects of support on health and well-being (see reviews by Broadhead *et al.*, 1983;

Leavy, 1983; Chapters 11 through 15 of this book), relatively little work has focused on *how* increased support improves health.

Etiology of Disease

During the last five years, there has been considerable interest in determining whether positive relationships between social support and health occur because support enhances health and well-being irrespective of stress level (direct or main effect hypothesis) *or* because support protects people from the pathogenic effects of stressful events (buffering hypothesis). (See Chapter 13 by Gore and Chapter 11 by Kessler & McLeod in this volume.) Although this issue is posed as if only one of these mechanisms is correct, recent research provides evidence for *both* direct and buffering effects of social support on health and well-being (see reviews by Cohen & Wills, 1984; Kessler & McLeod, chapter 11 in this volume). The direct and buffering processes may, however, be linked with different conceptions (and hence types of measures) of social support (Cohen & Wills, 1984; Reis, 1984; Thoits, in press). Direct effects generally occur when the support measure assesses the degree to which a person is integrated within a social network, while buffering effects occur when the support measure assesses the availability of resources that help one respond to stressful events.

It is our position that further emphasis on the comparison of the direct effect and buffering models will not significantly increase our understanding of how social support prevents illness and/or enhances health. Instead, future work should examine more specific hypotheses about how social support relates to various behavioral, emotional, and physiological mediators of health. Some specific hypotheses that provide possible explanations for the direct effect and buffering models follow.

The *direct effect hypothesis* argues that support enhances health and well-being irrespective of stress level. Such a direct benefit could occur as a result of the perception that others will provide aid in the event of stressful occurrences or merely as a result of integrated membership in a social network. The perception that others are willing to help could result in increased overall positive affect and in elevated senses of self-esteem, stability, and control over the environment. These psychological states may in turn influence susceptibility to physical illness through their effects on neuroendocrine or immune system functioning (Jemmott and Locke, 1984), or through changes in health-promoting behaviors (e.g., decreased cigarette smoking, decreased alcohol use, and improved diet or exercise patterns). Membership in social networks may also result in increased senses of predictability, stability, and control because they provide the opportunity for regularized social interaction and the concomittant feedback that allows adoption of appropriate roles and behaviors (Cassel, 1976; Hammer, 1983; Hirsch, 1981; Thoits, 1983). Again, these psychological states may affect health through their influence on behavior and physiological response. Feedback and direction from others may also aid in the avoidance of life stressors that would otherwise increase the risk of both psychological and physical disorder.

In a sociological view of this process, Thoits (in press) suggests an alternative link between role involvement and health. According to this view, role relationships provide a set of identities, a source of positive self-evaluation, and the basis for a sense of control and mastery. Health is enhanced because role involvement gives meaning and purpose to one's life, and hence reduces the liklihood that profound anxiety and despair will be experienced.

In the extreme, the mechanisms just described suggest that support and health are linearly related; that is, an increase in support will be beneficial to health irrespective of the existing level of support. (See Broadhead *et al.*, 1983 for a review of evidence for such a gradient.) There is at least some evidence, however, that only very low levels of support are associated with decreases in well-being (cf. Berkman & Syme, 1979; House, 1981; House, Robbins & Metzner, 1982; Kahn & Antonucci, 1982). Hence, there may be some minimum threshold of social contact required for health maintenance, and increases above that level may be unimportant. These data also suggest an alternative causal model in which isolation (possibly acting as a stressor) causes ill health rather than support promoting better health (see Berkman, Chapter 12 in this volume).

In contrast to the direct effect model, the *buffering hypothesis* argues that support exerts its beneficial effects in the presence of stress by protecting people from the pathogenic effects of such stress. In this model, support may play a role at two different points in the stress–pathology causal chain (Cohen & McKay, 1984; Gore, 1981; House, 1981). First, support may intervene between the stressful event (or expectation of that event) and the stress experience by attenuating or preventing a stress response. In short, resources provided by others may redefine and reduce the potential for harm posed by a situation and/or bolster the ability to cope with imposed demands, hence preventing the appraisal of a situation as stressful. Second, support may intervene between the experience of stress and the onset of the pathological outcome by reducing or eliminating the stress experience or by directly influencing responsible illness behaviors or physiological processes. House (1981) suggested three ways in which support may alleviate the impact of the stress experience: Support may reduce the importance of the perception that a situation is stressful, it may in some way tranquilize the neuroendocrine system so that people are less reactive to perceived stress (Bovard, 1959; Cassel, 1976), of it may facilitate healthful behaviors such as exercising or attending to personal hygiene, proper nutrition, and sufficient rest.

Support and Symptom Reporting

Much social support research on disease etiology has focused on self-reported symptomatology rather than on clinical pathology. Evaluation of such research must include a caution regarding the use of self-reports of symptoms as "objective" measures of disease symptomatology. Awareness of internal sensations and reporting of symptoms do not necessarily represent an exact correspondence to actual physiological change. Symptom reporting is influenced by a variety of physiological, personality, social, and cultural factors (Mechanic, 1972; Pennebaker, 1982). Social support may affect symptom reporting by altering physiological states (pathology) as described earlier, or by affecting psychosocial factors. For example, support may influence perceptions of whether reporting more symptoms will elicit reinforcement or punishment from others. It may also affect self-image, which in turn influences what symptoms are encoded and reported. Although work on the effect of support on symptoms is interesting in its own right, symptom measures cannot be viewed as proxies for direct measures of clinical pathology. Evaluation of the association between social support and disease must therefore include further research using more "objective" measures of pathology.

Recovery from Illness

A relationship between social support and recovery from physical illness may be mediated by the effects of support on health behavior and/or the mobilization of the immune system. In the case of health behaviors, information from others about proper health care and about coping with illness may influence perceived and actual ability to affect health status. Instrumental aid, such as nonprofessional patient care, may also have a direct impact on the patient's well-being, and information about the esteem in which a person is held by others may influence motivation to get well and consequently increase compliance with medical regimens and performance of health care behaviors. Feelings of belonging, elevated self-esteem, and security engendered by social support may also directly aid in recovery from physical illness by facilitating mobilization of the immune system (Jemmott & Locke, 1984). Support-induced elevations in self-esteem, ability to cope, and motivation to get well may similarly aid in recovery from mental health problems by directly influencing emotional and cognitive states

associated with the disorder or by increasing compliance with medical regimens.

It is likely that the role of social support in both etiology and recovery
are, to some degree, similarly mediated. In both cases, support may influence health through the promotion of self-care and immunologic competence. Future work should focus on these mediators and on the emotional
and psychological states that trigger these mechanisms. This work should
also recognize that support is a complex concept that can only be understood when research is designed to investigate specific conceptions of support that are theoretically linked to the processes under consideration.

Issues in the Study and Application
of Social Support

This volume contains over a dozen chapters that include detailed discussions of both conceptual and methodological issues as they apply to multiple settings, multiple age groups, and multiple perspectives. It is beyond
the scope of this chapter to provide a thorough or even a representative
preview of these issues. Instead, our goal is to highlight some issues that
we view as important across disciplines and across perspectives. In general,
we raise conceptual and methodological questions and suggest alternative
approaches but do not provide answers.

Issues Related to a Contextual Perspective

One of the attractive aspects of studying the role of social support in
health and health maintenance is its seemingly simple, magic-bullet-like
quality. Unfortunately, but predictably, this simplicity is more illusion than
reality. An adequate (predictive) model of the relationship between social
support and well-being must consider individual differences in need or desire for such support, as well as the social and environmental contexts in
which support is perceived, mobilized, given, and taken. Following are some
of the questions that a realistic conception of the support process must
address (cf. House, 1981; Pearlin, Chapter 3 in this volume). Our intent here
is not to define a list of variables to be included in every study of support,
but rather to indicate the complexity of the process, to suggest a range of
theoretical issues, and to provide a list of issues that may be critical in the
design of successful interventions. The emphasis here is on the buffering
model; that is, support as a resource to aid in response to stressful events.

However, a number of the issues we raise are also relevant to the direct effect model.

Who is providing the support? The same resource may be acceptable from one giver but unacceptable from another. Roles of the giver and receiver, norms for these roles, and issues of the perceived equity, reciprocity, and appropriateness of the transaction are all relevant in determining if a supportive behavior from a particular giver will have a positive impact. For example, a person overwhelmed by job demands may be more affected by support from a co-worker or supervisor who has relevant information about the situation than by support from a nonjob friend or a spouse.

What kind of support is being provided? The specific resource that is provided may or may not beneficially affect well-being, depending on its appropriateness for the situation and person. For example, a monetary gift or loan may be invaluable in the face of unemployment and worthless in the face of bereavement.

To whom is the support provided? Characteristics of the recipient that may be important in determining the effectiveness of a supportive behavior include personality, social and cultural roles, and resources available to the receiver from alternative sources. The recipient's ability to attract, mobilize, and sustain support is also critical to the support process.

For which problem is support provided? The appropriateness of a specific kind of social support may be dependent on a match between the type of support offered and the type of problem encountered. For example, marital conflict, unemployment, and bereavement may elicit very different support needs.

When is the support provided? Social support that may be optimally effective at one point may be useless or even harmful at another. Consider, for example, the course of the need for support for self-esteem elicited by job loss. Workers who lose their jobs when a plant closes may attribute their loss to the economy or poor plant management and not suffer any initial threat to self-esteem. However, after several months of unemployment they may start to question their self-worth. At this point, support for self-esteem may become crucial.

For how long is support provided? Although many networks function well in providing short-term aid, long-term provision of support may place demands on a network that are beyond its capacity. The ability of givers to sustain support and/or change the kinds of support offered over a prolonged period is central to questions about the role of support for the chronically ill or those suffering long-term stress.

What are the costs of giving and receiving support? The cost of giving and receiving support and perceptions of these costs can be critical in determining whether it is asked for, whether it is given, and the impact of support-giving on the relationship between giver and receiver. It is likely that perceptions of support availability, often measured by support scales, are strongly influenced by the respondents' estimates of the cost of giving and whether they can "afford" to solicit such support.

How do these various issues interact in determining support level? An adequate model of support must recognize the complex interactions of the various factors just discussed. For example, the availability of long-term support is likely moderated by the roles of persons providing the support. Thus, the obligations of spouse and family to provide support over prolonged periods may make these sources more stable in long-term situations than are friends, acquaintances, and fellow workers. This relationship can be further complicated when one considers the kind of support being provided. Hence, an acquaintance at work might lend money for a short period but provide self-esteem support for a long period, whereas a family member may lend one money for a long period but provide support for self-esteem over only a short period. Clearly, a thorough understanding of the support process requires further conceptual and empirical consideration of the questions just raised and of the complex means by which these factors are related to one another.

Structural versus Functional Perspectives

The support process has been studied from two rather different perspectives. The issue is whether support is conceptualized in terms of the *structure* of an interpersonal relationship or social network or in terms of the *functions* that a relationship or network serve. The choice of perspective has a striking effect on the way a researcher studies support since each requires a different kind of support measure (see House & Kahn, Chapter 5 in this volume). Structural measures describe the existence of and interconnections between social ties (e.g., marital status, number of relationships, or number of relations who know one another). Functional measures assess whether interpersonal relationships serve particular functions (e.g., provide affection, feelings of belonging, or material aid). Although conceptually the issue of whether a measure is structural or functional is not necessarily tied to whether it is objective or subjective, practically the objectivity–subjectivity and structural–functional dimensions have been confounded. Structural measures (although mostly self-report) are generally considered to measure objective characteristics of social networks, while functional measures generally ask persons about their perceptions of the availability or adequacy of resources provided by other persons. (To our knowledge there is no existing research in which investigators objectively determined the availability of existing resources.

What can be learned from investigating "objective" support structures?
Because these measures are objective, they provide information about
properties of networks around an individual, independent of personal characteristics (Hammer, 1983). Structural indices of social integration that include number of contacts with family, friends, and community, as well as
number of active memberships in formal and informal groups, provide
measures of embeddedness in a social system. As discussed earlier, being
embedded in such a system implies that one receives the feedback from
others that helps form self-identities and feelings of stability, predictability,
and control over individuals' lives. Individual characteristics of network
structure (e.g., marital status, number of network members, network density) can be used to determine whether various quantities and forms of
social contact influence health. Structural measures also allow investigation
of the effects of support defined in terms of the characteristics of networks
in a group or society in addition to those at an individual level (see Hall &
Wellman, Chapter 2 in this volume). Hence they can be used to specify the
social characteristics of groups having higher (or lower) rates of disease
than others.

Structural measures (individual or group) should not be viewed as proxies for measures of available resources. For example, a spouse may be a
source of support but may instead, or also, be a source of conflict and
stress. Having more social contacts not only provides more potential resources but also may create additional demands on time and increase the
probability of interpersonal conflicts.

What can be learned from investigating "subjective" support functions?
Subjective–functional measurement helps to tap individuals' psychological
representations of their support systems. Since perceptions of support resources are affected by personal and environmental characteristics other
than objective network structure, these representations may or may not
be correlated with structural measures. Subjective–functional instruments
are used in testing theories of the support process that emphasize the role
of perceived (as opposed to objectively available) resources in determining
whether support will affect health (see Cohen & McKay, 1984). To the degree that the relationship between support and health is mediated by psychological representations of available support, as opposed to objective
structural relations, functional measures would be expected to provide better predictors of health and health behavior.

Measurement of multiple independent support functions can also help
determine the particular resources that affect health and behavior and
hence shed light on the mechanisms linking social support to health. For
example, Schaefer, Coyne, and Lazarus (1981) found that instrumental support was more important than either informational or emotional support

in predicting depression in older persons. Seeman (1984) similarly found that greater instrumental support from family and friends, but not emotional support, was associated with less coronary artery disease. Such results suggest the possibility that the provision of services, financial aid, and so forth helps persons avoid stressful situations that may increase the risk of depression and/or CAD. On the other hand, studies of support functions that protect college students from the potentially pathogenic effects of stressful life events find that instrumental support is not an effective buffer, while informational and emotional support are effective (see Cohen, Mermelstein, Kamarck & Hoberman, in press). In short, measurement of multiple support functions can help isolate potentially operative mechanisms. Moreover, these mechanisms may differ across populations and situations.

Unfortunately, there is little systematic work characterizing network structures in terms of the functions that they normally provide. An increased understanding of structure–function relationships would help integrate existing literature and facilitate the development of effective interventions, since undoubtedly certain network structures are more effective sources of certain functions than others.

Kinds of Social Support

We believe that further advances in the ability to conceptualize and assess the *kinds of support being provided* are necessary before it will be possible to understand the support process and realize its clinical possibilities. In order to assess, manipulate, or intervene with the appropriate kind of social support, a typology that categorizes interpersonal resources into classes that are relevant to the support process is required. This is easily said, but the task is not easily accomplished. Various typologies of supportive behaviors or acts have been proposed by Antonucci and Depner (1982), Barrera and Ainlay (1983), Caplan (1979), Cohen and McKay (1984), Gottlieb (1978), Henderson (1977), House (1981), Moos and Mitchell (1982), Kaplan, Cassel, and Gore (1977), Shumaker and Brownell (in press), Silver and Wortman (1980), and Wills (Chapter 4) and Wortman and Conway (Chapter 14) in this volume.

As noted earlier, the multidimensional measurement of support functions is essential in determining the mechanisms by which support affects health and well-being. Type of support may be especially important in understanding when social support buffers the pathogenic effects of stress. Hence, buffering effects may occur only when the kinds of available support match the needs elicited by the stress a person is experiencing (Cohen & McKay, 1984). This issue is complicated somewhat in that, in many cases, multiple needs are elicited by the same stressor and needs may shift over the course of the stress experience. Consider, for example, the role of the various sources of support following the death of a spouse. If the spouse provided a significant portion of the family income, then material support would be relatively more important. Information about the meaning of the loss may operate in terms of evaluating ability to cope. Emotional support may be operative in terms of convincing bereaved persons that there are still people who care. The need for each of these kinds of support may shift over the course of the bereavement period. For example, the need for informational support may come into play first, with needs for emotional support and material aid becoming important as the bereavement progresses.

As alluded to earlier, work investigating the impact of different kinds of support is in its infancy. Our purpose is not to offer any conclusions regarding the important categories of support, but rather to emphasize the importance of the development and use of representative typologies in solving the support puzzle. Understanding which supportive acts cause direct and/or buffering effects on health is especially important for planning interventions, since an efficient and powerful intervention would attempt to provide the kind of support most likely to be beneficial.

Measuring Social Support

Anyone attempting to review research on the relationship between social support and health faces the problem of trying to integrate a literature that has almost as many measures as studies. There are few or no data available on the psychometric qualities of most of these measures or on their relationships to one another. The development of sophisticated psychometric support instruments is imperative for further understanding of the support process. Scales that have demonstrated discriminative validity (e.g., are not highly correlated with social anxiety, personal competence, and social desirability) permit increased confidence that researchers are assessing social support and not some related personality factor. Moreover, internal and test–retest reliabilities allow increased accuracy in estimating the relationship of social support to various outcomes.

In addition to psychometric qualities, it is important to consider the method of choosing or designing an appropriate scale. It is no longer useful merely to use the available support measure or the one that worked for someone else. Support measures must be chosen (and designed) because they are tools to answer specific questions. Before selecting a scale, it is important to conceptualize clearly *what* about the support process one wants to learn from a study. Instruments differ on multiple dimensions, including whether they assess (1) structure or function, (2) subjective or objective support, (3) availability or adequacy of support, (4) individual structures or functions or global indices, (5) several individual structures or functions versus simply one, (6) the role of persons providing support or simply whether support is available, and (7) the number of persons available to provide support or simply the availability of support (irrespective of the number of people). It is worth reemphasizing that the appropriate measurement technique depends on matching the measurement instrument to the question being posed. Only through use of appropriate instruments will we be able to provide clear answers to our questions.

Assessing Processes Linking Social Support to Health

The chapters in this book review a growing literature that links social support to health. In general, there is fairly strong evidence for an association between support and mental health (Kessler & McLeod, Chapter 11) and for a link between support and mortality (Berkman, Chapter 12). The evidence is less convincing, however, regarding a relationship between social support and physical illness (Berkman, Chapter 12; Wallston, Alagna, DeVillis & DeVillis, 1983).

It is not known why social support is associated with health. The correlational nature of existing data makes causal interpretations difficult. But even if social support is a causal factor in the etiology of illness or the maintenance of health, existing data provide little evidence as to what underlies these links. It is our position that significant advances in the understanding of support–health relationships will occur only if future studies focus on the *process* by which support is linked to well-being instead of on determining merely whether a link exists. It must be asked whether the effects of social support on health and well-being are mediated by behavioral change, physiological change, perceptual change, or some combination of these three.

Questions to be answered include the following: Does social support enhance or inhibit health promoting behaviors? Does support influence the operation of the immune system or other processes that trigger and maintain physiological responses associated with disease etiology (e.g., release of catecholamines or corticosteroids)? Does support influence the occurrence of (or perception of) potentially stressful events or the abilities or perceived abilities to cope with such events? Decisions on ways to operationalize social support and to specify hypothetical intervening processes should be based on *theoretical conceptions* or the process by which support is related to the outcome under consideration.

Longitudinal–prospective designs in which biological and behavioral changes are continuously monitored provide a powerful tool to pursue these issues. The prospective emphasis on *changes* in health helps to exclude the possibility that results are attributable to an influence of health status on social support. Continuous monitoring of the variables under consideration allows a time-linked examination of the covariation of support, hypothetical mediators, and health. Moreover, longitudinal data permit investigation of the changes that occur in the processes linking social support to health as stressors and/or support needs persist over time (cf. Schulz & Rau, Chapter 7 in this volume).

An important issue in designing such studies is the time course of the development of a disease outcome. For example, although short-term changes in health-promoting behaviors may affect the etiology of a cold or the flu, such changes may be inconsequential in the course of a disease with a long developmental period, such as coronary heart disease. Hence, hypotheses regarding the link between support and illness must include consideration of the course of the diseases under study. In this light, it is worth noting that the lack of established relationships between social support and physical illness may be attributable to an insensitivity to the time course of disease etiology. In many cases, measures that assess social support at a particular point are compared with illness outcomes assessed at that same time or a short time later. These illness outcomes, however, may be determined by a process that spans a very long period.

Another critical issue in the design of prospective support research is the stability of support over the duration of the study. Measures of some conceptions of support, especially perceived availability, may fluctuate considerably over long periods. Moreover, for some populations, such as freshman college students and armed forces recruits, support will fluctuate as people are socialized into a new environment. In these cases, prediction from an initial assessment of support to an outcome occuring several years later would not provide a true prospective analysis. Hence, it is critical to consider the correspondence between longitudinal intervals and the stability of social support in the population under study when designing prospective support research.

Social Support and/or Personality?

There are two important questions regarding the role of personality in the relationship between social support and health. First, are there any effects of social support on health that occur above and beyond the effects of stable individual differences in sociability? This question addresses the possibility that social support is merely a proxy for personality factors, such as social competence and social anxiety, that are highly correlated with support. Second, does personality play a role in the need for, development of, maintenance of, and mobilization of social support? In this section, we emphasize the first issue, since it is critical to interpreting existing literature, but we also comment on the second issue.

Existing research on the relationship between social support and health is almost entirely correlational. Some prospective studies have attempted to exclude the possibility that reported associations are attributable to illness determining support levels; however, the possibility still exists that some stable individual difference factor accounts for changes both in social support and in health. For example, Heller (1979) has pointed to the possibility that social competence affects both support levels and well-being, and others have implicated feelings of personal control, social anxiety, and intraversion–extraversion. In addition to the scientific importance of the possibility that support measures are merely proxies for personality factors, as Kiesler (Chapter 17) has noted, this problem needs to be solved before social support research can affect public policy. In short, if the association between support and health is actually attributable to the influence of personality on both support and health, social support interventions would be fruitless.

The ultimate solution to this problem lies in experimental (intervention) studies in which persons are randomly assigned to support conditions (see Gottlieb, Chapter 15 in this volume). Intervention studies are imperative and those that are done with both theoretical and methodological sophistication will have an important impact on conceptions of the processes by which support affects health and well-being. However, these studies are expensive and difficult to carry out. The effectiveness of such manipulations depends on the appropriateness of the resources provided by the system, the interpersonal context in which those resources are made available, and whether persons perceive access to these resources in the way intended by the intervenor. In short, even if social support is causally related to health and well-being, proving it (and subsequently applying it) will require sophisticated methodological and clinical techniques. Despite the complexity of conducting intervention studies, the yield from such research is invaluable, and hence the extensive investment of time and effort is justified.

Although personality may provide a better explanation than support in some situations, it is likely that personality is not equally responsible for all sources and functions of social support. Research comparing multiple functions of support has found associations between support and well-being for some functions but not others, depending on the population and the situation (e.g., Cohen & Hoberman, 1983; Cohen et al., in press; Henderson et al., 1980; Schaefer et al., 1981; Seeman, 1984). If it is assumed that these various support functions are merely proxies for stable personality factors, different factors would need to be postulated for each kind of support. Although not impossible, this suggests that a single alternative personality factor explanation is probably invalid.

The second question raised earlier is whether personality plays a role in determining support levels. It would be naive to assume that the availability of support is determined totally by the social environment. Personality factors associated with sociability must play a significant role in the development of social networks, in the perceptions of support availability, and in the maintenance and mobilization of support (see Heller & Swindle, 1983).

It is also reasonable to expect that certain sources of support are less dependent on the supportee's personality than others. For example, personality is probably of relatively greater importance in making and maintaining friendships (kith) than in maintaining family (kin) ties, since support from kin often is viewed as an obligation implied by the relationship.

In sum, personality factors must be considered in the attempt to understand the relationship between social support and well-being. First, we need to examine the possibility that personality factors associated with sociability are primarily responsible for the relationships between social support and well-being that have been attributed to support-caused changes. There is suggestive evidence, however, that social support does play an important role—independent of personality—in this relationship. Second, we need to understand how personality factors influence the development and maintainence of support networks. In pursuing this issue, it is important to recognize that the roles of stable individual differences probably vary somewhat across situations and across sources of support.

The Individual versus the Group as the Unit of Analysis

The discussion so far has focused on research issues that derive from an approach viewing social support as a characteristic of individuals. In this view, individuals receive or give support to others under specific circumstances and with specific consequences. It is possible, however, to view social support as a characteristic of a group. One reason to adopt this perspective is the observation that rates of health and disease are patterned among social groups. Thus, while it is true that individuals get sick, it is also true that social groups exhibit consistent and patterned differences in rates of disease even though individuals come and go from them. For example, people in lower socioeconomic status groups have higher rates of virtually all diseases and disabilities than those in higher socioeconomic groups. Other such patterned and consistent differences in disease occurrence have been observed according to marital status, religious groups, occupation, and so on. Similarly, people living in particular states in the United States consistently have higher morbidity and mortality rates for virtually every disease than people living in other states. Further, this difference persists over time even as people are born, die, and migrate. Since these differences in disease rates persist over time in spite of individual movement in and out of groups, there must be some persistent characteristic of groups themselves that should be considered in studies of health and disease.

An individual perspective on social support addresses the question of why one person gets sick while another person does not. A social perspective addresses the question of why one group or aggregation has a higher rate of disease than another. Clearly, interventions to strengthen supports can also be viewed from both of these perspectives. Individuals can be helped to strengthen supportive interpersonal relationships, just as environmental or occupational circumstances can be changed to encourage a greater frequency of supportive relationships on a group-wide basis. The latter perspective is of particular value in dealing with diseases and conditions of enormous magnitude and where an individual approach is logistically difficult. Thus, it is probably more efficient to improve supportive relationships in a group of elderly nursing home residents by environmental intervention than by individual counseling. The issue here, of course, is not whether one approach is better than another but the usefulness of different approaches depending on their purpose.

Social Support and Disease Prevention

Is it possible to prevent disease by modifying the supportive characteristics of social environments? Theoretically, such interventions would be more cost effective than either treating disease after it occurs or, in the case of the buffering hypothesis, trying to reduce people's exposure to stressors (see Cassel, 1976). As Gottlieb (Chapter 15) has pointed out, interventions can be directed. at creating a new support system, strengthening an existing one, or training individuals in the social skills that would help them strengthen their own support systems.

Nonexperimental interventions—that is, interventions that are not being evaluated—are difficult to justify at this time. As noted earlier, there are plausible causal alternatives for correlational data linking support to health and well-being, and a lack of theoretically driven experimental interventions to clarify causality and direct intervention development. Kiesler (Chapter 17) has rightly argued that existing data are not sufficient to convince those forming health policy that social support interventions are an effective mode of health promotion. He has argued that not only is there a lack of intervention research that is adequate from a scientific perspective, but also a lack of evidence on the impact of social support interventions on variables critical to public policy decisions—impacts such as reduced incidence of disease, lower medical costs, and reduced mortality.

Conclusion

In the early years of research on a concept, the published evidence tends to be uniformly positive and enthusiastic. It is only after a concept has generated some credibility that the complexities and inconsistencies in the literature become issues. Enough evidence has now accumulated regarding the concept of social support that these issues are worth raising. We have provided an overview of some current problems and questions facing those studying and implementing the social support concept. The remainder of this book builds on these questions, assesses the current status of social support research, and plots a course for future research and practice.

We hope this book will provide a timely appraisal of the substantial body of work on social support that has accumulated. As noted earlier, we have deliberately emphasized a broad approach to the field so that common denominators could be observed. For this reason, we have defined the concepts of social support and of health and disease very broadly, we have included as diverse a disciplinary perspective as possible, and we have attempted to address the roles of social support in varied settings and circumstances.

It is our hope that the approach we have chosen will permit a critical assessment of the work that has been done as well as provide a guide for work that yet needs to be done. While the challenge is substantial, the possible benefits are equally great. Progress in understanding the meaning and significance of social support holds important promise for improving our understanding of the causes of disease as well as for improving clinical practice and enhancing policy decisions regarding the prevention and treatment of disease and disability. Clearly, this task deserves our best efforts.

References

Antonucci, T. C., & Depner, C. E. (1982). Social support and informal helping relationships. In T. A. Wills (Ed.), *Basic processes in helping relationships.* New York: Academic Press.

Barrera, Jr., M., & Ainlay, S. L. (1983). The structure of social support: A conceptual and empirical analysis. *Journal of Community Psychology, 11,* 133–143.

Berkman, L. F., & Syme, S. L. (1979). Social networks, host resistance, and mortality: A nine-year follow-up study of Alameda County residents. *American Journal of Epidemiology, 109,* 186–204.

Bovard, E. W. (1959). The effects of social stimuli on the response to stress. *The Psychological Review 66*, 267–277.

Broadhead, W. E., Kaplan, B. H., James, S. A., Wagner, E. H., Schoenbach, V. J., Grimson, R., Heyden, S., Tibblin, G., & Gehlbach, S. H. (1983). The epidemiologic evidence for a relationship between social support and health. *American Journal of Epidemiology, 117*, 521–537.

Caplan, R. D. (1979). Social support, person-environment fit, and coping. In L. A. Ferman & J. P. Gordus (Ed.), *Mental health and the economy*. Kalamazoo, MI: Upjohn, Institute for Employment Research.

Cassel, J. (1976). The contribution of the social environment to host resistance. *American Journal of Epidemiology 104*, 107–123.

Cohen, S., & Hoberman, H. (1983). Positive events and social supports as buffers of life change stress. *Journal of Applied Social Psychology, 13*, 99–125.

Cohen, S., & McKay, G. (1984). Social support, stress and the buffering hypothesis: A theoretical analysis. In A. Baum, J. E. Singer, & S. E. Taylor (Eds.), *Handbook of psychology and health* (Vol. 4). Hillsdale, NJ: Erlbaum.

Cohen, S., Mermelstein, R., Kamarck, T., & Hoberman, H. (in press). Measuring the functional components of social support. In I. G. Sarason & B. Sarason (Eds.), *Social Support: Theory, research and applications*. The Hague, Holland: Martinus Nijhoff.

Cohen, S., & Wills, T. A. (1984). Stress, social support, and the buffering hypothesis: A critical review. Unpublished manuscript, Department of Psychology, Carnegie-Mellon University, Pittsburgh.

Gore, S. (1981). Stress-buffering functions of social support: An appraisal and clarification of research models. In B. S. Dohrenwend & B. P. Dohrenwend (Eds.), *Stressful life events and their contexts*. New York: Prodist.

Gottlieb, B. H. (1978). The development and application of a classification scheme of informal helping behaviors. *Canadian Journal of Behavioral Science, 10*, 105–115.

Hammer, M. (1983). "Core" and "extended" social networks in relation to health and illness. *Social Science and Medicine, 17*, 405–411.

Heller, K. (1979). The effects of social support: Prevention and treatment implications. In A. P. Goldstein & F. H. Kanfer (Ed.), *Maximizing treatment gains: Transfer enhancement in psychotherapy*. New York: Academic Press.

Heller, K., & Swindle, R. W. (1983). Social networks, perceived social support and coping with stress. In R. D. Felner, L. A. Jason, J. Moritsugu, & S. S. Farber (Eds.), *Preventive psychology: Theory, research, and practice in community intervention* (pp. 87–103). New York: Pergamon Press.

Henderson, S. (1977). The social network support and neurosis: The function of attachment in adult life. *British Journal of Psychiatry, 131*, 185–191.

Henderson, S., Byrne, D. G., Duncan-Jones, P., Scott, R., & Adcock, S. (1980). Social relationships, adversity, and neurosis: A study of associations in a general population sample. *British Journal of Psychiatry, 136*, 574–583.

Hirsch, B. J. (1981). Social network and the coping process: Creating personal communities. In B. H. Gottlieb (Ed.), *Social networks and social support* (pp. 149–170). Beverly Hills, CA: Sage.

House, J. S. (1981). *Work stress and social support*. Reading, MA: Addison-Wesley.

House, J. S., Robbins, C., & Metzner, H. L. (1982). The association of social relationships and activities with mortality: Prospective evidence from the Tecumseh Community Health Study. *American Journal of Epidemiology, 116*, 123–140.

Jemmott, J. B., & Locke, S. E. (1984). Psychosocial factors, immunologic mediation, and human susceptibility to infectious diseases: How much do we know? *Psychological Bulletin, 95*, 78–108.

Kahn, R. L., & Antonucci, T. C. (1982). Convoys over the life course: Attachment, roles and social support. In P. B. Baltes & O. G. Brim (Ed.), *Life-span development and behavior.* New York: Academic.

Kaplan, B. H., Cassel, J. C., & Gore, S. (1977). Social support and health. *Medical Care, 15,* 47–58.

Leavy, R. L. (1983). Social support and psychological disorder: A review. *Journal of Community Psychology, 11,* 3–21.

Mechanic, D. (1972). Social psychologic factors in presentation of bodily complaints. *New England Journal of Medicine, 286,* 1132–1139.

Moos, R. H., & Mitchell, R. E. (1982). Social network resources and adaptation: A conceptual framework. In T. A. Wills (Ed.), *Basic processes in helping relationships.* New York: Academic Press.

Pennebaker, J. W. (1982). *The psychology of physical symptoms.* New York: Springer-Verlag.

Reis, H. T. (1984). Social interaction and well-being. In S. Duck (Ed.), *Personal relationships: Vol. 5. Repairing personal relationships.* London: Academic Press.

Schaefer, C., Coyne, J. C., & Lazarus, R. S. (1981). The health-related functions of social support. *Journal of Behavioral Medicine, 4,* 381–406.

Seeman, Teresa (1984). Social networks and coronary artery disease. Unpublished doctoral dissertation, University of California, Berkeley.

Shumaker, S., & Brownell, A. (in press). A social psychological theory of social support. *Journal of Social Issues.*

Silver, R. L., & Wortman, C. B. (1980). Coping with undesirable life events. In J. Garber & M. E. P. Seligman (Ed.), *Human helplessness.* New York: Academic Press.

Thoits, P. A. (1983). Multiple identities and psychological well-being: A reformulation and test of the social isolation hypothesis. *American Sociological Review, 48,* 174–187.

Thoits, P. A. (in press). Social support processes and psychological well-being: Theoretical possibilities. In I. G. Sarason & B. Sarason (Eds.), *Social support: Theory, research and applications* The Hague, Holland: Martinus Nijhoff.

Wallston B. S., Alagna, S. W., DeVellis, B. Mc., & DeVellis, R. F. (1983). Social support and physical health. *Health Psychology, 4,* 367–391.

CHAPTER 2

Social Networks and Social Support*

Alan Hall and Barry Wellman

Rediscovering Social Connections

Since the 1960s, social studies of health have participated in a major sociological event: the rediscovery of interpersonal ties. These relationships had not actually been lost, but social scientists, as well as the public at large, had lost track of them. Most people knew that they had abundant and useful ties with friends, relatives, neighbors, co-workers, and acquaintances, but they often believed that most others did not. They feared that such large-scale social changes as the growth of capitalism, bureaucratization, industrialization, urbanization, and accelerated technological change had eroded the broadly based intimate ties that traditionally formed the bases of interpersonal relations. Friendship, they believed, had become a residual relationship, little more than a game to be played in small groups.

Until the mid-1960s, social scientists continued to wonder if things had fallen apart in communities. Were interpersonal ties now likely to be few

*The research associated with this chapter has been supported by a Canada Health and Welfare fellowship to Alan Hall and research grants to Barry Wellman from the Social Sciences and Humanities Research Council of Canada (regular research grant and special aging program), the Joint Program in Transportation of York University and the University of Toronto, the U.S. National Institute of Mental Health (Center for Studies of Metropolitan Problems), and the Structural Analysis and Gerontology Programmes of the University of Toronto. Throughout, the Centre for Urban and Community Studies at the University of Toronto has been a sociable and supportive base.

in number, short in duration, and specialized in content? Did these ties
provide much help in dealing with acute or chronic problems? Had the
networks of these ties so withered away that those few that remained func-
tioned only as isolated relationships, rather than as integral parts of communities? Much writing on the subject suffered from the pastoral syndrome:
analysts nostalgically compared contemporary relationships to those in the
supposed good old days when villagers danced around maypoles, family
groups brought in the hay, and artisans whistled while they worked together.

Health care sociologists were as affected by this syndrome as those who
wrote about cities, families, workplaces, developing countries, and political
movements. Epidemiologists worried that those persons who lacked social
support from their few weak, specialized ties would both experience more
illness and suffer more seriously from its effects (e.g., Faris & Dunham,
1939; Jaco, 1954). Gerontologists feared that old age would bring further
disengagement from supportive relationships—a process heightened by the
alleged disappearance of stable, solidary communities (e.g., Cumming &
Henry, 1961).

These concerns that community had been lost have not stood up well to
the systematic data-gathering techniques of the 1970s and 1980s. A major
sociological industry has developed, devoted to discovering supportive relationships in cities and towns, bureaucracies and shops, rich countries and
poor, and among migrants, rioters, and suburbanites (see the review in
Wellman & Leighton, 1979). Health care sociologists have participated actively in this work, showing that these newly rediscovered ties do indeed
affect the experiencing of illness, the buffering of its effects, and the nature
of informal and formal health care (see reviews in Hammer, 1981; Mc-
Kinlay, 1980; Thoits, 1982).

It has become clear that if social scientists actually search for ties they
will find them. They will also find that such relationships provide supportive resources. Not only do such ties help people stay healthy, they also
play an important role in helping people deal with the pressures, opportunities, and contingencies emanating from large-scale social systems (e.g.,
getting a job, dealing with bureaucracies). Yet current knowledge of the
structure and functioning of small-scale interpersonal ties in large-scale divisions of labor is much like the terra incognita, or "unknown land," of early
mapmakers.

Until very recently, analysts have tended to see all interpersonal ties
as supportive and support itself as a global, unidimensional phenomenon.
Moreover, although analysts often talk about "helping" or "support networks," in practice they have often treated ties as discrete relationships
between two persons. Yet both common sense and data suggest that not

all ties are supportive, that support itself is not a single phenomenon (and perhaps not even a set of coherently related phenomena), and that the ways in which ties fit together in networks affect the nature of relationships between two individuals.

In this chapter we argue the advantages of social network analysis for describing systematically the composition, structure, and content of inter-personal ties in naturally occurring settings and for relating these network descriptions to the study of stress, social support, and other health care issues. Social network analysts have developed a battery of concepts and methods for studying how structures of relationships in social systems al-locate resources. The model provides powerful tools for getting beyond current surface descriptions of support systems to understand how the complexities of ties and networks affect health care. We first review the development of social network analysis from a sensitizing metaphor to its current paradigmatic approach to analyzing social structure. We then as-sess the state of social support research and suggest some ways in which the network analytic model may aid this work.

The Network Analytic Model

Development

Social scientists throughout the twentieth century have used the meta-phor of the social network to connote complex sets of relationships be-tween members of social systems (e.g., Radcliffe-Brown, 1940; Simmel, 1922/1955). Yet not until the 1950s did they begin to use the term system-atically and self-consciously to denote relationships that cut across the bounded groups (e.g., tribes, families) and social categories (e.g., gender, social class) traditionally used by social scientists to organize their data.

These network analysts defined a social network as a set of *nodes* that are *tied* by one or more specific types of *relations* between them. In most health research the nodes are individual persons, but they can just as easily be groups, corporations, households, nation–states or other collectivities. The ties are defined by the flow of resources from one node (or network member) to another. These resources can vary in *quality* (whether the tie provides emotional aid or companionship), *quantity* (whether it provides much emotional aid, frequent companionship), *multiplexity* (whether it pro-vides only emotional aid or both emotional aid and companionship), and *symmetry* (whether both parties to a tie exchange roughly equivalent amounts of emotional aid or whether the resource tends to flow only in one direction). Thus the criteria for including the nodes and ties that comprise a network are infinitely varied in principle, and researchers must designate the specific relations in which they are interested. For example, to study the influence of social class on health, researchers might want to include measures of power (e.g., control over the means of production), economic (e.g., landlord–tenant), and social (e.g., kin–friend) relations.

Network analyses focus on the characteristics of the patterns of ties between actors in a social system rather than on the characteristics of the individual actors themselves. Analysts search for regular structures of ties underlying often incoherent surface appearances and use their descriptions to study how these social structures constrain network members' behavior.

In many cases analysts do this by studying *whole networks,* all of the ties containing one or a few kinds of relation linking all of the members of a population. For example, a number of sociologists have analyzed interlocking corporate directorships (who sits on whose boards) to describe the structure of dominant institutions in Western industrial societies and to relate variations in these structures to variations in corporate profitability (see Berkowitz, 1982).

A basic strength of whole network analysis is that it permits a simultaneous view of both the social system as a whole and the parts that make up the system. This helps analysts to trace lateral and vertical flows of information, identify sources and targets, and to detect structural constraints operating on the flow of resources. Thus whole network analysis is directly applicable to the study of flows of clients, money, and personnel among health care agencies. Moreover, through manipulation of matrices representing who is connected with whom, it can discover densely knit clusters of heavily interconnected health care agents or find agents whose similar role relationships show up in a "blockmodel" (White, Boorman, & Breiger, 1976). Yet whole network studies are not always feasible because they demand complete lists of all members of a population and all of their ties. Indeed, prior specification of population boundaries may often be inappropriate, as when analysts want to discover the search pathways used by help-seekers (Erickson, 1978).

Hence, many analysts study egocentric or *personal networks* whose composition, structure, and contents are defined from the standpoint of a (usually large) sample of focal individuals. Investigators typically gather information about the networks' composition (e.g., the members' social class or gender), structure (e.g., which of the network members directly tied with a focal individual are also tied directly with each other), and contents (e.g., the flow of specific resources to and from the focal individual and network members). Such information not only provides data about dyadic ties (the two-person relationship between a focal individual and a network member treated in isolation) but also about the overall networks in which these ties are embedded: aggregate information about network composition (e.g., percent kin) and structural information about the arrangements of ties (e.g., clustering). Personal network studies lend themselves readily to large-scale survey research techniques, although investigators often must assume that respondents are accurate reporters of the relevant character-istics of their networks.[1] Investigators since Bott (1957) have developed a variety of measures to study both tie and network characteristics (Table 2.1; see also Mitchell, 1969; Mitchell & Trickett, 1980; Pilisuk & Froland, 1978).

The personal network approach is especially relevant to the study of social support because it focuses attention on how the properties of net-works affect the flow of resources to focal individuals. For example, not only do urban network studies describe the supportive resources available to city dwellers, they also show how such ties and networks affect the ways in which these individuals link up with the resources of larger-scale social systems (e.g., Fischer, 1982; Wellman, Carrington, & Hall, in press). Several search network studies (i.e., studies that trace the sequence of ties used to obtain particular resources) have shown how network properties affect the ways in which individuals seek and get jobs, social services, and other re-sources (e.g., Granovetter, 1974, 1982; Liu & Duff, 1972).

Some Basic Principles

While many investigators have continued to use network variables as additional explanations for the variance of otherwise conventional studies, a number of analysts have been working to interpret all social structure from within a broadly based network analytic model. Such analysts do not restrict their conceptualization of network nodes (or actors) to individual persons; relations among groups, organizations, and clusters of ties (treated as one node) have become an integral part of the model. These analysts no longer look just at friendship and kinship ties, they study how relations of power and dependency link together in stratified social systems.

The development of this comprehensive network analytic model has been influencing the ways researchers pose questions, collect information, and analyze data. Although the methods these network analysts use are often

---

[1]Several studies have shown that respondents underestimate the number of ties they have and the frequency of interactions with them (e.g., Conrath, Higgins, & McClean, 1983). It is not clear whether such problems affect validity and reliability more than the biases involved in respondent reporting of other forms of behavior and attitudes. It appears, as well, that respondents are more likely to forget less significant events.

Table 2.1

Some Measures of Tie and Network Characteristics

Characteristic	Measure
Ties	
Strength	The quantity of resources characterizing a relation
Frequency	The quantity of contact between two network members (i.e., the number of times a resource flows between the two)
Multiplexity	The number of different resources exchanged by two network members in a tie (i.e., the number of relationships between the two)
Duration	The length of time a tie or a relation has existed
Symmetry (reciprocity)	The extent to which resources are both given and received
Intimacy	The perceived social closeness (emotional attachment) of one network member by another
Networks	
Range (size)	The number of network members (nodes)
Density	The extent to which a network is interconnected overall by means of direct ties, measured by comparing the actual number of direct ties between network members with the number of ties that would exist if all members were directly connected
Degree	The extent to which a network member is tied directly to other network members
Boundedness	The proportion of all ties of network members that stay within the network's boundary
Reachability	The average number of ties required to link any two network members
Homogeneity	The extent to which network members have similar personal attributes (e.g., gender)
Cliques	Portions of networks in which all members are tied directly; has a density of 1.0
Clusters	Portions of networks with high density, but defined by less stringent connectivity criteria than cliques
Components	Portion of networks in which all members are tied directly or indirectly

different from those of mainstream sociologists, the real difference lies in four fundamental aspects of their analytic approach:

1. Network analysts set up analyses in terms of relations between actors instead of trying to sort actors into categories defined by the inner attributes (or essences) or these actors.
2. They interpret behavior in terms of structural constraints on activity instead of assuming that inner forces (e.g., socialization to norms) impel actors in voluntaristic, sometimes teleological, behavior toward a desired goal.

3. They interpret all dyadic relations in the light of the dyadic partners' additional relations with other network members.
4. They treat social structure as a network of networks that may (or may not) be partitioned into discrete groups, not assuming a priori that tightly bounded groups are the intrinsic building blocks of a social structure.[2]

Aggregated Categories and Relational Structures

Mainstream sociological studies have long relied on categorical analyses that treat social processes as the sum of individual actors' personal attributes and internalized norms. Yet their key assumption of unit independence, which makes their statistics so usable and powerful, detaches actors from social structures and forces analysts to treat them as disconnected masses. The analyst begins with actors as disconnected, independent units of analysis, groups them together into social categories (e.g., socioeconomic status) based on similarities in their attributes (e.g., education) and norms (e.g., working class values), and then treats the resulting categories as structural measures.

This approach destroys structural information in the same way that centrifuging genes destroys structure while retaining information about composition. The boundaries of the social categories are defined ultimately by reference to the personal attributes of the individual actors and not by reference to the structural relationship of these actors to one another and to large-scale divisions of labor.

As a consequence, analysts are led away from studying how structural location in social systems allocates the possession and flow of scarce resources. They often interpret social behavior as emanating only from actors' common possession of norms and attributes. Because such analyses assume random network linkages, they cannot take into account the extent to which coordinating ties among members of the same category may be responsible for their similar behavior.

Thus the categorical approach leads to the treatment of inherently structural phenomena, such as social class and social isolation, as personal attributes, such as socioeconomic status and alienation (e.g., Turner & Noh, 1983). This in turn can lead analysts to discount the ways in which variation in control over their own labor power may affect poor people's behavior. They equate isolation with alienation (and perhaps depression) without taking into account the extent to which interpersonally isolated individuals use

[2]More extensive reviews of the contemporary network analytic approach appear in Berkowitz (1982), Burt (1980), and Wellman (1983).

resources from formal organizations or their households to control their own lives (e.g., Brown, Bhrolchain, & Harris, 1975).

It is easier to see what is wrong with categorical modes of analysis than to develop concepts and methods for analyzing social structure directly. Although ethnographic and archival accounts have been important since the early days of network analysis (see the reviews in Barnes, 1972; Mitchell, 1969), most methodological work has been quantitative, using measures derived from simple graph theory and matrix algebra to describe and analyze networks. Some analysts (e.g., Erickson, 1978) have defined populations relationally rather than categorically, tracing chains of network members. Others have manipulated matrices to identify clusters of densely knit ties within networks or used "blockmodels" to discover members of social systems with similar role relations (White *et al.*, 1976). Some analysts have begun using determinate mathematics (in preference to statistics) to model social structure (see Berkowitz, 1982). In general, studies of social support have continued to rely on a few similar measures of tie and network properties, integrating these with traditional statistical data bases (see, e.g., Mueller, 1980).

Norms and Structures

Network analysts try to avoid normative explanations of social behavior, arguing that such analyses do not take into direct account the ways in which structured access to scarce resources determines opportunities and constraints for such behavior. They criticize as nonstructural explanations that find social regularities when actors in the same social categories (having similar attributes) behave similarly in response to shared norms. Such analyses inherently treat social integration as the normal state, defining the relation of individuals to social systems "in terms of shared consciousness, commitments, normative orientations, values, systems of expectation" (Howard, 1974, p. 5).

For example, disengagement theory assumes that both the aged and others in their personal networks limit their ties in response to attitude shifts associated with the aged's retirement, reduced roles, and preparation for death (e.g., Cumming & Henry, 1961). Yet research has suggested that normative changes come after shifts in the aged's social relations, such as movement to a retirement home, loss of job, and illness or death of other network members. Moreover, many aged experience continuity in their relationships, some even obtaining more social support (see Marshall, 1980).

In contrast, network analysts treat norms as effects, not causes. They try to study regularities in how actors behave rather than regularities in beliefs about how they ought to behave. This leads to the study of how the structure of relations of exchange, power, and dependency allocates the flow of resources in a social system. It suggests that the study of social support could be aided by analysis of the social distribution of possibilities—the unequal availability of such resources as information, wealth, time, and emotional skills—and the structures through which network members have access to such resources.

Dyads and Structures

When analysts treat interaction between two persons as the basic relational unit of analysis (e.g., Berscheid & Walster, 1978), they make an implicit assumption that they can analyze ties adequately in structural isolation. This occurs in social support studies that assume the number of interpersonal ties is, by itself, an adequate predictor of social support (e.g., Evans & Northwood, 1979). Such studies see support as emerging from multiple duets with separate others.

In contrast, network analysts argue that the proper analytic project is "Tinkertoys" and not "Pick-up Sticks." For one thing, most ties do not exist or operate in splendid structural isolation. Our East York study (see Wellman, 1979), for example, found fully 81% of the respondents' interpersonal ties to be structurally embedded in mutual ties to third parties. (Indeed, 46% of the ties operated only as parts of larger network structures.) Such ties are to persons with whom the respondents must deal in their neighborhoods, kinship groups, friendship circles, or on their jobs—whether they are attracted to them or not. Although interpersonal attraction often affects the intensity and breadth of these ties, the ties themselves are a consequence of social structure and not their cause (Wellman, Carrington, & Hall, in press).

Network analysts point out that investigators cannot discover such emergent structural properties as coalition formation or clustering from the study of dyads. Yet the pattern of ties in a network can affect the flow of supportive resources through these ties (Hirsch, 1979). Moreover, the structure of networks can affect the extent to which individuals have indirect access to the supportive resources to which their tie partners are connected. We suspect, for example, that while densely knit, tightly bounded networks are structurally efficient for conserving existing resources, more sparsely knit, loosely bounded networks are more efficient for accessing new and more varied resources.

Groups and Networks

Some of the earliest network studies investigated the condition of African migrants from rural villages to urban industrial areas (see the reviews in Peil, 1981). Many mainstream social scientists feared that such migrants, cut off from traditional village and kinship groups, would become alienated and distressed in the modernizing cities (see Korhnhauser, 1968, on mass society). Yet analysts were able to show that such migrants maintained strong supportive ties within the cities (often cutting across traditional village and kinship boundaries) as well as back to their homelands. Their complex network structure gave them appreciable interpersonal support and helped them to operate within the demands of capitalistic, urbanizing, industrializing divisions of labor.

Thus the network model facilitates the study of ties that are not organized into discrete groups while permitting the discovery of networks that are bounded and densely knit enough to be considered groups. For example, this allows the analyst to look for social support among the more than 50% of North American strong interpersonal ties that stretch beyond neighborhood and kinship groups (see Fischer, 1982; Wellman *et al.,* in press).

Network analysts further caution that focusing on bounded groups oversimplifies descriptions of complex social structures into organizational trees, whereas it is the network members' crosscutting memberships in multiple social circles that weave social systems together. They point out that shifts in analysis from small-scale to large-scale systems can be facilitated by treating large-scale systems as networks of networks in which clusters of actors in small-scale (interpersonal) systems are treated as single nodes in large-scale (interorganizational) systems (Craven & Wellman, 1973). Such an approach could easily be used to study links among agents, agencies, and clients in health care systems (e.g., Liu & Duff, 1972; McKinlay, 1973, 1980).

The Uses of Network Analysis in Studying Support

Network as Formalism, Metaphor, or Mediator

As social network analysis has developed, social support analysts have increasingly turned to it to understand the nature of supportive ties and networks (see the papers in Gottlieb, 1981). The network approach has become especially important to investigators who want to predict the circumstances under which support is given. Yet even many of those analysts who start with support and want to predict its consequences for health have tried to use network analysis to understand the circumstances under which support occurs and the implications of such support for relations with interpersonal networks and larger-scale social systems. Although most of this work has focused on the provision of supportive resources themselves (e.g., Thoits, 1982), the network approach also seems applicable to studies of the ways in which support is perceived by recipients and givers (e.g., Tapping, 1983).

Yet while all social support analysts seem aware of network analysis, not all use it; and many of those who do use it do so in limited and programmatic ways. Many support analysts continue to rely on mainstream sociological and psychological variables, dealing with relationships between support and health in terms of individual differences (e.g., some persons can "cope" better with less support, some persons "know" how to get access to more support) and membership in social groups and categories (e.g., lower socioeconomic class males living in an urban setting are more likely to use tangible supportive resources; see *Journal of Community Psychology*, 1982). Although detailed critiques are lacking, several support analysts appear to view network analysis as too formalistically reductionist, that is, as seeking to explain the giving and experiencing of support solely in terms of the patterns of ties that link actors (e.g., Leavy, 1982; Turner, Frankel, & Levin, 1983). Such formalism is undoubtedly part of network analysis (e.g., Holland & Leinhardt, 1979), but it is a mistake to reject the broader network model because of one limited usage.

Some other support analysts laud the benefits of network analysis, but in practice tend to use it metaphorically.[3] Although they have translated their label from "support system" to "social network," their analyses ignore the battery of available concepts and methods. Such metaphoric usage tends to see social support as a single, unidimensional concept that defines both the social network and the social process operating through the network. The approach leads either to a vaccination model of support (an individual either has it or not as a defense against stress and strain) or to an additive model (the more ties, the more support).

However, many support studies have gone beyond such metaphoric usage (reminiscent of pre-1950s network analysis) to study how a variety of dyadic (tiewise) and structural (networkwise) characteristics of personal networks mediate "the effects of both personal variables (e.g., values, social competencies) and environmental variables (e.g., neighborhood socioeconomic level) on adaptation" (Hirsch, 1981, p. 165). Where support research originally focused solely on examining the effects (direct and buffering) of supportive resources on health, the network-mediating model takes the analysis one step further, asking an additional set of questions regarding the availability of support resources from others. Analysts using this sort of network model treat support as a set of contingent resources flowing through ties and networks, rather than as an inherent characteristic of ties and networks. They seek to identify the dyadic and structural characteristics of networks that are the major determinants of supportive resource flow (and use) to focal individuals—resources that either mediate the health ef-

---

[3] See, for example, Syrotuik and D'Arcy (1983), Turner, Levin, and Noh (1982), Wan (1982), and Young, Giles, and Plantz (1982).

fects of stressful life events and circumstances or provide direct health benefits (see Figure 2.1).[4]

Some network analyses of support have studied comparative populations, seeking to distinguish the personal networks of psychiatric (or ex-psychiatric) patients from those of "normal" populations. For example, Tolsdorf (1976) found that psychiatric patients had smaller, more kinship-based networks with fewer multistranded, reciprocal, and symmetric relationships (see also reviews in Mueller, 1980; Perrucci & Torg, 1982).

In contrast, community studies have sought to identify the phenomena within target community populations that best explain the distribution of health and well-being in those populations. For example, one Toronto study (Dellcrest, 1981) found that low-income mothers with sparsely knit networks were more likely to use formal support services (like health care professionals) and receive emotional support. Studies by Hirsch (1979, 1980) found that women with sparsely knit, multistranded networks adjusted better to stressful events. Such networks may provide a greater range of access to nonfamily roles and activities, allowing a less drastic reorganization of life-style when changes are required (see also Fischer, 1982; Kadushin, Ziviani, Roth, Martin, & Boulanger, 1980; Wellman, 1979).

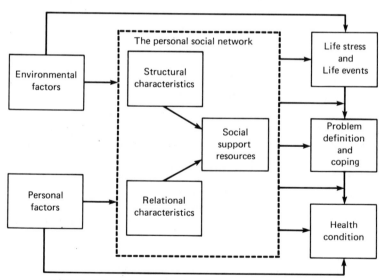

Figure 2.1.   The social network as a mediating construct.

[4]See reviews in Gottlieb (1981), Leavy (1982), Mitchell and Trickett (1980), Mueller (1980), and Pilisuk and Froland (1978).

Both the comparative and the community studies have contributed significantly to the analysis of social support by

1. debunking the assumption that integrated sets of social ties (i.e., densely knit networks) are necessarily related to access to more support and better health;
2. forcing the recognition that social ties can perform multiple functions, both positive and negative, with varying implications for health (see Wellman, 1984);
3. demonstrating that supportive aid can be understood in terms of network structures and compositional features;
4. indicating that any given network characteristic can have contradictory implications for access to social support and for health (e.g., strong ties may provide a good deal of direct emotional and material aid but they may restrict access to new information and exert greater pressure for conformity).

Network Analysis as a Structural Approach to the Study of Support

Although the application of network concepts and methods to health care research has been an important step, it is just a beginning step. For the most part, analysts have incorporated a limited set of network variables into a research strategy that essentially maintains the traditional astructural logic of mainstream sociology and social psychology. Yet the analytical power of network analysis lies in its distinctive structuralist approach to social behavior and social problems. We believe that the time is right for comprehensively applying this more broadly based network analytic model to the analysis of health care, informing the ways in which questions are posed, information is collected, and data are analyzed. Such a development would entail a threefold change in the ways health care analysts approach their research: defining nodes relationally, defining ties structurally, and taking structures seriously.

Defining Nodes Relationally

Many support studies look only at supportive ties, either assuming that all interpersonal ties are supportive or, more often, assuming that it is conceptually and methodologically more efficient to analyze supportive ties (e.g., McLanahan, Wedemeyer, & Adelberg, 1981; Wilcox, 1981). Yet such a strategy has important conceptual and methodological dangers because the distinction between support networks and social networks is more than semantic, even though analysts casually interchange the two terms.[5]

First, most persons have some ties which are not supportive, in whole or in part. Not only is there a large body of psychotherapeutic evidence for this, but social network studies themselves show that not nearly all ties are supportive. Thus, we have found that 18% of the East Yorkers' active ties do not supply any of 15 surveyed kinds of emotional aid, services, material goods, financial aid, or information (Wellman, 1984; see also Hammer, 1981; Mitchell & Trickett, 1980).

Second, looking only at support networks transforms support from a variable to a constant. A new a priori category—support—bounds the network. This precludes the study of the circumstances under which support may be given and limits analysts to looking only at the effects of support.

Third, it distorts analysis by wrenching supportive ties out of context. For example, it is unlikely that having five supportive ties has the same implications for one person whose active network consists of only these five ties than for another whose active network also includes five nonsupportive others. Such nonsupportive persons are not just neuters to be grieved over, but active network members linked to the support-givers and influencing their activities in a number of ways. Thus the support network is an analytic abstraction that too often does not reflect the ways in which social networks—even functionally specific parts of networks—operate.

Fourth, nonsupporters must be taken into account because they may be indirect sources of resources through their ties with other network members. This is often the case in job searches, where information about vacancies flows through chains of relationships (Granovetter, 1982). Nonsupporters may also influence the availability and use of support by acting as "network police," demanding conformity and restricting behavioral alternatives (e.g., Liu & Duff, 1972).

Fifth, the support network–social network distinction can affect the comparability of results. For example, support networks—inherently smaller in size and usually containing a higher proportion of intimates—are more likely to be densely knit. Yet analysts often compare inconsistent density findings with little reference to how the networks are defined (e.g., Killilea, 1982; McLanahan, Wedemeyer, & Adelberg, 1981).

Defining Ties Structurally

When analyses assume the existence of support, they implicity detach ties from networks because they make support into a personal attribute of

---

[5]The same basic argument can be applied to the reliance on networks defined by intimacy or closeness. The analytical advantages of network analysis are immediately confused by the narrow way in which the boundaries of the networks are drawn (see Hammer, 1981).

the dyadic other, rather than a set of resources this dyadic other has obtained through the larger social structure.

The network approach avoids such dyadic myopia by situating the specific ties within larger structures of relationships. This allows the study of social support as phenomena embedded within the power, influence, and communication channels of the social network, rather than as phenomena dependent on the interpersonal attraction of two persons who may or may not like each other. It leads to the definition of the contents of ties as strands of resource flows, leaving open the question of which resources are being conveyed instead of assuming that all ties convey a undimensional thing called "support." (Our East York study has found that ties are quite specialized in the supportive resources they convey, with clear distinctions between many of those ties that provide emotional aid, companionship, services, information, and financial aid, Wellman, 1984; see also Barrera & Ainley, 1983; Gottlieb, 1978). Moreover, by accepting that network members often have access to different kinds and quantities of resources, the network model handles unequal relationships routinely, encouraging analysts to conceptualize health processes in terms of the hierarchical, and sometimes stratified, nature of large-scale social systems. For example, our study has found that East Yorkers with different locations in the large-scale social structure (i.e., employed men, employed women, homemaking women) have networks with quite different compositions, structures, and contents (Wellman, 1985).

Taking Structures Seriously

Support analysts have tended to rely on simple measures of social structure, such as network size and density. Whereas having a large network does seem to bring more support, the effects of density on support and health are less clear. Unfortunately, this has led some (e.g., Aday & Anderson, 1975) to question the general utility of structural measures in explaining support processes.

Both network size and density are summary measures of overall network characteristics that do not take into account the structure of relationships within networks. Indeed, an exclusive reliance on density—ignoring the possibilities for structural complexity—essentially reproduces the same assumption network analysts had originally criticized: that an actor can only be treated as a member of a single group. For example, many of the East Yorkers' personal networks contain several densely knit clusters of ties, regions of more sparsely knit relations, one or two disconnected isolates, and a few dyadic ties (Wellman et al., in press).

Thus overall summary measures, such as density, are only pale and distorted reflections of those aspects of network structure that actually impinge directly on network members. Network analysts have developed many methods to make such microstructures identifiable and usable (see Burt & Minor, 1983), but such methods have been largely ignored in support analyses. It is disappointing that a field that has devoted so much attention to the proper description of support itself (see the papers in Sarason, 1984) should take so lightly the description of the ties and networks that bring such support.

Finally, it may be useful for support analysts to broaden their structural perspective and to treat personal networks also as partial views of whole networks, seen from the standpoints of focal individuals. When the personal network perspective is used, a system property, such as network size or density, becomes a personal attribute of the focal individual, just like gender.

The problem with relying on this strategy alone is that it reinterprets a system property, such as network density, in individual terms (Berkowitz, 1982). It uses an aggregative model of social structure in which structural properties are treated, more or less equally, as elements in a system that can be arranged along with all other elements in a random or a priori order. All of the inferences from such analyses are drawn ultimately from the behavior of the elements of the system, whether or not some of those elements are labeled as structural properties.

In contrast, a more comprehensive network model would draw inferences about the behavior of the elements from the structural aspects of the system (the pattern of social relations) rather than from the aggregated behavior of the elements of the system. A basic thrust of methodological development in network analysis has been to develop ways of examining both the elements of a network and the structured relationships between and among these elements. These graphs and matrices are no more formidable than the battery of multivariate statistical techniques that support analysts routinely employ. With them, analysts can go beyond using network concepts as variables toward a structural analysis of the origins, provisions, use, and perceptions of social support.

If analyses are expanded beyond support to the network as a whole, the practical implications that can be drawn from analysis are ultimately expanded. The focus on intimacy or support and the use of network concepts in a conventional individualistic manner both reinforce a tendency to seek solutions for health problems by changing individuals (e.g., Froland et al., 1981). A broader structuralist approach, however, expands the scope of investigation toward an understanding of why stress and attendant health problems develop in various social contexts (e.g., the social class–health relationship). The very nature of this approach forces researchers to consider the larger structural constraints operating on the provision of support and encourages them to recognize the limitations of common-sense social network interventions strategies that try to add more or better support ties (D'Augelli & Vallence, 1982). In health research generally it represents a return to an intervention logic, which includes structural as well as individual changes.

References

Aday, L., & Anderson, R. (1975). *A framework for the study of access to medical care.* University of Chicago: Robert Wood Johnson Foundation.

Barnes, J. (1972). *Social networks.* Reading, MA: Addison-Wesley.

Barrera, M., Jr., & Ainley, S. (1983). The structure of social support: A conceptual and empirical analysis. *Journal of Community Psychology, 2,* 133–141.

Berkowitz, S. (1982). *An introduction to structural analysis: The network approach to social research.* Toronto: Butterworths.

Berscheid, E., & Walster, E. (1978). *Interpersonal attraction* (2nd ed). Reading, MA: Addison-Wesley.

Bott E. (1957). *Family and social networks.* London: Tavistock.

Brown, G., Bhrolchain, M., & Harris, T. (1975). Social class and psychiatric disturbance among women in an urban population. *Sociology, 9,* 225–249.

Burt, R. (1980). Models of network structure. *Annual Review of Sociology, 6,* 79–141.

Burt, R., & Minor, M. (Eds.). (1983). *Applied network analysis.* Beverly Hills: Sage.

Conrath, D., Higgins, C., & McClean, R. (1983). A comparison of the reliability of questionnaire versus diary data. *Social Networks, 5* (September), 315–22.

Craven, P., & Wellman, B. (1973). The network city. *Sociological Inquiry, 43,* 57–88.

Cumming, E., & Henry, W. (1961). *Growing old: The process of disengagement.* New York: Basic Books.

D'Augelli, A., & Vallence, T. (1982). The helping community: Issues in the evaluation of preventive intervention to promote informal helping. *Journal of Community Psychology, 10,* 199–208.

Dellcrest Children's Centre. (1981). *An investigation into the use of formal and informal helping resources by low-income families.* Unpublished manuscript.

Erickson, B. (1978). Some problems of inference from chain data. In K. F. Schuessler (Ed.) *Sociological methodology* (pp. 276–302). San Francisco: Jossey-Bass.

Evans, R. L., & Northwood, L. K. (1979). The utility of natural help relationships. *Social Science and Medicine, 13A,* 789–795.

Faris, R., & Dunham, H. (1939). *Mental disorders in urban areas.* Chicago: University of Chicago Press.

Fischer, C. (1982). *To dwell among friends.* Chicago: University of Chicago Press.

Froland, C., Pancoast, D., Chapman, N., & Kimboko, P. (1981). *Helping networks and human services.* Beverly Hills, CA: Sage.

Gottlieb, B. (1978). The development and application of a classification scheme of informal helping behaviours. *Canadian Journal of Behavioural Science, 10,* 105–115.

Gottlieb, B. (Ed.). (1981). *Social networks and social support.* Beverly Hills, CA: Sage.

Granovetter, M. (1974). *Getting a job.* Cambridge, MA: Harvard University Press.

Granovetter, M. (1982). The strength of weak ties: A network theory revisited. In P. Marsden & N. Lin (Eds.). *Social structure and network analysis.* Beverly Hills, CA: Sage.

Hammer, M. (1981). Social supports, social networks and schizophrenia. *Schizophrenia Bulletin, 7,* 45–57.

Hirsch, B. (1979). Psychological dimensions of social networks: A multi-method analysis. *American Journal of Community Psychology, 7,* 263–277.

Hirsch, B. (1980). Natural support systems and coping with major life changes. *American Journal of Community Psychology, 8,* 159–172.

Hirsch, B. (1981). Coping and adaptations in high risk populations: Toward an integrative model. *Schizophrenia Bulletin, 7,* 164–172.

Holland, P., & Leinhardt, S. V., (Eds.). (1979). *Perspectives on social network research.* New York: Academic Press.

Howard, L. (1974). *Industrialization and community in Chotangapur.* Unpublished Ph.D. dissertation, Department of Sociology, Harvard University.

Jaco, R. (1954). The social isolation hypothesis and schizophrenia. *American Sociological Review, 19,* 567–577.

Journal of Community Psychology. (1982). [Special issue]. *10* (October).

Kadushin, C., Ziviani, C., Roth, L., Martin, J., & Boulanger, G. (1980). *Social density and mental health.* Center for Social Research of the Graduate Center City University of New York, Center for Policy Research, Inc., and Teacher's College, Columbia University.

Killilea, M. (1982). Interaction of crisis theory, coping strategies and social support systems. In H. Schulberg & M. Killilea (Eds.). *The modern practice of community mental health.* San Francisco: Jossey-Bass.

Kornhauser, W. (1968). Mass society. *International Encyclopedia of the Social Sciences, 10,* 58–64.

Leavy, R. (1982). Social support and psychological disorder: A review. *Journal of Community Psychology, 10,* 3–21.

Liu, W., & Duff, R. (1972). The strength in weak ties. *Public Opinion Quarterly, 78,* 361–366.

Marshall, V. (1980). State of the art lecture: The sociology of aging. In J. Crawford (Ed.). *Canadian Gerontological Collection III.* Winnipeg: Canadian Association on Gerontology.

McLanahan, S., Wedemeyer, N., & Adelberg, T. (1981). Network structure, social support, and psychological well-being in the single-parent family. *Journal of Marriage and the Family, 43,* 601–612.

McKinlay, J. (1973). Social networks, lay consultation and help-seeking behavior. *Social Forces, 51,* 275–292.

McKinlay, J. (1980). Social network influences on morbid episodes and the career of help seeking. In L. Eisenberg & A. Kleinman (Eds.), *The relevance of social science for medicine* (pp. 77–107). Dordrecht: Reidel.

Mitchell, J. (1969). The concept and use of social networks. In J. Mitchell (Ed.), Social networks in urban situations (pp. 1–50). Manchester: University of Manchester Press.

Mitchell, R., & Trickett E. (1980). Task force report: Social networks as mediators of social support. *Community Mental Health Journal, 16,* 27–44.

Mueller, D. (1980). Social networks: A promising direction for research on the relationship of the social environment to psychiatric disorder. *Social Science and Medicine, 14A,* 147–161.

Peil, M. (1981). *Cities and suburbs: Urban life in West Africa.* New York: Holmes & Meier.

Perrucci, R., & Targ, D. (1982). *Mental patients and social networks.* Boston: Auburn House.

Pilisuk, M., & Froland, C. (1978). Kinship, social networks, social support and health. *Social Science and Medicine, 12A,* 273–280.

Radcliffe-Brown, A. (1940). On social structure. *Journal of the Royal Anthropological Society of Great Britain and Ireland, 70,* 1–12.

Sarason, I., & Sarason, B. (Eds.). (1984). *Social support.* The Hague: Martinus Nijhoff.

Simmel, G. (1922/1955). The web of group affiliations. In G. Simmel *Conflict and the web of group affiliations* (R. Bendix, Trans.), pp. 125–195. New York: Free Press.

Syrotuik, J., & D'Arcy, C. (1983). *The relationship between social support and psychological distress: Direct, protective and compensatory effects.* Paper presented at the Annual Meeting of the Canadian Sociology and Anthropology Association, Vancouver.

Tapping, C. (1983). *Social support and asthma.* Paper presented at the Annual Meeting of the Canadian Sociology and Anthropology Association, Vancouver.

Thoits, P. (1982). Conceptual, methodological, and theoretical problems in studying social support as a buffer against life stress. *Journal of Health and Social Behavior, 23,* 145–159.

Tolsdorf, C. (1976). Social networks, support, and coping. *Family Process, 15,* 407–417.

Turner, R., Frankel, B., & Levin, D. (1983). Social support: Conceptualization, measurement, and implications for mental health. In J. Greenley (Ed.), *Research in community and mental health* (Vol. III), Greenwich: JAI Press.

Turner, R., Levin, D., & Noh, S. (1982, August). *Variations in psychological well-being across the life course: The significance of social support and stress among the physically disabled.* Paper presented at the International Sociology Association Annual Meeting, Mexico City.

Turner, R., & Noh, S. (1983). Class and psychological vulnerability among women: The significance of social support and personal control. *Journal of Health and Social Behavior, 24,* 2–15.

Wan, T. (1982). *Stressful life events, social support networks and gerontological health.* Lexington, MA: Lexington Books.

Wellman, B. (1979). The community question. *American Journal of Sociology, 84,* 1201–1231.

Wellman, B. (1983). Network analysis: Some basic principles. In R. Collins (Ed.), *Sociological theory* (pp. 144–200). San Francisco: Jossey-Bass.

Wellman, B. (1984). From social support to social network. In I. Sarason & B. Sarason (Eds.), *Social support.* The Hague: Martinus Nijhoff.

Wellman, B. (1985). Domestic work, paid work and net work. In S. Duck & D. Perlman (Eds.) *Understanding personal relationship* (Vol. I). London: Sage.

Wellman, B., Carrington, P., & Hall, A. (in press). Networks as personal communities. In S. Berkowitz & B. Wellman, (Eds.), *Social structures.* Cambridge, England: Cambridge University Press.

Wellman, B., & Leighton, B. (1979). Networks, neighborhoods, and communities. *Urban Affairs Quarterly, 14,* 363–390.

White, H., Boorman, S., & Breiger, R. (1976). Social structure from multiple networks: I. Blockmodels of roles and positions. *American Journal of Sociology, 81,* 730–880.

Wilcox, B. (1981). Social support in the adjusting to marital disruptions: A network analysis. In B. Gottlieb (Ed.), *Social networks and social support* (pp. 97–116). Beverly Hills, CA: Sage.

Young, C., Giles, Jr., D., & Plantz, M. (1982). Natural networks: Help-giving and help-seeking in two rural communities. *American Journal of Community Psychology, 10,* 457–469.

CHAPTER 3

Social Structure and Processes of Social Support

Leonard I. Pearlin

Introduction

The intensive interest in social supports among social scientists and policymakers is justified. Any set of circumstances that promises to contribute to the prevention or alleviation of suffering or distress certainly merits close scrutiny. Yet the very intensity of our interest must also serve as a warning to monitor and restrain our judgments of supports: We should not magnify their efficacy, we should not ignore their limits, and we should not fail to establish as a prominent part of our research task the identification of conditions under which they exercise their effects. The almost eruptive upsurge of research into social supports makes it imperative that we pause and take stock of what they can and cannot do and of the circumstances that regulate their influences on behavior and well-being. Much of this chapter is in the spirit of such stock taking.

Any appraisal of the current state of knowledge about social supports and any attempt to specify directions for future research must depend, of course, on what it is we are seeking to learn. From the perspectives of a stress researcher, social supports present an opportunity to explain the seemingly inconsistent findings emerging from research. Briefly, it is a construct that helps to make sense out of the differences observed in people's responses to common problems. As we learn more about the circumstances

43

that adversely affect people, we also learn that not everyone facing the same circumstances is adversely affected by them. The very conditions that produce distress in some people leave other people seemingly untouched. Variations in the consequences of difficult life conditions, therefore, lead us to posit the presence of factors that mediate the relationship between these conditions and their outcomes. The concept of social supports—along with that of coping—serves this function.

Although it is relatively simple to identify the explanatory functions social supports ought to serve, it is far from a simple matter to recognize what can be done to enhance these functions. On the contrary, there is considerable conceptual and methodological confusion pervading research into social supports. In part, this confusion results because social supports represent a rather broad and varied area of research rather than a focused research problem. As a consequence, a discussion of one part of this complex area necessarily implicates other, interrelated parts. As will be seen in the course of this chapter, the identification of the problems and promises of social supports entails a sifting and sorting of intricately linked issues. In addressing this task, I make no effort to assemble a review of these issues. For example, I shall largely ignore measurement and definitional problems. Instead, I shall be very selective, emphasizing those social structural considerations that might either help to clarify some issues or to bring issues into view that have been ignored.

Support Systems: Boundaries and Functions

I begin by considering the sources of support, for much of the discussion that follows hinges on this topic. There are several critical ways to approach the question of who provides support (see Turner, 1983), but probably none is more common than that which, implicitly or explicitly, distinguishes among networks, group affiliations, and interpersonal interactions. The network perspective is the broadest, of course, calling attention to an entire web of relationships of which individuals are a direct or indirect part (Berkman & Syme, 1979; Mitchell & Trickett, 1980; Mueller, 1980; Wellman, 1981). A network may be seen as defining the outer boundaries of supports upon which an individual can draw. People are not likely to reach out at any one time to all the resources encompassed by their networks; on the other hand, they are certainly not able to call on more resources than are provided by the network. Sociologically, the concept of the network is of great importance, because it draws attention to the institutional and organizational resources that societies make available to their members. And just as the distribution of wealth, power, and status are unequally distributed in societies, the extensiveness and resourcefulness of networks are unequally distributed, too. That is, the scope of networks and what they can offer to their participants varies from one stratum of society to another. Indeed, variations in the scope and richness of networks may be as important to the study of social stratification as they are to the study of social supports.

A second perspective on sources of supports, nestled within that of networks, centers on the groups to which individuals have active attachments. This is probably the perspective most commonly adopted in research (e.g., Eaton, 1978; Eckenrode & Gore, 1981; Gore, 1978). Whereas knowledge of networks informs researchers which supports individuals *can* potentially call upon, individuals' active social relations represent the supports to which they are *likely* to turn. Moreover, it is reasonable to assume that the greater level of attachment to and interaction with membership groups, the greater is the likelihood that they will provide the most fertile harvest of supports of various kinds. It is for this reason that, when we seek to identify active affiliations within the boundaries of networks, we typically ask not only with whom people interact—family, friends, colleagues, and associates—but also about their residential proximity to the subject, the frequency of face-to-face visits with them, patterns of communication, and so on. Within a person's network, the subset of relationships where interactions are most direct, active, and intense presumably represents the most viable source of support.

A third approach to support looks within active affiliations in an attempt to make certain distinctions based more on qualitative than quantitative properties of relationships. The search for the qualities that are associated with supportive relationships, moreover, is likely to direct attention to specific individuals rather than to groups. For example, there is some indication that supports, especially of an emotional character, are likely to be found in interpersonal relations marked by trust and intimate exchange (e.g., Brown, 1978; Brown, Bhrolchain, & Harris, 1975; Lowenthal & Haven, 1968; Pearlin, Lieberman, Menaghan, & Mullan, 1981). These kinds of qualities, in turn, are usually found in what Cooley (1915) referred to as primary relations: those that are important to people for noninstrumental reasons, that are nonspecialized and continuous, and that encompass broad areas of interest and concern. Such qualities, of course, are often found in wife–husband relationships or in friendships of special closeness. Furthermore, in relationships distinguished by trust and intimacy, the getters of support may be entirely unaware that they are in fact its recipients. Thus Brown (1978) learned that people embedded in primary relationships often think of themselves as entirely self-reliant, suggesting that emotional support is something built into such relationships rather than something that needs to be consciously sought from them. Effective getters of support, I propose, are people who have the ability to form and sustain relationships marked by intimate exchange and by communication that penetrates beneath superficial levels. Moreover, in such relationships people can often get support without having to ask for it.

My purpose in outlining these general orientations to the study of social supports is to provide a necessary background for much of the discussion that follows. It should be clear that these approaches involve a complex web of issues that are either bypassed or treated lightly here. More detailed discussions of these issues can be found in other chapters of this volume and in work reported elsewhere (e.g., House, 1981; Turner, 1983). However, it should be quite evident from what I have set forth here that these perspectives do not compete; each provides distinctly useful knowledge about the sources and nature of social supports and, beginning with the organization of networks, each is embedded in the preceding. But, as important as they are in their own right, the conceptual and research problems surrounding social supports only begin with these orientations. They are but the stage on which a host of other issues come into play.

Specialization of Giving and Getting

One of these issues concerns the specialization of supports. There are two dimensions of specialization that can be recognized. One concerns the fact that supports may be drawn from different sources for different problems; the other pertains to the shifts in supports that occur between the onset of a problem and its final resolution. With regard to the first, it is clear that the people from whom support is derived for one set of difficulties may be entirely inappropriate for other difficulties. Someone looking for a job would go to an employment agency or, perhaps, to a friend of an uncle who owns a machine shop; but someone grieving over the death of an aged parent might turn to a spouse and siblings. There may be systems of support that are activated for all exigencies, regardless of their nature. But, certainly, the activation of other systems varies in some specialized way with the type of problem being confronted.

I suggest, then, that there is a specialized division of labor among various sources of support that would entail distinctly different supports for different types of problems. An extension of this specialized fit between supports and problems may be seen by looking at different aspects of the same basic problem. This is an important issue and deserves clarification. Essentially, serious life problems rarely arise singly, separate from other problems. For example, an unemployed person would reach out to the limits of his or her networks—from public bureaucracies to friends of friends—to find another job. At the same time, unemployment sets in motion circumstances that lead to other difficulties. Thus job loss is likely to result in financial difficulties, and a person might borrow money from a brother to make a monthly car payment. Perhaps being unemployed has also raised some disquieting doubts about competence, and in a subtle way the individual looks to a spouse to restore self-confidence. One problem, then, is likely to lead to another and another, and for each spin-off the individual might turn to a different source of support.

Different problems, therefore, call for the specialized kinds of supports from specialized sources. Occasionally, different life problems are independent of one another and occasionally there may be interrelated constellations of problems that are satellite spin-offs of a core problem. In both types of cases, each problem may mobilize a distinct source to provide a distinct type of support. There is a third variant of specialization, which is best observed longitudinally. The same basic problem may evoke different supports as it moves through various stages and transformations. Here I am emphasizing that the nature and character of a problem can change over time, and with each change there can be a corresponding shift in the nature and character of supports utilized. Illnesses provide an obvious illustration of this point, especially those that begin with the appearance of being acute or episodic but emerge as chronic and life threatening. Following a cardiac infarction, for example, a patient may be exclusively in the care of specialized hospital personnel. As the patient improves, his family may begin to bring him news of the outside, try to express their confidence in his future, relate stories of others who have had successful outcomes from the same exigencies, suggest coping mechanisms he should adopt, and warn him away from excesses, express love and caring, and so on. When the patient returns home, an expanded set of supports is activated: Friends, neighbors, fellow club members, workmates, and the minister come to visit, bringing gifts, information, and good cheer from their respective sectors. The medical bureaucracy, which at this point has a much reduced role, gives way to a mixture of secondary and primary relationships. Another hypothetical patient may have a recovery that is slower than anticipated and serious complications indefinitely put off her return to normal roles. Under these circumstances, perhaps, there will be a contraction of both the sources and the nature of the supports. As the patient's assumption of activities outside the home is deferred, her support becomes increasingly the responsibility of family and friends. Her needs will be overwhelmingly centered on the logistics of daily care and on emotional buttressing. Should she later recover to the point where she can again anticipate being active outside the home, representatives of secondary relationships will once more surface to provide information, reassert that she is wanted, and in other respects ease the transition back to former roles outside the family domain.

Obviously, the relevant aspects of the infinite number of scenarios can and do vary widely. But the main points to be recognized with regard to the specialization of supports are, first, that people rarely have single problems; they are typically multiple. Even where a problem surfaces in an otherwise untroubled life, that problem can spawn other problems and a constellation of secondary problems develop. Each of these may then activate a range of supports, from the outer reaches of the network to the small intimate circle of relationships having special qualities. Second, each problem for which supports are mobilized may have its own natural history. As the nature of the problem changes, so, too, do the significant sources of supports. To observe this, the researcher ideally needs to track problems through time, because the critical nature of problems may shift from their first appearance to their final resolution. Each shift, in turn, may obviate one set of supports and bring others into greater prominence.

Clearly, it is not enough to argue about which is the most important source of support–network, affiliate, or intimate. The real task is to see the dynamic use of each of these systems as people attempt to grapple with problems across the space and over the span of their lives. From the beginning to the end of this process, all sources of supports are likely to be involved.

Interactional Aspects of Support

There is a very important issue that in some respects overshadows those just discussed. Simply put, it is necessary to stop thinking of support *either* as something received by individuals *or* as something given by individuals or groups. Instead, support for a problem often involves both giving and receiving by the same individual and it must be seen in terms of an interactional exchange between donors and recipients (Pearlin, 1983a). Most research implicitly or explicitly regards support as flowing either from the bountifulness or duty of the donor or from the cleverness or resourcefulness of the recipient. In some instances, assumptions of this order may be essentially correct. There is very little interaction, to take an exaggerated example, between the surgeon and the inert patient whose appendix is being removed. The "support" is being given in response to the dictates of professional obligations and norms; it is being received in response to a prior demonstration of the ability to pay a fee. The giver and getter roles are rigidly fixed and noninterchangeable.

In many instances, however, support takes place in continuing relationships in which the giving and getting functions are less clearly separated and, in fact, may be reciprocally exchanged. The exchange of giver and getter roles has its structural roots in role sets, that is, the roles around which people interact (Merton, 1959). Thus a family constitutes a role set, as does a work group or any set of roles that are functionally linked. The very integration of roles within a set makes it unlikely that serious life problems can beset one party without also affecting that person's inter-actions with the other closely related parties who share the role set. Indeed, one person's problems may quickly become the problem of others. When this happens, the boundaries between the giving and the getting of support may become quite blurred. If a mother and father, for example, have a child who is seriously ill, there may be between them a dynamic exchange of giver and getter roles over time. They would not necessarily exchange the same form of support for the exchange to be reciprocal; thus one might be primarily expressive and the other instrumental in the supports they give to each other. The equity of the exchange, therefore, cannot be judged solely on the basis of whether an individual returns to the other precisely what had previously been received.

Aside from issues of reciprocity, powerful imperatives for providing sup-port typically develop within continuing role sets, particularly those that constitute primary groups. The helping norms that develop may be but-tressed not only by concern for the well-being of the recipient of the sup-port but by concern for the sustained integrity of the group itself. The wife of an unemployed worker may desperately try to cheer up her husband as much out of a general desire to maintain a quality of family life as out of a particular desire to help her husband. The norms of helping and sup-port also rest on the recognition by the donor that he or she may very well be a recipient at a later time. Although people within role sets do not nec-essarily engage in a conscious calculus, there is no doubt that being an available and bountiful donor provides the license for being a getter of support if the need arises.

Even someone embedded in a role set within a primary group cannot take support for granted. Whether or not support is received ultimately rests on how the donor reads and defines the situation of need. Specifically, need has to be seen as legitimate, reasonable, and meriting concern if sup-port is given, at least in a sustained fashion. I can only speculate about the kinds of considerations that influence judgments of legitimacy. Probable factors are the extent to which the difficulty is seen as the person's "own fault," whether it is a recurring difficulty, and whether the recipient is perceived as having the capacity to benefit from the support. Whatever may shape the legitimization of need, it is clear that these kinds of judg-ments ultimately regulate the availability of supports. And despite the limits of our current knowledge about these issues, it is necessary to begin thinking of support in terms of interpersonal relations rather than of the actions of separate and unrelated individuals. In this way, the availability, duration, and efficacy of social supports should be more clearly understood.

This leads to a closely related point. Most research is primarily and justifiably concerned with the person considered to be in need, but it would be useful to consider also the consequences of support for the relationship. What, for example, are the costs of the supports, emotional and otherwise, to the donor and what is the impact of these costs on the interaction between the giver and the getter? What happens to the relationship if support is one-sided, lacking in the reciprocity and exchange that was discussed earlier? And what happens when the best efforts to provide effective support fail? Do providers become burned out and withdraw from the relationship because it stands as a painful reminder of failure? When the same problem repeatedly surfaces, is caring replaced with anger; does the frustrated donor now both withhold help from and direct ire toward the recipient? Obviously, the giving and getting of supports can be an important and highly charged component of social interaction, one that can have a powerful impact on the relationship itself.

Once again, this is an area in which it is much easier to ask questions than to find answers. Nevertheless, it is obvious that our thinking about supports must be adjusted to bring relationships—as distinct from individual recipients—under consideration. Whether support will be forthcoming, what it will be, how long it will last, the nature of its qualities—all of these aspects of support are determined not solely by the actions of the recipient nor solely by the status of the donor, but by the nature of their relationship and the interactions it encompasses.

Latent Social Ingredients of Support

I wish now to address directly a topic that is woven into some of the preceding discussions and that has an important bearing on the study of the effects of supports: the substance and types of support, a topic that is prominent in the literature. The matter of identifying what is given when supports are received is of vital importance. Without such identification there can be no measurement; without measuring the various components of support, it would not be possible to specify and account for the effects of supports. Furthermore, any attempt to understand the specialized sources of support described earlier must necessarily go hand in hand with the recognition of variations in the types of support. Considerable attention has been devoted to these matters (e.g., Caplan & Killilea, 1976; Cobb, 1976,

1979; Gottlieb, 1978) and I shall not attempt to summarize this material. Instead I shall briefly speculate on forms of supports that are potentially powerful but that, because they are somewhat subtle and latent, have received little recognition.

Perhaps the sheer sense of attachment is among the more important forms of support; this observation, Turner (1983) has pointed out, that goes back to biblical times. A person who is supported is also likely to feel that he or she matters to others. And mattering is important (Rosenberg & McCullaugh, 1981). Since the work of Durkheim, it has been known that the well-being of people lacking solidary ties are at risk. It is not always clear, of course, whether the isolation creates the disorder or the disorder leads to isolation, or both. However, research dealing with events that disrupt attachments, such as residential changes (Stokols & Shumaker, 1982) and divorce (Pearlin & Johnson, 1977), has indicated that the loss of attachments is accompanied by psychological distress. This kind of work suggests that support systems, whatever else they provide in time of crises and need, impart to people a general and abiding sense of security and well-being. It is good to have supports during times of travail, but it is also good to have them when nothing is needed but a sense of place and belongingness. This is essentially the point at issue when researchers distinguish between the main effects and the buffering effects of social supports (La Rocco, House, & French, 1980; Thoits, 1982).

A different component of support involves the rich array of norms that people acquire from their membership groups. Among these norms are those that give meaning to potentially stressful situations (Pearlin & Schooler, 1978). Simply put, social relationships are the source of norms that help people appraise situations and identify those of which to be wary. Once situations that do threaten well-being are distinguished, socially acquired norms also provide the coping repertoires that help people avoid or minimize stress. Supportive relationships, then, are supportive because of the *direct* help that people draw from them. But they are also supportive *indirectly* to the extent that they are the source of coping norms that enable people to help themselves—to cope as individuals in their own behalf. Supports can be the social basis of individual actions taken to mediate psychological stress.

Somewhat akin to what I have been discussing is another form of support. A support system, I believe, can be a selective source of appropriate models on which people pattern their actions. If someone suffers from a particular illness, for example, someone else from the system is likely to step forward as having had, or knowing someone who has had, the same ailment—or, better yet, the same ailment in more severe form. That person then can be used as a reference figure against whom the seriousness of the case can be judged, the prognosis weighed, and the most appropriate course of treatment chosen. Indeed, people may be so eager to offer themselves as models to others as a way to inspire optimism and encouragement that they may exaggerate or otherwise distort the relevance of their problems to those of the person whom they want to support. At any rate, it is known (Pearlin & Schooler, 1978) that people actively seek reference figures to evaluate the significance of their problems, and the support system often offers itself as a supplier of such figures.

In this brief consideration of the nature and substance of social supports, I have attempted not to catalog all forms of social support but to draw attention to those that are likely to be overlooked. I am underscoring, essentially, that the main effects of social supports should not be ignored; the existence of relationships of which people feel an important part and with which they identify in a positive manner are by themselves supportive of mental health and well-being regardless of the problems people face. It should be recognized, therefore, that the forms of support are often indistinguishable from the forms of normal social process. When we look at the natural products of social interaction—that is, at group integration and solidarity, at norms and the use of reference figures—we are looking, too, at ingredients of social support. Much support is sought, recognized, and contracted for in response to concrete problems. But much of it has a general presence, is beyond the level of awareness, and is embedded in the everyday transactions that take place between people in their prosaic pursuits.

Giving and Getting and the Life Course

Virtually every important aspect of people's social supports is subject to change as they traverse the life course, moving from one life stage to another: The sorts of problems they are likely to confront, the sources of support that are available to them, the forms and nature of the supports that they receive, their ability to reciprocate by switching into a donor role, and, perhaps, the effects of supports. Yet, it must be emphasized that these assertions are based far less on the fruits of empirical research than on what appears to be logical imperatives of the life course and the alterations it entails in the conditions of life. With limited exception (Cobb, 1979; Kahn & Antonucci, 1980; Lowenthal & Haven, 1968), social supports have been studied without benefit of a life course perspective.

There are a number of reasons why, on prima facie grounds alone, the structure of support systems can be expected to change along the life course. There are periods of life in which the abandonment of old roles and statuses and the achievement of new ones take place at a fairly rapid pace, particularly in the earlier and later phases of adult life. Each time a transition occurs, furthermore, there is change in role sets. To the extent that the sources of supports are located within role sets, movement out of and into roles necessarily have some repercussions on the support systems. Consider for illustration these transitions in a life-scenario: A person is married, enters into the labor force, changes jobs, has children, comes to be recognized as adult by his or her parents (perhaps the most elusive, hard-to-achieve transition), eventually presides over an empty nest, has grandchildren, resigns from one club but joins another, retires, moves to the Sun Belt, is left alone because of the spouse's death, reluctantly takes up residence with an adult child, and, finally, moves to a nursing home when health fails. At each turn of this hypothetical though familiar life cycle there can be a contraction, expansion, or substitution of social supports. Thus, supports are mobilized not only in response to unscheduled, eruptive crises; changes that are scheduled and built into the normative changes along the life course act also as forces in structuring and restructuring each aspect of the support system.

Obviously, the inherently dynamic character of social supports across time has not yet been captured by the research that has been done. Of the rich array of life course changes that do take place I would like to consider two, one involving age and the other gender. The first is represented in the reversal of roles that occasionally occurs between elderly parents and their adult children. This exchange of support is interesting, in part, because the role set remains intact while the distribution of tasks and responsibilities among the participants may undergo dramatic alteration, a situation quite different from those transitions that entail movement out of or into role sets. In the case of parents and their children, the question of who does what for whom will bring very different answers as the parents become aged and their children middle-aged (Lieberman, 1978). There can be, and often is, a gradual reversal of support functions: Where parents were the encouragers, guides, emotional pillars, and material providers, these functions may inexorably shift to children as physical and economic frailty encroaches upon the parents.

It is noteworthy not only that former givers of support now become primarily getters, but also that this role reversal itself may become a life strain for which support is needed (Pearlin, 1983b). Thus, these family relations are at once a source of strain and pain and the source of relief from the distress. Particularly where primary relations are concerned, the very systems that distress can also be those that bring relief from the distress. Within role sets, the nature and sources of both the distress and its alleviation can go through rather profound changes as participants move through the life course.

In addition to the exchange of need and of support between the young and the old, there is also some evidence of exchange between men and women along the life course. Presumably, the norms governing support are built into the relationships between men and women, husbands and wives. It is an embedded assumption of social theory that women are the nurturant and supportive members of the family and men the more instrumental providers (Belle, 1982; Zelditch, 1955). To the extent that this assumption is correct, it might be expected that males, at least with regard to emotional support, are more often the beneficiaries than the givers. As in the case of age relations among donors and recipients, however, there may be a turnabout in support functions between men and women during the life course. Specifically, there is some indication that after children are grown and parents are no longer needed as socializing role models, men become more expressive and nurturant while women become more assertive about their own needs and dispositions (Gutmann, 1975). These findings are not yet developed to a point where they can be accepted as fact. Nevertheless, they suggest it might be misleading to characterize support relationships between men and women in ways that do not take into account shifts across the life span.

Many more illustrations could be drawn that highlight the changes in supports that unfold at different points of the life course. There are many distinct patterns of change across the life course and its age ranks: changes in who is giving and who is receiving support, in whether support is coming mainly from primary or secondary relationships, in the form and substance of the support, and in the problems that have stimulated it. The point to be underscored again is that supports do not stand apart from social life. To understand social supports it is also necessary to understand social organization, the structure of interpersonal relations, the norms and values that regulate behavior, and the changes that take place along each of these dimensions. Clearly, to think of social supports as fixed responses to needs of the recipient or as a reflection of the skillfulness of the recipient to form and use support systems is to ignore the complexity of the issues.

The Effects of Support: How and Where to Look for Them

Thus far I have discussed four aspects of social supports: (1) the broad social contexts from which they stem (i.e., whether they are drawn from the outer reaches of a social network, that part of the network composed of interacting affiliates, or the smaller part of it made up of confidantes between whom there are special qualities of trust and intimacy), (2) the specialization of the giving and getting process, (3) the forms and ingredients of support, and (4) changes in support systems concomitant with life course changes. Obviously, each of these aspects of social supports is interconnected with each of the others. Just as obviously, these interconnections form a process that ends in producing certain outcomes or effects. From the perspective of those who do research into social stress, it is the mediating effects of supports that are of ultimate interest. The major reason that other aspects of social supports are studied is because they help reveal such effects. Bluntly put, the bottom line for research on social supports is the difference they make in the stress process. If they make no difference, much of the reason for their study is obviated.

However, it is no easy task to determine what difference they do make, because the evaluation and assessment of the mediating effects of supports is itself ambiguous and difficult. Most scholarly effort to remove the conceptual and methodological obstacles to understanding the effects of social supports has centered on issues of main versus buffering consequences of supports. However, there are other issues and problems surrounding the study of effects of social supports that, although they have received less attention, merit close consideration. I shall try to delineate some of them.

I believe that one of the serious (but not obvious) obstacles in the assessment of the effects of supports is that often the nature of the problems whose effects the supports are supposed to buffer is insufficiently understood. This is quite critical, for the only way we can ascertain whether supports make a difference is by observing how the supports govern the relationship between the problem and its outcome. What is done, operationally, is to compare the well-being of people with equivalent life problems but who differ with regard to their social supports. Because the life problems are presumably the same, differences in well-being can be attributed to differences in the supports that people enjoy. The accuracy of the attribution, however, depends on the accuracy of the judgments of whether or not the life problems are truly equivalent. But, for reasons already discussed, there may be more to a problem than readily meets the eye.

One reason it is difficult to recognize the problems people face is because problems beget problems. Again, in studying the mediating effects of supports on the relationship between myocardial infarction and psychological depression, a group all suffering the same health problem would be observed and then the ways different conditions of support are related to differences in depression would be studied. But are they all experiencing the same problem? All subjects may have suffered an infarction, but perhaps not all of their suffering is physical. Some subjects, for example, may be also exposed to extreme social and economic problems that are concomitants of the illness, whereas others may be more shielded from these kinds of spin-offs. In some instances the illness may intensify marital strains; for others this may not be the case. Where there are such variations, then, the comparison would not really be of people with equivalent life problems. Inadvertently, people who in critical respects are quite different from one another would be compared. Further, in attempting to determine if social supports make any difference in protecting people from the depressive after-effects of myocardial infarction, it would be misleading to accept a finding of no appreciable effects; such a study would really be trying to judge the efficacy of supports among people who are facing life problems that in major respects are quite different. One conclusion to be drawn from this is clear: The study of the effects of social supports requires identifying the constellations of interrelated problems that impinge on the lives of people.

However, once such constellations of life problems are identified, the job is not yet done; it is necessary also to establish the relationship among these problems. The reason for this lies in the rather convincing evidence that the constellation of problems can form a complex antecedent process that leads to the outcome. Several examples could be used to explicate this matter, but I shall draw from the results of some of our research involving involuntary job disruption and its stressful outcomes (Pearlin et al., 1981). Briefly, the loss of a job can be seen as initiating a process that eventually results in psychological depression. The linkages between loss of job and depression are as follows: The job loss leads to a decrease in earnings and the decreased earnings result in an increase in the level of economic strain that is experienced; the economic strain, in turn, diminishes positive self-concepts, self-esteem and mastery; the diminution of the self, finally, results in depression. What should be recognized in this brief account is that the problems that are antecedent to depression may be sequentially linked, with each problem contributing to depression indirectly through its causative relationship to a subsequent problem.

What does this mean with regard to evaluating the efficacy of social supports? It means that if evaluations rely exclusively on determining how supports directly reduce or constrain depression, the possible mediations that the supports can have at earlier points in the antecedent process are ignored. Thus, in the job loss example, it is possible to see if supports minimize the economic strain that would otherwise appear, if they reduce the erosion of self-concept that ordinarily ensues from economic strains, or if they mediate the depression that would follow from the assault on self-concepts. Note, too, that these points of intervention can be observed by looking either at the main effects of the supports or at the buffering effects. In the illustration used here (Pearlin et al., 1981), we actually found that social supports appear to have little or no direct efficacy in reducing depression. However, they do have a rather special and important indirect effect. Specifically, within the context of the problems under scrutiny in this example, supports function primarily to buttress self-esteem and mastery in the face of hardship; the effects of social supports in protecting against psychological depression are very important but entirely indirect. Were we not in a position to observe these indirect effects, we would have judged that supports lacked efficacy in barricading people from the depressive impact of job loss.

Clearly the techniques for assessing the effects of supports can advance no further than the boundaries of comprehension of the complex antecedent process that results in distress or otherwise undermines well-being. The more we come to think of the antecedents of distress and illness in terms of processes that unfold over time rather than as single episodes, events, or conditions, the more we shall be able to search for a variety of social supports.

Consider now the multiple directions of the effects of social supports. I think it is fair to state that current research is typically disposed to find good effects, those that prevent, minimize, or alleviate pain and threats to well-being. However, it is fruitful to recognize that effects may be entirely negative or that there may be deleterious effects mixed with those that are salubrious. There are reported instances of boomerang effects, where the very outcome that is expected to be eased is in fact exacerbated. It is not known if the support itself induces negative effects or if, instead, it is the support combined with selected subjective dispositions of people making use of it that creates such effects. To take a hypothetical example, a person who is disposed to dependency may use support in a way that reinforces this personality trait, with the result that whatever help the person receives is accompanied by some emotional damage.

Although at this time I can only speculate why more is not known about negative and mixed effects of social supports, several reasons can be suggested. First, as noted earlier, studies characteristically focus exclusively on the recipient of support, ignoring the consequences of supports for their donor. However, when supports are mobilized in response to problems that are slow to change and resistant to intervention, the donors may be subject to frustration, feelings of impatience, loss of mastery, and burnout. Under these conditions , it might be that whatever benefits the recipient enjoys are at the expense of the donor. Thus, the favorable–unfavorable mix of effects may be distributed between the givers and the getters; however, these cannot be discerned when one is observed but not the other.

Similarly, it should be recognized that the recipient is likely to be called upon to pay dues as a donor. That is, in return for the support received, an open-ended debt can be incurred whose payment can be called for frequently and endlessly. This is the case in societies where family systems are the primary secure sources of support, such as in Italy (Banfield, 1958; Pearlin, 1971). The price for this security is an obligation to familial benefactors for an entire lifetime. The more that research encompasses both the donor and the recipient of supports, the more likely it is that mixed effects will be encountered.

Such effects are also more likely to be revealed as research extends over longer spans of time. The advantages of long-run, multiwave research hardly need to be extolled. Such research is likely to reveal that the long- and short-run mediation by social supports can produce very different consequences. Easy availability of supports, for example, might relieve short-term pressures but stimulate long-term dependency. Or, support that is primarily emotional may inadvertently inhibit the recipient's acquisition of problem-solving skills. Like much else in life, social supports are not necessarily an unmixed blessing.

Conclusions

House has stated (1981, p. 22) that the issues of research into social supports are captured in a simple question: Who gives what to whom regarding which problem? This comes close to being a succinct summary of this chapter. To it I would add one more question, perhaps the most critical: With what effects? It should be amply evident at this point that it is much easier to be succinct in asking the questions than in providing the answers. This probably reflects accurately the present state of the field.

The accumulated knowledge is quite convincing that social supports can and do mediate the effects of stressful conditions. But it is not yet known how or under what conditions they do act as successful mediators. That these queries cannot be answered should not be interpreted as failure; it bespeaks more the complexity of the issues. Indeed, it was a goal of this chapter to convey some of these complexities. In considering the sources and recipients of support, the various forms it can take, the problems for which it is mobilized, or its multiple effects, there is no shortage of theoretical and methodological hurdles. However, the major difficulties stem from the fact that the answers to each one of these questions depend on each of the others. Thus, *who* is giving support will depend on who the recipient is and their relationship, the nature of the problem, and the form of support required for its alleviation. It is not possible to focus on one of these issues without simultaneously focusing on all others. And that is what is both very complicated and very challenging.

Of course, it must be recognized that there are several ways to conceptualize the various interlocking issues involved in support and its mediating effects. In this chapter I have chosen to approach the issues from the perspective of a sociologist–social psychologist. I do this not to raise a disciplinary flag. Rather, it is out of the conviction that support, itself intrinsically social and interactional, takes place within larger structured social and cultural contexts. These contexts, in turn, help to shape the character and outcomes of supports. It is good to call attention to these matters, even at the risk of emphasizing the obvious. The giving and exchange of supports as people deal with life problems can be a lonely struggle, and even the outside observer might be tempted to view what is going on as reflecting only the involved individuals and their personalities. Although forces of personality can certainly be at work, they should not obscure the fact that each component of House's question can be addressed in social and economic terms. As in virtually all instances where the well-being of people is at stake, personal problems overlap with social problems and personal support systems are shaped by social resources.

References

Banfield, E. C. (1958). *The moral basis of backward society*. Glencoe, IL: The Free Press.

Belle, D. (1982). The stress of caring: Women as providers of social support. In Leo Goldberger & Shlomo Breznitz (Eds.), *Handbook of stress* (pp. 496–505). New York: Free Press.

Berkman, L., & Syme, S. L. (1979). Social networks, host resistance and mortality: A nine-year follow-up study of Alameda County residents. *American Journal of Epidemiology, 9,* 225–254.

Brown, B. B. (1978). Social and psychological correlates of help-seeking behavior among urban adults. *American Journal of Community Psychology, 6,* 425–439.

Brown, G. W., Bhrolchain, M., & Harris, T. (1975). Social class and psychiatric disturbance among women in an urban population. *Sociology, 9,* 225–254.

Caplan, G., & Killilea, M. (1976). *Support systems and mutual help*. New York: Grune and Stratton.

Cobb, S. (1976). Social support as a mediator of life stress. *Psychosomatic Medicine, 38,* 300–314.

Cobb, S. (1979). Social support and health through the life course. In Matilda White Riley (Ed.), *Aging from birth to death: Interdisciplinary perspectives* (pp. 93–106). Washington, D.C.: American Association for the Advancement of Science.

Cooley, C. H. (1915). *Social organization*. New York: Scribner.

Eaton, W. W. (1978). Life events, social supports, and psychiatric symptoms: A re-analysis of the New Haven data. *Journal of Health and Social Behavior, 19,* 230–234.

Eckenrode, J., & Gore, S. (1981). Stressful events and social supports: The significance of context. In B. H. Gottlieb (Ed.), *Social networks and social supports*. Beverly Hills, CA: Sage.

Gore, S. (1978). The effect of social support in moderating the health consequences of unemployment. *Journal of Health and Social Behavior, 19,* 157–165.

Gottlieb, B. H. (1978). The development and application of a classification scheme of informal helping behaviors. *Canadian Journal of Science, 10,* 105–115.

Gutmann, D. (1975). Parenthood: A key to the comparative study of the life cycle. In Nancy

Datan & Leon H. Ginsberg (Eds.), *Life-span developmental psychology.* New York: Academic Press.

House, J. S. (1981). *Work stress and social support.* Reading, MA: Addison-Wesley.

Kahn, R. L., & Antonucci, T. C. (1980). Convoys over the life course: Attachment, roles and social support. In Paul B. Baltes & Orville Brim (Eds.), *Life-span development and behavior* (Vol. 3). New York: Academic Press.

La Rocco, J., House, J. S., & French, Jr., J. (1980). Social support, occupational stress and health. *Journal of Health and Social Behavior, 21,* 202–219.

Lieberman, G. L. (1978). Children of the elderly as natural helpers: Some demographic differences. *American Journal of Community Psychology, 6,* 425–439.

Lowenthal, M. F., & Haven, C. (1968). Interaction and adaptation: Intimacy as a critical variable. *American Sociological Review, 33,* 20–30.

Merton, R. K. (1959). The role set: Problems in sociological theory. *British Journal of Sociology, 8,* 106–120.

Mitchell, R., & Trickett, E. (1980). Task force report: Social networks as mediators of social supports. *Journal of Community Mental Health, 16,* 27–44.

Mueller, D. P. (1980). Social networks: A promising direction for research on the relationship of the social environment to psychiatric disorder. *Social Science and Medicine, 14A,* 147–161.

Pearlin, L. I. (1971). *Class context and family relations: A cross national study.* Boston: Little, Brown and Company.

Pearlin, L. I. (1983a, April). *Developmental perspectives on family and mental health.* Unpublished report, Behavioral sciences research in mental health, Department of Health and Human Services, Washington, DC.

Pearlin, L. I. (1983b). Role strains and personal stress. In Howard B. Kaplan (Ed.), *Psychosocial stress: Trends in theory and research.* New York: Academic Press.

Pearlin, L. I., & Johnson, J. (1977). Marital status, life strains and depression. *American Sociological Review, 42,* 704–715.

Pearlin, L. I., Lieberman, M. A., Menaghan, E., & Mullan, J. T. (1981). The stress process. *Journal of Health and Social Behavior, 22,* 337–356.

Pearlin, L. I., & Schooler, C. (1978). The structure of coping. *Journal of Health and Social Behavior, 19,* 2–21.

Rosenberg, M., & McCullaugh, B. C. (1981). Mattering: Inferred significance and mental health. In Roberta Simmons (Ed.), *Research in community and mental health.* Greenwich, CT: JAI Press.

Stokols, D., & Shumaker, S. A. (1982). The psychological context of residential mobility and well-being. *Journal of Social Issues, 38,* 149–171.

Thoits, P. A. (1982). Conceptual, methodological and theoretical problems in studying social support as a buffer against life stress. *Journal of Health and Social Behavior, 23,* 145–158.

Turner, R. J. (1983). Direct, indirect, and moderating effects of social support on psychological distress and associated conditions. In Howard B. Kaplan (Ed.), *Psychosocial stress: Trends in theory and research.* New York: Academic Press.

Wellman, B. (1981). Applying network analysis to the study of support. In Benjamin H. Gottlieb (Ed.), *Social networks and social support.* Beverly Hills: Sage.

Zelditch, Jr., M. (1955). Role differentiation in the nuclear family: A comparative study. In Talcott Parsons & Robert F. Bales (Eds.), *Family, socialization and interaction process* (pp. 307–315). Glencoe, IL: The Free Press.

CHAPTER 4

Supportive Functions
of Interpersonal Relationships*

Thomas Ashby Wills

Introduction

A considerable body of literature has shown that social support is related
to increased psychological well-being and to a lower probability of physical
illness (see Cohen & Wills, 1984; Wallston, Whitcher-Alagna, DeVellis, &
DeVellis, 1983). It is evident that resources provided by interpersonal relationships play an important role in determining people's adaptive functioning and health outcomes. To clarify the theoretical basis of this
phenomenon, two questions can be posed: First, what are the specific supportive functions provided by interpersonal relationships, and second, what
are the psychological processes through which these functions have their
effects?

This chapter focuses on these two issues. I begin with a discussion of
social–psychological theories relevant to supportive functions and then consider a model of psychosocial stress that delineates the functions most relevant for coping effectively with stressful occurrences. From this theoretical
background I distinguish several different functions that can be provided
through interpersonal relationships: *esteem support*, which increases feel-

*The author wishes to thank Peggy Clark, Jeffrey D. Fisher, George Levinger, and the
editors for their incisive comments on a draft of this chapter.

61

ings of self-esteem; *informational support,* which involves providing necessary information; *instrumental support,* defined as providing assistance
with instrumental tasks; and *social companionship,* which involves various
kinds of social activities. I discuss how these different functions may be
indexed in current measures of social support. Finally, I suggest which
functions probably are involved in *main effect* processes, which operate
irrespective of stress level, and *buffering* processes, which have their benefit primarily for persons who are experiencing a high level of stress.[1]

Theories Relevant for Support Relationships

Several different social–psychological theories are relevant for considering the supportive aspects of interpersonal relationships, and in the following section I discuss the major approaches. Because these theories were
not always developed to specifically address social support relationships,
and because social support research has not always been designed with
reference to theory, the linkage between the two is less direct than in some
other areas of research. I shall note the linkages where possible.

Social Exchange Theory

Behavioral theories have considered interpersonal relationships in terms
of their capacity for providing rewards that a person values. In theory, it
would be expected that the more rewards provided, the more supportive
the relationship would be. A crucial issue, however, is to have specific pos-
tulates about the nature of the rewards provided and a theory that emphasizes the reciprocal aspects of social behavior. Merging concepts from
behavioral theory and economic theory, several frameworks have considered interpersonal relationships as a system in which rewards are exchanged between participants. The rewards exchanged within the system
were assumed to be things such as simple economic goods or services, interpersonal rewards such as expressions of liking, or more general social
rewards such as status enhancement. The original theory of Homans(1961),

---

[1]Although this chapter focuses on the supportive functions of interpersonal relationships,
it should be noted that there are both positive and negative aspects. Studies of personal relationships have shown that positive (satisfying) and negative (dissatisfying or conflictual) variables represent statistically orthogonal dimensions (e.g., Argyle & Furnham, 1983; Braiker &
Kelley, 1979; Wills, Weiss, & Patterson, 1974; see also Diener, 1984). On the whole, relationships such as marriage are supportive, but both positive and negative aspects of a relationship
should be considered.

which derived from research on sociometry and group relations, also included a principle of equity or distributive justice, specifying that the rewards gained by each participant should be proportional to his or her investments and costs. A later extension by Foa (1971) suggested that the rewards exchanged were love, status, information, money, goods, and services.

Several predictions about interpersonal relationships were derived from social exchange theories. For example, it was predicted that equity in exchanges (of any particular resource) would produce greater relationship satisfaction, and this has been demonstrated in dating relationships (Hatfield, Utne, & Traupmann, 1979). Further, several formulations suggested that interpersonal exchanges of self-disclosure information increase as relationships develop (Altman & Taylor, 1973) or that the general exchange of social rewards determines the progression of a relationship (Levinger & Huesmann, 1980). Such theories were important for suggesting that shared interactions and exchanges within a relationship are supportive not only because more rewards are available, but also because the history of reciprocal exchanges makes individuals more confident that others would provide assistance in times of need. Foa and Foa (1980) also suggested that resources were not wholly interchangeable; their research indicated that money could be exchanged with almost any other resource, but love was typically exchanged only with love in return.

Work in the tradition of family sociology has used social exchange models to account for satisfaction with, and stability of, marital relationships (see Burr, Hill, Nye, & Reiss, 1979; Nye, 1982). These models emphasize fulfilment of mutual role performance expectations in various areas of marriage, usually defined as emotional expression, child rearing, household management, financial provision, sexual satisfaction, and social companionship. These theories have been supported by an extensive body of research on the determinants of marital satisfaction (Spanier & Lewis, 1980), and the lack of these supportive aspects of marital relationships almost perfectly describes the predictors of divorce (e.g., Kitson & Sussman, 1982). Thus it is evident that the defined properties represent significant rewarding aspects of interpersonal relationships. Moreover, this work has shown some differential correlations, indicating that the strongest determinant of marital satisfaction is a dimension, called understanding, communication, or emotional gratification, which reflects spouses' ability to understand and listen sympathetically to each others' concerns and problems (Barker & Lemle, 1984; Nye & McLaughlin, 1982; Spanier & Lewis, 1980). The relation of this dimension to support seeking is straightforward, and naturalistic studies indicate that spouses are a primary avenue of help seeking for persons experiencing psychological distress (see Wills, 1983).

There is one theoretical complication for social exchange formulations because another facet of exchange theory predicts that persons who receive aid may experience a state of indebtedness, which is perceived as aversive and can discourage further help seeking (see Greenberg, 1980). A resolution has been suggested by Clark and Mills (1979), who proposed a theoretical distinction between *exchange* relationships (such as everyday economic transactions) and *communal* relationships (such as marriage and friendship). Their research indicates that in communal relationships, interpersonal behavior is governed more by a felt desire to respond to the other's needs and less by exchange principles. Consistent with this position, other investigators (Braiker & Kelley, 1979; Huston & Burgess, 1979) have noted that as close relationships develop, members feel increasingly interdependent and perceive themselves more as a unit than as a set of exchanging parties.[2] This perceived absence of exchange concerns is hypothesized to enhance the supportiveness of communal relationships because it encourages help seeking from the other person (see Clark, 1983).

Social Comparison Theory

The theory of social comparison presented by Festinger (1954) posited that people are motivated to validate their notions of social reality by comparing their own performances and opinions with those of other persons. This provides a theoretical mechanism through which interpersonal relationships may provide a type of cognitive support. The original social comparison theory posited upward comparison (i.e., comparison with more competent or better-off others) and received some confirmation in laboratory studies with nonstressed subjects (see Gruder, 1977). It is probable that social relationships serve under ordinary conditions to provide some kinds of informational comparisons. The limitation of upward comparison theory is that it does not apply to persons who are stressed, who display a quite different type of comparison (see Wills, 1981).

Self-Esteem Theories

Several formulations based on the concept of self-esteem maintenance have been developed for various areas of social-psychological research. For

---

[2]Assuredly there are limits on this, and there is evidence that relationships with a marked imbalance between positive and negative behaviors are at risk for dissolution (e.g., Birchler, Weiss, & Vincent, 1975). The shift from strict exchange perceptions to a more altruistic concept of the relationship does not seem to eliminate the necessity for providing a balance of experiences. There is evidence that married couples spontaneously provide each other with positive experiences (Wills *et al.*, 1974), and more research is needed on how a shift from exchange to communal perceptions is related to changes in behaviors.

example, downward comparison theory (Wills, 1981), which posits that distressed persons may obtain self-enhancement through comparison with worse-off others, has been applied to areas such as the fear-affiliation effect and choice of others for social comparison. Self-esteem maintenance has also been a successful formulation in accounting for evidence on help-seeking decisions (DePaulo, 1982), reactions to receiving help (Fisher, Nadler, & Whitcher-Alagna, 1982), and coping with negative life events (Snyder, Higgins, & Stucky, 1983). The application of these formulations to diverse areas of research has suggested the general importance of self-esteem maintenance as a social motive, and thus self-esteem formulations seem particularly relevant for research on the functions provided for distressed persons by social networks.

Personal Control Theories

Theories of personal control have focused on the perception of control over events as a determinant of psychological well-being. This may be construed as a perception of internal locus of control (Lefcourt, 1981) or as a perception of general self-efficacy and control over events (Bandura, 1977; Schorr & Rodin, 1982), which is the opposite of the state of perceived helplessness (see Garber & Seligman, 1980). Social networks may enhance feelings of personal control because of their availability for providing needed aid and resources in times of crisis; this formulation, then, predicts that it is the perceived *reliability* of networks rather than any current exchanges that provides a supportive function. In addition, perceived stress is generally posited to be related to an appraisal of the current balance between environmental demands and available resources (e.g., Coyne & Lazarus, 1980), so the availability of a reliable network of social relationships might affect the appraisal of stressful situations.

Dimensions of Psychosocial Stress

To understand which support functions are most relevant for highly stressed persons, it is necessary to consider some basic propositions about the nature of psychosocial stress. Conceptual analyses (e.g., Coyne & Lazarus, 1980; Wills & Langner, 1980) have noted that stress occurs when the demands posed by negative environmental occurrences exceed the pres coping abilities and resources of an individual. The consequenc appraisal include lowered self-esteem, perceptions of low s perceived lack of control over important events. To counter stress, a support function should be capable of avoiding or reducing these consequences.

Research on the structure of negative life occurrences (Billings & Moos, 1982; Lewinsohn & Amenson, 1978; Williams, Ware, & Donald, 1981) suggests that these fall into several major categories. Primary among these is interpersonal discord: conflict and rejection in relationships with significant others. Marital discord, involving arguments with and criticism by the spouse, is a source of stress for a significant proportion of persons in community samples, and may be based on dissatisfaction either with role performance or with personality characteristics. Conflicts with work supervisors, which are probably an analogous combination of instrumental role performance and personality compatibility, are also an important source of enduring stress (see Billings & Moos, 1982; House, 1981).

Other types of stressors are more diverse. Difficulties in relationships with society, such as going deeply into debt or having problems with the legal system, are a major source of stress for some persons. Job characteristics such as work overload, time pressure, and role ambiguity have been shown to be significant stressors in the occupational area (House, 1981). Serious physical illness (especially chronic illness) is an occurrence that presents instrumental, financial, and other problems. Overall income is undoubtedly a factor in personal and social functioning because of its role in providing access to pleasurable activities and avoiding (or quickly resolving) negative occurrences, and low income is a consistent correlate of psychological distress in community studies (Wills & Langner, 1980).

It is useful to consider common elements through which diverse events produce stress reactions. As previously noted, threat to self-esteem is probably involved in many stressors. Threats to self-esteem may occur because of explicit personal criticism by other persons, or because of the social comparison problem presented by the fact that an individual is experiencing significant difficulties in role performance while other persons are apparently having no problems. For example, although divorce involves a number of instrumental difficulties such as lowered income and child care problems, the empirical correlation between divorce and emotional disorder is apparently accounted for primarily by the feelings of failure, lowered self-esteem, and sense of incompetence that are frequently experienced by divorced persons (see Bloom, Asher, & White, 1978). It can similarly be noted that whereas job problems such as demotion or unemployment present financial difficulty, they also have profound implications for a person's self-esteem, and several authors (e.g., Kasl, 1974) have noted the adverse effect that unemployment has on a worker's self-esteem, even when due to factors beyond the person's control.

It also seems likely that enduring strains prompt a search for information about the nature of the problem and a consideration of suggestions about problem-solving approaches. Just as professional helpers begin therapeutic work by posing questions about the locus of the problem and then provide feedback about the personality and behavior of the client, so troubled persons probably search for information and guidance about the nature of, and solution to, their problems, and the evidence on help-seeking suggests that social networks play an important role in problem definition (Wills, 1983).

Following from this discussion are three predictions. First, if stressful events have common elements, functions relevant to these would display generalized buffering properties. Also, some stressors (e.g., economic difficulty) might be resolved only by specific supportive resources (in this case, financial or legal assistance). Of course it is unlikely that any particular stressful event or string of events evokes only one psychological need, and the examples noted previously illustrate how a given event such as unemployment probably involves some combination of ego-threat, doubts about the future, financial difficulties, and needs for information. Analogously, it is probable that a given social relationship (e.g., a marriage relationship) provides more than one supportive function, so distinctions among functions are not meant to imply that these functions are necessarily derived from different sources.[3]

Supportive Functions

Esteem Support

In the course of human existence, people encounter threats to their self-esteem: occurrences that raise doubts about their own ability, social attractiveness, or career performance. An interpersonal resource with a strong effect for counteracting self-esteem threats is having someone available with whom one can talk about problems; this supportive function has variously been termed *esteem support,* emotional support, ventilation, or a confidant relationship. Because talking about important problems gen-

---

[3]For several types of interpersonal difficulties, such as problems with children, help seeking from formal helping agencies is an important resource (e.g., Veroff, Kulka, & Douvan, 1981), but because this chapter focuses on informal support systems I shall not give extensive consideration to support from professional helpers. It should be noted that an extensive period of problem discussion within informal social networks apparently precedes the decision to seek professional help (see Wills, 1983), and hence informal supporters may play an important role in providing discussion about problem definition, information about referral sources, and so on.

erally involves revealing negative aspects of the self, most people tend to confine serious problem discussions to a person they feel particularly close to, who may be a husband or wife, a family member, or a close friend with whom there has been a mutually respectful and long-standing relationship. Studies of social support typically show a large difference in symptomatology between persons who have no such relationship and persons who have at least one such relationship (see Cohen & Wills, 1984).

The mechanism through which discussions about problems serve to enhance or restore self-esteem is not known in detail. Probably an important element in this resource is the experience of feeling accepted and valued by another person, even though one is having difficulties in other life areas. This is the process that in professional helping relationships has been termed unconditional positive regard, and the evidence suggests that it is an important facilitative condition in formal helping relationships (Wills, 1982) as well as in social network support (Wills, 1983). There is relatively little evidence on the actual helping behaviors that bring about this function, but several studies have suggested that supportive interactions include listening attentively and reflecting respondents' statements, offering sympathy and reassurance, sharing personal experiences, and avoiding criticism or exhortatory advice-giving (Cowen, 1982; Elliott, Stiles, Shiffman, Barker, Burstein, & Goodman, 1982). Alternatively, conversations with supporters may show that a person's problems are shared by others and perhaps are relatively frequent in the population, which according to attribution theory (where it is called consensus information) should decrease the perceived severity and threat value of the negative events. Consensus information has in fact been shown to facilitate help seeking (Snyder & Ingram, 1983).

In terms of psychological theory, esteem support is best conceptualized with reference to the self-esteem theories discussed previously. By receiving acceptance and approval from significant others, a person's own self-evaluation and self-esteem are enhanced. Esteem support is probably relevant for a wide variety of stressors, both because ego-threat is a common element in stressful life events and because a large proportion of negative events involve conflict in interpersonal relationships, which implicitly or explicitly involves criticism or devaluation by other persons. Relationships in which a person is esteemed and valued provide both a source of active self-enhancement and a set of alternative, accepting relationships, which may serve as an antidote to a relationship where there is unresolved conflict. This type of support would be expected to have its greatest effect primarily for persons who are under considerable stress, and the literature on help seeking suggests that self-esteem maintenance is the primary function sought by distressed persons within social networks (Wills, 1983).

Status Support

It is possible that social relationships serve a supportive function simply because of their existence. For example, Levinger and Huesmann (1980) have made a theoretical distinction between behavioral rewards (based on specific behavioral exchanges of the participants) and relational rewards, which derive from the mere existence of the relationship. Relational rewards may be correlated with psychological well-being because of attributions made by observers about the participant's personality characteristics. Participation in certain formal social relationships provides evidence that a person is capable of fulfilling normative role obligations. Marriage is an example of a role that may provide some relational reward by demonstrating that one person has the ability to initiate and maintain a close relationship with another and to assume responsibility for raising children. Status rewards may also accrue through participation in community activities such as school boards, service organizations, social clubs, and cultural or religious organizations. Participation in such activities, which often involves some element of selection or formal approval, provides evidence of being a valued member of the community and of having the capacity to work effectively with other community members. This aspect of support has been discussed by researchers using terms such as social regulation, social integration, or embeddedness in social roles (Antonucci & Depner, 1982; Moos & Mitchell, 1982). When this type of support is measured by structural indices (e.g., marital status, number of organizations a person belongs to), buffering effects would not be expected, because by definition the support derives simply from the existence of the relationship and not from any esteem-supporting interactions provided by the relationship.

Informational Support

If problems cannot be resolved easily and quickly, people probably begin a search for information about the nature of the problem, knowledge about resources relevant to the problem, and guidance about alternative courses of action. *Informational support* is the term applied to a process through which other persons may provide information, advice, and guidance. Network members may serve a supportive function by providing independent assessments of the locus of the problem (for example, which party is more at fault in a marital or parent–child conflict), by giving suggestions about the respondent's decisions or problem-solving approach, or by giving information about community helping agencies. The literature on help seeking in fact indicates that social networks are an important source of referral information for both medical and psychological treatment (Wills, 1983).

In theoretical construal of the role of informational support, it is important for several reasons to obtain careful measurement of specific support behaviors and perceptions. One reason is that in actual help-giving interactions, esteem-enhancing behaviors and advice giving typically occur together (Barker & Lemle, 1984), so esteem support and informational support probably derive to some extent from the same sources. Indeed, studies that have obtained separate measures of these two dimensions of support have found that they are highly intercorrelated (Norbeck & Tilden, 1983; Schaefer, Coyne, & Lazarus, 1981; Wethington, 1982). This may occur not only because of behavioral co-occurrence in helping interactions but also because provision of advice may be perceived by the recipient as an expression of caring and concern by the other person, which would tend to be interpreted as esteem support. Thus, although the theoretical distinction between esteem and informational support is clear cut, it is not so simple to measure these as completely independent dimensions.

A further issue is that theories need to define mechanisms of informational support specifically. For example, social comparison theory as originally formulated (Festinger, 1954) posited what is essentially a self-evaluation process, in which persons obtain an objective assessment of their own ability through comparison with the performances of other persons. Laboratory research, however, has shown clearly that persons who are under stress tend to pursue self-enhancing rather than self-evaluative comparisons (Wills, 1981). It is true that people want to evaluate their own performance, but it is also true that they want the evaluation to turn out favorably for themselves, and comparisons pursued by stressed persons in naturalistic settings often involve a search for dimensions on which the distressed person is better off than others (Taylor, Wood, & Lichtman, 1983). Thus a search for causal information may be motivated by a need for reassurance that a person's problems are not due to personal deficiencies, and a search for consensus information may have as its goal the impression that these problems are relatively common in the population. How people's search for information is influenced by self-enhancement or self-evaluation motivations and how people process feedback that is not favorable to the self are topics that need further investigation.

In general, it can be predicted that informational support will operate primarily as a buffering process. Under ordinary circumstances, most people probably have the information necessary for effective functioning. It is only when environmental stresses exceed the person's available knowledge and problem-solving ability that additional information and guidance become necessary, and network members may provide valuable assistance under these conditions. Thus, this type of support should be most relevant for persons who are highly stressed.

Instrumental Support

People may be a source of support through providing assistance with instrumental tasks. *Instrumental support* (also termed aid, tangible support, or material support) can include a wide range of activities such as providing assistance with household chores, taking care of children, lending or donating money, running errands, providing transportation, helping with practical tasks (e.g., carpentry, plumbing, moving), looking after a household when the owner is away, and providing material goods such as furniture, tools, or books. Providing help in times of physical injury or illness, which encompasses most of these activities, is a particularly important form of instrumental support because in this case the recipient is almost completely unable to perform necessary instrumental tasks. Under ordinary circumstances, instrumental support could be related to well-being because it reduces task load or provides increased time for leisure activities. There is some evidence that instrumental support is a relevant function in general population samples (Paykel, Emms, Fletcher, & Rassaby, 1980; Schaefer *et al.,* 1981), and instrumental role performance is an important determinant of marital satisfaction (e.g., Argyle & Furnham, 1983; Nye & McLaughlin, 1982; Wills, Weiss, & Patterson, 1974). This type of support is probably particularly relevant for low-income persons, who often are overburdened with instrumental chores, have smaller social networks to begin with, and are financially unable to buy assistance (see Pelton, 1982; Wills & Langner, 1980).

From a theoretical standpoint, in one sense the relationship between instrumental support and well-being is straightforward: People have a specific instrumental need, and other persons can help them to resolve that need. There are, however, several theoretical issues that bear on the effectiveness of instrumental support. One issue is that under ordinary conditions people have a general reluctance to seek help, even for simple instrumental tasks (see DePaulo, 1982). This reluctance may be reduced if a person is imbedded in a network of reciprocal exchanges (Wills, 1983) or, as Clark (1983) has suggested, when there is a communal relationship.

Another issue is that ratings by respondents of instrumental support are perhaps based not so much on recalled instances of specific assistance behaviors but on the perception that network members are dependable, that they could and would provide instrumental assistance if called on. These observations suggest that what persons are responding to when considering instrumental support is the dimension of reliability or predictability, the perception that if something goes really wrong there is someone who is likely to help if called on; this seems more closely related to the construct of personal control (Garber & Seligman, 1980; Schorr & Rodin, 1982). These considerations lead to a somewhat mixed prediction about the relationship between instrumental support and psychological well-being, which is strongly dependent on measurement approach. To the extent that a support measure tapped simple assistance with everyday tasks, only a small main effect would be predicted. To the extent that a measure of instrumental support tapped the perception that networks are reliable and predictable, this variable would be predicted to show some buffering effect. To the extent that the support measure indexed the provision of instrumental assistance that was directly relevant to a particular stressor, a strong buffering effect would be predicted, as for example when relatives and family provide financial assistance to an unemployed person or when friends and neighbors provide crisis assistance that would make it easier to care for a chronically ill family member.

Social Companionship

Social relationships may provide an important supportive function because of the possibility for *social companionship*: enjoyable social activities such as social visiting, dinners, parties, films and concerts, excursions and outdoor activities, or informal athletics. This dimension of relationships has been shown to be of significant importance both in the marital literature, where variables usually termed companionship, friends, or sociability are empirical correlates of marital satisfaction (e.g., Spanier & Lewis, 1980), and in research on pleasurable everyday events, which show social activity as being a major contributor to positive mood (e.g., Lewinsohn & Amenson, 1978). Additionally, studies of overall life satisfaction typically show leisure and recreational activity as making a major contribution to global satisfaction (London, Crandall, & Seals, 1977). Having more social relationships increases the probability of pleasurable activities in general, and entering into a new, significant interpersonal relationship typically combines several social networks (e.g., friends, family, in-laws) which may be available for social and other activities. Thus, a relationship between the social companionship function and indices of well-being can be predicted.

There are, however, some complications in relating evidence on social companionship to current research on social support. For one, studies of major life events have typically found no relationship between positive events and symptomatology measures, and accordingly have tended to focus on negative events (see Cohen & Wills, 1984). This approach, however, ignores the considerable body of evidence on the contribution of everyday positive events to subjective well-being (Diener, 1984). Moreover, it has been shown (Cohen & Hoberman, 1983) that the interaction between positive and negative major events makes an independent contribution to symptomatology, suggesting renewed attention to the ongoing balance between positive and negative experiences (see Diener, 1984).

From a measurement standpoint, it should be noted that people who engage in more social companionship activity probably have access to more instrumental support and probably more esteem support, because shared activities and interests undoubtedly lead to perceptions of reciprocity and in some cases to closer friendships. The suggestion is that measurement strategies should attempt to obtain measures of social companionship activities that are separate from measures of esteem support, expecting that there probably will be some intercorrelation of companionship, esteem, and instrumental support but that each dimension may make an independent contribution to different aspects of psychological well-being. Companionship can be predicted to show primarily a main effect relationship to well-being, because the kinds of activities represented in this dimension do not seem directly relevant to the esteem-threatening aspects of negative life events. Social companionship may, however, show an interaction with negative occurrences.

Motivational Support

Discussion of the ability of social networks to provide *motivational support* enters the realm of conjecture, but on theoretical grounds this may be an important function. One basis for such thinking is that, as several commentators (e.g., Brown, 1981; Miller & Ingham, 1979) have emphasized, many psychosocial stressors are chronic in nature. They derive from problems that are not easily resolved, have significant implications for the future, and require persistence and endurance before they are finally overcome. For example, a person in a dissatisfying job typically does not simply leave immediately on discovering the situation, but insteads waits and looks for a position with better conditions; this process may take a considerable length of time, and for the duration of the present position the unfortunate jobholder will have to endure a lot of frustration. For another example, problems in relationships with children or a spouse usually do not resolve quickly, but often straighten out as attitudes, behaviors, or life cycles change; this also requires patience until the problems begin to ameliorate.

Another part of the theoretical background is a body of work construing psychological disorder as essentially a motivational phenomenon, based on a person's perception that he or she is unable to overcome ongoing difficulties, that the process is no longer interesting or challenging, and that things are not going to get any better with time (see Dohrenwend, Shrout, Egri, & Mendelsohn, 1980; Frank, 1976). Against this background it can be posited that social networks may play an important role by providing what is essentially motivation enhancement: encouraging persons to persist in their efforts at problem solution, reassuring them that their efforts will ultimately be successful and that better things will come, helping them to endure frustration, and communicating their belief that "we can ride it through." By providing continuing support that is there every day, network members may help to avoid the downward spirals that lead to serious depression. The suggestion that this is an important support function is not purely hypothetical, because expectation variables are apparently an element in the therapeutic benefit derived from professional helping relationships (Wills, 1982). In view of the generally equivalent effectiveness of professional and lay helpers it seems likely that this same process occurs in informal social network helping. What is happening in the interactions called confidant relationships perhaps includes a large element of motivational support in addition to esteem-supporting behaviors.

Testing hypotheses about the contribution of motivational support will require methodology somewhat different from that now used to index esteem or instrumental support. Separate measures could be included to index respondents' perceptions that network members encourage them to endure transient distress, communicate a sense of commitment to maintaining the support relationship (cf. Lemkau, Bryant, & Brickman, 1982), and generate positive expectations for the future. Such measures could be similar to those used in research on expectancy changes in psychotherapy (e.g., Kazdin, 1979). The measures could be validated by comparing persons experiencing inherently limited difficulties (e.g., paying off a loan) with those experiencing more long-term problems such as chronic illness of a family member, and could be related to general measures of persistence and optimism. It would also be informative to conduct observational studies of actual helping interactions to determine if reliable distinctions can be made between esteem-enhancing and motivation-supporting behaviors and how each category is related to the perceived helpfulness of the interaction (cf. Elliot *et al.*, 1982).

On the basis of the preceding theoretical analysis it can be predicted that motivational support operates as a pure buffering process. It may prove difficult to obtain strictly independent measures of esteem support and motivational support, because they probably are intercorrelated and tend to occur in the same helping transactions. Nonetheless, from a theoretical standpoint it would be interesting to examine the question.

Summary and Discussion

This chapter has outlined the theoretical basis of social support processes and delineated specific support functions that may contribute to general well-being and may also serve to buffer the impact of particular life stressors. Evidence from epidemiological studies is compelling in linking social support to physical and psychological well-being and is suggestive with regard to the types of functions that may be responsible for these effects. Studies of social networks indicate that spouses, friends, and family members are a primary avenue of help seeking for distressed persons, and this evidence suggests that a primary function sought through informal help seeking is self-esteem maintenance. Other functions that have been implicated in the support–well-being relationship are informational support, instrumental support, social companionship, and possibly motivational support.

The available literature provides confirmation for two general theoretical formulations of supportive functions. Self-esteem maintenance formulations (e.g., Fisher *et al.,* 1982; Greenwald, 1980; Wills, 1983) are successful in accounting for the contribution of esteem support to well-being, and this appears to be the most consistent relationship in the social support literature. Social exchange formulations (Foa & Foa, 1980; Huston & Burgess, 1979; Kelley, 1979) have emphasized the importance of reciprocal exchanges of affection, goods, and services, and in some respects the results of social support research are consistent with this view. Direct links can be seen in the marriage literature, which shows clearly the importance of instrumental and emotional role performance for marital relationship satisfaction (Nye, 1982; Spanier & Lewis, 1980). Personal control formulations also appear relevant because of the suggestion that an important aspect of social support may be the perception that network members will respond if needed, a process that seems more closely related to a theory of predictability or perceived control (Garber & Seligman, 1980; Schorr & Rodin, 1982).

Overall, this formulation is consistent with research on the dimensions of interpersonal relationships (Huston & Levinger, 1978; La Gaipa, 1981) and with suggestions of support needs for particular populations (Antonucci & Depner, 1982; Dunkel-Schetter & Wortman, 1981; House, 1981). It appears that a basic distinction between instrumental and emotional (self-related) aspects of interpersonal relationships is productive for understanding different aspects of supportive functions, and it also seems necessary to distinguish between activities that provide enjoyable or diverting experiences (e.g., social companionship) from those that provide an opportunity to communicate with another person about personal problems. In most cases, though, the links between theory and research are somewhat tenuous. It is not at all clear in most current empirical studies what type of support function was measured and what theoretical model was used to predict a correlation between support and well-being. Understanding of support relationships will be advanced if research is designed to test theoretically derived predictions about the supportive functions available from social networks and interpersonal relationships.

On the basis of current theory, I have suggested which support functions probably operate primarily as main effect processes or as buffering processes. This formulation is summarized in Table 4.1. Esteem support is regarded as a buffering process that protects against the self-esteem threat involved in many stressful events, but this prediction is made only for functional measures that validly index the availability of this function; measures that simply show the existence of a social status are predicted to produce main effect findings only. Informational support is predicted to operate primarily as a buffering process, although there are many theoretical ambiguities about existing measures of this function. Predictions for instrumental support are qualified, depending on the relevance of the instrumental support measured with respect to the specific needs of the population under study. Social companionship, if indexed with a specific measure, should operate as a main effect process. Finally, motivational support (which has not been measured as such in previous research) is predicted to operate as a pure buffering agent. Again it should be noted that these various support functions probably are empirically correlated, deliv-

Table 4.1

Summary of Effects for Different Support Functions[a]

Function	Type of effect	
	Main effect	Interaction effect
Esteem support		
Functional measure		X
Status measure	X	
Informational support		X
Instrumental support	X	X[b]
Social companionship	X	
Motivational support		X

[a] X indicates that function is predicted to show the given type of effect.
[b] Qualified prediction, contingent on match between stressor and type of instrumental assistance.

ered concurrently within essentially the same set of close relationships. It is unlikely that it will be easy to obtain completely independent measures of support functions, but the challenge for further research is to develop functional measures that are as specific as possible.

Suggestions for Support Measurement

The present discussion has emphasized the need for specificity in measuring different functions of social support. The theoretical development presented here and in other discussions (Cohen & McKay, 1984; Cohen & Wills, 1984) has suggested that buffering effects depend on a relationship between the specific need evoked by a particular stressor and the function(s) provided by available supporters. The functions defined here are posited to vary considerably with regard to whether they operate as main effect or as buffering processes, and further research will not be able to test buffering hypotheses clearly unless specific measures of both stressors and support functions are employed. For example, several studies (e.g., Brown & Harris, 1978; Henderson, Byrne, Duncan-Jones, Scott, & Adcock, 1980) have used systematic measures of the existence of a confidant relationship, but because several different functions (e.g., discussion of problems, social companionship, instrumental support, sex) may be confounded in the types of relationships identified by this type of measure, it is not clear which one or more of these functions is the efficacious agent. Because of such ambiguities in measurement, it is conceivable that functions such as instrumental support or social companionship are more important than has generally been suggested by the available literature.

Another recommendation for specific functional measures is that they allow tests of individual differences in support needs. For example, several studies have shown different patterns of findings for men and women, with men deriving more benefit both from a marital relationship and from a diffuse network of community involvements where there are shared activities and interests; women appear to derive more benefit from relationships where there is intense discussion of intimate problems (confidant or "close support" measures—see, e.g., Henderson *et al.*, 1980; House, Robbins, & Metzner, 1982; Huston & Levinger, 1978). It is not clear, however, what types of support functions actually occur in diffuse support networks: whether it is social companionship, or instrumental support, or problem discussion carried on in different settings and contexts. Specific functional measures would help to clarify the basis for these individual differences in support–well-being correlations.

The present argument also suggests ways in which structural measures of social support can be made to yield more information. In addition to establishing the existence or number of social relationships, measures can attempt to index the functions provided by the relationships. For example, studies of general population samples have consistently shown marital relationships to be an important determinant of overall life satisfaction (Freedman, 1978; Glenn & Weaver, 1981). A more fine-grained analysis, however, shows that it is really the quality of the marital relationship that accounts for most of the variance in this effect (Gove, Hughes, & Style, 1983). Because even a moderately successful marriage provides a number of different supportive aspects (esteem, instrumental, companionship, status, and sex), marital relationships tend to be supportive; but a significant minority are not, and so it is important to measure the level and quality of various types of marital role performance. There are several multidimensional measures of marital satisfaction available (e.g., Haynes, Follingstad, & Sullivan, 1979; Snyder, 1979), and these would provide more precise information about why marital relationships are supportive.

A similar argument can be applied to structural measures. For example, a considerable body of literature shows that persons who belong to a church have lower disease rates than those who do not, and that this difference exists regardless of denomination, time, or place. There are, however, several possible reasons for this effect. People may go to church to pray for guidance and strength, to assist in helping persons who are poor or distressed, to meet people, to participate in a regular and socially respectable activity, or for other reasons. Measures providing information about the specific supportive functions that persons derive from church attendance or other community involvements would add considerably to the understanding of the beneficial effects of social support.

References

Altman, I., & Taylor, D. A. (1973). *Social penetration: The development of interpersonal relationships.* New York: Holt.

Antonucci, T. C., & Depner, C. E. (1982). Social support and informal helping relationships. In T. A. Wills (Ed.), *Basic processes in helping relationships.* New York: Academic Press.

Argyle, M., & Furnham, A. (1983). Sources of satisfaction and conflict in long-term relationships. *Journal of Marriage and the Family, 45,* 481–493.

Bandura, A. (1977). Self-efficacy: Toward a unifying theory of behavioral change. *Psychological Review, 84,* 191–215.

Barker, C., & Lemle, R. (1984). The helping process in couples. *American Journal of Community Psychology, 12,* 321–336.

Billings, A. G., & Moos, R. H. (1982). Stressful life events and symptoms: A longitudinal model. *Health Psychology, 1,* 99–117.

Birchler, G. R., Weiss, R. L., & Vincent, J. P. (1975). Multidimensional analysis of social reinforcement exchange between maritally distressed and nondistressed spouse and stranger dyads. *Journal of Personality and Social Psychology, 31,* 349–360.

Bloom, B. L., Asher, S. J., & White, S. W. (1978). Marital disruption as a stressor: A review and analysis. *Psychological Bulletin, 85,* 867–894.

Braiker, H. B., & Kelley, H. H. (1979). Conflict in the development of close relationships. In R. L. Burgess & T. L. Huston (Eds.), *Social exchange in developing relationships.* New York: Academic Press.

Brown, G. W. (1981). Contextual measures of life events. In B. S. Dohrenwend & B. P. Dohrenwend (Eds.), *Stressful life events and their contexts.* New York: Prodist.

Brown, G. W., & Harris, T. (1978). *Social origins of depression: A study of psychiatric disorder in women.* London: Tavistock.

Burr, W. R., Hill, R., Nye, F. I., & Reiss, I. L. (Eds.), (1979). *Contemporary theories about the family* (Vols. 1, 2). New York: Free Press.

Clark, M. S. (1983). Some implications of close social bonds for help-seeking. In B. M. DePaulo, A. Nadler, & J. D. Fisher (Eds.), *New directions in helping* (Vol. 2): *Help-seeking.* New York: Academic Press.

Clark, M. S., & Mills, J. (1979). Interpersonal attraction in exchange and communal relationships. *Journal of Personality and Social Psychology, 37,* 12–24.

Cohen, S., & Hoberman, H. M. (1983). Positive events and social supports as buffers of life change stress. *Journal of Applied Social Psychology, 13,* 99–125.

Cohen, S., & McKay, G. (1984). Social support, stress, and the buffering hypothesis: A theoretical analysis. In A. Baum, J. E. Singer, & S. E. Taylor (Eds.), *Handbook of psychology and health* (Vol. 4). Hillsdale, NJ: Erlbaum.

Cohen, S., & Wills, T. A. (1984). *Stress, social support, and the buffering hypothesis: An integrative review.* Manuscript submitted for publication.

Cowen, E. L. (1982). Help is where you find it: Four informal helping groups. *American Psychologist, 37,* 385–395.

Coyne, J. C., & Holroyd, K. (1982). Stress, coping, and illness: A transactional perspective. In T. Millon, C. Green, & R. Meagher (Eds.), *Handbook of health care clinical psychology.* New York: Plenum.

Coyne, J. C., & Lazarus, R. S. (1980). Cognitive style, stress perception, and coping. In I. L. Kutash & L. B. Schlesinger (Eds.), *Handbook on stress and anxiety.* San Francisco: Jossey-Bass.

DePaulo, B. M. (1982). Social-psychological processes in informal help seeking. In T. A. Wills (Ed.), *Basic processes in helping relationships.* New York: Academic Press.

Diener, E. (1984). Subjective well-being. *Psychological Bulletin, 95,* 542–575.

Dohrenwend, B. P., Shrout, P. E., Egri, G., & Mendelsohn, F. S. (1980). Nonspecific psychological distress and other dimensions of psychopathology. *Archives of General Psychiatry, 37,* 1229–1236.

Dunkel-Schetter, C., & Wortman, C. B. (1981). Dilemmas of social support: Parallels between victimization and aging. In S. B. Kiesler, J. N. Morgan, & V. K. Oppenheimer (Eds.), *Aging: Social change.* New York: Academic Press.

Elliott, R., Stiles, W. B., Shiffman, S., Barker, C. B., Burstein, B., & Goodman, G. (1982). The empirical analysis of help-intended communications. In T. A. Wills (Ed.), *Basic processes in helping relationships.* New York: Academic Press.

Festinger, L. (1954). A theory of social comparison processes. *Human Relations, 7,* 117–140.

Fisher, J. D., Nadler, A., & Whitcher-Alagna, S. (1982). Recipient reactions to aid. *Psychological Bulletin, 91,* 27–54.

Foa, U. G. (1971). Interpersonal and economic resources. *Science, 171,* 345–351.

Foa, E. B., & Foa, U. G. (1980). Resource theory: Interpersonal behavior as exchange. In K. J.

Gergen, M. S. Greenberg, & R. H. Willis (Eds.), *Social exchange: Advances in theory and research.* New York: Plenum.

Frank, J. D. (1976). Restoration of morale and behavior change. In A. Burton (Ed.), *What makes behavior change possible?* New York: Brunner/Mazel.

Freedman, J. (1978). *Happy people: What happiness is, who has it, and why.* New York: Harcourt.

Garber, J., & Seligman, M. E. P. (Eds.). (1980). *Human helplessness: Theory and applications.* New York: Academic Press.

Glenn, N. D., & Weaver, C. N. (1981). The contribution of marital happiness to global happiness. *Journal of Marriage and the Family, 43,* 161–168.

Gove, W. R., Hughes, M., & Style, C. B. (1983). Does marriage have positive effects on the psychological well-being of the individual? *Journal of Health and Social Behavior, 24,* 122–131.

Greenberg, M. S. (1980). A theory of indebtedness. In K. J. Gergen, M. S. Greenberg, & R. H. Willis (Eds.), *Social exchange: Advances in theory and research.* New York: Plenum.

Greenwald, A. G. (1980). The totalitarian ego: Fabrication and revision of personal history. *American Psychologist, 35,* 603–618.

Gruder, C. L. (1977). Choice of comparison persons in evaluating oneself. In J. M. Suls & R. L. Miller (Eds.), *Social comparison processes: Theoretical and empirical perspectives.* Washington, DC: Hemisphere.

Hatfield, E., Utne, M. K., & Traupmann, J. (1979). Equity theory and intimate relationships. In R. L. Burgess & T. L. Huston (Eds.), *Social exchange in developing relationships.* New York: Academic Press.

Haynes, S. N., Follingstad, D. R., & Sullivan, J. C. (1979). Assessment of marital satisfaction and interaction. *Journal of Consulting and Clinical Psychology, 47,* 789–791.

Henderson, S., Byrne, D. G., Duncan-Jones, P., Scott, R., & Adcock, S. (1980). Social relationships, adversity and neurosis: A study of associations in a general population sample. *British Journal of Psychiatry, 136,* 574–583.

Homans, G. C. (1961). *Social behavior: Its elementary forms.* New York: Harcourt.

House, J. (1981). *Work stress and social support.* Reading, MA: Addison-Wesley.

House, J. S., Robbins, C., & Metzner, H. L. (1982). The association of social relationships and activities with mortality: Prospective evidence from the Tecumseh Community Health Study. *American Journal of Epidemiology, 116,* 123–140.

Huston, T. L., & Burgess, R. L. (1979). Social exchange in developing relationships: An overview. In R. L. Burgess & T. L. Huston (Eds.), *Social exchange in developing relationships.* New York: Academic Press.

Huston, T. L., & Levinger, G. (1978). Interpersonal attraction and relationships. *Annual Review of Psychology, 29,* 115–156.

Kasl, S. (1974). Work and mental health. In J. O'Toole (Ed.), *Work and the quality of life.* Cambridge, MA: MIT Press.

Kazdin, A. E. (1979). Nonspecific treatment factors in psychotherapy outcome research. *Journal of Consulting and Clinical Psychology, 47,* 846–851.

Kelley, H. H. (1979). *Personal relationships: Their structures and processes.* Hillsdale, NJ: Erlbaum.

Kitson, G. C., & Sussman, M. B. (1982). Marital complaints, demographic characteristics, and symptoms of mental distress in divorce. *Journal of Marriage and the Family, 44,* 87–101.

La Gaipa, J. J. (1981). A systems approach to personal relationships. In S. Duck & R. Gilmour (Eds.), *Personal relationships* (Vol. 1). London: Academic Press.

Lefcourt, H. M. (Ed.). (1981). *Research with the locus of control construct.* New York: Academic Press.

Lemkau, J. P., Bryant, F. B., & Brickman, P. (1982). Client commitment to the helping relationship. In T. A. Wills (Ed.), *Basic processes in helping relationships*. New York: Academic Press.

Levinger, G., & Huesmann, L. R. (1980). An "incremental exchange" perspective on the pair relationship: Interpersonal reward and level of involvement. In K. J. Gergen, M. S. Greenberg, & R. H. Willis (Eds.), *Social exchange: Advances in theory and research*. New York: Plenum.

Lewinsohn, P. M., & Amenson, C. S. (1978). Some relations between pleasant and unpleasant mood-related events and depression. *Journal of Abnormal Psychology, 87,* 644–654.

London, M., Crandall, R., & Seals, G. W. (1977). The contribution of job and leisure satisfaction to quality of life. *Journal of Applied Psychology, 62,* 328–334.

Miller, P. McC., & Ingham, J. G. (1979). Reflections on the life-events-to-illness link with some preliminary findings. In I. G. Sarason & C. D. Spielberger (Eds.), *Stress and anxiety* (Vol. 6). New York: Hemisphere.

Moos, R. H., & Mitchell, R. E. (1982). Social network resources and adaptation: A conceptual framework. In T. A. Wills (Ed.), *Basic processes in helping relationships*. New York: Academic Press.

Norbeck, J. S., & Tilden, V. P. (1983). Life stress, social support, and emotional disequilibrium in complications of pregnancy. *Journal of Health and Social Behavior, 24,* 30–46.

Nye, F. I. (Ed.). (1982). *Family relationships: Rewards and costs*. Beverly Hills, CA: Sage.

Nye, F. I., & McLaughlin, S. (1982). Role competence and marital satisfaction. In F. I. Nye (Ed.), *Family relationships: Rewards and costs*. Beverly Hills, CA: Sage.

Paykel, E. S., Emms, E. M., Fletcher, J., & Rassaby, E. S. (1980). Life events and social support in puerperal depression. *British Journal of Psychiatry, 136,* 339–346.

Pelton, L. (1982). Personalistic attributions and client perspectives in child welfare cases. In T. A. Wills (Ed.), *Basic processes in helping relationships*. New York: Academic Press.

Schaefer, C., Coyne, J. C., & Lazarus, R. S. (1981). The health-related functions of social support. *Journal of Behavioral Medicine, 4,* 381–406.

Schorr, D., & Rodin, J. (1982). The role of perceived control in practitioner-patient relationships. In T. A. Wills (Ed.), *Basic processes in helping relationships*. New York: Academic Press.

Snyder, C. R., Higgins, R. L., & Stucky, R. J. (1983). *Excuses: Masquerades in search of grace*. New York: Wiley.

Snyder, C. R., & Ingram, R. E. (1983). "Company motivates the miserable": The impact of consensus information on help seeking for psychological problems. *Journal of Personality and Social Psychology, 45,* 1118–1126.

Snyder, D. K. (1979). Multidimensional assessment of marital satisfaction. *Journal of Marriage and the Family, 41,* 813–823.

Spanier, G. B., & Lewis, R. A. (1980). Marital quality: A review of the seventies. *Journal of Marriage and the Family, 42,* 825–840.

Taylor, S. E., Wood, J. V., & Lichtman, R. R. (1983). It could be worse: Selective evaluation as a response to victimization. *Journal of Social Issues, 39* (2), 19–40.

Veroff, J., Kulka, R. A., & Douvan, E. (1981). *Mental health in America: Patterns of help-seeking from 1957 to 1976*. New York: Basic Books.

Wallston, B. S., Whitcher-Alagna, S., DeVellis, B. M., & DeVellis, R. F. (1983). Social support and physical health. *Health Psychology, 2,* 367–391.

Warheit, G. J. (1979). Life events, coping, stress, and depressive symptomatology. *American Journal of Psychiatry, 136,* 502–507.

Wethington, E. (1982, August). *Can social support functions be differentiated? A multivariate model*. Paper presented at the American Psychological Association Meeting, Washington, DC.

Williams, A. W., Ware, Jr., J. E., & Donald, C. A. (1981). A model of mental health, life events, and social supports applicable to general populations. *Journal of Health and Social Behavior, 22,* 324–336.

Wills, T. A. (1981). Downward comparison principles in social psychology. *Psychological Bulletin, 90,* 245–271.

Wills, T. A. (1982). Nonspecific factors in helping relationships. In T. A. Wills (Ed.), *Basic processes in helping relationships.* New York: Academic Press.

Wills, T. A. (1983). Social comparison in coping and help-seeking. In B. M. DePaulo, A. Nadler, & J. D. Fisher (Eds.), *New directions in helping* (Vol. 2): *Help-seeking.* New York: Academic Press.

Wills, T. A., & Langner, T. S. (1980). Socioeconomic status and stress. In I. L. Kutash & L. B. Schlesinger (Eds.), *Handbook on stress and anxiety.* San Francisco: Jossey-Bass.

Wills, T. A., Weiss, R. L., & Patterson, G. R. (1974). A behavioral analysis of the determinants of marital satisfaction. *Journal of Consulting and Clinical Psychology, 42,* 802–811.

CHAPTER 5

Measures and Concepts
of Social Support*

James S. House and Robert L. Kahn
with the assistance of
Jane D. McLeod and David Williams

Introduction

The study of social support emerged, seemingly out of nowhere, during the 1970s. The impression of novelty, however, is not wholly accurate. At least twice before, support has been proposed as a central concept in social science. Likert argued in 1961 that the core element in supervisory success was the principle of supportive relations, the ability of some supervisors to conduct each transaction with subordinates in such a way that the individual's sense of personal worth and importance was enhanced. And Rogers (1942), 20 years earlier, had put supportive behavior at the center of his theory of psychotherapy and counseling.

*Preparation of this chapter has been supported by grants No. 1 P01 AG03981 from the National Institute on Aging and No. 5T32 MH16806 from the National Institute on Mental Health. We are indebted to Sheldon Cohen, Victor Hawthorne, Barbara Israel, Jane Norbeck, Richard Price, Leonard Syme, Camille Wortman, and Elaine Wethington for comments on a previous draft and to members of the Social Environment and Health Program and the seminar of the Research Training Program in Psychosocial Factors in Mental Health and Illness for discussions that have contributed to the development of our thinking over a period of years. Marie Klatt has shepherded the manuscript through the vagaries of authors, editors, and word processors. We much appreciate her patience, skill, and good humor.

Whether or not the interest is new, its current magnitude and manifestations are impressive. The *Social Sciences Citation Index* shows a rapidly accelerating, almost geometric, growth in the number of articles with the term *social support* in their titles, from 2 in 1972 to 50 in 1982. This rate of publication is naturally spawning a growing number of review articles and monographs (e.g., Antonucci, in press; Broadhead *et al.*, 1983; House, 1981; Israel, 1982; Leavy, 1983; Mueller, 1980; Turner, 1983; Wallston *et al.*, 1983). Such rapid scientific development often reflects the influence of a specific theoretical concept or empirical measure (e.g., the literature on life events or the type A and type B behavior patterns).

The research appeal of social support, however, is based neither on the specificity of the concept nor on the emergence of some uniquely successful empirical measure. Rather, like the related concept of stress, social support has attracted researchers and stimulated research across the biomedical, behavioral, and social sciences because of its integrative promise and intuitive appeal. It suggests an underlying common element in seemingly diverse phenomena and it captures something that all of us have experienced. The term connotes enough that it has proved fruitful even in the absence of denotation. Indeed, one of the most influential review papers on social support (Cassel, 1976) offered neither an explicit definition of support nor any specifications regarding measurement. At this point, however, generality has served its purpose and lack of specificity in conceptualization and measurement poses increasingly serious problems for research on social support.

The basic task of this chapter is to evaluate existing measures of social support, to suggest directions for their future use, and to propose the development of new measures as needed. However, assessment of the adequacy of existing or proposed measures, especially their *construct validity*, requires a theoretical framework to give clarity and meaning to the concepts being measured. Such a framework must specify the nature of and the relationships among the various concepts and measures now used interchangeably within the broad domain of social support research. It must also state the relationship of key social support variables to their causes and consequences.

The Domain of Social Support

The term *social support* (like the terms *social network* and *social integration*) refers to a number of different aspects of social relationships. Social support is sometimes defined conceptually or operationally in terms of the *existence or quantity* of social relationships in general, or of a particular type such as marriage, friendship, or organizational membership. Social support is also sometimes defined and measured in terms of the *structure* of a person's social relationships. In addition, social support is sometimes defined in terms of the *functional content* of relationships, such as the degree to which the relationships involve flows of affect or emotional concern, instrumental or tangible aid, information, and the like.

Because the term *social support* has been used to refer to each of these aspects of relationships, each must be considered part of the general domain of social support. *Social support* is, however, most commonly used to mean the last of these aspects of social relationships—their functional content. Similarly, the term *social network* is most often used to refer to the structures existing among a set of relationships (e.g., their density, homogeneity, or range). Finally, terms such as *social integration* or *isolation* are most often used to refer to the existence or quantity of relationships. Such designations are used throughout this chapter.

It is necessary to consider all three aspects of social relations—quantity, structure, and function—because they are logically and empirically interrelated. Moreover, they may constitute distinctive explanations of the effects of social support or social networks as these terms are used more generically. The existence or quantity of relationships is a necessary condition for, and hence a partial determinant of, both the network structure of those relationships and their functional content or qualities. Similarly, network structure may partially determine the functional content or qualities of relationships within the network. The potential connections among these different aspects of social relations are shown in Figure 5.1.

It is desirable on both substantive and methodological grounds that at least two, and preferably all three, of these aspects of social relationships be explicitly conceptualized and measured within a single study. Only then can the relationships both among these aspects of social relations and between them and health be understood. Figure 5.1 suggests, for example, that the connection between the existence of a social relationship (e.g., marriage) and health may be explainable wholly or in part by the different network structures or functional content associated with marriage. Conversely, the figure also suggests that some apparent effects of network structure or relationship content on health may be spurious products of the mere existence of the relationship (or of some other unspecified variable associated with the existence of a relationship).

Assessing the Quality of Measures: A Focus on Validity

How can researchers decide what is known and what needs to be known, or what is good and bad, about a measure of social relationships, network structure, or support? The standard, if incomplete, answer is by evaluation

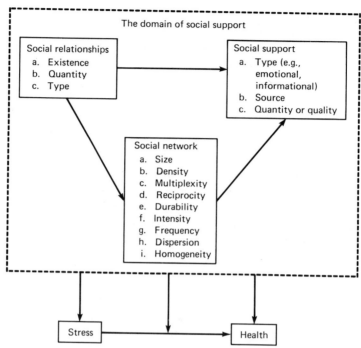

Figure 5.1. Theoretical framework for assessing the quality of measures of social support.

of the reliability and validity of the measure. This is easier said than done, because there are multiple forms of reliability and validity. High reliability, in terms of both internal consistency and test–retest stability, is a desirable feature of any measure and a crucial precondition of validity.

But validity remains the essential problem, and a complex one. There is no criterion validity against which measures of social relationships, networks, and support can be assessed. Of course, evidence of face validity, content validity, and convergent and discriminant validity is desired. Most critical, however, is evidence of construct validity (see Campbell, 1960; Nunnally, 1978). The meaning of a scientific concept is really defined by its place in a theoretical system of relationships with other variables (see Cronbach & Meehl, 1955). What is most novel and critical about the concept of social support, as it has emerged since the early 1970s, is the idea that it is beneficial to health and well-being, either directly or because it moderates the negative effects of stress and other hazards on individual health and well-being as shown in Figure 5.1 (See Broadhead *et al.*, 1983; Cassel, 1976; Cobb, 1976; House, 1981; Kahn, 1981). Thus, assessing the validity of measures of social support involves consideration of the substantive relationships found between those measures and health, most notably the degree to which social support contributes to the ability to predict health outcomes.

If an empirical study uses a particular measure and finds that the relationships predicted within the framework are nonexistent or contrary to prediction, the reasons for the failure of prediction may be difficult to interpret. Especially when neither the measure nor the theory has been well established in previous empirical work, the negative results may mean that either or both are deficient. On the other hand, when well-designed empirical research confirms theoretical ideas about the relation between social support and health, confidence in both the theory and the measures used to test it is enhanced.

In the absence of a dominant, well-validated measure of social support, diverse proposed measures have proliferated almost as rapidly as have new empirical studies. It is easy to become preoccupied with comparisons of these measures and their psychometric properties. It must be remembered, however, that the litmus test of the validity of any measure of social support is its relationship to the major causes and consequences of social support.

A Note on Method

In this chapter we will review available measures of the existence or quantity of social relations, the network structure of those relations, and their functional content, paying attention not only to the formal psychometric properties of measures but also to the extent to which they have been shown to relate meaningfully to theoretically expected causes and health consequences of social support.

In the course of the review, we will show that the measures of social support used in prior studies range from one or two global items to questionnaires of from 50 to 100 or more differentiated items taking up to a half-hour to administer. Because both time and money are at a premium in most research, issues of cost-effectiveness must be considered—that is, how much is gained by using a longer, more differentiated, and more complicated measure rather than a shorter, less complex, and more global measure? In the end we try to recommend how an investigator might choose or construct measures of social support for different purposes and under different constraints of time and resources.

In reviewing existing measures of social support we have tried to examine all empirical studies of support and health published between 1972 and mid-1983. Our basic universe was all studies that contained the term *social support* in their title and that appeared in the *Social Sciences Citation Index* between 1971 and 1982. This list was supplemented by a parallel search of *Psychological Abstracts* and by information obtained through informal networks. We have reviewed not only studies focused on measurement but also empirical studies of social relationships, social networks, and social support in relation to physical and mental health.

Social Relationships as Measures of Support

The relation of the existence or quantity of an individual's social contacts or relationships to health and well-being has long been a focus of both experimental and nonexperimental research. Measures of the existence or quantity of social contacts or relationships are relatively objective, reliable, and easy to obtain. Such information can sometimes be obtained by observation or from behavioral records (e.g., marriage or organizational membership). Even if obtained by self-report, information on whether or not persons are married, live alone, or belong to a church or other organizations is generally simple to collect, stable over time, and accurate. Donald and Ware (1982, p. 110), for example, found 1-year test–retest correlations of .80 for church attendance and of from .64 to .66 for group membership and activity. Reports of marital status and living alone are probably even more stable and accurate.

People also report quite easily on the frequency of contacts with friends and relatives, and on the number of such relationships. These quantitative reports, however, are not as obviously accurate and stable as reports of formal membership and status. Donald and Ware (1982) report 1-year test–retest reliabilities of from .4 to .6 for reports of social contacts. Yet such reports appear objective and stable compared to reports of the functional quality of relationships, which are likely to be more labile and confounded with mental health status. This combination of objectivity, stability, and ease of assessment undoubtedly accounts for the popularity of measures of the existence and quantity of relationships in empirical research.

Measures and studies of social relationships are relevant to the study of social support in several ways. Often studies that purport to measure social supports or social networks operationalize these concepts in terms of the existence or quantity of social relationships (e.g., Berkman & Syme, 1979; Eaton, 1978; Funch & Marshall, 1983; Wan & Weissert, 1981). Even where such measures are more accurately described as social relationships or social contacts and resources (e.g., Donald & Ware, 1982; House, Robbins, & Metzner, 1982), they are hypothesized and often found to behave as measures of social support should behave. Finally, social relationships must exist in some quantity before they can have a structure and supportive content or function. And some have argued that it is the sheer existence or quantity of relationships that is consequential for health, rather than their structure or functional content (e.g., Syme, 1982). The underlying idea here might be considered a social isolation hypothesis, although what exactly is consequential about social isolation is not spelled out.

Data relating the existence and quantity of relationships to health are impressive in quality as well as in volume. These associations have as yet not been fully accounted for in terms of more specific and theoretically satisfying measures of the structure or quality of relationships. Nevertheless, they present a coherent pattern.

Of all social relationships, marital status has been the most studied and most consistently related to health. Beginning with Durkheim's (1951) evidence that unmarried men and women are more likely to commit suicide than those who are married, numerous cross-sectional, retrospective, and longitudinal or prospective studies have shown a higher prevalence and incidence of many psychological and physical disorders and a lower life expectancy (or higher mortality risk) among the unmarried than the married. The benefits of marriage in these respects are almost always greater for men than women. There is also some evidence that not all unmarried states are equally deleterious, though evidence here is lower in quality and quantity and less consistent (see Berkman & Syme, 1979; Gove, 1972; Gove & Tudor, 1973; Gove, Hughes, & Style, 1983; House *et al.*, 1982; Ortmeyer, 1974).

The existence and quantity of contacts with friends and relatives have also been found to relate cross-sectionally, retrospectively, and prospectively to lower rates of psychological and physical disorders and mortality. Membership and attendance in church and participation in other voluntary organizations show positive relationships to well-being. These results are somewhat more sparse and variable than in the case of marital status, but still relatively consistent (see Berkman & Syme, 1979; Donald & Ware, 1982; Henderson, Byrne, & Duncan-Jones, 1982; House *et al.*, 1981; Wan & Weissert, 1981; Williams, Ware, & Donald, 1981).

In a number of studies, indexes were formed of the total number of social relationships or the frequency of social contacts. Three prospective mortality studies of broad community samples have shown independently that people with low levels of social relationships have at least twice the risk of mortality from all causes as persons with moderate to high levels of relationships (Berkman & Syme, 1979; Blazer, 1982; House *et al.*, 1982). Among women with breast cancer (Stage 3), those with higher levels of organizational involvement had a significantly longer survival period (Funch & Marshall, 1983). Medicare patients living alone or not having grandchildren were significantly more likely to be institutionalized over a follow-up period of

1 year (Wan & Weissert, 1981). Lower levels of social relationships and activities have also been associated cross-sectionally and longitudinally with symptoms of poor mental health (Henderson *et al.*, 1982; Williams *et al.*, 1981). Several studies have suggested that relatively isolated persons with few or no social relationships are especially at risk; increases above a moderate number of relationships appear to produce diminishing returns to health (see Berkman & Syme, 1979; Blazer, 1982; House *et al.*, 1982).

These findings are especially impressive because they consistently show effects of social relationships on health, including "hard" outcomes such as mortality, in well-designed and well-controlled, prospective studies of large and broad-based samples. The results on human populations are reinforced by experimental studies showing the health-protective effects of social relationships in a variety of animal species. They are also reinforced by the frequent finding (discussed subsequently) that the size of social networks is predictive of health. All of these effects are, however, main or additive effects. The hypothesis that social relationships can buffer people against effects of stress has not really been tested in most cases, and when tested has been sometimes confirmed (Eaton, 1978) and sometimes not confirmed (e.g., Williams *et al.*, 1981).[1]

In sum, although they represent very crude assessments of the nature of individuals' social worlds, simple measures of the existence and quantity of social relationships are relatively objective, reliable, and not artifactually confounded with measures of other relevant variables such as stress and health. There is also substantial evidence for their construct validity in terms of their relationships with health outcomes. Selected studies (Blazer, 1982; Gove *et al.*, 1983) have presented evidence that it is the quality of these relationships, particularly the perceived support they offer, that largely accounts for their effects. The majority of studies, however, have not gone beyond assessment of the existence and quantity of relationships, and some that have (House *et al.*, 1982) did not find these other measures to be predictive of health outcomes.

It seems logical that the beneficial effects of social relationships derive from the content and quality of those relationships. That presumption should not, however, lead to neglect of measures of existence and quantity. At least until the effects of social relationships on health can be empirically accounted for, assessment of the existence, quantity, and contact frequency of major social relationships should be a standard part of studies of social

---

[1]The Williams *et al.* (1981) specification of the buffering effect in their regression models appears invalid, because a product term was created from two variables, neither of which has a real zero point (see Kessler & Cleary, 1980). One figure they presented, however, suggests little buffering.

support. Most important among these relationships are marital status, number and frequency of contacts with friends and relatives, church membership and attendance, and participation in other voluntary organizations. The Social Network Index of Berkman and Syme (1979) covers all these aspects of social relationships, and can readily be adapted and expanded for other studies. House *et al.* (1982) and Donald and Ware (1982) have provided other relatively brief batteries of questions on these topics.

Social Network Measures of Support

There has been a growing interest in using social network analysis to study the ways in which social relationships are linked to individual health and well-being. Some researchers have even urged "that we transmute support system analysis into social network analysis" (Wellman, 1981, p. 171). The purported advantages of network analysis are several: (1) It broadens the range of social relationships examined, (2) it encourages attention to multiple aspects and effects of these relationships, both positive and negative, and (3) it provides a method for describing the structural pattern of ties and for analyzing the effects of different patterns (Wellman, 1981; see also d'Abbs, 1982; Wilcox, 1981).

In our view, the unique features of a social network approach, as compared to the social relationships approach described earlier and the social support approach described subsequently, lie in its emphasis on (1) analyzing the structure of social relationships (as opposed to their mere existence or their functional content), (2) mapping a broad range of social contacts and relationships, and (3) attending not only to the focal person and his or her relationship to others but also to relationships among the other persons in the network of the focal person. That is, the issue is not just who are a person's friends, but who are the friends of those friends (Boissevain, 1974).

Social network analysis has a long history of application to a wide range of problems. At issue is how useful it has proved, or may prove, in analyses of the association between aspects of social relationships and health or well-being. Our sense is that the utility of network analysis for mapping individual's social worlds and studying a broad range of social processes (e.g., communication and influence, power structures) is clear; the utility of many aspects of network analysis in understanding the etiologic pathways that link social relationships to health and illness remains to be established. Network analysis may be more useful to the understanding of health or illness behavior, where access to information and providers of care is crucial.

Our reading of the literature concurs with that of Israel (1982), who identified a set of network characteristics she called structural and interactional: (1) size or range, (2) density (i.e., the extent to which all members of a network are linked with each other), (3) content (i.e., uniplexity versus multiplexity, or the extent to which relationships involve more than one type of content or transaction), (4) directedness or reciprocity, (5) durability, (6) intensity or emotional closeness, (7) frequency, (8) dispersion, and (9) homogeneity. These are distinguished from functional characteristics, or the functional content and quality of relationships (e.g., affective, instrumental, and cognitive support).[2]

Israel (1982, p. 71) concluded that "quantitative structural and interactional characteristics of networks have been found to have conflicting associations with well-being." The only exception to this is network size, which is generally found to be positively associated with health and well-being (e.g., Froland *et al.,* 1979; Gallo, 1982; Phillips, 1981), but which is really just a measure of the quantity of relationships people have (as are such measures as number of social contexts and range of socializing, used by Phillips, 1981). Many studies of social relationships and health (e.g., Berkman & Syme, 1979) have used the term *network,* but only a limited number, usually based on small and idiosyncratic samples, have actually assessed the kinds of structural network properties emphasized by Israel and other network analysts. The substantial costs involved in fully mapping social networks militates against systematic analysis of network properties in large samples. In short, the network characteristics considered and the method of assessment vary so greatly across studies that it is presently impossible to draw firm conclusions about the utility of the network approach for predicting and explaining health or illness.

After size, density is probably the network property most frequently and uniformly studied. Some studies (Gallo, 1982) have reported a positive association between density and indicators of mental health and well-being, some have reported a negative association (Hirsch, 1980, 1981), and some have reported no relationship (Phillips, 1981). Such a pattern of conflicting results may, however, reflect some underlying regularities. Walker, MacBride, and Vachon (1977), among others, have argued that networks of small size, strong ties, high density and homogeneity, and low dispersion are helpful in maintaining social identity and hence well-being to the extent that well-being relies on maintenance of social identity. However, change in social roles and identities is facilitated by larger networks with weaker ties, lower density, and greater social and cultural heterogeneity. This interpretation is consistent with differences in the populations of the stud-

---

[2]We would argue that intensity, connoting as it does strong affect, is as much a functional as a structural feature of relationships.

ies just cited: Hirsch found density deleterious to mental health among women experiencing widowhood and divorce, whereas Gallo found density positively associated with health in a community sample of persons 60 and over. Phillips, who found neither relationship, analyzed a representative "normal" sample of 50 northern California communities.

Reciprocity, or directedness, is another property of relationships and perhaps networks that logically seems relevant to health, and there is some empirical support for such relevance (Gallo, 1982). Relationships in which both the focal person and the network member initiate contact are health-promotive, those in which the focal person usually initiates contact are not, and those in which the network member initiates contact are negatively associated with health status.

Network analysis also highlights the importance of considering the characteristics of the others with whom an individual has social relationships. A neglected but promising variable appears to be the sex of the other or others in a relationship or network. Evidence suggests that relationships with women may be more supportive and health promoting than relationships with men, and conversely that the degree to which others (perhaps men especially) rely on women for support may be deleterious to women's health (see Belle, 1982). Marriage is generally more beneficial to men then women, but women benefit more from relationships with friends and relatives (which run predominantly along same sex-lines). And Kessler and McLeod (in press) have found evidence that the higher rate of symptoms of psychological disorder among women, as compared to men, stems in substantial part from the life events occurring to people they know (presumably requiring women to provide support). Obviously, the issues of reciprocity and sex composition of relationships are related in that women may benefit more from relationships with other women not because such relationships are less demanding, but because they are more reciprocal.

In sum, network analysis suggests a number of promising leads for new measures of the characteristics of social relationships that are consequential for health. However, at this point the empirical evidence for the utility of such measures is much lower in quality and amount than that for the effects of the sheer existence and quantity of social relationships. This is especially true of the more complex measures of network structure. The reasons are in part methodological. It is quite costly to collect and process the amount of data necessary to characterize fully the structure of social networks. The cost-effectiveness of such an effort, in our view, has yet to be demonstrated. Moreover, the validity of network data reported by the focal person has yet to be assessed, although some such efforts have been undertaken (Kahn, Wethington, & Ingersoll, in press). Thus, we feel it is necessary to be selective in measuring and analyzing network properties in relation to health. For example, it is not yet known what the gains or losses are from focusing on smaller versus larger numbers of persons in obtaining data about social networks; however, some of our own work has suggested that at somewhere between 5 and 10 persons in a network, a point of greatly diminishing returns is reached in data collection.[3] Among network properties, density, reciprocity, and sex composition seem most promising—the latter two being properties of dyads as well as networks. If a researcher desires a full assessment of network properties, the approach of Fischer (1982; see also McCallister & Fischer, 1978) represents the state of the art.

Although the structural analysis of networks is most highly developed, at least in a quantitative sense, network analyses have often proved most informative when they have focused on the content and quality as well as the structure of relationships (see d'Abbs, 1982; Israel, 1982; Wellman, 1981). Such a focus bears directly on the domain to which the term *social support* commonly refers.

Measures of Social Support in Terms of the Functional Content of Relationships

Our review uncovered over 40 published studies that have attempted to measure social support in terms of the functional content of social relationships as opposed to their mere existence or structure. Most investigators develop their own scales, so there are almost as many different measures as there are studies. The studies vary greatly in their populations and methods and generally employ weak research designs (i.e., cross-sectional correlations between reported measures of social support and mental health within small and idiosyncratic samples). Most studies present reasonable evidence for the reliability of their social support measures, but the evidence for construct validity is limited. There are few negative results but the positive results may be somewhat artifactual and not very generalizable. Thus, we are unable to find a single measure that is so well validated and cost-effective that it is to be preferred above the others; various measures may be appropriate for various purposes and circumstances, and continued efforts at measurement development are needed.

---

[3]How many people are elected in a network depends greatly on the questions used to define membership in the network. On this issue, we see no clear consensus. Fischer (1982; also McCallister & Fischer, 1978) has provided the most exhaustive method, asking about a variety of types of social relationships. Others generally have asked people to name others who are "close" or "important" to them (e.g., Kahn & Antonucci, 1980).

The assessment of social support, like that of social networks, ranges from global to differentiated. Differentiations are usually made with respect to (1) quantity or availability of support versus quality or adequacy of support, (2) source of support, and (3) type of support. Measures also differ in whether they ask about the perceived availability of support or the occurrence of actual supportive behaviors. In the latter case it is possible to assess these behaviors by direct observation, by report of the person who enacts the supportive behavior, or by report of the recipient of the behavior. Thus far, almost all measures of support, and also of social relationships and networks, have relied on the self-report of a focal person (recipient) about how others behave or how the focal person perceives their behavior. We will focus on such measures here, although we recognize the need to understand how objective behavior relates to perceptions of that behavior and to feelings of support engendered by it (see House, 1981, Ch. 5; Kahn & Antonucci, 1980). In reviewing specific measures we will first focus on those that have been designed for and empirically tested in specific and limited populations, and then consider measures designed and used for more general and representative populations.

Social Support among College Students

Procidano and Heller (1983) and Sarason *et al.* (1983) have developed fairly lengthy scales (20–40 items) of the perceived availability of social support, which are potentially adaptable to general populations but have thus far been used mainly in small studies of college students. Procidano and Heller measured only a global concept of support but have separate scales for family and friends; Sarason distinguished only between the number of supporters and satisfaction with them. Barrera, Sandler, and Ramsay (1981) have developed a 40-item Index of Socially Supportive Behaviors, which also yields a single global score. Considerable data are available on the reliability of these measures and their cross-sectional correlations with measures of personality, social relations, and mental health. Some of these data are from experimental studies. The item pools may be of interest to other investigators, but their utility beyond college student populations remains to be determined. We also feel that the measures are not very cost-effective for use in general population surveys because they use 20–40 items to generate one or two global measures of support.

Cohen and Hoberman (1983) and their colleagues (Cohen, Mermelstein, Kamarck, & Hoberman, 1984) have developed a 48-item Interpersonal Support Evaluation List (ISEL), which assesses the perceived availability of four types of functions of social support—tangible, appraisal, self-esteem, and belonging. A 40-item ISEL has also been developed for noncollege populations, although it has been used only once on a sample of other than college students (64 persons in a university-based smoking cessation program). These authors reported cross-sectional and some longitudinal correlations of the ISEL (total score and subscales) with mental and, to a lesser degree, physical health. They found evidence that these measures, with the exception of tangible support, buffer the relationship between stress and health. In the smoking cessation study the intercorrelations among the appraisal, belonging, and self-esteem scales ranged from .61 to .73, very close to the maximum possible given the estimated reliabilities of these scales (.6–.8). Thus the ISEL seems to differentiate clearly only two functions of support (tangible versus the others, which appear to consist primarily of emotional support). This is a basic dichotomy that gives the ISEL an edge over the measures just discussed, which it otherwise resembles.

Social Support in Special Populations

A number of other investigators have developed and used measures of social support in small and specialized nonstudent populations. Although many of these measures have shown some promise, evidence for their reliability is limited and their content is often narrowly focused. Among the more promising measures of this type are those of Norbeck, Lindsey, and Carrieri (1981), Brandt and Weinert (1981), and Cronenwett (1983). The Norbeck measure developed an interesting set of questions, based on the theoretical scheme of Kahn and Antonucci (1981), to assess three aspects or forms of social support—aid, affirmation, and affect—from multiple sources. The way the measure attempts to distinguish both types and sources of support is very useful. The scaling procedures used by Norbeck are flawed, however, and result in no empirical discrimination among forms of support.[4] With different scaling procedures, the measure has promise and has been used in a small sample of employed adults (Norbeck, 1983).

Brandt and Weinert (1981) operationalized Weiss's (1974) five functions of support—indication of personal value, group membership, provision for attachment and intimacy, opportunity for nurturance, and availability of help (informational, emotional, and material). Empirical validation was, how-

---

[4]The error of Norbeck et al. (1981) is one common among measures that ask people to nominate persons in their network (e.g., who are "close to them" or provide different kinds of support). If the overall measures of different types of support are based on *numbers* of persons named, the size of the network is confounded with assessment of the content or quality of the relationships. Norbeck *added* responses to questions regarding the behavior of each person named, making the measure of each type of support largely a function of the number of persons in the network. Consequently, most of her measures intercorrelate in the .90s.

ever, limited to a study of spouses of multiple sclerosis victims. Cronenwett (1983) tried to operationalize House's (1981) conceptualization of four types of support—emotional, instrumental, informational, and appraisal—using the interesting approach of defining a type of support and asking who provided that kind of support. The measures suffer from a moderate contamination of the quantity and quality of relationships, as discussed in footnote 4 and subsequently. The measure has also been used only in a small study of relatively well-educated new parents.

Social Support Measures in General Populations

A number of measures have been developed for and used in studies of the general population. The simplest of them are one- or two-item assessments of the presence or absence of a confidant (e.g., Lowenthal & Haven, 1968). Pearlin *et al.* (1981) used a variant of this approach in their longitudinal study of the stress process in a representative sample of adults aged 18–65 in the Chicago area. They created a summative index of two confidant items, one referring to friends and relatives and the other to the spouse. The index was shown both to have main effects on measures of well-being, and to buffer the impact of job disruption in longitudinal analyses. Fleming, Baum, Gisrel, and Gatchel (1982) and Turner (1981) presented slightly more elaborate global measures of support, tested on smaller samples.

Moos and colleagues (Billings & Moos, 1981, 1982; Holahan & Moos, 1982) have developed both a Quantitative Social Support Index (QSSI), a measure of social relationships similar to those discussed in the section "Social Relationships as Measures of Support," and a Family Relations Index (FRI) and a Work Relations Index (WRI) derived from Moos's (1974) Family Environment and Work Environment Scales. They presented cross-sectional associations of these measures with mental health and coping. Although the measures show evidence of construct validity, they do not appear to have special virtues for other users. The QSSI is similar to measures discussed earlier, and the FRI and WRI are global measures of support from two sources, developed largely before the concept of support had been made explicit. They do illustrate that current concepts and measures of support have much in common with earlier concepts and measures (e.g., cohesion).

MacFarlane *et al.* (1981) developed an interesting measure that asks respondents to name individuals with whom they have discussed six types of problems and to indicate how helpful those discussions were. It also asks whether the other reciprocates by coming to the respondent to discuss problems. Thus far, however, only highly aggregated measures of the number of persons talked to and their average helpfulness across all problem areas have been reported empirically (MacFarlane, Norman, &. Streiner, 1983). The measures have the potential to yield a more differentiated picture of sources of support, but not of types. No evidence on the validity and utility of the reciprocity questions is available. The measure is suggestive but hardly definitive.

Henderson *et al.* (1982) have undertaken the most ambitious effort to measure forms of social support from many different sources. They developed a more than 50-item Interview Schedule for Social Interaction (ISSI), which assesses the availability and perceived adequacy of a wide range of social contacts and relationships (from people seen on the street to confidants). From this schedule they developed indexes of the availability and perceived adequacy of what they termed *social integration* and *attachment. Social integration* is really a measure of the number of relationships people have, whereas *attachment* refers to how much those relationships provide various types of support (emotional, tangible, etc.) Henderson *et al.* also constructed indexes of indifference to relationships and conflicts in relationships. In a broad community sample they examined the additive and interactive effects on neurotic symptoms of these variables in conjunction with life events. The analyses are both cross-sectional and longitudinal. Cross-sectionally, all four main indexes have both main and buffering effects on neurosis, though the effects of adequacy are stronger than those of availability. Longitudinally, the adequacy but not the availability measures produce both additive and buffering effects.

The results, about which Henderson and colleagues were unnecessarily skeptical, suggest substantial validity for these measures, and their work merits close examination. We have two related reservations about the ISSI, however. First, it is costly and probably not cost-effective. Second, it has so far been used only to create aggregated measures, which do not distinguish among types or sources of support, although the component items have the potential to generate some such distinctions. If the goal is this level of aggregation, a smaller number of items would suffice.

Finally, Schaefer, Coyne, and Lazarus (1981) have developed a measure of tangible, informational, and emotional support in a longitudinal study of 100 middle-aged and older persons. The respondent's tangible score was the number of situations (out of nine) in which he or she could count on help from another person. The situations ranged from minor (being able to borrow a cup of sugar) to major and demanding ones (such as needing care following an illness or injury).

Another section of the questionnaire asked participants to rate their spouse, close friends, relatives, co-workers, neighbors, and supervisors on five separate items designed to measure different types of support. Because ratings on four of the five items (i.e., caring, confiding, being reliable, and boosting spirits) were highly intercorrelated (average $r > .90$), the four items were summed into an index of emotional support. The fifth question, which asked explicitly about information, suggestions, and guidance, was designated as the measure of informational support.

The method of indexing appears to produce an artifactually high correlation (.85) between informational and emotional support, which makes it impossible to distinguish their separate effects. On the other hand, the measure of tangible support is very different, bordering on a measure of social isolation ("Is there anyone who. . ."). Thus this measure is also problematic, but among the few that distinguishes among both sources and types of support. Schaefer *et al.* (1981) did provide some evidence of construct validity.

Our own efforts at measurement have also met with mixed success at this point. In a study of workers in 23 occupations in multiple locations ($N = 636$), Caplan *et al.* (1975) developed a 12-item measure of perceived social support from work supervisors, co-workers, and persons outside of work with respect to work-related problems. In a study of white, male blue-collar workers in an industrial plant ($N = 1809$), House (1980) adapted this measure by adding several additional supervisor items and distinguishing persons outside of work into spouses versus friends and relatives. Both studies used items intended to distinguish between emotional and instrumental support, but empirically no such distinction emerged. Analyses by House and Wells (1978) and LaRocco, House, and French (1980), however, showed clearly that the importance of different sources of support varied with the context and the nature of the stresses being considered. Work-related sources of support were generally most consequential in alleviating occupational stress and buffering its effects on health, with the importance of supervisors versus coworkers varying by occupational setting. Spouses also proved to be important sources of support with respect to work-related problems, but friends and relatives were not consequential.

Two ongoing studies by Kahn and Antonucci (1978, 1984) and by Kahn, Antonucci, and Depner (1979) have attempted to measure some aspects of network structure and extensive supportive functions in two distinctive samples: a cross-sectional personal interview study of a national probability sample ($N = 718$) of persons aged 50 and over and a longitudinal mail survey of all persons first qualifed to teach secondary school in Michigan in 1980 ($N = 678$). In the study of new teachers, respondents reported their network structure and the supportive behavior of network members by means of written questionnaires administered annually over a 3-year period. Network structure was identified by asking respondents to write the first names or initials of people "who are important to you or to whom you are important" in each of six categories: spouse or partner, family member or relative, co-worker, supervisor, professional (doctor, psychologist, clergy member, psychiatrist, social worker), and friend (if not already mentioned). The supportive functions of aid, affect, and affirmation were measured by means of 12 five-point scales, each asking separately the extent to which the network as a whole and the most important network member in each of the six categories performed a specific function.

In the national survey, respondents were shown a diagram consisting of three concentric circles, with a center marked "you." Each respondent was asked to provide the first names or initials of network members who belonged in each of three circles—in the first circle people "to whom you are so close that it is hard to imagine life without them," in the second circle people who are "not that close but still very important," and in the third circle "people who are not as close as those in the second circle but still belong in your network." Demographic characteristics, category of relationship (friend, relative, etc.), frequency of contact, and other descriptors were measured for individual network members so that structural properties could be generated for the network as a whole.

Six specific support functions—intended to reflect the dimensions of aid, affirmation, and affect—were measured by means of 12 items, paired to assess the extent to which each of the six support functions was provided to the focal person by network members and the extent to which the focal person provided each of these forms of support to network members.

These studies attempted in different ways to operationalize the kind of matrix specification of sources and types of support illustrated in Table 5.1, which we feel provides the most useful broad framework for developing measures of social support. Thus far, we have had only partial success. Ongoing analyses of these data have succeeded in differentiating sources of support and showing their differential effects or correlates. Although we can, like others, construct indexes of different types of support with acceptable internal consistency, expressions of aid, affect, and affirmation, as measured in these studies, are so highly correlated with each other as not to be clearly empirically distinguishable. Moreover, in the national survey the amount of support of each type received by the focal person was measured by counting the number of network members who provided it. This method of estimating quantity of support, as we have pointed out, confounds support quantity with network size. Attempts have been made to deal with this problem in analysis (Kahn, Wethington, & Ingersoll, in press), but it seems advisable to avoid it by measuring quantity or magnitude of support independently of the number of providers. The concentric circle procedure for network mapping works well in personal interviews and provides rich network data. It is dependent on visual cues, however,

Table 5.1

Potential Forms of Social Support[a]

Content of supportive acts	Source of support								
	Spouse or partner	Other relatives	Friends	Neighbors	Work supervisor	Co-workers	Service or caregivers	Self-help groups	Health and welfare professionals
Emotional support: esteem, affect, trust, concern, listening									
Appraisal support: affirmation, feedback, social comparison									
Informational support: advice, suggestion, directives, information									
Instrumental support: aid in kind, money, labor, time, modifying environment									

Within this matrix of types of social support, each can be (1) general versus problem-focused and (2) objective versus subjective.

[a]From James R. House, *Work stress and social support*, © 1981, Addison-Wesley, Reading, MA. Table 2.2. Reprinted with permission.

and would require substantial modification for use in telephone interviews or written questionnaires.

Summary

Our review of published measures of the perceived availability or occurrence of specific types of supportive behaviors suggests to us that measurement in this area is still in a fairly primitive state. Most measurement efforts have not been guided by any explicit conceptual framework. Those that have been so guided have produced only preliminary results. Although we do not see one or a few standard measures to recommend for widespread use, we do feel there is a clear strategy to follow in developing better measures in this area, using existing measures as a source of ideas for items.

First, in any study the measurement of support must be guided by a theoretical conception of the nature of support and of how support relates to other variables in the study. Both for conceptual and methodological reasons, it is useful to distinguish among different *sources* of support (see LaRocco *et al.,* 1980) and among *types* of support (see Table 5–1). Which types and which sources are important depends on the nature of the problem under study. Most conceptual and empirical analyses of support, however, suggest that emotional support or affect should be distinguished from instrumental support or aid and that both of these should be distinguished from informational support and from affirmation or appraisal support (see House, 1981; Kahn & Antonucci, 1980). Relevant sources can be suggested both by stipulation of relevant roles (e.g., spouse, co-worker, supervisor) and by having respondents nominate persons who are important or close to them. We recommend letting respondents nominate a small number of persons and then adding critical role relationships they do not mention.

For each source of support, then, items should be written to assess the occurrence or availability of relevant types of support. It is important to ensure that the magnitude and quality of support received are clearly distinguished from the number of people who provide such support. Asking simply how many people do something confounds the number of relationships or network size with the functional content and quality of the relationship. Further, it artifactually inflates correlations among functional types of support.

Even with this common error avoided, it has proven difficult to achieve satisfactory discriminant validity among different types of support. To a considerable extent, this reflects reality. That is, people generally receive (or fail to receive) multiple types of support from the same persons. Those who give emotional support are the ones who also can be turned to for instrumental aid, information, and affirmation or appraisal. This does not mean, however, that the analysis of different types of support should be forsaken. Rather, theoretical analysis must be sharpened. Different types of support are most likely to be discriminable and to have different effects *as the nature of the problem requiring support varies.* Thus, those interested in measuring and demonstrating the empirical utility of different types of support must attend more to the problem specific nature of the support process. For example, the discriminability and effects of types of support may vary for the bereaved versus the critically ill or versus persons seeking to stop smoking or drinking.[5]

Finally, how elaborate and differentiated measures should be is largely determined by balancing research goals against available resources. If there are limited resources and limited interest in support, a simple confidant type of measure may suffice. Slightly more elaborate are efforts to assess a global concept of support from differentiated others or different types of support from undifferentiated others. Most elaborate is the kind of matrix specification shown in Table 5.1.

Conclusion

Clearly, behavioral scientists are still in process of developing measures of the generic concept of social support, including social relationships, their network structure, and the specific supportive functions or content of relationships. As we have indicated, the measures used in a given study should be tailored to the needs of that study. This is not to say, however, that investigators should all construct their own measures from scratch. The existing literature provides good models for most types of measures, which if not usable verbatim can be adapted to specific other purposes.

Table 5.2 presents a suggested battery of social support measures and a guide to good examples of each type of measure. Additional measures are cited in the text and references. How many and which measures an investigator chooses depend on the nature of the study and the resources available. We do, however, have a number of recommendations.

---

[5]Cohen *et al.* (1984), for example, found that among persons in a smoking cessation program appraisal support promotes sustained smoking reduction after the end of the program among those who were abstainers by the end, but it promoted a return to increased smoking among those who only had reduced their amount of smoking by the program's end. This is one illustration of how support may sometimes have negative effects—a topic of great interest but beyond the scope of this chapter.

Table 5.2

Suggested Battery of Social Support Measures

Type of item	Useful references
Measure of existence of social relationships (especially marriage, contacts with friends and relatives)	Berkman and Syme (1979) House, Robbins, and Metzner (1982) Donald and Ware (1982)
Confidant measure	Pearlin, Lieberman, Menaghan, and Mullan (1981)
Measure of network size and structure based on a limited number of persons (5–10)	McAllister and Fisher (1982)

Measures of basic types of support from different sources (and with respect to particular problems, if appropriate)
  Types (see Table 5.1)
  Sources
    Five closest persons
    Role-specific persons
      not among the five
      closest (see Table 5.1)
	Cohen and Hoberman (1983)
	House (1980)
	Schaefer, Cohen, and Lazarus (1981)
	Kahn, Wethington, and Ingersoll (in press)
	Norbeck, Lindsey, and Carrieri (1981)

1. *Studies should attempt wherever possible to measure at least two and preferably all three aspects of social relationships* considered in this chapter: (a) their *existence and quantity,* (b) *aspects of network structure,* and (c) the *functional content and quality of relationships.* It is critical to understand better how these aspects relate to each other and how important each is in relation to health.

2. *The number of persons or relationships considered should generally be limited to a range of from 5 to 10* because existing evidence suggests strongly diminishing returns above that level. Further analysis should be directed at determining the relative informational value of considering additional persons or roles even within this range. We have argued elsewhere that it is the absence of *any* supportive relationship that is most deleterious to health (House, 1981; Kahn & Antonucci, 1980). The incremental gain from each addition beyond the first such relationship has not yet been carefully studied.

3. *Measures of network structure should be used selectively.* Density, reciprocity, and aspects of network composition (e.g., gender) appear most promising. By limiting the number of persons considered and

the network properties considered, we feel, network analyses will be made more productive and cost-effective.

4. *The quantity and quality of specific types of support functions should be measured independently of the number of persons providing such types of support.* For example, it is not enough to ask how many people provide emotional support; how much (or how well) each or all of them provides such support should also be asked.

5. *Within types of support, priority should go first to measuring emotional support, and then to other aspects that are appropriate.* This is because emotional support has been most clearly linked to health, in terms of both direct effects and buffering effects.

6. *Within sources of support, respondents should be allowed to nominate a few people close to them, and that list should then be supplemented with roles that seem most crucial for a particular study.*

References

Antonucci, T. C. (in press). Personal characteristics, social support and behavior. In E. Shanas & R. H. Binstock (Eds.), *Handbook of aging and the social sciences.*

Barrera, M., Sandler, I., & Ramsay, T. (1981). Preliminary development of a scale of social support: Studies on college students. *American Journal of Community Psychology, 9* (4), 434–447.

Belle, D. (1982). The stress of caring: Women as providers of social support. In L. Goldberger & S. Breznitz (Eds.), *Handbook of stress: Theoretical and clinical aspects.* New York: The Free Press.

Berkman, L. F., & Syme, S. L. (1979). Social networks, host resistance, and mortality: A nine-year follow-up study of Alameda County residents. *American Journal of Epidemiology, 109* (2), 186–204.

Billings, A. G., & Moos, R. H. (1981). The role of coping resources in attenuating the stress of life events. *Journal of Behavioral Medicine, 7* (2), 139–157.

Billings, A. G., & Moos, R. H. (1982). Social support and functioning among community and clinical groups: A panel model. *Journal of Behavioral Medicine, 5* (3), 295–311.

Blazer, D. G. (1982). Social support and mortality in an elderly community population. *American Journal of Epidemoiology, 115* (5), 684–694.

Boissevain, J. (1974). *Friends of friends: Networks, manipulators, and coalitions.* Oxford: Blackwell.

Brandt, P. A., & Weinert, C. (1981). The PRQ—A social support measure. *Nursing Research, 30* (5), 277–280.

Broadhead, W. E., Kaplan, B., James, S. A., Wagner, E. H., Schoenbach, V. J., Grimson, R., Heyden, S., Tibblin, G., & Gehlbach, S. H. (1983). The epidemiologic evidence for a relationship between social support and health. *American Journal of Epidemiology, 117* (5), 521–537.

Campbell, D. T. (1960). Recommendation for APA test standards regarding construct, trait, or discriminant validity. *American Psychologist, 15,* 546–553.

Caplan, R. D., Cobb, S., French, Jr., J. R. P., Harrison, R. V., & Pinneau, Jr. S. R. (1975). *Job demands and worker health: Main effects and occupational differences* (USGPO

NO.HE7111-J57, USPO Stock 1733–0083). Washington, DC: United States Government Printing Office.

Cassel, J. (1976). The contribution of the social environment to host resistance. *American Journal of Epidemiology, 104* (2), 107–123.

Cobb, S. (1976). Social support as a moderator of life stress. *Psychosomatic Medicine, 38* (5), 300–314.

Cohen, S., & Hoberman, H. M. (1983). Positive events and social supports as buffers of life change stress. *Journal of Applied Social Psychology, 13* (2), 99–125.

Cohen, S., Mermelstein, R., Kamarck, T., & Hoberman, H. (1984). Measuring the functional components of social support. In I. Sarason (Ed.), *Social support: Theory, research and applications.* The Hague, Netherlands: Martines Niijhoff.

Cronbach, L., & Meehl, P. E. (1955). Construct validity in psychological tests. *Psychological Bulletin, 52,* 281–302.

Cronenwett, L. (1983). *Relationships among social network structure, perceived social support, and psychological outcomes of pregnancy.* Unpublished doctoral dissertation, University of Michigan, Ann Arbor.

d'Abbs, P. (1982). *Social support networks.* Melbourne: Institute of Family Studies.

Donald, C. A., & Ware, Jr., J. E. (1982). *The Quantification of Social Contacts and Resources.* Santa Monica, CA: Rand Corp.

Durkheim, E. (1951). *Suicide.* New York: Free Press.

Eaton, W. W. (1978). Life events, social supports, and psychiatric symptoms: a reanalysis of the New Haven data. *Journal of Health and Social Behavior, 19,* 230–234.

Fischer, C. (1982). *To dwell among friends.* Chicago: University of Chicago Press.

Fleming, R., Baum, A., Gisrel, M., & Gatchel, R. (1982). Mediating influences of social support on stress at Three Mile Island. *Journal of Human Stress, 8* (3), 14–22.

Froland, C., Brodsky, G., Olson, M., & Stewart, L. (1979). Social support and social adjustment— Implications for mental health professionals. *Community Mental Health Journal, 15* (2), 82–93.

Funch, D. P., & Marshall, J. (1983). The role of stress, social support and anger in survival from breast cancer. *Journal of Psychosomatic Research, 27* (1), 77–83.

Gallo, F. (1982). The effects of social support network on the health of the elderly. *Social Work in Health Care, 8* (2), 65–74.

Gove, W. R. (1972). The relationship between sex roles, marital status, and mental illness. *Social Forces, 51,* 34–44.

Gove, W. R., Hughes, M., & Style, C. B. (1983). Does marriage have positive effects on the psychological well-being of the individual? *Journal of Health and Social Behavior, 24* (2), 122–131.

Gove, W. R., & Tudor, J. F. (1973). Adult sex roles and mental illness. *American Journal of Sociology, 78,* 812–835.

Henderson, S., Byrne, D. G., & Duncan-Jones, P. (1982). *Neurosis and the social environment.* Sydney, Australia: Academic Press.

Hirsch, B. J. (1980). Natural support systems and coping with major life changes. *American Journal of Community Psychology, 8* (2), 159–172.

Hirsch, B. J. (1981). Social networks and the coping process. In B. H. Gottlieb (Ed.), *Social networks and social support.* Beverly Hills: Sage.

Holahan, C. J., & Moos, R. H. (1982). Social support and adjustment: Predictive benefits of social climate indices. *American Journal of Community Psychology, 10* (4), 403–413.

House, J. S. (1980). *Occupational Stress and the Physical and Mental Health of Factory Workers* (Report on NIMH Grant No. 1R02MH28902). Research Report Series: Institute for Social Research, University of Michigan, Ann Arbor.

House, J. S. (1981). *Work stress and social support.* Reading, MA: Addison-Wesley.

House, J. S., Robbins, C., & Metzner, H. L. (1982). The association of social relationships and activities with mortality: Prospective evidence from the Tecumseh Community Health Study. *American Journal of Epidemiology, 116,* 123–140.

House, J. S., & Wells, J. A. (1978). Occupational stress, social support, and health. In A. McLean, G. Black, & M. Colligan (Eds.), *Reducing occupational stress: Proceedings of a conference.* U.S. Department of Health, Education and Welfare, HEW (NIOSH) Publication No. 78–140.

Israel, B. A. (1982). Social networks and health status: Linking theory, research and practice. *Patient Counseling and Health Education, 4* (2), 65–79.

Kahn, R. L. (1981). *Work and health.* New York: Wiley.

Kahn, R. L., & Antonucci, T. C. (1978). *Social support networks among new teachers.* Technical proposal to the National Institute of Education.

Kahn, R. L., & Antonucci, T. C. (1980). Convoys over the life course: Attachments, roles and social support. In P. B. Baltes & O. Brim (Eds.), *Life-span development and behavior* (Vol. 3). New York: Academic Press.

Kahn, R. L., & Antonucci, T. C. (1981). Convoys of social support: A life course approach. In S. B. Kiesler, J. N. Morgan, & V. K. Oppenheimer (Eds.), *Aging: Social Change.* New York: Academic Press.

Kahn, R. L., & Antonucci, T. C. (1984). *Social supports of the elderly: Family/friends/professionals.* Final report to the National Institute on Aging, Grant No. AG01632–01.

Kahn, R. L., Wethington, E., & Ingersoll, B. N. (in press). Social networks: Determinants and effects. In R. Abeles (Ed.), *Implications of the life-span perspective for social psychology.* New York: Erlbaum.

Kessler, R. C., & Cleary, P. R. (1980). Social class and psychological distress. *American Sociological Review, 45,* 463–478.

Kessler, R. C., & McLeod, J. D. (in press). Sex differences in vulnerability to undesirable life events. *American Sociological Review.*

LaRocco, J. M., House, J. S., & French, Jr., J. R. P. (1980) Social support, occupational stress, and health. *Journal of Health and Social Behavior, 21,* 202–218.

Leavy, R. L. (1983). Social support and psychological disorder. *Journal of Community Psychology, 11,* 3–21.

Likert, R. (1961). *New patterns of management.* New York: McGraw-Hill.

Lowenthal, M. F., & Haven, C. (1968). Interaction and adaptation: Intimacy as a critical variable. *American Sociological Review, 33* (1), 20–30.

McCallister, L., & Fischer, C. S. (1978). A procedure for surveying personal networks. *Sociological methods and research, 7* (2), 131–148.

McFarlane, A., Neale, K. A., Norman, G. R., Roy, R. G., & Streiner, D. L. (1981). Methodological issues in developing a scale to measure social support. *Schizophrenia Bulletin, 7* (1), 90–100.

McFarlane, A. H., Norman, G. R., & Streiner, D. L. (1983). The process of social stress: Stable, reciprocal, and mediating relationships. *Journal of Health and Social Behavior, 24* (2), 160–173.

Moos, R. (1974). *The social climate scales: An overview.* Palo Alto, CA: Consulting Psychologists Press.

Mueller, D. P. (1980). Social networks: A promising direction for research on the relationship of the social environment to psychiatric disorder. *Social Science and Medicine, 4, 147, 161.*

Norbeck, J. S., Lindsey, A. M., & Carrieri, V. L. (1981). The development of an instrument to measure social support. *Nursing Research, 30* (5), 264–269.

Nunnally, J. C. (1978). *Psychometric theory*. New York: McGraw-Hill.

Ortmeyer, C. F. (1974). Variations in mortality, morbidity, and health care by marital status. In C. E. Erhardt, & J. E. Berlin (eds.), *Mortality and morbidity in the United States*. Cambridge, MA: Harvard University Press.

Pearlin, L. I., Lieberman, M. A., Menaghan, E. G., & Mullan, J. T. (1981). The stress process. *Journal of Health and Social Behavior, 22,* 337–356.

Phillips, S. L. (1981). Network characteristics related to the well-being of normals: A comparative base. *Schizophrenia Bulletin, 7* (1), 117–124.

Procidano, M. E., & Heller, K. (1983). Measures of perceived social support from friends and from family: Three validation studies. *American Journal of Community Psychology, 11* (1), 1–24.

Rogers, C. R. (1942). *Counseling and psychotherapy*. Boston: Houghton-Mifflin.

Sarason, I. G., Levine, H. M., Basham, R. B., & Sarason, B. R. (1983). Assessing social support: The social support questionnaire. *Journal of Personality and Social Psychology, 14,* 127–139.

Schaefer, C., Coyne, J. C., & Lazarus, R. S. (1981). The health-related functions of social support. *Journal of Behavioral Medicine, 4* (4), 381–406.

Syme, S. L. (1982). *Is social isolation a risk factor for coronary heart disease?* Paper presented at the 9th Science Writers Forum of the American Heart Association, Charleston, SC.

Turner, R. J. (1981). Social support as a contingency in psychological well-being. *Journal of Health and Social Behavior, 22,* 357–367.

Turner, R. J. (1983). Direct, indirect, and moderating effects of social support on psychological distress and associated conditions. In H. B. Kaplan (Ed.), *Psychosocial stress: Trends in theory and research* (pp. 105–155). New York: Academic Press.

Walker, K. N., MacBride, A., & Vachon, M. L. S. (1977). Social support networks and the crisis of bereavement. *Social Science and Medicine, 11,* 35–41.

Wallston, B. S., Alagna, S. W., DeVellis, B. M., & DeVellis, R. F. (1983). Social support and health. *Health Psychology, 2,* 367–391.

Wan, T. H., & Weissert, W. G. (1981). Social support networks, patient status, and institutionalization. *Research on Aging, 3* (2), 240–256.

Weiss, R. S. (1974). The provisions of social relationships. In Z. Rubin (Ed.), *Doing unto others* (pp. 17–26). Englewood Cliffs, NJ: Prentice-Hall.

Wellman, B. (1981). Applying network analysis to the study of support. In B. Gottlieb (Ed.), *Social networks and social support*. Beverly Hills: Sage.

Wilcox, B. L. (1981). Social support, life stress, and psychological adjustment: A test of the buffering hypothesis. *American Journal of Community Psychology, 9* (4), 371–386.

Williams, A. W., Ware, J. G., & Donald, C. A. (1981). A model of mental health, life events, and social supports applicable to general populations. *Journal of Health and Social Behavior, 22* (4), 324–336.

CHAPTER 6

Causal Inference in the Study of Social Support*

David Dooley

Introduction

This chapter reviews some of the methods that have been and can be used to estimate the effect of social support on health. In the interests of brevity and breadth, the coverage is necessarily condensed and introductory. The reader is referred to examples and to more technical coverage where appropriate.

The Social Support Questions

Reviews of the social support literature have generally concluded that social support is good for physical and mental health (e.g., Heller & Swindle, 1983; Mitchel, Billings, & Moos, 1982; Rook, 1983). In some cases this social support effect has been reported for all people without regard to the presence or absence of stressors (e.g., Williams, Ware, & Donald, 1981). Other studies have found the effect only among those experiencing some adaptive challanges usually operationalized as stressful life events (e.g., Pearlin, Menaghan, Lieberman, & Mullan, 1981). The former variant of the social sup-

*The author appreciates the helpful advice of Shel Cohen, David Kenny, Karen Rook, Leonard Syme, and R. Jay Turner and the manuscript preparation by Fran Renner.

109

port effect will be referred to as the *main* effect, and the latter variant will, following common usage, be referred to as the *buffering* effect. The buffering effect is usually indicated by the presence of a statistically significant interaction between support and life events. The two types of effects are summarized graphically in Figure 6.1.

In Figure 6.1(A), the main effect (with no buffering effect) appears as negatively sloping lines with *equal* slopes for high and low life-event groups. The buffering effect illustrated in Figure 6.1(B) and (C) is identified by the *unequal* slopes of the two lines. In Figure 6.1(B), the low stressor group's line has arbitrarily been drawn with a slope of zero to reflect the usual buffering hypothesis that social support has little or no effect in the absence of stress. Note that if the design fails to include a measure of stressors, there is no way to discriminate the main and buffering effects (see, e.g., Berkman & Syme, 1979). As illustrated in Figure 6.1(C) the existence of an interaction (i.e., unequal slopes) does not automatically mean that there is no social support effect in the absence of stress (note negative slope of low stress line). In both Figure 6.1(B) and 6.1(C) main and interaction effects can appear (as found by Wilcox, 1981), and the main effect can be interpreted only in the context of the interaction.

Careful attention must be given to the measurement of support and life change (Gore, 1981). Some life events (e.g., divorce, death of loved one) may be confounded with social support in a way that produces a spurious buffering effect (Thoits, 1982). One proposed solution is to conduct longitudinal research to control for the effect of earlier support on later life change and on the interaction of later life change and support (see Thoits, 1982, Figure II, p. 153). (For additional useful treatment of the analysis of the life event effect and the interaction of life events and support, see Finney, Mitchell, Cronkite, & Moos, 1984; House, 1981, pp. 131–140; Kessler, 1982.)

Drawing Causal Inferences from Correlational Data

Most social support research is correlational. That is, the independent variable (social support) is measured rather than experimentally set. As will be discussed, correlational designs are vulnerable to important threats to their internal validity—that is, to plausible alternative explanations. Different designs and different statistical controls can, to varying degrees, rule out these threats. As a result, differently designed or controlled studies can produce quite different results. Examples of how main or buffering effects of social support can appear and disappear as a function of design are those by Monroe (1983) and Thoits (1982). Of the various threats to internal validity, two are most prominent in correlational research: spuriousness and reverse causation. Figure 6.2 illustrates these two rival explanations.

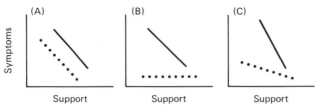

Figure 6.1. Main and buffering effects of social support. Dotted lines represent persons with few stressful events; solid lines persons with many stressful events.

An association between two variables is said to be spurious when it is produced by a third variable, as shown by Z in Figure 6.2(A). For example, some personal characteristic, such as poverty or age, may be the actual cause of both social network disintegration (i.e., decreased social support) and greater risk of health problems. Reverse causation occurs when the observed association is causal but the direction of causation is opposite from that hypothesized, as illustrated by Figure 6.2(B). For example, some kinds of illness may frighten away friends (e.g., terminal cancer) or prevent the social activity that leads to making and keeping friends (e.g., depression). The next section considers some strategies for dealing with spuriousness and reverse causation. In the final section, we consider some of the assumptions and inferential difficulties of different statistical approaches.

One way to avoid the spuriousness and reverse-causation rival hypotheses is to conduct controlled experiments. Experimental manipulation of the independent variable of social support assures that support is not caused by the dependent variable (i.e., reverse causation). Maximum control is provided by the random assignment of subjects to manipulated high-and-low support conditions. This type of assignment eliminates the association of irrelevant third variables with support (i.e., spuriousness).

Experimental manipulation has been rare in the social support field (for a few examples, see Felner, Ginter, & Primavera, 1982; McGuire & Gottlieb, 1979; Sarason & Stoops, 1978; Whitcher & Fisher, 1979). One reason may be that such manipulated support is, by definition, not "natural." However, researchers hoping to discover more effective public health interventions

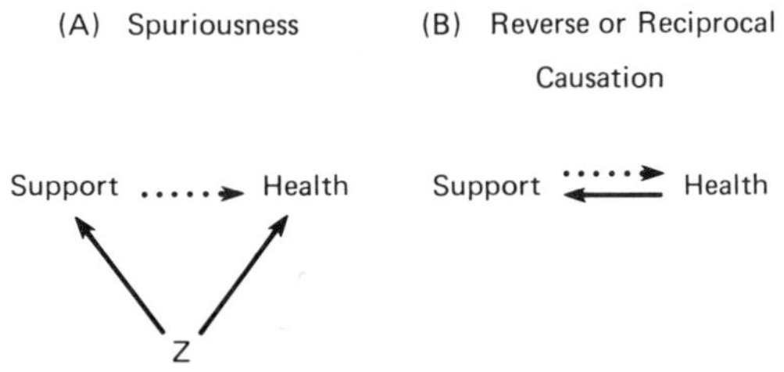

(A) Spuriousness

(B) Reverse or Reciprocal Causation

Figure 6.2. Common threats to internal validity in correlational designs. Dotted arrows represent expected causal paths; solid arrows actual causal paths.

Support ·····➤ Health

Support ⬅····➤ Health

Z

based on manipulated ("unnatural") social support should consider using experimental designs for both internal and construct validity reasons. Another reason for the rarity of social support experiments is the difficulty in manipulating support. The literature has concentrated on correlational methods, as the remainder of this chapter will do.

Strategies in Correlational Research

Controlling Spuriousness: Multivariate Analysis

   Correlational studies, both cross-sectional and longitudinal, can provide checks of the spuriousness threat if they include measures of supposed confounding variables. Because many such confounding variables can be imagined, such studies must be multivariate. The effect of the confounding variable can be statistically removed or partialled out. The unconfounded association of support and health is expressed as a partial correlation or regression coefficient. Ordinarily all control variables are entered into the regression equation first, before the explanatory power of support is measured. Some work has suggested that such control variables as social status may interact with support, thus requiring more complicated analyses within stratified levels of control variables (Turner & Noh, 1983).

   The inclusion of some variables to control for spuriousness is now standard procedure. Not yet standard is the listing of all the control variables that ought to be included. Not all variables are found to be confounding (e.g., marital status and occupational status were not associated with symptoms in Lin, Simeone, Ensel, and Kuo, 1979). However, it is always possible to argue that some uncontrolled variable accounts for the observed association of support and health. Although the inclusion of an unnecessary control variable causes little harm (e.g., wasted degrees of freedom), the omission of a confounding variable (i.e., one correlated with support and that causes health) leads to incorrect results.

Dealing with Reverse Causation: Longitudinal
Data Analysis

   Evidence has accumulated for the reverse causation of social support by disorder, especially psychological depression (e.g., Coyne, 1976; Gotlib & Robinson, 1982). Because later symptoms are usually highly correlated with earlier symptoms, the cross-sectional observation of an association of symptoms and support may be the effect of earlier symptoms on later symptoms and on both earlier and later support.

   The effect of prior symptoms on the association of prior support and later symptoms can be removed statistically if the design is longitudinal. Panel studies that measure symptoms over time allow such control, and in such studies prior symptom level is routinely included as a control variable. Two procedures for dealing with reverse causation are discussed in the following sections on cross-lag panel correlational analysis and path analysis.

One problem with partialling out prior symptom level is that doing so deals with only one direction of a potentially bidirectional relationship. Indeed, the support-with-health relationship seems likely to be reciprocal. Symptoms may lead to decreased support, which in turn leads to increased symptoms, and so forth. The difficulty with reciprocity hypotheses is in estimating the relative contribution of each path. One cross-sectional procedure for dealing with reciprocal causation is two-stage least-squares analysis. A more general procedure can accommodate multiwave longitudinal data, reciprocal causal paths, and theoretical constructs with multiple measures. Both procedures are discussed in subsequent sections.

Cross-Lag Panel Correlational Analysis of Longitudinal Data

A method that is intuitively appealing is cross-lag panel correlation analysis (CLPC). Figure 6.3 illustrates the data arrangement necessary for CLPC, as reproduced from Turner's study of two-wave panel data (1981).

The CLPC method has been controversial, and this controversy has produced increasingly sophisticated guidelines for its application. The least sophisticated approach simply compares the two cross-lag correlations (i.e., Support 1 with Well-Being 2, .39 and Well-Being 1 with Support 2, .40). In this approach, causal predominance is shown by the relative magnitudes of the two cross-lag correlations. Because, in the example of Figure 6.3, there is little difference, no predominance is indicated in these data. If these correlations were confused with path coefficients (standardized regression coefficients), it could be supposed that this is a case of approximately equal reciprocal causation.

Kenny (1975) has pointed out that such a CLPC comparison is really a test of spuriousness and rests on some crucial assumptions. By spurious-

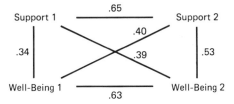

Figure 6.3. Cross-lag panel correlation of social support and psychological well-being; $n = 293$. Reproduced by permission from Turner, 1981, Figure 1.

ness Kenny meant that the two variables may not be causing each other at all, but rather they may both be caused by some unmeasured third variable. Only if the two cross-lag correlations are significantly different, he argued, can the spuriousness hypothesis be rejected. His test of spuriousness rested on the assumptions of synchronicity and stationarity. By synchronicity, he meant that the two Time-1 and the two Time-2 measures must be collected at the same times. If one of each pair of variables was retrospective for a longer period than the other, this assumption would be violated and the cross-lag correlations could be biased. Suppose support was recalled over the previous year while symptoms were recalled over the previous week, and further that there was a 1-year lag between interviews. In such a case, recalled Support 1 could be much farther in time from Well-Being 2 than Well-Being 1 from Support 2. Because temporally more proximate variables can be expected to be more strongly associated, this absence of synchronicity would tend to favor the Well-Being-1-with-Support-2 correlation.

By stationarity, Kenny meant that the causal structure of a variable is constant over time (i.e., its structural equation would have the same coefficients at each time point). One way of assessing this assumption is to test the equivalence of the two synchronous correlations (i.e., between the variables measured at the same point in time). One cause of unequal synchronous correlations is change in the reliability of measurement of one or both variables. For example, suppose that support was more reliably measured at Time 2 than at Time 1. This increased reliability will inflate any correlation with Support 2, including not only that between the two Time-2 variables but also that of Well-Being 1 with Support 2. This latter effect will make the Well-Being-1-to-Support-2 correlation appear, falsely, to be greater than the Support-1-to-Well-Being-2 correlation. Kenny provides a method for adjusting correlations for reliability shifts, but the method requires at least one other variable, measured at both time points, that is correlated with both variables of primary interest.

Using Kenny's strategy, one would first assess synchronicity (making sure that the measures reflect the same time periods), then test for stationarity (testing the equality of the two synchronous correlations), and finally test the equality of the two cross-lag correlations. The two latter tests require a special formula because the correlations are themselves correlated (see Steiger, 1980 for the updated formula). Assuming synchronicity and no change in reliability requiring adjustments, these two tests were conducted on the data in Figure 6.3. The test of the two synchronous correlations (.34 and .53) shows them to be unequal in violation of the stationarity assumption. Perhaps this inequality is due to a reliability shift, but this could be ascertained only with additional data, adjustment, and testing. Testing of the cross-lag correlations is inappropriate in this case because the stationarity assumption cannot be met.

A further complication for the CLPC method was raised by Rogosa (1980) who showed that not only must the synchronous correlations be equal, but also the autocorrelations or stabilities (i.e., correlation of variable with itself over time) must be equal for the cross-lag correlations to be evaluated. Rogosa showed that the less stable variable (i.e., lower autocorrelation) will tend to appear as the predominant cause even if the true causal coefficients are equal. Unequal stabilities do not appear to be a problem in Figure 6.3 (.65 and .63), but could be expected in studies matching highly stable symptom indicators with psychometrically primitive support measures.

In summary, CLPC analysis is based on a number of assumptions that cannot always be met. Even when these assumptions are met, CLPC may not be the best method. It allows for the assessment of buffering only by splitting the sample on stressful life events. As indicated earlier, most research on social support must be multivariate, whereas CLPC is typically bivariate. At best, CLPC is a rather low-power test and can only indicate predominance in reciprocal relationships.

Path Analysis of Longitudinal Data

Better than CLPC would be a method permitting inclusion of other variables including interaction terms, and that would assign coefficients to the reciprocal causal effects controlling for all the other variables. Such an approach will more suitably be pursued in path analysis, which decomposes linear relationships in the framework of a causal model, than in correlational analysis, which tends to blur spurious, direct, and indirect causal paths (see Heise, 1975, for the details of path analysis). In path analysis, the causal relationships in the assumed model can be presented visually as a path diagram consisting of variables linked by arrows representing the hypothetical causal paths. Estimates of the magnitudes of the relationships can be derived from regression analysis. One regression equation is fitted for each endogenous variable (i.e., a variable with causal paths leading to it from other variables in the diagram). The path coefficient estimated for each arrow in the diagram consists of the appropriate standardized regression coefficient from the relevant equation.

For example, when Turner (1983) applied multiple regression and path analysis to three-wave data, evidence was found for lagged (6-month) reciprocal relationships of support and distress. A synchronous relationship between these variables was also found, and the causal direction was assumed to be from support to distress. Another example of path analysis of panel data illustrates this method's arbitrariness in assessing reverse causation and reciprocity. Unlike Turner (1983), Billings and Moos (1982) found that reinterview depression was significantly related only to earlier depression in men and to earlier depression and reinterview support in women. The reverse path from reinterview depression to reinterview support was not tested. Only one path between reinterview depression and reinterview support can be tested at a time because simultaneous reciprocal paths (called a nonrecursive relationship) cannot be fitted unless additional data are provided. The two regression equations necessary for estimating two reciprocal synchronous paths are undersupplied with information (or under-identified) by a single bivariate coefficient and cannot be solved. As a result, only lagged reciprocity can be assessed in ordinary path analysis.

Unfortunately, reciprocity may operate nearly concurrently and thus not show up in lagged analysis. More importantly, ordinary least-squares regression, which is commonly used for estimating path coefficients, relies on assumptions that are commonly violated (see Rogosa, 1979). For example, causal variables such as first interview symptoms and social support are usually measured with error, and their fallibility usually leads to biased estimates of path coefficients. Even if the measures are perfect, lagged regression equations (e.g., predicting reinterview symptoms from initial symptoms) can produce biased estimates due to another assumption violation: serial correlation (i.e., correlation of residuals or estimation error; see Kessler & Greenberg, 1981, pp. 87–89).

Dealing with Reciprocity: Two-Stage Least-squares Analysis of Cross-Sectional Data

An alternative approach to the study of reciprocal causation in cross-sectional data is called two-stage least-squares analysis or 2SLS (see James & Singh, 1978, for more detail). The 2SLS method is so called because it involves two applications of least-squares regression. This procedure can provide estimates for concurrent reciprocal paths, but it does require that each of the reciprocally related variables (i.e., support and symptoms) has other measured variables related to it but not to the other. These related variables are called instruments, and they supply the extra information needed to identify the two reciprocal causal path equations.

The object of this method is to estimate two path coefficients—from support to symptoms and from symptoms to support—in cross-sectional data. Consider the path from support to symptoms. The problem in isolating this effect is avoiding the confounding effect of symptoms on support. What is needed is an estimate of support that excludes the influence of symptoms. The 2SLS solution is to measure other variables that are related to but not caused by support and that are not related, except via support, to symptoms. Suppose two such variables, X_1 and X_2, can be measured. In the first stage of 2SLS, these two instruments can be used to estimate support. This process consists of a regression of support on the instruments and then the use of the resulting coefficients to estimate support: Estimated Support $= b_1 X_1 + b_2 X_2$. This estimate of support is uncontaminated by symptoms. That is, it is the part of the value of support that is not the result of the symptoms.

In the second stage of 2SLS, the symptoms variable is regressed on its causal variables, including the new variable Estimated Support. This regression produces an estimate of the coefficient for the path from support to symptoms.

By a similar procedure, the effect of symptoms on support could be estimated in two stages, assuming instrumental variables for symptoms were available. First symptoms would be regressed on its instruments to produce Estimated Symptoms (the part not caused by support). Then support would be regressed on its predictors including Estimated Symptoms to estimate the path from symptoms to support.

Just as with CLPC and path analysis, 2SLS presents difficulties. The most obvious one is that of finding instrumental variables. The difficulty can be seen by trying to imagine variables that cause symptoms or support but that are not independently related to each other. One possible instrument for family-supplied support might be family size (i.e., number of living parents and siblings). One possible instrument for symptoms might be exposure to a risk factor for illness (e.g., employment in an industry with toxic chemicals or the experience of a stressful event such as job loss). Whether because of its unfamiliarity or because of the difficulty in finding instrumental variables, 2SLS has yet to be used in the social support literature.

There are numerous assumptions underlying the application of multiple regression in 2SLS (see James & Singh, 1978, p. 1113, for a summary). One such assumption is that the control variables (independent variables other than instruments) are measured without error. When these variables are highly but not perfectly reliable, the resulting bias in parameter estimation may not be excessive.

Structural Analysis with Latent Variables

To meet the need of 2SLS and path analysis for errorless variables, a different technique has emerged. Using this approach, path analysis can be performed on latent variables (i.e., unmeasured constructs) created by confirmatory factor analysis from observed variables. Latent variable analysis can be applied when there are multiple indicators of a construct, whether the indicators (e.g., items or subscales) were carefully designed to measure the construct or were assembled as an afterthought. This approach employs various statistical procedures (e.g., maximum likelihood analysis) for analyzing covariance structures. This procedure simultaneously fits a measurement model (i.e., the suspected relationships of observed variables to each unmeasured latent construct) and a structural or causal model (i.e., the suspected relationships among the latent constructs), which can include reciprocal paths.

A full introduction to this methodology exceeds the scope of this chapter (see instead Bentler, 1980; Kenny, 1979; Maruyama & McGarvey, 1980). The computer software most widely used to perform such analyses is Linear Structural Relations (LISREL), developed by Joreskog and Sorbom (see Joreskog & Sorbom, 1982, for an overview of LISREL V).

Both structural equation modeling with latent variables and 2SLS can produce similar results for simultaneous reciprocal causal paths (e.g., Schmitt & Bedeian, 1982, give an example that does not involve social support). The structural equation approach has some advantages in addition to including latent variables. It permits convenient tests of overall model fit and of contrasts between competing models; thus, whether one path between support and symptoms fits better than another can be empirically determined. It also allows for serial correlation in panel data.

A general and powerful analytic method such as LISREL is predicated on rather strong assumptions about the data (e.g., multivariate normal distribution). Because LISREL only entered widespread use in the early 1980s, its robustness against assumption violations is not yet fully understood. Nevertheless, its use has been growing. For example, Aneshensel and Frerichs (1982) applied LISREL to a panel study of depression. They reported a final trimmed model in which life events and support affect depression with no lag and depression affects support indirectly through life events with a lag of 4 months.

Statistical Issues

Level of Measurement and Regression Analysis

The conventional wisdom is that a statistical test must be appropriate to the level of measurement; for example, interval-level statistics can be applied only to interval-level measures and never to lower levels such as ordinal data (Siegel, 1956). Some authors have disputed the need to adhere to this matching of measurement level to statistical technique and have advocated the application of regression to ordinal-level measures, which reflect constructs with an underlying continuous nature (Borgatta & Bohrnstadt, 1980). In fact, the assumptions underlying regression are concerned more with the distribution than the measurement level of the data (e.g., Kerlinger & Pedhazur, 1973, pp. 47–48). Generally speaking, the calculation of descriptive statistics such as the Pearson r can be applied with little regard for assumptions, although the interpretation of such statistics does depend on certain assumptions (e.g., linearity of the relationship and normality of the variables' distributions),

Assumptions become more crucial in the case of inferential statistics. In multiple regression, the F test, for example, rests on the assumptions that (1) the values of the dependent variable are normally distributed in the population and at each level of each independent variable, (2) the dependent values have equal variances at each level of each independent variable, and (3) the residuals (difference of actual and estimated values) are random, normally distributed, and have equal variances at each value of the independent variable. Fortunately, regression statistics are fairly robust, that is, resistant to violation of some assumptions. One exception is the independence of the observations (e.g., two subjects from the same support network should not be sampled).

The robustness of regression inferential statistics is not a license to ignore the risk of assumption violation. Only by checking the distribution of the data can researchers know whether to transform the data. Note that the normality assumptions pertain only to the dependent variable. Categorical independent variables can be accommodated in regression analyses by use of dummy coded variables. Even curvilinear relationships can be studied by creating ordered categories out of continuous independent variables and using dummy codings. When the levels of categorical independent variables can be treated as fixed, the hierarchical multiple regression is equivalent to ANOVA. When continuous control variables are entered first, the analysis becomes ANCOVA. Note that in ANCOVA it is assumed that the covariates are measured without error and that they do not interact with the independent variables (i.e., that the regression lines of the dependent variable on the covariate have equal slopes at different levels of the independent variables).

As noted in the previous section, more sophisticated techniques such as structural equation analysis by maximum likelihood methods have qualitatively more demanding assumptions and may not be so robust. A potential rival hypothesis resides in every unchecked assumption. Thus, a borderline finding that social support is significantly associated with health in an ANCOVA may be doubted if it is found that the dependent variable is badly skewed or kurtotic, that it has unequal variance over cells, or that the covariate regression lines did not have equal slopes.

In the procedures that generate path coefficients (path analysis and structural equation modeling), the buffering effect can be tested by inclusion of a multiplicative term (support times stress). When one or both of the terms being multiplied is categorical with dummy coding (e.g., presence or absence of stressful event or of intimate relationship), the interpretation of the interaction coefficient is straightforward. The unstandardized regression coefficient can be disaggregated into separate slopes for each level of the dummy coded variable (see Kerlinger & Pedhauzer, 1973, p. 252); the analysis of the product of two continuous variables can be more difficult (see pp. 414–415).

Logit Analysis for Categorical Variables

Regression analysis is inappropriate when the dependent variable is dichotomous (e.g., hospitalization versus non hospitalization). The reasons for this are complex and are detailed elsewhere (e.g., Hanushek & Jackson, 1977), although it is obvious that the distribution of a dichotomous dependent variable grossly violates the assumptions stated earlier. This problem originally had no good solution; either multiple regression in violation of its assumptions or an awkward procedure, such as discriminant analysis or simple contingency table analysis, could be used. However, a sophisticated analogue to multivariate regression for multiway contingency table analysis has appeared (Fienberg, 1980). Logit analysis is a variant of log-linear analysis appropriate when one variable is regarded as dependent and is dichotomous. Coefficients are produced for the effect of each independent variable or interaction term. The dependent variable is expressed as the log of the odds ratio (i.e., risk of falling in one category rather than the other category of the dependent variable). The coefficients are additive for the log form of the ratio but can be transformed to multiplicative (antilog) coefficients (Swafford, 1980). The overall fit of a logit or log-linear model is given by a chi-square comparison of the observed and the expected (under the particular model) values in each cell.

Logit analysis avoids some of the problems raised by the numerous distribution assumptions underlying multiple regression. However, it is not without its own problems. The technique requires a large sample size if many variables are to be analyzed. Unless the levels of independent variables are naturally categorical (e.g., male versus female) or numerous (five or more), arbitrary cut points can introduce serious problems (Reynolds, 1978). When some of the independent variables are continuous but the dependent variable is dichotomous, the technique of logistic regression can be applied.

Contradictions between categorized and continuous treatments of the same data have appeared in the social support literature. For example, it has been noted (Mitchell et al., 1982, footnote 3), that both Turner (1981) and Lin *et al.* (1979) found support for buffering in analyses by subgroup categories but not in regressions on continuous data. An explanation that has been offered for these discrepancies in nonlogit analyses is that the arbitrary categorizing of the continuous variables somehow changed the apparent relationship (biasing transformation).

A different controversy illustrates the potential for discrepancy between log-linear and other sorts of analyses. An original study of life events, depression, and social support was interpreted by its authors to support buffering (Brown & Harris, 1978). When these data were reanalyzed using log-linear methods, the interaction of support and events was not significant (Tennent & Bebbington, 1978). Cleary and Kessler have clarified this dispute in terms of the underlying assumptions of the analysts (1982). The data at issue are expressed as proportions of the sample developing depression. For those with no events, this proportion is 1% for those with support and 3% for those without. In contrast, for those with life events the proportions are 10 and 32% respectively (Brown & Harris, 1978, p. 181, Table 3). Using an additive model, Brown and Harris argued that the suppressive effect of support on the risk of depression is much greater for those with events (22% = 32% − 10%) than those with no events (2% = 3% − 1%). But in using the log-linear model, Tennant and Bebbington tested not the additive but the ratio difference in relative risk and found the same 3:1 ratio in both those without events (3% to 1%) and those with events (32% to 10%).

At one level these two approaches differ on subjective preference. Because of the intuitively plausible preference for the additive approach, the 22% difference does seem much greater than the 2% difference. At another level, these two approaches can be understood to differ by choice of statistical analysis. In order to have the convenient feature of additive coefficients, the logit approach must analyze logarithms. It follows that the data in their raw (antilog) form are related multiplicatively and thus subject to the ratio criterion. In the absence of a statistically satisfactory alternative method for analyzing dichotomous data, Cleary and Kessler recommended the use of the logit approach with its implicit bias for the ratio criterion. However, they recommended choosing between conflicting results only on the basis of additional substantive or theoretical reasons.

Summary

Social support researchers have, in relying heavily on nonexperimental methods, accepted the burden of defending their findings from two major rival explanations: spuriousness and reverse causation. In order to deal with

Table 6.1

Summary of Correlational Methods

Method	Purpose	Technique	Requirements and limitations
Cross-lag panel correlation	To determine causal predominance	Sequence of tests of equality of pairs of correlations	Panel data; no test of buffering; low power; assumes synchronicity, stationarity, and equal stabilities
Longitudinal path analysis	To estimate direct and indirect effects, including reciprocal lagged relations in panel data; buffering	Estimation of standardized regression or path coefficients in equations determined by theory	No estimation of simultaneous reciprocity; requires errorless independent variables, no serial correlation of residuals of lagged variables, and no spuriousness
Two-stage least-squares analysis	To estimate reciprocal relations without lag	Regression equations for each simultaneous reciprocal path based on instrumental variables	Availability of instrumental variables, errorless control variables, and no spuriousness
Causal analysis with latent variables	To estimate structural equations, including buffering with errorless latent variables; simultaneous reciprocity possible if model is identified	Maximum likelihood estimates of coefficients and overall model fit statistics	Each latent variable needs multiple indicators; based on strong normality of distribution assumptions and no spuriousness
Logit analysis	Causal analysis when dependent variable is dichotomous; includes buffering	Log-linear analysis when all variables are categorical and logistic regression when some independent variables are continous	Large sample size necessary; no simultaneous reciprocity

these problems, researchers are obliged to use the strongest designs (longitudinal and/or multivariate) and the most appropriate statistics. Unfortunately, the theoretically best statistical methodologies are typically difficult to apply because of their assumptions. The methods described in this chapter are summarized in Table 6.1.

References

Aneshensel, C. S., & Frerichs, R. R. (1982). Stress, support, and depression: A longitudinal causal model. *Journal of Community Psychology, 10*, 363–376.

Bentler, P. M. (1980). Multivariate analysis with latent variables: Causal modeling. *Annual Review of Psychology, 31*, 419–456.

Berkman, L., & Syme, S. L. (1979). Social networks, host resistance, and mortality: A nine-year followup study of Alameda County residents. *American Journal of Epidemiology, 109* (2), 186–204.

Billings, A. C., & Moos, R. H. (1982). Social support and functioning among community and clinical groups: A panel model. *Journal of Behavioral Medicine, 5*, 295–311.

Borgatta, E. F., & Bohrnstadt, G. W. (1980). Level of measurement: Once over again. *Sociological Methods and Research, 9*, 147–160.

Brown, G. W., & Harris, T. (1978). *Social origins of depression: A study of psychiatric disorder in women.* New York: Free Press.

Cleary, P. D., & Kessler, R. L. (1982). The estimation and interpretation of modifier effects. *Journal of Health and Social Behavior, 23*, 159–169.

Coyne, J. C. (1976). Depression and the response of others. *Journal of Abnormal Psychology, 85*, 186–193.

Felner, R. D., Ginter, M., & Primavera, J. (1982). Primary prevention during school transitions: Social support and environmental structure. *American Journal of Community Psychology, 10*, 277–290.

Fienberg, S. E. (1980). *The analysis of cross-classified categorical data.* Cambridge, MA: MIT Press.

Finney, J. W., Mitchell, R. E., Cronkite, R. C., & Moos, R. H. (1984). Methodological issues in estimating main and interactive effects: Examples from coping/social support and stress field. *Journal of Health and Social Behavior, 25*, 85–98.

Gore, S. (1981). Stress-buffering functions of social supports: An appraisal and clarification of research methods. In B. S. Dohrenwend & B. P. Dohrenwend (Eds.), *Stressful life events and their contexts.* New York: Prodist.

Gotlib, I. H., & Robinson, L. A. (1982). Responses to depressed individuals: Discrepancies between self-report and observer-rated behavior. *Journal of Abnormal Psychology, 91*, 231–240.

Hanushek, E. A., & Jackson, J. E. (1977). *Statistical methods for social scientists.* New York: Academic Press.

Heise, D. R. (1975). *Causal analysis.* New York: Wiley.

Heller, K., & Swindle, R. W. (1983). Social networks, perceived social support and coping with stress. In R. D. Felner, L. A. Jason, J. Moritsugu, & S. S. Faber (Eds.), *Preventive psychology: Theory, research, and practice in community interventions.* New York: Pergamon.

House, J. S. (1981). *Work stress and social support.* Reading, MA: Addison-Wesley.

James, L. R., & Singh, B. K. (1978). An introduction to the logic, assumptions, and basic analytic procedures of two-stage least squares. *Psychological Bulletin, 85,* 1104–1122.

Joreskog, K. G., & Sorbom, D. (1982). Recent developments in structural equation modeling. *Journal of Marketing Research, 19,* 404–416.

Kenny, D. A. (1975). Cross-lagged panel correlation: A test for spuriousness. *Psychological Bulletin, 82,* 887–903.

Kenny, D. A. (1979). *Correlation and causality.* New York: Wiley.

Kerlinger, F. N., & Pedhazur, E. J. (1973). *Multiple regression in behavioral research.* New York: Holt.

Kessler, R. C. (1982). Life events, social supports, and mental health. In W. R. Gove (Ed.), *Deviance and mental illness.* Beverly Hills: Sage.

Kessler, R. C., & Greenberg, D. F. (1981). *Linear panel analysis.* New York: Academic Press.

Lin, N., Simeone, R. S., Ensel, W. M., & Kuo, W. (1979). Social support, stressful life events, and illness: A model and an empirical test. *Journal of Health and Social Behavior, 20,* 108–119.

Maruyama, G., & McGarvey, B. (1980). Evaluating causal models: An application of maximum-likelihood analysis of structural equations. *Psychological Bulletin, 87,* 502–512.

McGuire, J. C. & Gottlieb, B. H. (1979). Social support groups among new parents: An experimental study in primary prevention. *Journal of Clinical Child Psychology, 8,* 111–116.

Mitchell, R. E., Billings, A. G., & Moos, R. H. (1982). Social support and well-being: Implications for prevention programs. *Journal of Primary Prevention, 3,* 77–98.

Monroe, S. M. (1983). Social support and disorder: Toward an untangling of cause and effect. *American Journal of Community Psychology, 11,* 81–97.

Pearlin, L. I., Menaghan, E. G., Lieberman, M. A., & Mullan, J. T. (1981). The stress process. *Journal of Health and Social Behavior, 22,* 337–356.

Reynolds, H. T. (1978). Some comments on the causal analysis of surveys with log-linear models. *American Journal of Sociology, 83,* 127–143.

Rogosa, D. (1979). Causal models in longitudinal research: Rationale, formulation, and interpretation. In J. R. Nesselroade & P. B. Baltes (Eds.), *Longitudinal research in the study of behavior and development.* New York: Academic Press.

Rogosa, D. (1980). A critique of cross-lagged correlation. *Psychological Bulletin, 88,* 245–258.

Rook, K. S. (1983). *Social support, loneliness, and social isolation* (Technical Advisory Report). Office of Prevention, National Institute of Mental Health.

Sarason, I. G., & Stoops, R. (1978). Test anxiety and the passage of time. *Journal of Consulting and Clinical Psychology, 46,* 102–109.

Schmitt, N., & Bedeian, A. G. (1982). A comparison of LISREL and two-stage least squares analysis of a hypothesized life-job satisfaction reciprocal relationship. *Journal of Applied Psychology, 67,* 806–817.

Siegel, S. (1956). *Nonparametric statistics for the behavioral sciences.* New York: McGraw-Hill.

Steiger, J. H. (1980). Tests for comparing elements of a correlation matrix. *Psychological Bulletin, 87,* 245–251.

Swafford, M. (1980). Three parametric techniques for contingency table analysis: A nontechnical commentary. *American Sociological Review, 45,* 664–690.

Tennant, C., & Bebbington, P. (1978). The social causation of depression: A critique of the work of Brown and his colleagues. *Psychological Medicine, 8,* 565–575.

Thoits, P. A. (1982). Conceptual, methodological, and theoretical problems in studying social support as a buffer against life stress. *Journal of Health and Social Behavior, 23,* 145–159.

Turner, R. J. (1981). Social support as a contingency in psychological well-being. *Journal of Health and Social Behavior, 22,* 357–367.

Turner, R. J. (1983). Direct, indirect, and moderating effects of social support on psychological distress and associated conditions. In H. B. Kaplan (Ed.), *Psychosocial stress: Trends in theory and research.* New York: Academic Press.

Turner, R. J., & Noh, S. (1983). Class and psychological vulnerability among women: The significance of social support and personal control. *Journal of Health and Social Behavior, 24,* 2–15.

Whitcher, S. J., & Fisher, J. A. (1979). Multi-dimensional reaction to therapeutic touch in a hospital setting. *Journal of Personality and Social Psychology, 37,* 87–96.

Wilcox, B. L. (1981). Social support, life stress, and psychological adjustment: A test of the buffering hypothesis. *American Journal of Community Psychology, 9,* 371–386.

Williams, A. W., Ware, Jr., J. E., & Donald C. A. (1981). A model of mental health, life events and social supports applicable to general populations. *Journal of Health and Social Behavior, 22,* 324–336.

PART II

Social Support through the Life Cycle

CHAPTER 7

Social Support through
the Life Course*

Richard Schulz and Marie T. Rau

Introduction

One of the fundamental characteristics of human society is that roles, relationships, and behaviors change with age. Contemporaneous with these changes are both subtle and profound changes in health status. In this chapter we examine some of the complex interactions involving health, age, human relationships, and social support.

One of the difficulties of writing about social support through the life course is deciding what not to include. Virtually all of the empirical literature on social support is based on investigations of populations of identifiable chronological ages. This chapter might include therefore a discussion of all of the social support literature, organized by a life-course variable such as age. Such an undertaking would quickly exhaust both our space limitations and probably the reader's patience. We have opted, therefore, to examine and discuss selectively the literature on social support through the life course. The following guidelines were used to focus our discussion:

*We wish to thank Charlene Rhyne for her help in the preparation of this manuscript. Preparation of this manuscript was also supported by grants from the AARP Andrus Foundation, the Paralyzed Veterans of America Technology and Research Foundation, and from the National Institute on Aging, 1 RO1 AG04349.

1. Because the nature of the relationships among children, their kin, and their peers is in many ways unique and is addressed elsewhere in this book, we have decided to begin our examination of the life course with young adulthood.

2. Age-related changes in social support are best examined in longitudinal or cross-sectional studies that span relatively large chronological age ranges. We are especially interested in examining those studies that satisfy this criterion. The literature also contains many studies that examine social support among individuals within a specific chronological age range (e.g., the elderly) or individuals occupying an age-related role (e.g., motherhood).

The discussion that follows is divided into four parts. First, we develop a conceptual system for the life course, which is then used as a context within which we examine changes in social support and health. The next part focuses on changes in health and in structural aspects of social networks throughout the life course. Specific functional aspects of social networks as they relate to a life-course perspective are examined next. Finally, the implications of adopting a life-course perspective on social support and health are examined.

The Life Course

At the most basic level, the life course can be defined as the major life events and transitions an individual experiences between birth and death. Some theorists have claimed (Buhler, 1962; Erikson, 1963; Levinson, 1978) there is an invariant underlying structure to adult life within which the personal biographies of individuals are enacted. Levinson (1978), for example, has identified eight periods, each lasting about 5 years, that describe the major events and transitions of early and middle adulthood. Other researchers (Brim & Ryff, 1980; Danish, Smyer, & Nowak, 1980) have taken their cues from Holmes and Rahe (1967) and Dohrenwend and Dohrenwend (1974, 1981) and have partitioned the life course into critical or significant life events such as marriage, having a child, a son or daughter leaving home, and retirement. Because the empirical base for the latter approach is better developed, particularly with respect to the areas of health and social support, our discussion of the life course will be guided by the earlier work of Danish *et al.* (1980), Brim and Ryff (1980), and Hultsch and Plemons (1979).

We have developed a conceptual system for classifying life-course events and transitions based on two dimensions: statistical and temporal normativity. As illustrated by the examples in Table 7.1, events are defined to be

Table 7.1

Typology and Examples of Life-Course Events

	Temporally normative	Temporally nonnormative
Statistically normative	Marriage Birth of first child Retirement	Entering college at middle age Becoming widowed at young age Having first child late in life
Statistically nonnormative	Spinal cord injury Stroke Rape Inheriting estate Winning professional award	Cultural events: War Depression Natural disaster Individual events: Winning lottery Being fired from job Changing occupation

statistically normative when they happen to most individuals in a cultural group. Thus, events such as marriage and retirement are considered to be statistically normative because they are experienced by most individuals in our culture, whereas rape, inheriting a large estate, or winning a presitigious professional award are statistically nonnormative; they are experienced by only a small number of persons in our culture.

An event is *temporally normative* when it occurs within a predictable, limited age range, either because of biological constraints or because of cultural norms. Certain illnesses such as spinal cord injury and stroke are temporally normative when they occur during young adulthood and old age, respectively. Becoming widowed, according to this classification system, is defined as temporally normative when it occurs in late life but is temporally nonnormative when it occurs during young adulthood. As will be discussed in detail subsequently, how a particular event is classified has important implications regarding expectations for support and its availability, delivery, and impact.

Statistically and Temporally Normative Life Events

Despite the large individual variability in the way people live their daily lives, there exist strong biological and societal imperatives that define the major events in the human life cycle. Such events include marriage, birth of a child, and retirement. These events are normative in a statistical sense because they are experienced by most people, and they are also temporally normative or age-graded because their temporal location in the life cycle is determined by biological capacity and/or social norms.

Given the properties of these events, the following relationships among the triad of life-course events, social support, and health could be expected. First, because the events are temporally normative they are also predictable. This should help reduce the levels of subjective stress and negative health effects associated with the occurrence of these events (Schulz, 1976).

Second, to the extent that a culture judges an event to be both common and potentially stressful, it is likely to establish both formal and informal support systems to help the individual cope with the event. Widowhood support groups and preretirement counseling services are examples of formal support systems established to help an individual successfully navigate through a particular transition period. The tradition of giving monetary gifts to newlyweds is another example of informal support given to help ease a major life transition.

Third, the predictability and frequency of these events ensures widespread anticipatory socialization of both the individual experiencing the event and the potential support persons. Thus, expectations for support are likely to be high and the impact of receiving support relatively low. On the other hand, not receiving support when it is expected may have detrimental consequences for individuals who feel they need help.

Statistically Normative, Temporally Nonnormative Life Events

The pattern just described applies to many of the life-course events experienced by people in Western cultures, yet all of us have encountered individuals who do not fit the rhythm of the temporally normative life cycle. These are individuals who start their education at midlife, have a child either very early or late in their lives, or retire at a young age—in short, individuals who experience the same major life events that most people do, but at an atypical time (Neugarten, 1970). The lives of such individuals are likely to be less predictable and perhaps more stressful. Moreover, individuals who follow these less-traveled paths are likely to have unique social network and support system needs and may be at greater risk of negative health consequences. For example, individuals who begin their college education at the age of 45 may obtain little support from their same-aged network of friends simply because their networks lack the knowledge and/or the motivation to provide support.

Statistically Nonnormative, Temporally Normative Life Events

Statistically nonnormative but temporally normative events are experienced by relatively few people. Spinal cord injuries and strokes are examples of such events. Most spinal cord injuries occur in persons between the ages of 18 and 30, and most strokes occur after the age of 65. Because such events occur infrequently, neither the victim nor the support network acquires the specific knowledge and skills that might be useful in coping with the event. Even though potential support persons may be highly motivated to provide support they lack the appropriate helping skills and may be further inhibited from helping because they feel inadequate and helpless.

Dunkel-Schetter and Wortman (1982) pointed to a similar dynamic in explaining the inadequacy of the social support available to spinal cord injured persons, cancer patients, rape victims, and the elderly. They argued that the opportunities for ventilation and validation may be limited for members of each of these groups because they arouse feelings of vulnerability and helplessness among their support networks. Although we agree with this analysis as applied to victims of nonnormative events such as spinal cord injuries, cancer, and rape, we do not subscribe to its application to aging. To the extent that events associated with growing old are normative (e.g., retiring or losing one's spouse), we would expect both the victim and the support system to be appropriately socialized to deal with these events when they occur.

Statistically and Temporally Nonnormative Life Events

The final category of life events includes those events that occur infrequently and are not strongly related to age. This category can be further subdivided into cultural events, those that affect large populations, and individual events, those that affect individuals. Examples of cultural events include wars, depressions, and natural disasters such as earthquakes and tornadoes. Such events affect individuals of all ages in a given geographic locale. Examples of individual events include being fired from a job, changing occupations, losing a limb in an auto accident, or winning a lottery. The primary impact of these events is focused on the individual rather than on a large group.

Like nonnormative events in general, these occurrences are rare and unpredictable. We would expect, therefore that socialization for coping with these events and for providing support is minimal. Moreover, with cultural nonnormative events the negative impact is likely to be felt by the individual as well as by those who might provide support. For example, in a major economic depression friends and relatives may not be able to provide tangible aid simply because they do not have any to spare. We would predict, therefore, particularly adverse health consequences under such circumstances. When the event is geographically more isolated (e.g., a tornado or flood), its negative impact should be attenuated to the extent that neighboring unaffected areas or national support groups (e.g., the Red Cross) can provide support.

It should be apparent from the descriptions provided that the life course of an individual is likely to consist of events from each of the four quadrants described. Most people experience most of the statistically and temporally normative life events along with a smattering of nonnormative events.

Life-Course Events, Social Support, and Health

We have applied the descriptors *statistically* and *temporally normative* to life events because they can be easily linked to social support and to health. Whether or not a particular event is normative or not is likely to have both direct and indirect effects on health and social support. Nonnormative events are likely to be more stressful to the individual than normative events. This has direct consequences for the health of the individual. In addition, event type has direct effects on the need for and expectations of social support as well as the availability of social support, which may in turn affect the individual's health. In this section we will assess the validity of these assumptions by examining the empirical literature on the relationships among life course events, social support, and health.

A considerable literature has accumulated since the 1970s documenting the beneficial effects of social support in helping individuals cope with life-course events such as having a first child (Nuckolls *et al.*, 1972; Reibstein, 1981) adapting to college life (Cohen & Hoberman, 1983), and losing a spouse (Walker, MacBride, & Vachon, 1977). However, as Lieberman (1982) and others (Brehm, 1983; House, 1981) have pointed out, there is no simple and direct relationship between social support and health when examined in the context of important life transitions. The extensive and frequently contradictory findings on the role social support plays in a large variety of life events (such as widowhood, birth of a child, loss of a child, and severe illness) emphasizes the importance of determining who, what, for whom, when, and under what circumstances social support affects health outcomes. A critical question is what aspects of social networks or features of social support are related to health outcomes when examined from a life-course perspective.

Structural Aspects of Social Networks and the Life Course

The empirical literature on social support through the life course is sparse. As illustrated in Table 7.2, there are relatively few studies that span the complete adult life cycle; most of the studies are cross-sectional, and many of them emphasize structural aspects of social networks rather than the functions that networks might serve.

The consensus among most researchers is that network size and frequency of contact, especially with close kin, remain relatively stable across the life span (Antonucci, 1984; Babchuck, 1978–1979; Costa, Zonderman, & McCrae, 1983). For example, Kahn and Antonucci (Antonucci, 1984) sampled 719 adults aged 50 and over, and found that network size in this national sample did not decline with age, nor were there large age differences in the amount of support individuals reported receiving and providing. Costa *et al.* (1983) found that friendships and social participation did not decline in a longitudinal sample of males whose mean age was 50 when they were first interviewed and 64 when they were interviewed for the third time.

Fischer (1982), on the other hand, reported declines in network size for both men and women as they age, and Babchuck (1978–1979) showed that the frequency of certain types of social contacts decreases with age. Fischer *et al.* reported the greatest declines in the categories of co-workers and just friends. The number of kin in one's network, especially kin identified as very close friends, remains stable from ages 21 to 64 (Stueve & Gerson, 1977). In their sample of Detroit males, Stueve and Gerson (1977) also found that there was a great deal of turnover of best friends in the early adult years and relatively little turnover in late life. These data suggest a process whereby over time people sift through acquaintances and friends, and retain primarily those who are most valued.

Examining the literature on the relationship between network contacts and health outcomes yields a similarly complex picture. Berkman and Syme (1979), in their longitudinal study of an Alameda County, California, sample, found that larger network size and greater frequency of contact was related to decreased mortality for both men and women at all ages, even when other factors such as socioeconomic status, initial health status, and health practices were statistically controlled. Others have similarly found

Table 7.2

Major Life-Course Social Network Studies

Reference	Sample	Age range and breakdown	Type of study	Measures of health and well-being	Social network (NW) operationalized	Social support functions operationalized
Babchuck (1978–1979)	$N = 800$ Stratified probability sample, Midwest	45–89 45–54 55–64 65–74 74+	Cross-sectional	None	Number of primary and confidant kin and friends	Availability of confidant
Berkman and Syme (1979)	$N = 4725$: 2229 male, 2496 female Random sample, Alameda County, California	30–69 30–49 50–59 60–69	Longitudinal (one interview, with mortality follow-up data)	Mortality rates	Social Network Index: number of social ties and relative importance; four sources of social contact: Marital status, friends and relatives, church members, group members	
Campbell (1981)	$N = 3692$ National sample, 1978 (also several other years)	20–60+ 20–29 30–39 40–49 50–59 60+	Cross-sectional	Self-report	Marital status; number of friends, kin; frequency of contact; whether living alone	Supportiveness of marital relationship (four parts); availability of confidant; satisfaction with family and friend relationships
Fischer (1982)	$N = 1050$ Probability sample, English-speaking, Northern California	16–61+ 16–20 21–30 31–40 41–50 51–60 61+	Cross-sectional	Self-report	Overall size of NW; personal characteristics of NW members; type of relationship, frequency of contact, density of NW, geographical distance from respondent (some questions about	Three types of social support: counseling, companionship, practical

136

Study	N	Age	Design	Health measure	Social network/activity measure	Social support measure
Kahn and Antonucci (1983)	$N = 719$	50–95 50–64 65–74 75–95	Cross-sectional		Size of NW, other structural NW characteristics (all NW members, others about five key NW members)	Six types of social support; confiding; reassurance, respect, care when ill, talking with when upset, talking about health; amount of support; perceived adequacy of social support
Medley (1980)	$N = 1786$	22–65+ 22–34 35–44 45–64 65+	Cross-sectional	Self-report (satisfaction with health, other life domains)	Satisfaction with family life and family activities (one question)	
Palmore and Luikart (1972)	$N = 502$ Duke University adaptation study	45–71	Longitudinal	Self-rated; physician-rated performance status	Organizational activity; meetings per month; social activity: hours per week; productive hours per week, including volunteer activities	
Veroff, Douvan, and Kulka (1981)	1957: $N = 2460$ 1976: $N = 2267$ Two interview years	21+	Cross-sectional	Self-rated (mental health focus)	Marital status; membership in organizations; leisure activities; number, frequency of contact with relatives, friends, neighbors; nature of interactions	Formal and informal sources of support; resources when worried, concerned, unhappy; perceived availability of support; frequency of talking about problems; satisfaction with social security

that the size of the network is related to mental health and coping (Hirsch, 1981; McKinlay, 1981; Mitchell & Trickett, 1980).

On the other hand, Schaefer and her colleagues (1981), in a longitudinal study of persons aged 45–64, found network size to be unrelated to outcome measures of psychological symptomatology (depression, negative morale) and self-reported physical health status; however, level of social support, especially perceived tangible aid, was related to depression and negative morale. Lieberman (1982) summarized a series of life-transitions studies conducted at the University of Chicago and reported that neither network size nor frequency of contact were related to health and well-being.

Finally, there are a large number of studies demonstrating that structural social network variables such as the frequency of social interaction is correlated with life satisfaction throughout adulthood (e.g., George, 1978; Markides & Martin, 1979; Palmore & Kivett, 1977; Windley & Scheidt, 1982). Moreover, many of these studies include measures of health, allowing an examination of relationships among age, health, subjective well-being, and social support. The most consistent finding in this literature is that subjective well-being changes little with age, and that health, socioeconomic factors, and quantity of social interaction are strong correlates of subjective well-being at all ages (Larson, 1978).

The relationship between social interaction and well-being requires one qualification, however. In his extensive review of well-being in older persons, Larson (1978) reported that this relationship does not hold for interactions with family. Similar results are reported by Lee and Ihinger-Tallman (1980), Stephens et al. (1978), and Wood and Robertson (1978), who found either weak or no relationship between interaction with kin such as siblings and grandchildren and measures of well-being or morale. On the other hand, interactions with friends do appear to be beneficial (Arling, 1976; Spakes, 1979; Wood & Robertson, 1978). Spakes, for example, studied persons aged 55 and over in three North Carolina communities and found the frequency of contact with close friends to be significantly related to life satisfaction, whereas neither frequency of family contacts nor satisfaction with such contacts was related to life satisfaction.

Focusing on the role of networks in buffering individuals from the negative effects of nonnormative events yields a more consistent picture. Individuals who receive social support consistently cope better with events such as physical disability (Kemp & Vash, 1971; Schulz & Decker, 1983), rape (Burgess & Holmstrum, 1978), job loss (Cobb & Kasl, 1977), cancer (Vachon et al., 1977), loss of spouse (Kasl & Berkman, 1981; Lopata, 1973), and stroke (Fengler & Goodrich, 1979; Robertson & Suinn, 1968). It is not always clear from these studies to what extent size of network is a critical indicator of social support; however, size is frequently correlated with well-being. Schulz and Decker (in press), for example, found that depression among middle-aged and elderly spinal cord injured persons was related to network size.

The work of Hirsch (1980) provides insight into the role of network density as a contributor to health and self-reported well-being. He studied two populations of women who had recently experienced an off-time event. One group consisted of younger widows, and the other consisted of mature women returning to college. For both groups, Hirsch (1980) found that women with less dense networks reported significantly better support and better mental health. He also found that the presence of multidimensional or multiplex friendships was positively correlated with perceived support and mental health. Hirsch speculated that the greater access to salient non-familial roles and activities provided by low-density, multidimensional social networks contributed to a smoother reorganization of their lives. Similar negative effects of high-density networks have been found by Finlayson (1976), who studied the wives of men who had suffered a heart attack.

In terms of the life-course model presented earlier, it is likely that more diversified, less closely knit networks increase the probability of finding appropriate models and/or individuals who understand the types of support needed for coping with temporally nonnormative events. It can be further speculated that for certain types of events (e.g., an interracial marriage) a strong family network may not be associated with positive well-being; in fact, the reverse might be true.

The preceding discussion suggests four important points regarding structural aspects of social networks throughout the life course. First, the size of the network and the quantity of interaction among network members remains fairly constant throughout the adult life course. Depending on how the question is asked, most adults report having 8–15 persons in their network. Assuming that maintaining a network relationship requires a periodic investment of emotional and time resources, there is probably an upper limit to the number of persons in a network. The data of Fischer *et al.* (1977) furthermore suggest that over time individuals sift through their relationships and retain those that are valued most. If it is assumed that network size is related to the amount of social support received, then these data have important implications. Because health problems and the need for help increase with age, particularly in the 65-year-old and older category, an age-related increase in the size of the support network might be expected. That this does not happen suggests there are either some needs that are not met or the existing network provides more support to individuals who are old. This issue will be discussed in greater detail in the following section.

Second, the size of the network appears to be related to the health impact of specific life-course events. In particular, the negative impact of nonnormative events is attenuated by the presence of a sizable support network.

Third, a diverse social network may be a valuable asset to individuals experiencing normative off-time events, such as being widowed at a young age or going to college late in life. Such networks are more likely to contain individuals with the appropriate helping skills.

Fourth, nonnormative events are not only likely to be experienced as more stressful when they occur, but they may also permanently affect the size of a network for the rest of an individual's life. For example, our research on middle-aged and elderly spinal cord injured persons shows their networks to be very small compared to those of nondisabled persons of similar age (Schulz & Decker, in press). Although we cannot be sure of the reasons for this, it is likely that the limitations in mobility associated with the injury cause existing networks to shrink initially and then remain small in size throughout the individual's life. The absence of an extensive network may make an already at-risk population more susceptible to decline should the existing network be overtaxed or eliminated through illness of death.

Functional Aspects of Social Networks and the Life Course

Although early social network researchers frequently failed to distinguish between structural and functional aspects of social networks, there exists almost universal consensus among contemporary researchers that it is important to assess separately both of these components of social networks. Indeed, many researchers would agree that the number of people in a person's network may not be as important as what they do for the individual. Our focus in this section will be on the functional aspects of social support. General issues regarding the differentiation of types of support and variations in support given and received at different stages in the adult life course are discussed first, followed by an examination the unique supportive functions of marital and confidant relationships.

Types of Support

There are many different types of support that might be provided or received in a given relationship, but most of these can be classified into three or four generic categories. Schaefer *et al.* (1981) identified three types of support functions (emotional, informational, and tangible), whereas Cohen and McKay (1984) opted for four (tangible, appraisal, self-esteem, and belonging). These distinctions are based on the theoretically derived assumption that different types of support may independently affect health or psychological functioning. Furthermore, from a life-course perspective, we would hypothesize that support needs and the probability of receiving specific types of support vary as a function of the individual's temporal location in the life course. For example, we would expect a college student to have higher tangible aid needs and to receive more tangible aid than a middle-aged individual. Questions concerning the validity of the theoretical distinctions made regarding types of support have been addressed by several other contributors to this book who have examined the independent health-related effects of different types of support. For us, the important questions are what the normative intergenerational life-course support patterns are and how they are related to health and well-being. The work of Riley and Foner (1968), Streib (1965), Kahn and Antonucci (1983), Hill *et al.* (1970), and Shanas *et al.* (1968) has suggested that one of the common characteristics of intergenerational interaction is the provision of mutual aid. The aid provided may take the form of housework or babysitting, money or gifts, information, advice, and moral support. With respect to economic aid, the balance between generations is relatively even, although adult children tend to receive more than they give. Child care also favors the younger generation, whereas the provision of health-related services favors the older generation. All in all, it appears that parents continue to give to their children what they can for as long as they can, and this process reverses itself when the health and/or financial condition of the parents deteriorate.

It was pointed out earlier that large numbers of old persons suffer from debilitating chronic health conditions. One consequence is that younger kin frequently end up providing large amounts of personal care, sometimes at levels that are detrimental to their own health. Brody (1977) estimated that 70–80% of the health care received by old people is provided by their children. The large quantities of support provided in late life can be understood by invoking the concept of a support reserve or support bank (Antonucci, 1984). The idea behind a support bank is that individuals can collect later in life on the support they have provided earlier. Although there exist no data substantiating the validity of support transfers over the life course, it is probably not a bad idea to invest regularly in a support bank for possible later withdrawal.

Functions of Marital and Confidant Relationships

Historically, the provision of emotional support and feelings of intimacy have been presumed to be critical components of the health-protective effects of social support throughout the adult life course. The empirical support for this assumption is found in the literature on the differences in well-being between individuals who have a spouse and/or a nonspouse confidant and those who do not.

Probably the most powerful normative life-course supportive relationship, in terms of its health-protective functions, is the marital relationship. Several cross-sectional studies of large representative samples have shown a consistently strong relationship between marital status and reported well-being (Campbell, 1981; Veroff, Douvan, & Kulka, 1981). Epidemiological studies have repeatedly shown a relationship between being married and having lower rates of mortality (Berkman & Syme, 1979; House, Robins, & Metzner, 1982; Ortmeyer, 1974; Price, Slater, & Hare, 1971) and morbidity (Weiss, 1973).

Not only is marriage per se important to individual well-being, but the quality of the marital relationship may further enhance the protective effects of being married. In her study of a large, random sample of older women, Goldberg (1981) found a strong negative relationship between depressive symptomatology and the presence of a spouse who was also identified as a confidant. Similar positive effects have been reported for nonspouse confidants (Brown, 1981; Goldberg, 1981; Lowenthal & Haven, 1968).

The beneficial effects of a spouse–confidant have also been demonstrated in the context of specific normative and nonnormative life-course events. Several illustrative examples are found in the transitions study carried out by Lieberman and his colleagues (Lieberman, 1982) at the University of Chicago. For example, Reibstein (1981) found that spouses played a critical role in predicting the adjustment of highly educated and career-invested women to the birth of their first child. The more a spouse was perceived to be available to discuss important personal problems and the more he was perceived as approving of the wife's new role as mother and housewife, the more satisfied respondents were in their new roles and the less marital strain they reported. Moreover, for those women who did not report receiving support from their husbands, Reibstein found no evidence that other sources of social support, such as peer support, were effective substitutes. Other researchers have also found a supportive marital relationship to be a powerful mediating factor in reducing the negative health consequences of such nonnormative events as job loss (Cobb & Kasl, 1977; Gore, 1978) and death of a child (Lieberman, 1982).

Another approach to assessing the effects of marital status on health examines the impact of losing a spouse either through divorce or death. This literature is particularly relevant to our focus because such a loss may occur at either unexpected or expected points in the life course. Death of a spouse is unexpected when it occurs early in adulthood and expected when it occurs late in life. The reverse is true for divorce. Late-life divorces are very rare, whereas divorces during the first 5 years of marriage are relatively common.

In general, evidence suggests that the mortality and morbidity rates of the widowed are higher than those of married controls of comparable age and sex (Stroebe *et al.*, 1982). However, the magnitude of the excess mortality and morbidity depends in part on the age at which the individual becomes widowed. Kraus and Lilienfeld (1959) and McNeil (1973) showed that there is a decreased relative risk of negative health consequences when widowhood occurs at older ages. Morgan (1976), in a cross-sectional study of widows aged 45–74, found that in contrast to younger widows—who showed significantly lower morale than their married-age peers—older widows had morale scores equal to and slightly higher than married women in the same age group. Morgan suggested that the higher morale among widows over age 70 is consistent with the notion that the older widow experiences fewer negative outcomes because she has available a reference group of supportive, empathic individuals (i.e., other widows).

Divorce in many ways presents a mirror image of widowhood. Whereas the negative effects of widowhood are greater at young ages, divorce takes a greater toll at older ages. Chiriboga (1982) investigated the effects of divorce on both men and women ranging in age from the 20s through the 70s. He found that those in their 40s reported significantly lower overall happiness than those in their 20s or 30s; individuals over 50 were the least happy of all. Older divorced persons also reported more difficulty dealing with their social world, greater long-term dissatisfaction, and fewer positive emotional experiences, and they exhibited more signs of personal discomfort. One possible reason for these negative effects is that, unlike the case of widowhood, there exists no empathic support group that might provide help for the older divorced individual.

Although all the data identifying who provides what type of support to whom and when are not yet in, it is possible to construct a rough outline of support exchanges for the normative, age-graded life course. Using three generic categories of support (tangible aid, informational support, and emotional support) and three age stages (young adulthood, middle age, and old age) the following picture can be drawn:

1. For the young adult, the parents are the primary source of tangible aid and friends are the major source of informational and emotional support, with other relatives playing a secondary role.
2. For middle-aged individuals, the spouse is a primary provider of both tangible aid and emotional support, with friends, colleagues, and neighbors providing most of the informational support.

3. In old age, adult children and the spouse, if living, provide most of the tangible aid. Informational and emotional support is provided by a variety of sources, including children, formal organizations such as organized religions, specialized support groups such as widowhood groups, and friends.

This summary is obviously only a rough approximation of reality, and is very cohort-specific at that. The support exchanges that occur in subsequent generations of young, middle-aged, and old persons may be altogether different from the description provided here.

Social Support and the Life Course: Themes and Metaphors

For a social network to provide support to an individual, it must not only exist in a structural sense, but its members must also possess the ability, knowledge, and motivation to act when necessary. One of the central themes of this chapter is that the necessary conditions for the occurrence of a supportive act vary systematically with the type of life course event the individual is experiencing.

Those life transitions that are experienced by most people and that occur within narrow age ranges are not likely to be troublesome because they are predictable—and therefore the individual has an opportunity to prepare for them—but also because the social network has the ability, knowledge, and motivation to provide support. Ability and knowledge are acquired through socialization. The motivation to act has its source in societal sanctions regarding interpersonal exchanges within and across generations; parents are supposed to help their college-aged children, husbands are supposed to be supportive of their wives during pregnancy and the birth of a child, children are supposed to help care for their frail parents, and so forth. On the other hand, the expectations for support for such events are likely to be high as well. As a result, there may not be many health-related benefits associated with receiving support, but there may be negative effects associated with not having it.

Life-course events that are unexpected either because they occur off-time or because they are statistically infrequent are likely to be more problematic. Because the individual often does not have the opportunity to prepare for them, they are likely to be inherently more stressful. Moreover, members of the support network are less likely to have the appropriate abilities or knowledge to provide support even if they have the motivation. Expectations for support are probably more uncertain for these events; when support is provided, it is likely to be beneficial to the individual's well-being.

A second theme of this chapter is that relatively little is known about social support through the life course, particularly in a longitudinal sense. With the exception of the work of Kahn and his colleagues (in press), Fischer (1982), Lieberman (1982), and Costa *et al.* (1983), there have been relatively few attempts to examine support empirically in the context of the life course. Theoretical models of support through the life course are even rarer. Kahn's convoy model is one attempt to describe the structure and function of social networks and their relation to the individual over the life course. It is a useful model for organizing the personal and contextual variables that affect individuals as they move through life, and as a metaphor it captures some of the dynamics of social support through the life course.

Our own analysis of the social support literature suggests another metaphor appropriate to a life-course analysis of social support. We have come to think of the social network and the support it provides as a musical ensemble, such as a string quartet. A good musical ensemble consists of several instrumentalists who have different functions but who work together to produce a unified whole. A good support system consists of different actors—friends, relatives, colleagues—each of whom has assigned functions and who together cover the full range of support needs.

Each player in an ensemble must have the ability to take a lead role at the appropriate time and to recede into the background when others take the lead. No one player can always be the soloist. In a small ensemble neither the players nor the parts are interchangeable, and a weak or absent player cannot be compensated for by the others. In a good support system different individuals also play primary supportive roles at different times. For young adults, parents are the primary providers of tangible aid but not informational support. The latter has to come from friends. Similarly, the person relegated to the spouse–confidant role has specific functions that cannot be performed by substitutes.

Finally, creating a good ensemble requires time to find the proper mix of performers and then more time to coordinate individual performance to yield an integrated and well-balanced whole. A support system also evolves over time. New individuals are recruited while others are lost, although as in a good musical ensemble there must be some stability in order to achieve high-quality performances.

References

Antonucci, T. C. (1984). Personal characteristics, social support, and social behavior. In E. Shanas & R. H. Binstock (Eds.), *Handbook of aging and the social sciences* (2nd ed.). New York: Van Nostrand.

Arling, G. (1976). The elderly widow and her family, neighbors, and friends. *Journal of Marriage and the Family, 38,* 757–768.

Babchuck, N. (1978–1979). Aging and primary relations. *International Journal of Aging and Human Development, 9,* 137–151.

Berkman, L. F., & Syme, S. L. (1979). Social networks, host resistance, and mortality: A nine year follow-up study of Alameda County residents. *American Journal of Epidemiology, 109,* 186–204.

Brehm, S. S. (1983, May). *Social support processes: Problems and perspectives.* Paper presented at the Annual Meeting of Midwestern Psychological Association, Chicago.

Brim, Jr., O. G., & Ryff, C. D. (1980). On the properties of life events. In P. B. Baltes & O. G. Brim, Jr. (Eds.), *Life-span development and behavior* (Vol. 3, pp. 368–387). New York: Academic Press.

Brody, E. M. (1977). Health and its social implications. In M. Marvis (Ed.), *Le vieillisement: Un defi à la science et à la politique sociale.* Paris: Institute de la Vie.

Brown, B. B. (1981). *A friend in need: The impact of having a confidant.* Unpublished paper, Department of Educational Psychology, University of Wisconsin.

Buhler, C. (1962). Genetic aspects of the self. *Annals of the New York Academy of Applied Science, 62,* 730–764.

Burgess, A. W., & Holmstrum, L. L. (1978). Recovery from rape and prior life stress. *Research in Nursing and Health, 1,* 165–174.

Campbell, A. (1981). *The sense of well-being in America.* New York: McGraw-Hill.

Chiriboga, D. A. (1982). Adaptation to marital separation in later and earlier life. *Journal of Gerontology, 37,* 109–114.

Cobb, S., & Kasl, S. V. (1977). *Termination: The consequences of job loss* (NIOSH, Publication No. 77–224). Cincinnati, OH: U.S. Department of Health, Education, and Welfare.

Cohen, S., & Hoberman, H. M. (1983). Positive events and social supports as buffers of life change stress. *Journal of Applied Social Psychology, 13,* 99–125.

Cohen, S., & McKay, G. (1984). Social support, stress and the buffering hypothesis: A theoretical analysis. In A. Baum, J. E. Singer, & S. E. Taylor (Eds.), *Handbook of psychology and health* (Vol. 4). Hillsdale, N.J.: Erlbaum.

Costa, Jr., P. T., Zonderman, A. B., & McCrae, R. R. (1983). *Longitudinal course of social support in the Baltimore Longitudinal Study of Aging.* Paper presented at the NATO Advanced Workshop: Social Support-Theory, Research and Application, Chateau de Bonas, France.

Danish, S. J., Smyer, M. A., & Nowak, C. A. (1980). Developmental intervention: Enhancing life-event processes. In P. B. Baltes & O. G. Brim, Jr. (Eds.), *Life-span development and and behavior.* New York: Academic Press.

Dohrenwend, B. S., & Dohrenwend, B. P. (Eds.). (1974). *Stressful life events: Their nature and effects.* New York: Wiley.

Dohrenwend, B. S., & Dohrenwend, B. P. (Eds.). (1981). *Stressful life events and their contexts.* New York: Prodist.

Dunkel-Schetter, C., & Wortman, C. B. (1982). Parallels between victimization and aging. In S. B. Kiesler, J. N. Morgan, & V. K. Oppenheimer (Eds.), *Aging: Social change* (pp. 349–381). New York: Academic Press.

Erikson, E. H. (1963). *Childhood and society.* New York: Norton.

Fengler, A. P., & Goodrich, N. (1979). Wives of elderly disabled men: The hidden patients. *The Gerontologist, 19,* 175–183.

Finlayson, A. (1976). Social networks as coping resources. *Social Science and Medicine, 10,* 97–103.

Fischer, C. S. (1982). *To dwell among friends.* University of Chicago Press.

Fischer, C. S., Jackson, R. M., Stueve, C. A., Gerson, K., Jones, L. M., & Baldassare, M. (1977). *Networks and places: Social relations in the urban setting.* New York: Free Press.

George, L. K. (1978). The impact of personality and social status factors upon levels of activity and psychological well-being. *Journal of Gerontology, 33,* 840–847.

Glick, I. O., Weiss, R. D., & Parkes, C. M. (1974). *The first year of bereavement.* New York: Wiley.

Goldberg, E. L. (1981, October). *Health effects of becoming widowed.* Paper delivered at The Changing Risk of Disease in Women: An Epidemiologic Approach Symposium. Johns Hopkins University, Department of Epidemiology.

Gore, S. (1978). The effect of social support in moderating the health consequences of unemployment. *Journal of Health and Social Behavior, 19,* 157–165.

Hill, R., Foote, N., Aldous, J., Carlson, R., & Macdonald, R. (1970). *Family development in three generations.* Cambridge, MA: Schenkman.

Hirsch, B. J. (1980). Natural support systems and coping with major life changes. *American Journal of Community Psychology, 8,* 159–172.

Hirsch, B. J. (1981). Social networks and the coping process: Creating personal communities. In B. H. Gottlieb (Ed.), *Social networks and social support,* (pp. 149–170). Beverly Hills, CA: Sage.

Holmes, T. H., & Rahe, R. H. (1967). The social readjustment rating scale. *Journal of Psychosomatic Research, 11,* 213–218.

House, J. S. (1981). *Work stress and social support.* Reading, MA: Addison-Wesley.

House, J. S., Robbins, C., & Metzner, H. L. (1982). The association of social relationships and activities with mortality: Prospective evidence from the Tecumseh Community Health Study. *American Journal of Epidemiology, 116,* 123–140.

Hultsch, D. F., & Plemons, J. K. (1979). Life events and life-span development. In P. B. Baltes & O. G. Brim, Jr. (Eds.), *Life-span development and behavior* (pp. 1–31). New York: Academic Press.

Kahn, R. L., & Antonucci, T. C. (1983). *Supports of the elderly: Family, friends, professionals.* Final report to the National Institute on Aging.

Kahn, R. L., Wethington, E., & Ingersoll, B. (in press). Social support and social networks: Determinants, effects, and interactions. In R. Abeles (Ed.), *Life-span developmental issues in social support.*

Kasl, S. V., & Berkman, L. F. (1981). Some psychosocial influences on the health status of the elderly: The perspective of social epidemiology. In J. L. McGaugh & S. B. Kiesler (Eds.), *Aging: Biology and behavior* (pp. 345–385). New York: Academic Press.

Kemp, B. J., & Vash, C. L. (1971). Productivity after injury in a sample of spinal cord injured persons: A pilot study. *Journal of Chronic Disease, 24,* 259–275.

Kraus, A. S., & Lilienfeld, A. N. (1959). Some epidemiologic aspects of the high mortality rate in the young widowed group. *Journal of Chronic Diseases, 10,* 207–217.

Larson, R. (1978). Thirty years of research on the subjective well-being of older Americans. *Journal of Gerontology, 33,* 109–125.

Lee, G. R., & Ihinger-Tallman, N. (1980). Sibling interaction and morale: The effects of family relations on older people. *Research on Aging, 2,* 367–391.

Levinson, D. J. (1978). *The seasons of a man's life.* New York: Basic Books.

Lieberman, M. A. (1982). The effects of social supports on response to stress. In L. Goldberger & S. Breznitz (Eds.), *Handbook of stress* (pp. 764–784). New York: Free Press.

Lopata, H. Z. (1973). *Widowhood in an American city.* Cambridge, MA: Schenkman.

Lopata, H. Z. (1979). *Women as widows: Support systems.* New York: Elsevier.

Lowenthal, M. F., & Haven C. (1968). Interaction and adaptation: Intimacy as a critical variable. *American Sociological Review, 33,* 20–30.

McKinlay, J. B. (1981). Social network influences on morbid episodes and the career of help seeking. In L. Eisenberg & A. Kleinman (Eds.), *The relevance of social science for medicine* (pp. 77–107) Dordrecht, Holland: Reidel.

McNeil, D. N. (1973). Mortality among the widowed in Connecticut. New Haven, CT: Yale University, M. P. H. Essay.

Markides, K. S., & Martin, H. W. (1979). A causal model of life satisfaction among the elderly. *Journal of Gerontology, 34,* 86–89.

Medley, M. L. (1980). Life satisfaction across four stages of adult life. *International Journal of Aging and Human Development, 11,* 193–209.

Mitchell, R. E. & Trickett, E. J. (1980). Social network research and psychosocial adaptation: Implications for community mental health practice. In P. Insel (Ed.), *Environmental variables and the prevention of mental illness* (pp. 43–68). Lexington, MA: Heath.

Morgan, L. A. (1976). A re-examination of widowhood and morale. *Journal of Gerontology, 31,* 687–695.

Neugarten, B. L. (1964). Personality in middle and late life. New York: Atherton Press.

Neugarten, B. L. (1970). Adaptation and the life cycle. *Journal of Geriatric Psychiatry, 4,* 71–87.

Nuckolls, K. B., Cassel, J., & Kaplan, B. H. (1972). Psychosocial assets, life crisis and the prognosis of pregnancy. *American Journal of Epidemiology, 5,* 431–441.

Ortmeyer, C. (1974). Variations in mortality, morbidity, and health care by marital status. In C. F. Erhardt & J. E. Berlin (Eds.), *Mortality and morbidity in the United States,* (pp. 159–188). Cambridge, MA: Harvard University Press.

Palmore, E. B., & Kivett, V. (1977). Change in life satisfaction: A longitudinal study of persons aged 46–70. *Journal of Gerontology, 32,* 311–316.

Palmore, E. B., & Luikart, C. (1972). Health and social factors related to life satisfaction. *Journal of Health and Social Behavior, 13,* 68–80.

Price, J. S., Slater, E., & Hare, E. H. (1971). Marital status of first admissions to psychiatric beds in England and Wales in 1965 and 1966. *Social Biology, 18,* 574–594.

Reibstein, J. (1981). *Adjustment to the maternal role in mothers leaving careers: The impact of their interaction with role colleagues.* Doctoral dissertation, University of Chicago.

Riley, M. W., & Foner, A. (1968). *Aging and society* (Vol. 1): *An inventory of research findings.* New York: Russell Sage Foundation.

Robertson, E. K., & Suinn, R. M. (1968). The determination of rate of progress of stroke patients through empathy measures of patient and family. *Journal of Psychosomatic Research, 12,* 189–191.

Schaefer, C., Coyne, J., & Lazarus, R. (1981). The health related functions of social support. *Journal of Behavioral Medicine, 4,* 381–406.

Schulz, R. (1976). The effects of control and predictability on the psychological and physical well-being of the institutionalized aged. *Journal of Personality and Social Psychology, 33,* 563–573.

Schulz, R., & Decker, S. (in press). Long-term adjustment to physical disability: The role of social support, perceived control, and self-blame. *Journal of Personality and Social Psychology.*

Shanas, E., Townsend, P., Wedderburn, D., Friis, H., Milhoj, P., & Stehouwer, J. (1968). *Older people in three industrial societies.* New York: Atherton.

Spakes, P. R. (1979). Family, friendship, and community interaction as related to life satisfaction of the elderly. *Journal of Gerontological Social Work, 1,* 279–294.

Stephens, R. C., Blau, Z. S., Oser, G. T., & Millar, M. D. (1978). Aging, social support systems, and social policy. *Journal of Gerontological Social Work, 1,* 33–45.

Streib, G. F. (1965). Intergenerational relations: Perspectives of the two generations on the older parent. *Journal of Marriage and the Family, 27,* 469–476.

Stroebe, W., Stroebe, M. S., Gergen, K. J., & Gergen, M. (1982). The effects of bereavement on mortality: A social psychological analysis. In J. R. Eiser (Ed.), *Social psychology and behavioral medicine.* New York: Wiley.

Stueve, C. A., & Gerson, K. (1977). Personal relations across the life cycle. In C. S. Fischer, R. M. Jackson, C. A. Stueve, K. Gerson, L. M. Jones, & M. Baldassare (Eds.), *Networks and places: Social relations in the urban setting* (pp. 79–98). New York: Free Press.

Tallmer, M., & Kutner, B. (1970). Disengagement and morale. *The Gerontologist, 10,* 317–320.

Vachon, M. L. S., Freedman, K., Formo, A., Rodgers, J. Lyall, W. A. L., & Freeman, S. J. J. (1977). The final illness in cancer: The widow's perspective. *Canadian Medical Association Journal, 177,* 1151–1154.

Veroff, J., Douvan, E., & Kulka, R. (1981). *The inner American.* New York: Basic Books.

Walker, K. N., MacBride, A., & Vachon, M. L. S. (1977). Social support networks and the crisis of bereavement. *Social Science and Medicine, 11,* 35–41.

Weiss, N. S. (1973). Marital status and risk factors in coronary heart disease. *British Journal of Preventive and Social Medicine, 27,* 41–43.

Windley, P. G., & Scheidt, R. J. (1982). An ecological model of mental health among small-town rural elderly. *Journal of Gerontology, 37,* 235–242.

Wood, V., & Robertson, J. F. (1978). Friendship and kinship interaction: Differential effects on the morale of the elderly. *Journal of Marriage and the Family, 40,* 367–375.

CHAPTER 8

Social Support, Family Relations, and Children*

W. Thomas Boyce

Introduction

The effect of social support on the health and well-being of children has remained a relatively unexplored area within social epidemiologic research. Nonetheless, a growing body of work suggests that social determinants of disease and disability are as important to the childhood years as they are to later stages in the human life cycle. The central thesis of this chapter is that mutual, interactive social support emerges from a child's earliest experiences in the context of its family and that such support—and its meaning to the child—figure prominently in the maintenance of health and the progression of normal development. The chapter reviews evidence in support of this thesis and sums up collective observations on the character and function of social support in childhood, beginning with an examination of general evidence for an association between child health and the character of the social environment.

*This work was supported in part by a grant from the W. T. Grant Foundation, New York.

151

Child Health and the Social Environment

For centuries, it has been observed that persons from lower socioeconomic conditions sustain a disproportionate burden of the disease and mortality within a given population. Syme and Berkman (1976) have reviewed contemporary work supporting this association and have documented higher morbidity and mortality rates for almost every disease within lower social class groups. Few studies, however, have specifically addressed socioeconomic effects on child health. Engels(1887), in one of the earlier observations of this kind, noted the markedly increased mortality among working class children in nineteenth-century Manchester. More recent work, such as that by Brenner (1973) and Mare (1982), has confirmed that socioeconomic differentials in mortality among children from lower social classes have persisted in modern societies. Children from poorer families experience significantly increased risks of deaths from all causes and are particularly likely to die as a result of injury, poisoning, or violence. Further, studies such as those of Starfield *et al.* (1980) and Egbuonu and Starfield (1982) have demonstrated both an increased prevalence of nearly all major pediatric diseases and an increased severity of disease among U.S. children of lower socioeconomic status. One line of evidence supporting the social environment's influence on child health is the variety of such work documenting socioeconomic effects on children's illness experience and risk of mortality.

A second source of general evidence relating child health to social experience is a series of publications reporting longitudinal, community-based studies of childhood populations. Miller's (1960) work, for example, with children born in the late 1940s in Newcastle-upon-Tyne suggested that social adversity in the form of deprivation or inadequate family functioning was strongly related to a wide range of childhood diseases and disabilities. In a 10-year follow-up of children born on Kauai, Werner, Bierman, and French (1971) found that many times more children developed problems attributable to the effects of a poor social or family environment than developed problems related to the effects of perinatal complications. They concluded that family stability was a major predictor of subsequent biological and behavioral disorders. Finally, both Elder's (1974) analysis of the lives of children growing up in the Great Depression and Rutter's (1979) studies of British children raised in disadvantaged homes point to the central role of the social environment in influencing child health under conditions of adversity.

Common to each of the longitudinal studies just cited is the observation that families appear to serve as a principal environmental source of social support in children's lives. Social support is defined here as the resources (affective, cognitive, and instrumental) provided to the child through relationships and social interactions. From this definition a powerful argument can be raised that families represent the primary social context from which children's experience of social support is derived. The reviews of Haggerty, Roghmann, and Pless (1975), Kaplan and Cassel (1975), and Litman (1974) summarize a large number of studies relating child health to the character and quality of life within families. Various investigators have described family determinants of health in terms of family competence (Boardman, Zyzanski, & Cottrell, 1975), disorganization (Aponte, 1976), structural characteristics such as size (Chen & Cobb, 1960), and qualitative aspects of the family's internal and external relationships (Pless & Satterwhite, 1973). Other work has related aspects of family structure and function to specific illness outcomes (Hunter, Kilstrom, Kraybill, & Loda, 1978; Meyer & Haggerty, 1962; Plionis, 1977); resilience in periods of stress (Hansen & Johnson, 1979), and utilization of child health services (Roghmann & Haggerty, 1973; Fergusson, Horwood & Shannon, 1981). The effects of broader social connections such as those between a child and its peers or its parents' peers have not gone unrecognized (Cochran & Brassard, 1979), and Boocock (1975) has decried the paucity of linkages between contemporary children and the larger society lying outside the boundaries of their nuclear families. It has become increasingly clear that in modern societies children's families serve, throughout much of their developmental years, as the central, enduring source of supportive social interaction. The family can therefore be plausibly regarded as the social environment's primary agent of influence on the health and development of children.

A variety of epidemiologic observations thus support a general impression that the social and family environment may represent an important determinant of child health. Beyond the emerging recognition of this association, however, little is known of the origins and character of the social support that children receive and provide. Only limited information is available regarding the evolution of supportive interactions in families, and even less is known of the specific aspects of social support that bear upon the maintenance of child health and the prevention of disease. How early does recognizable parent–child support begin to appear in the lives of young families? What are the consequences of a supportive versus a nonsupportive social environment in early childhood? Is there a common link among the multiplicity of social factors, both stressful and protective, that may account for their effects on child health?

Questions such as these constitute issues of critical concern in the study of social support—for both child and adult populations. In what follows, a set of early and approximate answers to such questions is proposed, based on collective observations from past and more recent work. Attention is first directed to the origins of social support in families, focusing on the role of parent–child attachment as an elemental process in the evolution of supportive exchange.

The Origins of Social Support in Families

The Capabilities of the Human Infant
for Social Interaction

In almost every culture, the relationship between mother and infant has been regarded as one of the decisive social interactions in the human life cycle (Wolff, 1976). In spite of this, the human infant has traditionally been regarded, from the standpoint of developmental theory, as a relatively ineffective social creature with a limited repertoire of interactive abilities. However, a large number of contemporary observations have concluded that the infant's behavioral organization and capacity for social interaction are remarkably complex, even at birth.

As summarized by Lozoff, Brittenham, Trause, Kennell, and Klaus (1977) and others (Brazelton & Als, 1979; Stone, Smith, & Murphy, 1973), experimental studies have suggested that the human infant is born with an elaborate and highly sophisticated set of receptive and interactive capabilities. Contrary to early beliefs, the neonate has strong visual acuity and is able to focus, follow objects, and even exhibit visual preferences. There is evidence, for example, that newborns selectively attend to facelike configurations, suggesting an innate predisposition toward response to their human environment (Goren, Sarty, & Wu, 1975). The neonate's motor and auditory systems also appear organized for responsive interactions even in the first several days of life. Newborn babies are now known, for example, to demonstrate imitative behaviors that approximate the facial expressions of an adult to which they are attending (Meltzoff & Moore, 1977). A neonate will preferentially respond to the auditory frequencies and rhythmic patterns characteristic of human speech, further suggesting an intrinsic responsivity to the elements of social interaction (Eisenberg, 1976). Finally, analyses of infant crying suggest that newborns utilize an assortment of audibly distinct cries to communicate with their caregivers (Wolff, 1969). Parents, in turn, appear almost from their infant's birth to understand the distinguishable meanings of these cries and to respond differentially to their various characters and intensities (Bernal, 1972).

There is now an abundance of observational and experimental data attesting to remarkable complexity in a human infant's ability to monitor, respond to, and even shape the subtleties of primitive social interactions. In the first hours and days of life, infants appear physiologically and organizationally competent to engage in a rudimentary, but highly elaborate, exchange with their human environment. Such capabilities are the substrates for the development of increasingly complex social interactions, ultimately recognizable as the attachment or bond between parent and child.

Attachment and Reciprocity in the Evolution of Social Support

By the end of their first year, human infants have typically established a strong, resilient, and enduring bond with their parents. Every parent is vividly aware of their infant's smiling recognition, clinging protests on separation, and enthusiastic greetings—all bearing witness to the powerful attachment that has evolved in the first months of the baby's life. Bowlby (1969) and Ainsworth (1972) both proposed that infants are born with a biological tendency to behave in ways that promote proximity and contact with their parents. According to Bowlby, this behavioral propensity to seek and evoke closeness with parents constitutes a primitive biological imperative, which has served to foster infant survival over the history of the human species. Empirical studies such as those by Ainsworth (1962) and Schaffer and Emerson (1964) have focused attention on the attachment between mothers and infants as a developmental event with important consequences for the infant's well-being. The work of Spitz (1946), Bowlby (1952), and others (Ainsworth, 1962; Provence & Lipton, 1962) with institutionalized infants also affirmed the emotional and developmental importance of a nurturing involvement with other human beings. Finally, the more recent work of Brazelton and Als (1979) has emphasized the earliest origins of attachment in the interactive exchanges between mother and infant in the first postpartum days.

Pertinent to the phenomenon of childhood social support, developmental theorists have advanced the hypothesis that an infant's early attachments may represent the primitive basis for all subsequent social relationships (Bowlby, 1969; Rutter, 1978). Three characteristics of attachment behavior are relevant to a consideration of this hypothesis. First, such behavior is clearly interactional, involving subtle, two-way communication and response between mother (or parent) and child. Brazelton, Koslowski, and Main (1974) and others have used the term *reciprocity* to describe the mutuality and dialogistic character of face-to-face interaction between mother and her infant. In such settings, the baby's social behavior appears highly dependent on the mother's ability to recognize and respond to subtle interactive signals conveyed by the infant in the first several days of life. Rutter (1981) summarized knowledge of the various factors capable of influencing these behaviors, noting their sensitivity to elements such as the infant's temperament and state and the character and promptness of the mother's response.

Second, although many studies have focused on the older infant's tie to its mother, some investigators have argued that the process of attachment begins early in infancy, perhaps during a critical, sensitive stage in the postpartum period. Lozoff *et al.* (1977), for example, have discussed the newborn's almost immediate ability to recognize and differentially respond to the mother's smell, voice, and appearance. Such sensitivity to the mother's presence is presumably connected at some level to observations relating subsequent infant behavior to early maternal interactions. Infants exposed more continuously and intensively to a single caregiver during the first few days of life become more readily organized into sleep–wake cycles and cry less frequently than infants experiencing fewer or more random maternal contacts (Sander, Julia, Stechler, & Burns, 1972). Maternal behaviors, such as nurturing and protecting, also appear to be favorably altered by early, continuous contact with the baby (Egeland & Sroufe, 1981; Klaus, Jerauld, Kreger, McAlpine, Steffa, & Kennell, 1972).

A third aspect of attachment behavior relevant to its consideration as a precursor of social support is the development of the so-called secure base effect. Following and seeking closeness are characteristic attachment behaviors that markedly increase under conditions of threat or uncertainty, such as in the presence of a stranger (Lamb, 1977). However, many investigators have described the increasing willingness of infants to explore and experiment with their surroundings as their attachment to their mother becomes more firm and secure. Infants play and speak more actively in their mother's presence than in her absence, and having a parent nearby markedly diminishes the intensity of stranger anxiety (Ainsworth, 1962; Rutter, 1981). The infant's mother therefore appears to operate in part as a base of security from which forays into a more threatening world can be safely undertaken.

The reciprocity of early mother–infant interactions serves as a stimulus to the development of a close affective and protective bond, a process known as attachment. From a number of perspectives, the behaviors involved in mother–infant attachment suggest that this relationship functions as a psychological anlage in the child's developing capacity for social interaction. In the mutuality of early maternal–infant exchanges, the infant learns the subtleties and conventions of human interaction and acquires the security that constitutes the basis for all later social relationships.

Children in the Broader Social Environment

Until the 1970s, nearly all formative work on the nature of social bonds between children and their social environments focused principally on the mother–infant relationship. Moreover, most studies of attachment and its consequences have been dominated by interest in the effects of that relationship on the child, with few attempts to evaluate effects on the parent. More recent work such as that by Lamb (1977) has acknowledged and assessed the role of other, perhaps less biologically central, members of the young child's social network, such as fathers, peers, and extended family. In addition, a number of workers (Lerner & Spanier, 1978; Lewis & Rosenblum, 1974) have broadened the consideration of the effects of social attachments to include the influences of such affiliations on parents.

As reviewed by Rutter (1981), it is now clear that infants form attachments to a variety of people in their broader social networks and that such attachments do not differ qualitatively from the primary relationship with the mother. The specific qualities of attachment discussed earlier have been shown to apply equally to the infant's relationship with siblings, peers, father, and adult caretakers. Nearly all studies agree that young infants are most strongly attached to their mothers, but it is increasingly clear that a child's social and intellectual development are not solely determined by the mother–infant relationship (Lewis & Weinraub, 1976). Nonmaternal relationships have both direct and indirect effects on the child's health and development. Fathers, for example, can directly affect their children through father–child activities and patterns of interaction but may also have indirect effects through their influences in the marital relationship. Bronfenbrenner (cited in Lewis & Weinraub, 1976. p. 174) referred to the latter as second-order effects and stressed the importance of the father's emotional and economic support to the well-being of the mother–child relationship. By providing both emotional and tangible support to his wife, a father may have important secondary effects on his child's development and health (Lynn, 1974).

Although most work in this area has been concerned with parent effects on children's lives, a number of investigators have explored the presence of children as a determinant of social and psychological health in the lives of adults (Lerner & Spanier, 1978; Lewis & Rosenblum, 1974). The child is not only affected by but also affects its social, economic, and biological world. Bell (1974) summarized the various behavioral contributions of the infant and young child to the initiation and maintenance of social interactions with its parents. Hoffman and Manis (1978) presented data suggesting that, in general, children appear to enhance marital closeness and stability, and Hammer, Gutwirth, and Phillips (1982) studied the effects of children on parental social networks, noting a tendency for the birth of a child to alter both the character and quantity of network connections. The presence of children may result, for example, in more extensive interactions with kin but produce a concomitant reduction in the number of peer or other nonfamilial interactions.

What is clear from these and other studies is that isolated examination of dyadic mother–infant interactions has a definable but limited utility in understanding the social context in which children live and grow up. From a general systems theoretical perspective (Maluccio, 1981), the child's family should be viewed as an organic unit, characterized by a diverse and interdependent network of influence among its members. Children's social worlds are often filled with a colorful and changing assortment of caretaking adults, siblings, friends, distant relatives, and peers—each of which influences, and in turn is influenced by, the child and its way of being in the world.

Consequences of Attachment to the Social Environment

However diverse the child's affiliations with its social environment, no doubt can remain that such attachments have important and enduring consequences. The previously cited work of Spitz (1946), Bowlby (1952), and Ainsworth (1962) called attention to the early developmental effects of maternal deprivation, and the studies of Rutter (1978, 1979, 1981) have elegantly documented the more long-term consequences of being raised under conditions of social and family adversity. These investigators have provided useful insights into the effects of extreme disadvantage and social isolation; others have begun to assess the correlates of more normative levels of attachment and its lack. Lieberman's (1977) longitudinal study of 3-year-olds showed that children's competence in peer interactions was a function in part of the level of security in their attachments, as measured in home- and laboratory-based observations. Hartup's (1981) review of early socialization literature also concluded that a child's degree of security in its family's home produces a strong effect on its adaptation in peer relations. Moreover, work such as that by Beckwith and her colleagues (Beckwith, Cohen, Kopp, Parmelee, & Marcy, 1976) and others (Bee et al., 1982) has indicated that the quality of parent–child relations are predictive of long-term intellectual and language skill outcomes.

Finally, a number of longitudinal studies have demonstrated significant effects of childhood attachments on emotional and biological health in later adult life. The Midtown Manhattan Study of Srole, Langner, and Michael (1962) indicated that adverse parent–child experiences, such as separation from a parent, were strongly predictive of psychological impairment in adulthood. Further, the work of Thomas and Duszynski (1974) showed that a child's degree of closeness to parents was significantly related to the subsequent likelihood of early disability or death from suicide, mental illness, hypertension, coronary heart disease, and tumor. Although the evidence in this area is not unequivocal (Crook & Eliot, 1980), a child's strong and successful attachment to its family appears to be among the important determinants of social, developmental, and biological outcomes, both in childhood and in later life.

The Function of Attachment and Social Support

An argument has been proposed that the phenomenon of social support originates in the earliest social interactions that occur between parent and child. A child's attachment to its family is regarded as a critical process in the evolution of social support, and the absence of attachment carries profound and deleterious consequences for the child's health, development, and capacity for successful social interactions. A question of even greater theoretical importance is the issue of how attachment and social support are etiologically linked to the development of a healthy child. Work showing an association between various aspects of social support and child health has failed to provide a unifying account of the principles that may underlie the association. In the following section observations from social epidemiologic research and developmental theory are reviewed in an attempt to develop such an account, beginning with a consideration of the character of social support as revealed in epidemiologic reports.

Social Support and Child Health: The Nature of the Etiologic Link

Epidemiologic Studies of Social Support

A variety of epidemiologic and developmental observations suggest the possibility that the health effects of childhood social support reflect the operation of an underlying psychological principle. A striking feature of social epidemiologic investigations is the diversity of phenomena subsumed under the rubric of social support. As indicated in one review (Broadhead, Kaplan, James, Wagner, Schoenbach, Grimson, Heyden, Tibblin, & Gehlbach, 1983), varied social supports have been shown to have both direct health effects and interactive (buffering) effects in the presence of major stressors. Most impressive, however, is the range of resources for which such effects have been demonstrated. Measures of social support have included broadly defined psychosocial assets (Nuckolls, Cassel, & Kaplan, 1972), family competence (Boardman *et al.*, 1975), social network affiliation (Berkman & Syme, 1979), perceived social support (Schaefer, Coyne, & Lazarus, 1981), and strong cultural ties (Marmot & Syme, 1976). Such diversity in the operational definitions of social support prompted Schaefer *et al,* (1981, p. 382) to conclude that "some of the most frequently cited studies treat social network, psychosocial assets and perceived social support as interchangeable concepts, suggesting a more basic confusion about the nature of social support."

Perhaps as important as such conceptual confusion, however, is the fact that so many seemingly unrelated aspects of social experience have similar dependable effects on health and illness. Boyce (1981), for example, pointed out the basic similarity in the effects of social network support, psychosocial assets, and family routines in three distinct study populations (see Figure 8.1). In the case of each social support measure, a low score combined with high levels of life change was associated with a marked parallel increase in illness outcomes, suggesting an undisclosed commonality among the various experiences of social support. What is missing is a plausible conceptual link between the various aspects of social experience that seem to operate as support.

Similarly, a multiplicity of events is represented under the general concept of stressful life change. Hurst, Jenkins, and Rose (1978), for example, pointed out the broad range of events and transitions that appear to invoke

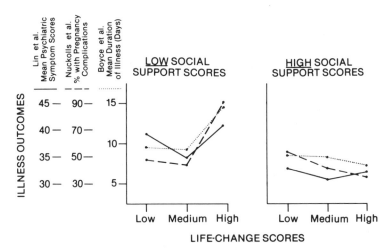

Figure 8.1. Interactions between social support and stressful life change in three study populations. From Boyce, 1981.

stress in human populations. They noted the marked inconsistency in investigators' designation of events as life change and the lack of a coherent approach to the common properties of such events. Also, current models within social epidemiology provide only a weak theoretical account of the interaction between life change and social support in their influence on disease. It is not immediately or easily apparent why stress and support should generate opposing effects on illness occurrence. What is the common ground among the protective resources known as social support, and how do these resources influence the connection between stressful change and disease?

One way of accounting for the observed similarity in the effects of various social supports is by postulating an elemental human need for stability. Such an account would explain parallel effects of the diverse social supports by their common tendency to promote an awareness of the enduring aspects of life experience. In the case of childhood social support, a child's evolving attachment to its social environment would be viewed as a critical element in fulfilling the need for stability. Further, within such a frame of reference stressful life events could be usefully viewed as acting on health through their capacity to undermine the child's sense of stability and permanence. Social support and life change would thus operate through their common, but opposing, effects on the perception and awareness of stability.

Developmental Theory

From the standpoint of developmental theory, there have been persuasive observations in support of such a claim for the basic need for stability. Erikson (1963), in his pioneering formulation of critical periods in psychological development, speaks of basic trust as the first crucial accomplishment in the life of a human infant:

> The infant's first social achievement, then, is his willingness to let the mother out of sight without undue anxiety or rage, because she has become an inner certainty as well as an outer predictability. Such consistency, continuity, and sameness of experience provide a rudimentary sense of ego identity. . . . we feel and act as if an outer goodness had become an inner certainty. (Erikson, 1963, pp. 247–249)

For Erikson, the acquisition of basic trust, awareness of continuity, and inner certainty represents a fundamental transformation in human consciousness. Through attachment to its mother and family, the infant becomes progressively aware of a permanence and changelessness that characterize at least some of its central life experiences.

Erikson's thesis is closely allied, as noted by Bowlby (1969), to Benedek's (1938) idea of a relationship of confidence, Klein's (1948) concept of introjection of the good object, and Ainsworth's (1972) dimension of security in a child's attachment to its parents. Common to each is an understanding of continuity and predictability as a core concept in the development of early social relations. Further, the secure base effect noted previously in the writings of Rutter (1981) and others (Lieberman, 1977) suggests that a central function of the attachment process is to invoke an awareness of the parent's stable presence, thereby allowing increasing comfort with the broader social world. Here again, the operational concept appears to be the child's developing sense of permanence and continuity.

In the perspective of cognitive development, Piaget (1973) in the later years of his work wrote of the relationship between cognitive object permanence and the evolution of interpersonal object relations in the psychoanalytic sense. Toward the end of its first year, an infant develops an expanding awareness of an object's stable existence, even after the object has passed out of the perceptual field. When an object is dropped behind a screen and disappears from the infant's view, a 9-month-old (but not a 4-month-old) will begin hunting for the vanished, but presumably still available, object. The baby has therefore learned that objects have, in a sense, a life of their own, that there is a kind of permanence or stability in the existence of things. At almost the same time, the infant's changing behavior appears to reflect an emerging consciousness of stability in the existence of persons and relationships. The infant becomes attached to the significant, enduring people in its environment, shows anxiety in the presence of strangers, and cries for its mother when she disappears from view. Piaget suggested that there is a meaningful connection between these two forms of development and claimed that the first "object" to be endowed with cognitive permanence is the child's primary caregiver. What is salient to a consideration of social support is the observation that cognitive and affective development seem to arrive concurrently at a growing awareness of the continuity inherent in social relations. The infant's enlarging capacities for social exchange move progressively toward a consciousness of the enduring and changeless features of its social world. In Erikson's terms, the infant establishes basic trust in the stability and permanence of its family environment.

Permanence and Continuity

Two lines of evidence thus converge on a single hypothesis. First, a search for commonalities in the array of preventive social factors known as social supports suggests that such factors may operate by promoting an individual's sense of permanence and continuity. A plausible means of accounting for the health effects of various social supports is their theoretical capacity for augmenting a sense of the stability contained in life experience. Second, it can be argued that a key transition in a child's evolving capacity for social exchange is the development of a secure and relatively resilient awareness of continuity and "sameness." From the standpoint of childhood social support, the hypothesized account offers an explanatory construct that is consistent with important dimensions of developmental theory.

Such a construct might be defined as follows: A sense of permanence is the perception that certain central elements of life experience are stable and changeless. It is a conviction that there are aspects of one's self and one's life that remain durable and relatively unchanging, even in the face of major events and transitions. Thus defined, the construct provides one useful conceptual approach to a broad arena of social epidemiologic findings. It asserts that what is common to the protective effects of social networks, cultural affiliation, and family competence is the capacity to promote and sustain a sense of permanence. In addition, the construct provides a plausible theoretical account for the interaction between life change and social support in their effects on disease. The opposing influences of stressful life events and social supports on health can thus be viewed as the bidirectional effects of such factors on a common medium: the individual's sense of permanence and continuity in life experience.

This thesis is closely allied with the work of Antonovsky (1979), who similarly endorsed the search for a unifying conceptual approach to social support. At the center of Antonovsky's proposal is a way of seeing the world, a consciousness of life as understandable and choate. His operational principle is the comprehensibility and coherence of the world, in all its cognitive and affective representations. A sense of permanence, on the other hand, specifies more narrowly the dimension in which the world is viewed and focuses on the stability and continuity it is perceived to contain.

What categories of experience might be expected to affect an individual's sense of permanence? As shown in Table 8.1, five general sources are proposed as possible contributors to the perception of permanence and continuity. Examples are given of experiences or social processes corresponding to each of the proposed sources. Interpersonal processes, for example, may affect the degree to which relationships are experienced as stable and dependable, and behavioral factors, such as routines and rituals, may influence an awareness of continuity through the establishment of patterned activity in day-to-day life. Each dimension is viewed as fostering an underlying sense of stability and continuity.

If the health effects of childhood social experience depend in part on the sense of permanence and its components, then certain important aspects of family life should figure prominently in a child's health and well-being. Marital instability, residential mobility, and lack of dependable family rou-

Table 8.1

Proposed Sources for a Sense of Permanence and Continuity

Sources	Contributory experiences and processes
Self: the awareness of self as capable and predictable from one place and time to the next	Experience of mastery: the perception of controlling to some extent the factors that affect one's life (Kobasa, Maddi, and Courington, 1981)
Interpersonal: the perception of stability and continuity in relationships	Social network membership, marriage, intimacy (Berkman and Syme, 1979)
Environmental: the identification of certain places or geographic locations as points of reference; a sense of place	Residential stability or mobility, modernization (Gerson, Stueve, and Fischer, 1977)
Behavioral: the awareness of patterns within day-to-day activity that foster feelings of predictability and persistence	Family routines, habits, rituals (Boyce, Jensen, James, and Peacock, 1983)
Spiritual: the consciousness of principles or a being that underlie the sense of universal permanence	Religious activities or their equivalents (Comstock and Partridge, 1972)

tines are, for example, three family attributes that would be expected to have deleterious effects on child health on the basis of the proposed thesis. Each of these characteristics would be expected to undermine children's sense of permanence, thereby increasing the likelihood of disease or disability. To examine this hypothesis further, literature on each of the three family descriptors will be briefly reviewed, ascertaining available evidence for such effects on child health.

Marital and Residential Instability

Evidence has accumulated suggesting that both marital and residential instability may have deleterious effects on physical and emotional well-being in childhood. Jellinek and Slovik (1981) reviewed literature on the effects of parental divorce on children and concluded that, although reactions are highly dependent on their developmental stages, children almost universally experience divorce as a profound personal, familial, and social loss. Depression and psychosomatic disorders (Jellinek & Slovik, 1981), aggressive behavior problems (Kalter, 1977), developmental regression (Wallerstein & Kelly, 1975), and delinquency (Offord, Abrams, Allen, & Poushinsky, 1979) are among the emotional and behavioral disturbances found with increased frequency among children from broken homes. In addition, work such as that by Coddington (1972) and others (Beautrais, Fergusson, & Shannon, 1982; Boyce, Jensen, Cassel, Collier, Smith, & Ramey, 1977; Heisel, Ream, Raitz, Rappaport, & Coddington, 1973) has suggested that divorce is one of the most disruptive life events children experience and that such events may be associated with alterations in biological health.

Not all children of divorced parents, however, experience the same degree of disruption and distress. Wallerstein (1977) and Felner, Farber, and Primavera (1981), for example, have found that a substantial subgroup of children in the midst of divorce remain resilient and healthy, apparently protected by factors such as the maintenance of daily routines, the emotional stability of the care-taking parent, or the persistence of ties to people and friends outside the nuclear family. Further, studies such as that by Wilcox (1981) have indicated that the maintenance of extrafamilial social bonds plays an important role in the family's adjustment in the postdivorce period.

Often closely tied to the experience of divorce is a child's loss of social and geographic ties to the neighborhood in which the family lived (Hancock, 1980; Jellinek & Slovik, 1981). Even in the absence of divorce, breaking residential bonds can have powerful and distressing effects in the life of a child. The early studies of Switzer, Hirschberg, Myers, Gray, Evers, and Forman (1961) and Mogey and Winokur (1965) prompted numerous investigations into the mental and physical health consequences of geographic mobility. Family moves have been implicated as precipitating factors in a variety of childhood disorders, ranging from problems in interpersonal relationships (McKain, 1976; Werkman, Farley, Butler, & Quayhagen, 1981) and difficulties in school adjustment or educational attainment (Levine, 1966) to childhood cancer (Jacobs & Charles, 1980) and other alterations in physical health as a result of injury (Knudson-Cooper & Leuchtag, 1982). Although overviews of this research have revealed areas of contradictory findings (Brett, 1980; Micklin & Leon, 1978), evidence linking residential mobility to changes in child health is clearly compatible with more general observations on the relationship of spatial or geographic identity to health and illness behavior. Shannon (1977), for example, posited "identity with one's surroundings" as a central determinant of the individual's perception, evaluation, and treatment of illness. Others, such as Tuan (1974) and Gerson *et al.* (1977), also regarded attachment to place as one of the critical dimensions of human experience. For children especially, stable identification with a place and home seems to represent an important protector of health.

Family Routinization

The degree of routinization in a family's day-to-day life is another dimension that might logically be expected to affect a child's sense of permanence and stability. Prompted by a study of family routines and childhood respiratory illness (Boyce *et al.*, 1977), the more recent work of Boyce, Jensen, and colleagues (Boyce *et al.*, 1983; Jensen, James, Boyce, & Hartnett, 1983) has examined in detail the possible connection between routinization and health. In the earlier study of Boyce *et al.* (1977), 58 children were followed prospectively for a 1-year period, assessing the predictive effects of life change and family routinization on patterns of respiratory disease experience. Family routines were defined as the observable, repetitive behaviors that involve several family members. and that occur with predictable regularity in the ongoing life of the family. Analysis of data demonstrated that the severity of respiratory illness was strongly related to the combined influence of major life change and the degree of family routinization. A subsequent reanalysis of the same data showed that for preschool children the mean duration of illness was highest among the subpopulation with high life change scores and few family routines (Boyce, 1981). The results suggest that family routinization constitutes an important moderator in the general relationship between stress and illness.

In addition, ethnographic observations and a series of related papers reviewed by Boyce *et al.* (1983) suggest that routines function as behavioral units providing structural integrity to family life and having important consequences for the overall health of the family. Merton (1968) identified ritual and routine as potential means of adapting to the experience of anomie, and Mead (1934) noted the basic human tendency to search for order in the immediate surroundings during periods of uncertainty and strain. Aponte (1976) viewed underorganization as a central problem in poor families, and Wallerstein (1977) and others (Hetherington, Cox, & Cox, 1978) suggested that the maintenance of family organization and stable household routines may foster a child's successful adaptation in the months following divorce. Also, Wolin, Bennett, and Noonan (1979) showed a strong inverse relationship between routines or rituals in the families of alcoholics and the transmission of alcoholism to a second generation. Alcoholism occurred least frequently in the second generation among those families in which rituals were unaltered by the alcoholic member's periods of heaviest drinking.

In a manner similar to the experiences of marital and residential instability, a child's experience in a disorganized and underroutinized family may plausibly be regarded as a potential threat to the child's sense of permanence and stability, thereby enhancing vulnerability to changes in health. Taken together, the studies of Boyce *et al.* (1977, 1981, 1983) along with other work reviewed herein offer additional support for the hypothesis that continuity and changelessness represent a critical dimension in the link between social experience and health.

Biological Mechanisms

A final issue worth considering is the problem of biological mediators in the connection between social factors and health: Given current knowledge of pathophysiologic processes, how might the individual's awareness of continuity and permanence influence the course or occurrence of disease? The mechanisms that mediate relationships between social experience and illness appear at present to be complex and largely unknown. What is known is that, in both animal and human subjects, psychological stressors can effect measurable change in endocrine and immunologic markers (Ader, 1981). There is evidence, for example, that stressful psychosocial experience, processed by the central nervous system and mediated by alterations in hypothalamic function, is accompanied by a variety of immunologic and reticuloendothelial changes ranging from involution of the thymus and spleen to suppression of interferon production and impairment of lymphocyte cytotoxicity (Stein, Schiavi, & Camerino, 1976). However, as noted by Palmblad (1981), much work relating stress to immunologic competence is uninterpretable because of retrospective designs, inadequate monitoring of immunologic parameters, and vagaries in the character of the immunologic response. Cell-mediated immunity, for example, may be either depressed or enhanced by experimentally induced stress, depending on variables such as the timing and the nature of the stressor event.

Furthermore, almost no studies have addressed the neuroendocrine and immunologic correlates of social support. As in the case of early social epidemiologic investigations, work on the biological mediators of social experience has been dominated by studies of stress alone. It is not unreasonable, however, to speculate that the same physiologic pathways may be operative in the effects of social support on host resistance. Further elucidation of biological mechanisms awaits both a more coherent understanding of the immunologic processes involved and greater clarity in the conceptual approach to psychosocial factors in disease etiology. Future studies relating immunocompetence to social experience may benefit from a more unified theoretical orientation, such as that proposed herein.

Summary and Conclusions

The purpose of this chapter has been to summarize evidence that social support represents an important and epidemiologically relevant dimension in the lives of children. It has been argued that the experience of social support originates in the earliest interpersonal transactions between a new-born and its parents and that the process of attachment is a source and template for all subsequent supportive exchange. In the primitive but ex-traordinarily complex interaction between a mother and her newly born infant, the earliest signs of human social support are revealed. It has been further argued that one of the critical elements in a child's evolving rela-tionship with its social world is the acquisition of a sense of the permanence and continuity inherent in its ongoing life experience. A hypothesis has been proposed that the direct and stress-modifying effects of social support reflect underlying effects on the child's sense of permanence, which in turn influences and modifies generalized susceptibility to disease. Thus, a child's perception of stability and continuity is regarded as an elemental attribute of its developing capacity for supportive social interaction.

More explicitly, it has been suggested that the sense of permanence is a representation of the *meaning* of social support in children's lives. Char-acteristically missing from much of the literature on social support is an interest in the phenomenological or experiential aspects of supportive ex-change. There is perhaps much to be learned by exploring social support as a system of meaning, as a frame of reference from which personal ex-perience is organized and upheld. The sense of permanence has been taken here as a category of what Polanyi called tacit knowledge (Polanyi & Prosch, 1975), that is, an awareness or understanding grounded in, but transcend-ing, the particulars of experience. In the same way that reading involves a tacit transformation from recognition of the printed word to an awareness of its meaning, social support involves a transcendence from the particulars of social interaction to a consciousness of its meaning in individuals' lives. It is as if people look *through* the subsidiary elements of social support to an understanding of their full and transcendent significance. Mother–infant interactions, family routines, affiliations with friends, and observances of cultural traditions—each becomes regarded as a particular manifestation of social support, all bound together by their common capacity to suggest and sustain a single meaning: a sense of what is permanent and enduring.

The notion of sense of permanence is offered here as one of many po-tential approaches to the multiple and complex issues in the study of social support. Particularly with regard to childhood, the rudimentary state of knowledge of social support and its effects on health suggests a profusion of questions that still await even preliminary investigation. Beyond the new-born period, how can attachment between parent and child be fostered and maintained? What are the commonalities and differences between so-cial support in childhood and in adult life? How do children of various ages generate or invoke social support? Do the deleterious effects of social dis-connection in childhood have counterparts in salutogenic effects of social connection? When do the benefits of peer support become equal in importance to those of family support? Are there endocrine and immunologic concomitants of social support in childhood? These are questions that deserve a new share of the attention and concern of both child health professionals and social epidemiologists. Childhood social experience is the developmental cradle of social support. And knowledge of the health-protective effects of such support will undoubtedly be advanced in important and unexpected ways by the study of the childhood origins of social interaction.

References

Ader, R. (Ed.) (1981). *Psychoneuroimmunology*. New York: Academic Press.

Ainsworth, M. D. (1962). The effects of maternal deprivation: A review of findings and controversy in the context of research strategy. In *Deprivation of maternal care: A reassessment of its effects* (Public Health Paper No. 14). Geneva: World Health Organization.

Ainsworth, M. D. (1972). Attachment and dependency: A comparison. In J. L. Gewitz (Ed.), *Attachment and dependency*. Washington, DC: Winston.

Antonovsky, A. (1979). *Health, stress, and coping*. San Francisco: Jossey-Bass.

Aponte, H. J. (1976). Underorganization in the poor family. In J. D. Guerin (Ed.) *Family therapy: Theory and practice*. New York: Gardner Press.

Beautrais, A. L., Fergusson, D. M., & Shannon, F. T. (1982). Life events and childhood morbidity: A prospective study. *Pediatrics, 70*, 935–940.

Beckwith, L., Cohen, S. E., Kopp, C. B., Parmelee, A. H., & Marcy, T. G. (1976). Caregiver-infant interaction and early cognitive development in pre-term infants. *Child Development, 47*, 579–587.

Bee, H. L., Barnard, K. E., Eyres, S. J., Gray, C. A., Hammond, M. A., Spietz, A. L., Snyder, C., & Clark, B. (1982). Prediction of IQ and language skill from perinatal status, child performance, family characteristics, and mother-infant interaction. *Child Development, 53*, 1134–1156.

Bell, R. Q. (1974). Contributions of human infants to caregiving and social interaction. In M. Lewis & L. A. Rosenblum (Eds.), *The effect of the infant on its caregiver*. New York: Wiley.

Benedek, T. (1938). Adaptation to reality in early infancy. *Psychoanalytic Quarterly, 7*, 200–15.

Berkman, L. F., & Syme, S. L. (1979). Social networks, host resistance, and mortality: A nine-year follow-up study of Alameda County residents. *American Journal of Epidemiology, 109*, 186–204.

Bernal, J. (1972). Crying during the first 10 days of life, and maternal responses. *Developmental Medicine and Child Neurology, 14*, 362.

Boardman, V., Zyzanski, S. J., & Cottrell, L. S. (1975). School absences, illness, and family competence. In B. H. Kaplan, & J. C. Cassel (Eds.), *Family and health: An epidemiological approach*. Chapel Hill, NC: Institute for Research in Social Science.

Boocock, S. S. (1975). The social context of childhood. *Proceedings of the American Philosophical Society, 119*, 419–429.

Bowlby, J. (1952). *Maternal care and mental health* (2nd ed.). Geneva: World Health Organization.

Bowlby, J. (1969). *Attachment and loss* (Vol. 1). New York: Basic Books.

Boyce, W. T. (1981). Interaction between social variables in stress research. *Journal of Health and Social Behavior, 22*, 194–195.

Boyce, W. T., Jensen, E. W., Cassel, J. C., Collier, A. M., Smith, A. H., & Ramey, C. T. (1977). Influence of life events and family routines on childhood respiratory tract illness. *Pediatrics, 60*, 609–615.

Boyce, W. T., Jensen, E. W., James S. A., & Peacock, J. L. (1983). The Family Routines Inventory: Theoretical origins. *Social Science and Medicine, 17*, 193–200.

Brazelton, T. B., & Als, H. (1979). Four early stages in the development of mother-infant interaction. *Psychoanalytic Study of the Child, 34*, 349–369.

Brazelton, T. B., Koslowski, B., & Main, M. (1974). The origins of reciprocity: The early mother-infant interaction. In M. Lewis & L. A. Rosenblum (Eds.), *The effect of the infant on its caregiver.* New York: Wiley.

Brenner, M. H. (1973). Fetal, infant, and maternal mortality during periods of economic instability. *International Journal of Health Services, 3*, 145–159.

Brett, J. M. (1980). The effect of job transfer on employees and their families. In C. L. Cooper & R. Payne (Eds.), *Current concerns in occupational stress.* New York: Wiley.

Broadhead, W. E., Kaplan, B. H., James, S. A., Wagner, E. H., Schoenback, V. J., Grimson, R., Heyden, S., Tibblin, G., & Gehlbach, S. H. (1983). The epidemiologic evidence for a relationship between social support and health. *American Journal of Epidemiology, 117*, 521–537.

Chen, E., & Cobb, S. (1960). Family structure in relation to health and disease. *Journal of Chronic disease, 12*, 544–567.

Cochran, M. M., & Brassard, J. A. (1979). Child development and personal social networks. *Child Development, 50*, 601–616.

Coddington, R. D. (1972). The significance of life events as etiologic factors in the diseases of children. *Journal of Psychosomatic Research, 16*, 7–18.

Comstock, G. W., & Partridge, K. B. (1972). Church attendance and health. *Journal of Chronic Disease, 25*, 665.

Crook, T., & Eliot, J. (1980). Parental death during childhood and adult depression: A critical review of the literature. *Psychological Bulletin, 87*, 252.

Egbuonu, L., & Starfield, B. (1982). Child health and social status. *Pediatrics, 69*, 550–557.

Egeland, B., & Sroufe, L. A. (1981). Attachment and early maltreatment. *Child Development, 52*, 44–52.

Eisenberg, R. B. (1976). *Auditory competence in early life: The roots of communicative behavior.* Baltimore: University Park Press.

Elder, G. H. (1974). *Children of the Great Depression.* Chicago: University of Chicago Press.

Engels, F. (1887). *The condition of the working class in England in 1844.* New York: Lovell.

Erikson, E. H. (1963). *Childhood and society* (2nd ed.) New York: Norton.

Felner, R. D., Farber, S. S., & Primavera, J. (1981). Children of divorce, stressful life events, and transitions. In R. H. Price (Ed.), *Prevention in mental health: Research, policy, and practice.* London: Sage.

Fergusson, D. M., Horwood, L. J., & Shannon, F. T. (1981). Birth placement and childhood disadvantage. *Social Science and Medicine, 15E*, 315–326.

Gerson, K., Stueve, C. A., & Fischer, C. S. (1977). Attachment to place. In C. S. Fischer (Ed.), *Networks and places: Social relations in the urban setting.* New York: The Free Press.

Goren, C. C., Sarty, M., & Wu, P. Y. K. (1975). Visual following and pattern discrimination of face-like stimuli by newborn infants. *Pediatrics, 56*, 544.

Haggerty, R. J., Roghmann, K. J., & Pless, F. B. (1975). *Child health and the community.* New York: Wiley.

Hammer, M., Gutwirth, L., & Phillips, S. L. (1982). Parenthood and social networks: A preliminary view. *Social Science and Medicine, 16*, 2091–2100.

Hancock, E. (1980). The dimensions of meaning and belonging in the process of divorce. *American Journal of Orthopsychiatry, 50*, 18–27.

Hansen, D. A., & Johnson, V. A. (1979). Rethinking family stress theory: Definitional aspects. In W. R. Burr, R. Hill, F. I. Nye, & I. L. Reiss (Eds.), *Contemporary theories about the family*. New York: The Free Press.

Hartup, W. W. (1981). Peer relations and family relations: Two social worlds. In M. Rutter (Ed.), *Scientific foundations of developmental psychiatry*. Baltimore: University Park Press.

Heisel, J. S., Ream, S., Raitz, R., Rappaport, M., & Coddington, R. D. (1973). The significance of life events as contributing factors in the diseases of children. *Journal of Pediatrics, 83*, 119–123.

Hetherington, E. M., Cox, M., & Cox, R. (1978). The aftermath of divorce. In J. H. Stevens, & M. Matthews (Eds.), *Mother/child father/child relationships*. Washington, DC: National Association for the Education of Young Children.

Hoffman, L. W., & Manis, J. D. (1978). Influences of children on marital interaction and parental satisfactions and dissatisfactions. In R. M. Lerner, & G. B. Spanier (Eds.), *Child influences on marital and family interactions: A life-span perspective*. New York: Academic Press.

Hunter, R. S., Kilstrom, N., Kraybill, E. N., & Loda, F. (1978). Antecedents of child abuse and neglect in premature infants: A prospective study in a newborn intensive care unit. *Pediatrics, 61*, 629–635.

Hurst, M. W., Jenkins, C. D., & Rose, S. M. (1978). The assessment of life change stress: A comparative and methodological inquiry. *Psychosomatic Medicine, 40*, 126–141.

Jacobs, T. J., & Charles, E. (1980). Life events and the occurrence of cancer in children. *Psychosomatic Medicine, 42*, 11.

Jellinek, M. S., & Slovik, L. S. (1981). Divorce: Impact on children. *New England Journal of Medicine, 305*, 557–560.

Jensen, E. W., James, S. A., Boyce, W. T., & Hartnett, S. A. (1983). The Family Routines Inventory: Development and validation. *Social Science and Medicine, 17*, 201–211.

Kalter, N. (1977). Children of divorce in an outpatient psychiatric population. *American Journal of Orthopsychiatry, 47*, 40–51.

Kaplan, B. H., & Cassel, J. C. (1975). *Family and health: An epidemiological approach*. Chapel Hill: Institute for Research in Social Science.

Klaus, M. H., Jerauld, R., Kreger, N. C., McAlpine, W., Steffa, M., & Kennell, J. H. (1972). Maternal attachment: Importance of the first post-partum days. *New England Journal of Medicine, 286*, 460–463.

Klein, M. (1948). *Contributions to psycho-analysis 1921–1945*. London: Hogarth.

Knudson-Cooper, M. S., & Leuchtag, A. K. (1982). The stress of a family move as a precipitating factor in children's burn accidents. *Journal of Human Stress, 8* (2), 32–38.

Kobasa, S. C., Maddi, S. R., & Courington, S. (1981). Personality and constitution as mediators in the stress-illness relationship. *Journal of Health and Social Behavior, 22*, 368.

Lamb, M. E. (1977). Father-infant and mother-infant interaction in the first year of life. *Child Development, 48*, 167.

Lerner, R. M., & Spanier G. B. (Eds.). (1978). *Child influences on marital and family interaction: A life-span perspective*. New York: Academic Press.

Levine, M. (1966). Residential change and school adjustment. *Community Mental Health Journal, 2*, 61–69.

Lewis, M., & Rosenblum, L. (Eds.). (1974). *The effect of the infant on its caregiver: The origins of behavior*. New York: Wiley.

Lewis, M., & Weinraub, M. (1976). The father's role in the child's social network. In M. E. Lamb (Ed.), *The role of the father in child development*. New York: Wiley.

Lieberman, A. F. (1977). Preschoolers' competence with a peer: Relations with attachment and peer experience. *Child Development, 48,* 1277–1287.

Litman, T. J. (1974). The family as a basic unit in health and medical care: A social-behavioral overview. *Social Science and Medicine, 8,* 495–519.

Lozoff, B., Brittenham, G. M., Trause, M. A., Kennell, J. H., & Klaus, M. H. (1977). The mother-newborn relationship: Limits of adaptability. *Journal of Pediatrics, 91,* 1–12.

Lynn, D. B. (1974). *The father: His role in child development.* Monterey, CA: Brooks-Cole.

McKain, J. L. (1976). Alienation: A function of geographical mobility among families. In H. I. McCubbin, B. B. Dahl, & E. J. Hunter (Eds.), *Families in the military system.* London: Sage.

Maluccio, A. N. (1981). Introduction: A life-model perspective on the family. In C. Getty, & W. Humphreys (Eds.), *Understanding the family: Stress and change in American family life.* New York: Appleton-Century-Crofts.

Mare, R. D. (1982). Socioeconomic effects on child mortality in the United States. *American Journal of Public Health, 72,* 539–547.

Marmot, M. D., & Syme, S. L. (1976). Acculturation and coronary heart disease in Japanese-Americans. *American Journal of Epidemiology, 104,* 225–247.

Mead, G. H. (1934). *Mind, self, and society.* Chicago: University of Chicago Press.

Meltzoff, A. N., & Moore, M. K. (1977). Imitation of facial and manual gestures by human neonates. *Science, 198,* 74–78.

Merton, R. K. (1968). *Social theory and social structure.* New York: The Free Press.

Meyer, R. J., & Haggerty, R. J. (1962). Streptococcal infections in families: Factors altering individual susceptibility. *Pediatrics, 29,* 539–549.

Micklin, M., & Leon, C. A. (1978). Life change and psychiatric disturbance in a South American city: The effects of geographic and social mobility. *Journal of Health and Social Behavior, 19,* 92–107.

Miller, F. J. W. (1960). *Growing up in Newcastle-upon-Tyne.* London: Oxford University Press.

Mogey, J., & Winokur, G. (1965). Sociology, mobility, and mental health. In M. B. Kantor (Ed.), *Mobility and mental health.* Springfield, IL: Thomas.

Nuckolls, K. B., Cassel, J., & Kaplan, B. H. (1972). Psychosocial assets, life crisis, and the prognosis of pregnancy. *American Journal of Epidemiology, 1972, 95,* 431.

Offord, D. R., Abrams, N., Allen, N., & Poushinsky, M. (1979). Broken homes, parental psychiatric illness, and female delinquency. *American Journal of Orthopsychiatry, 49,* 252–264.

Palmblad, J. (1981). Stress and immunologic competence: Studies in man. In R. Ader, (Ed.), *Psychoneuroimmunology.* New York: Academic Press.

Piaget, J. (1973). The affective unconscious and the cognitive unconscious. *Journal of the American Psychoanalytic Association, 21,* 249–261.

Pless, I. B., & Satterwhite, B. (1973). A measure of family functioning and its application. *Social Science and Medicine, 7,* 613–621.

Plionis, E. M. (1977). Family functioning and childhood accident occurrence. *American Journal of Orthopsychiatry, 47,* 250–263.

Polanyi, M., & Prosch, H. (1975). *Meaning.* Chicago: University of Chicago Press.

Provence, S., & Lipton, R. C. (1962). *Infants in institutions: A comparison of their development with family-reared infants during the first year of life.* New York: International Universities Press.

Roghmann, K. J., & Haggerty, R. J. (1973). Daily stress, illness, and use of health services in young families. *Pediatric Research, 7,* 520–526.

Rutter, M. (1978). Early sources of security and competence. In J. S. Bruner & A. Garton (Eds.), *Human growth and development.* Oxford: Clarendon Press.

Rutter, M. (1979). Protective factors in children's responses to stress and disadvantage. In

M. W. Kent & J. E. Rolf (Eds.), *Primary prevention of psychopathology. Vol. III: Social competence in children.* Hanover, NH: University Press of New England.

Rutter, M. (1981). Attachment and the development of social relationships. In M. Rutter (Ed.), *Scientific foundations of development psychiatry.* Baltimore: University Park Press.

Sander, L. W., Julia, H. L., Stechler, G., & Burns, P. (1972). Continuous 24-hour interactional monitoring in infants reared in two caretaking environments. *Psychosomatic Medicine, 34,* 270.

Schaefer, C., Coyne, J. C., & Lazarus, R. S. (1981). The health-related functions of social support. *Journal of Behavioral Medicine, 4,* 381.

Schaffer, H., & Emerson, P. (1964). The development of social attachments in infancy. *Monographs of Society for Research in Child Development, 29(3).*

Shannon, G. W. (1977). Space, time, and illness behavior. *Social Science and Medicine, 11,* 683–689.

Spitz, R. A. (1946). Anaclitic depression. *Psychoanalytic Study of the Child, 2,* 313–342.

Srole, L., Langner, T. S., & Michael, S. T. (1962). *Mental health in the metropolis—The Midtown Manhattan Study.* New York: McGraw-Hill.

Starfield, B., Gross, E., Wood, M., Pantell, R., Allen, C., Gordon, I. B., Moffatt, P., Drachman, R., & Katz, H. (1980). Psychosocial and psychosomatic diagnoses in primary care of children. *Pediatrics, 66,* 159–167.

Stein, M., Schiavi, R. C., & Camerino, M. (1976). Influence of brain and behavior on the immune system. *Science, 191,* 435–440.

Stone, L. J., Smith, H. T., & Murphy, L. B. (Eds.). (1973). *The competent infant: Research and commentary.* New York: Basic Books.

Switzer, R. E., Hirschberg, J. C., Myers, L., Gray, E., Evers, N. H., & Forman, R. (1961). The effect of family moves on children. *Mental Hygiene, 45,* 528–536.

Syme, S. L. & Berkman, L. F. (1976). Social class, susceptibility and sickness. *American Journal of Epidemiology, 104,* 1–8.

Thomas, C. B., & Duszynski, K. R. (1974). Closeness to parents and the family constellation in a prospective study of five disease states: Suicide, mental illness, malignant tumor, hypertension and coronary heart disease. *Johns Hopkins Medical Journal, 134,* 251–270.

Tuan, Y. (1974). *Topophilia: A study of environmental perception, attitudes, and values.* Englewood Cliffs, NJ: Prentice-Hall.

Wallerstein, J. S. (1977). Responses of the preschool child to divorce: Those who cope. In M. F. McMillan & S. Henao (Eds.), *Child psychiatry: Treatment and research.* New York: Brunner-Mazel.

Wallerstein, J. S., & Kelly, J. B. (1975). The effects of parental divorce: Experiences of the preschool child. *Journal of the American Academy of Child Psychiatry, 14,* 600–616.

Werkman, S., Farley, G. K., Butler, C., & Quayhagen, M. (1981). The psychological effects of moving and living overseas. *Journal of the American Academy of Child Psychiatry, 20,* 645–657.

Werner, E. E., Bierman, J. M., & French, F. F. (1971). *Children of Kauai: A longitudinal study from the prenatal period to age ten.* Honolulu: University of Hawaii Press.

Wilcox, B. L. (1981). Social support in adjusting to marital disruption. In B. H. Gottlieb (Ed.), *Social networks and social support.* London: Sage.

Wolff, P. H. (1969). The natural history of crying and other vocalizations in early infancy. In B. M. Foss (Ed.), *Determinants of infant behavior* (Vol. 4). London: Methuen.

Wolff, P. H. (1976). Mother-infant interactions in the first year. *New England Journal of Medicine, 295,* 999–1001.

Wolin, S. J., Bennett, L. A., & Noonan, D. L. (1979). Family rituals and the recurrence of alcoholism over generations. *American Journal of Psychiatry, 136,* 589–593.

CHAPTER 9

Social Support and Health in the Middle Years: Work and the Family

Stanislav V. Kasl and James A. Wells

Introduction

In this chapter we shall first offer some comments about conceptualization of social support; these represent some of the issues that have impressed us in the course of our readings. Next, we wish to provide a quick overview of the results from general social support studies. This will provide a useful background for the core of this chapter—research on the work environment. Most of the empirical evidence is concerned with the male work force, a variety of work stress factors, and a small set of support variables. There are a few studies integrating the work and family settings and these are examined next. Finally, we shall deal briefly with two transitions involving work and family roles: loss of job and return to work, and divorce. The chapter concludes with comments on future research directions.

This organization of the material and its scope reflect both the constraints on the length of this chapter and the availability of empirical evidence for review. This means that other social roles (such as leisure) and other environments (such as the residential one) will be neglected; the evidence is sparse and attempts to extend the scope to include these would only create a diffuse discussion.

The rapid growth of research on social support and health represents, in part, an extension and redirection of older research on stress and health. The concept of stress frequently provides the setting for carrying out the social support studies and, as will be shown, the two themes—stress and support—are closely intermingled in many of the investigations.

Some Issues in the Conceptualization of Social Support

Reviews of the social support literature have appeared in a wide variety of journals (e.g., Broadhead *et al.*, 1983; Cobb, 1976; Dean & Lin, 1977; Gottlieb, 1983; Henderson, 1980; Kaplan, Cassel, & Gore, 1977; Mueller, 1980; Pilisuk, 1982), which suggests that the concept is of great interest to a number of disciplines. One consequence is that new conceptual developments (refinements, distinctions, partitioning of the concept) and measurement methodologies are usually tied to a particular discipline and its own currently dominant research topics. As a result, confrontation with considerable diversity of social support concepts and measures appears inevitable, and it is likely that attempts to bring about a rapid convergence of concepts and measures might not serve all disciplines equally well.

In large-scale, prospective epidemiologic studies, relatively global and stable measures are likely to prove most useful as predictors of disease outcomes. However, in such study designs the additional goal of studying the details of process and mechanisms is generally unrealistic. Thus, such prospective studies have shown that (1) higher incidence of angina pectoris is found among men who report lack of appreciation, and feel hurt, by co-workers and superiors (Medalie *et al.*, 1973); (2) wife's love and support buffers the effects of high anxiety on elevated incidence of angina (Medalie & Goldbourt, 1976); and (3) female clerical workers who report having a nonsupportive supervisor have a considerable greater incidence of coronary heart disease than other working women and housewives (Haynes & Feinleib, 1980). These are relatively opaque associations but the findings are "clean" (prospective, independent of known biological risk factors), an acceptable tradeoff in epidemiology.

On the other hand, when we are studying, say, psychiatric patients— where the condition and its vicissitudes are exquisitely intertwined with the social support process (Henderson, 1980; Lipton, Cohen, Fisher, & Katz, 1981; Marsella & Snyder, 1981; Mueller, 1980)—then perhaps all of the published exhortations for greater conceptual richness, clarity, distinction, and detail are applicable. Among the recommendations mentioned in the literature are those concerning the conceptualization and measurement of (1) individual differences in need for support, (2) costs of receiving support (e.g., on self-esteem), (3) costs to family or network members of providing support, (4) stability and change in support and the process of its mobilization, (5) support under everyday circumstances versus chronic stress versus acute events versus emergencies, (6) availability of support versus utilization of support, (7) supportive behaviors versus supportive relationships, and (8) objective versus perceived psychological support (Belle, 1982; Caplan, 1979; DiMatteo & Hays, 1981; Dohrenwend *et al.*, 1982; Eckenrode & Gore, 1981; Gore, 1981; Lieberman, 1982; Liem & Liem, 1979).

The research context of social support is overwhelmingly the stress and disease framework, and this has major consequences for the past and future developments of the support concept that must be fully appreciated. At its simplest, the stress and disease framework contains three components (Elliott & Eisdorfer, 1982; Pearlin, Lieberman, Menaghan, & Mullan, 1981): (1) sources of stress or potential activators, (2) mediating processes and reactions (above all, coping), and (3) manifestations or consequences of stress. Social support seriously overlaps with all three components—conceptually, empirically, and methodologically. The overlap of stress and support can be seen at the conceptual level by juxtaposing a typical definition of stress, imbalance between demand and response capability (e.g., McGrath, 1970), and the definition of support proposed for this volume, namely, that it is a resource. Presumably, resource is part of response capability (otherwise it is an irrelevant resource and/or there is now a problem with defining *resource*) and thus part of the stress equation. Empirically and methodologically, various life events (such as loss of spouse or child, moving away, or job promotion) can contribute both to a measure of stress and an index of support, either by the scoring itself or as an empirical observation. Correlated predictors make it difficult to estimate regression coefficients for interaction effects (Southwood, 1978) and the empirical confounding makes it difficult to interpret alleged buffering effects (Thoits, 1982a). The overlap of social support and coping can be seen in the fact that the goals or objectives of coping (Folkman & Lazarus, 1980; Pearlin & Schooler, 1978) and of social support are pretty much the same. Many authors, especially those in the stress-at-work domain (e.g., Payne, 1980), explicitly view social support as a category of coping. Pearlin and Schooler (1978) did distinguish between specific coping responses and resources, that is, what is available to people in developing their coping repertoire. However, this is a difficult distinction operationally and an interpretive confusion of distress, helpseeking, coping, and support remains (see Gore, 1979; Pearlin & Schooler, 1979). The overlap of support and indicators of stress outcomes is perhaps the one that is least intended, namely, methodological and causal confounding. Levels of support indicators may reflect the outcome or consequence of a disease process or be an integral part of it, as in some psychiatric conditions (e.g., Lipton *et al.*, 1981; Tolsdorf, 1976), rather than antecedent processes. Measures of environmental support may be confounded with personal competence (Dohrenwend *et al.*, 1982) and, in general, subjective measures of perceived (low) support may tap into the same underlying psychological processes as do distress indicators, particularly depression. For example, two-thirds of the items in Blazer's (1982) index, perception of social support, can be found in many of the older measures of neuroticism.

Future developments in conceptualization and measurement of social support will undoubtedly take many different directions. Ideally, investigators should examine closely the overlap with other existing concepts and measures and refine the concept of social support in an incremental way: by accepting current formulations about the relationship of stress and disease to the extent that they are serviceable although incomplete, and then introducing specific and limited social support concepts that are compatible with (and linkable to) existing formulations and knowledge and are maximally responsive to current gaps. Instead, however, investigators will probably struggle for territorial control, with social support workers conquering large chunks of the stress and coping domain, often relabeling old findings but adding no new knowledge, as in the case of the rediscovery of the very old knowledge of the broad health correlates of marital status under new labels of support networks.

Overview of Results from General Surveys

Some salient findings from a number of studies, mostly cross-sectional surveys of community residents, will be summarized to provide a background for the discussion of work-specific studies in the next section. However, the summarizing statements are somewhat indeterminate because of the great variety of social support measures actually used.

In terms of univariate relationships, social support measures tend to show moderate negative associations (r values generally around .35) with a variety of measures of psychological symptoms or distress, whereas associations with self-report indices of physical health status are weaker or often not significant (Andrews, Tenant, Hewson, & Schonell, 1978; Aneshensel & Stone, 1982; Lin, Dean, & Ensel, 1981; Miller, Ingham, & Davidson, 1976; Schaefer, Coyne, & Lazarus, 1981; Turner, 1981; Turner & Noh, 1983; Vanfossen, 1981; Williams, Ware, & Donald, 1981). In multivariate analyses, when social support is introduced after selected sociodemographic indices and some measure of stress (generally stressful life events) its contribution may diminish into insignificance (Andrews *et al.*, 1978). Generally, however, the partial effect remains (Billings & Moos, 1981; Lin, Ensel, Simeone, & Kuo, 1979), partly because the measures of stress tend to be uncorrelated with social support (Aneshensel & Stone, 1982; Lin *et al.,* 1979).

In many of these surveys, the testing of the buffer hypothesis—showing that there is an interaction between stress and social support so that the benefits of social support are seen only among subjects high in stress—is a major goal. On balance the results favor an absence of detectable buffer effects (Andrews, Tennant, Hewson, & Vaillant, 1978; Aneshensel & Stone, 1982; Lin *et al.,* 1979; Norbeck & Tilden, 1983; Schaefer *et al.,* 1981; Turner, 1981; Williams *et al.,* 1981). Among the studies that have found a buffer effect, a clear-cut strong effect is rather rare (e.g., Brown, 1979); mostly, the results are weak and often further compromised by inadequate data analysis strategies (Frydman, 1981; Habif & Lahey, 1980; Paykel, Emms, Fletcher, & Rassaby, 1980; Vanfossen, 1981). One author (Boyce, 1981) has pointed out the possibility that the buffering may be more easily detected by zeroing in on the very high levels of stress. There is also a study that searched for a buffering effect between "objective" stress (actually, stressful life events) and strains in the financial, marital, and work domains, but found none (Aneshensel & Stone, 1982).

Most of these studies are cross-sectional in nature. Of two reports on longitudinal data sets, one study concluded that initial levels of social support were predictive of changes in mental health in the expected direction (Williams *et al.,* 1981); in the other study the longitudinal data were completely ambiguous with respect to causality between social support and well-being (Turner, 1981).

An interesting relationship between social support and coping has been noted in a few reports (Billings & Moos, 1981; Menaghan, 1982): People with fewer social resources or lower support in the marriage use ineffective coping strategies (avoidance, ignoring, resignation), which are associated with higher levels of distress, both cross-sectionally and longitudinally.

A series of papers has appeared that represent a sophisticated analysis of the possible mediating processes between disadvantaged status (particularly low social class and being unmarried) and higher distress levels. The initial proposition that such groups are exposed to greater number of stressors (e.g., Liem & Liem, 1978) was supported, but the differences in stressors were insufficient to account for the high distress levels (Eaton, 1978; Kessler & Essex, 1982; Pearlin & Johnson, 1977; Thoits, 1982b, 1982c). This, in effect, represents an interaction between disadvantaged status and stress, and can be interpreted as greater vulnerability or reactivity of the disadvantaged. The question then posed is whether social support differences account for this greater vulnerability. Kessler and Essex (1982), working with the initial wave of the Chicago survey data (Pearlin & Schooler, 1978), provide an affirmative answer: The greater resilience of the married is seen as due to greater intimacy of primary relationships. On the other hand, Thoits (1982b, 1982c) analyzed longitudinal data from the Chicago and New Haven surveys and concluded that the greater vulnerability of the disadvantaged could not be explained by differences in support. In fact, when controlling for initial levels of distress, even the evidence for the higher vulnerability of the disadvantaged began to crumble. But the longitudinal analysis confirmed a main effect: Persons who maintain intimate confiding relations experience reduced psychological distress, irrespective of stressful events.

The Work Environment

The findings in the previous section can obviously offer no closure and are unsatisfying; social support is worth pursuing but in which direction is the increased payoff? In this section we will examine a narrower set of socioenvironmental conditions with the hope that the greater specificity of focus will provide more insights. Most of the studies reviewed are of specific occupational groups and the subjects are invariably male. The state of the evidence on women, work stress, and social support is so limited (see Haw, 1982) that no review can be attempted. However, in the next section we will consider studies that examine the interplay of work and family roles, and those do have a greater breadth of coverage.

The vast majority of social support studies in the work setting are embedded in the stress-at-work context. This is a relatively accessible literature, generously compiled and reviewed (e.g., Cooper & Marshall, 1980; Cooper & Payne, 1978, 1980; Holt, 1982; House, 1981; Kahn, 1981; Kahn, Hein, House, Kasl, & McLean, 1982; Kasl, 1978; Levi, Frankenhaeuser, & Gardell, 1982; McGrath, 1976). A dominant theoretical formulation within this literature has been the so-called Institute for Social Research (ISR) model of stress (e.g., Kahn, 1981). This model depicts a presumptive causal schema in a sequence from (1) objective work environmental characteristics to (2) the perceived environment to (3) short-term responses (physiological, behavioral, affective) to (4) health and disease outcomes. The role of social support can be easily grafted onto this model (e.g., House, 1981): Social support can either act as a modifier of each of the three links in the chain, or as an independent (main) effect on any of the four categories of variables. More elaborate models have been offered, utilizing the person–environment fit formulation (Caplan, 1979). The latest version of this is so elaborate (Caplan, 1983) that satisfactory assessment and research design technology is unlikely ever to catch up with it. Under the impetus from

Cobb's (1976) buffer formulation, much of the research emphasis has been on buffering effects. However, Cobb's (1979) turning away from a dominating concern with buffer effects only is a welcome corrective.

House (1981) offered a four-dimensional matrix conceptualization of social support: (1) four types of supportive acts (emotional, appraisal, informational, and instrumental) by (2) nine types of sources (spouse, relatives, friends, supervisor, coworkers, etc.) by (3) general versus problem-focused support by (4) objective versus subjective assessments. Many of the measures for this complete typology are still unavailable. In fact, the types of measures that were often utilized were derived from the influential volume *Job Demands and Worker Health* (Caplan, Cobb, French, Harrison, &. Pinneau, 1975) and were quite limited, when compared with House's much richer but more recent formulation. Four identical questions were asked about: "your immediate supervisor," "other people at work," and "your wife, friends, and relatives." The second way of asking the items failed to distinguish subordinates, same-level co-workers, and those two or more levels above the respondent; the pooling of the different sources of support in the nonwork setting also appears undesirable. Also, two of the items are work-specific and two are quite general, again making the total scales a bit too heterogeneous.

There are several important data sets and reports from which a good deal of information about social support at work can be derived: (1) a study of 23 occupations (Caplan *et al.,* 1975; French, Caplan, &. Harrison, 1982; LaRocco, House, &. French, 1980); (2) a study of hourly workers at a large manufacturing plant (House, McMichael, Wells, Kaplan, &. Landerman, 1979; House &. Wells, 1978; Wells, 1982); (3) a Dutch study of 13 organizations (Winnbust, Marcelissen, &. Kleber, 1982); (4) a reanalysis of the 1972 U.S. Quality of Employment Survey (Karasek, Triantis, &. Chaudhry, 1982); and (5) a study of U.S. Navy enlisted men (LaRocco &. Jones, 1978).

At the purely descriptive level, several findings from these studies may be noted.

1. Supervisor, co-worker, and home support are only moderately intercorrelated (average *r* under .30); associations with education and occupational status are mostly between .10 and .20.

2. There is greater variance across occupations on supervisor and co-worker support indices than on the measures of home support. Occupations particularly low on work-setting support include forklift drivers, machine tenders, and assemblers, particularly machine paced.

3. Zero-order correlations of support with subjective indices of work stress tend to range mostly between 0 and low − .30s. Home support generally shows negligible correlations; supervisor support tends to yield somewhat higher associations than co-worker support. This is particularly

true of such measures as role conflict and role ambiguity, where the supervisor may be both the source of the stress and its remedy. Conversely, other stresses such as workload show negligible associations, perhaps because these are conditions intrinsic to the job and not easily modified.

4. Work-related psychological outcome measures, such as job satisfaction or boredom, show very low correlations with home support, moderately low (.20–.30) with coworker support, and somewhat higher correlations with supervisor support (.25–.40).

5. Measures of psychological distress (such as anxiety, depression, or irritation) show negligible relationships with home support and correlations in the .20–.30 range for work-based support (with co-worker support specifically showing some of the higher correlations).

6. Self-report measures of physical symptoms or of diagnostic categories, illness measures based on medical care contacts, physiological data (such as blood pressure, cholesterol, or uric acid), and health-threatening behaviors (smoking or alcohol consumption) all show a consistent picture of negligible associations with the support indices. The one possible exception are symptom indices that include a lot of psychophysiological symptoms, but even then the correlations are not as high as those for indexes of psychological distress.

Older studies (i.e., before social support became a focal concept) of job satisfaction and mental health are reasonably compatible with this picture (see Kasl, 1974). For example, such work group characteristics as lack of opportunity for interaction with co-workers, groups that are large and lack cohesiveness, and nonacceptance by co-workers have all been linked to low job satisfaction. Characteristics of supervision that relate to low job satisfaction include absence of participation in decision making, inability to provide feedback to supervisor, lack of recognition for good performance, and supervisors who are not considerate or understanding. Associations with poor mental health (psychological distress) tend to be reported only for supervision characteristics and include demands that are unclear or conflicting and close supervision with no autonomy. It is interesting to speculate to what extent the older concepts describing co-workers and supervisory characteristics are to be subsumed under the umbrella conceptualization of social support—and why such a relabeling would be useful. Payne (1980), for example, noted the large literature on the benefits of participation in decision making and wondered to what extent this is to be seen as an aspect of social support. Of course, participation in decision making is related both to formal organizational characteristics as well as individual variations in supervisory styles.

The independent contribution of social support variables, in the presence of a large number of other predictors reflecting job demands and person–

environment fit, was examined in a rigorous analysis involving split-sample replication (French *et al.*, 1982). The results revealed no independent contribution of supervisor and home support on a variety of work-related and psychological distress measures and physiological parameters. Other worker support did come through as a significant contributor, but only for depression and irritation.

The buffer hypothesis has been vigorously pursued. We shall set aside the studies in which no buffer effect was noted (Blau, 1981; LaRocco & Jones, 1978) and examine the nature of the positive results for the three studies in which the methodology is most similar (House & Wells, 1978; LaRocco *et al.*, 1980; Winnbust *et al.*, 1982). Two outcomes stand out. A large number of tests have been run but only a few are significant—probably more than chance, but it does propel one onto the unwanted narrowness of the path between type I and type II errors (see Schaefer, 1982). Also, the significant interactions are largely in the predicted direction (benefits of social support at higher levels of stress), but the effects are quite small, accounting predominantly for less than 1% of the variance. The Dutch study findings are not impressive (about 15% significant at the 10% level and in the predicted direction, involving intercorrelated predictors and outcomes), but the buffer effects of supervisor support on irritation and diastolic blood pressure are worth some attention (Winnbust *et al.*, 1982). In the House and Wells (1978) analysis, also about 15% of the runs were significant at the 10% level and in the expected direction; the most suggestive pattern involved wife support buffering stress effects on neurosis and supervisor support buffering effects on ulcers, with co-worker support appearing unimportant. The LaRocco *et al.* (1980) data revealed 27% of runs as significant; most of the buffering effects involved psychological distress variables and not job-related strains, and co-worker support appeared most important. Wells (1982) also examined the possible buffering of the link from objective job conditions to perceived stresses. Most of the small but significant effects involved commensurate pairs of objective and subjective conditions (as one would hope) and supervisory support appeared particularly relevant.

The analysis of the U.S. Quality of Employment survey data (Karasek *et al.*, 1982) involved several aspects of supervisory support (tolerant, attentive, instrumental, and demanding–authoritarian) and co-worker support (instrumental, co-workers as friends); the job stressor variable was an additive combination of high job demands and low decision latitude. About half of the tests of the buffer hypothesis were significant. Curiously, the majority of these involved the paradoxical finding that at lowest levels of stress, higher social support was associated with higher distress (job or life dissatisfaction and depressed mood). The authors referred to it as "stress-transfer buffer"; a convincing theoretical or even intuitive explanation is as yet lacking. An interesting observation, not related to the buffer hypothesis, was the rather strong association ($r = .47$) between instrumental support from supervisors and perceptions of them as demanding–authoritarian. Apparently, task relevant help from the supervisor is difficult to deliver in an unambiguously positive way.

It should be noted that the extent to which the other studies discussed might have also observed the stress-transfer buffer phenomenon is not clear. They appear to have been concerned only with differential slopes but not their intersection. In this connection it helps to remember the caution, expressed by Cleary and Kessler (1982) that whereas the interpretation of interaction effects is aided greatly by the presence of a true zero point, most scales do not actually have a clear-cut zero point.

These findings from the major surveys appear weak and unexciting. It is possible that they are, in fact, underestimates of the role of social support. For one, they are cross-sectional data on unselected workers; longitudinal data, particularly if collected around major transitions (such as initial adaptation to a high job demand work setting or promotion from worker to supervisor), might reveal much more about the dynamics of social support. These cross-sectional data only hint at the remnants of adaptation dynamics, much attenuated by passage of time and unmeasured selective attrition. Second, many of these large data sets lump together a great diversity of work settings in which a great diversity of specific social support processes are possibly being averaged out. For example, individuals reducing communication with their role senders tends to negate the effects of chronic role conflict and role overload (Kahn, Wolfe, Quinn, Snoek, & Rosenthal, 1964), even though they are also presumably cutting themselves off from possible sources of social support at work. However, such an intimate interplay between stress and support probably characterizes a minority of jobs—perhaps those involving management, administrative, or professional positions—but not most blue collar jobs. In fact, even just the measures of role conflict and ambiguity must have different meaning for incumbents of routine blue collar jobs versus white collar managers.

The promise of examining specific work settings for obtaining more striking social support effects is difficult to assess because it means scanning the research literature for possible isolated and unstable results. Nevertheless, some illustrative findings can shore up interest in social support at work.

1. Shift workers with a constant set of co-workers had considerably lower levels of cholesterol than those whose co-workers were ever-changing (Cassel, 1963); presumably co-worker friendship and support networks were difficult to establish in the latter case.
2. Workers paid on a piecework basis (pay proportional to output) or

switched from salary to piecework showed chronically higher or stably increased levels of epinephrine and norepinephrine (Levi, 1974; Timio & Gentili, 1976); piecework basis of pay could, among others, adversely affect worker cohesion, socializing, and support.

3. Among National Aeronautics and Space Administration (NASA) scientists and administrators, good interpersonal relations with co-workers, subordinates, and supervisors buffered the effects of job stresses on physiological outcomes (blood pressure, serum glucose, cortisol); similar buffering was not observed for psychological outcomes (Caplan, 1971; French, 1974).

4. Administrators of NASA tended to have lower blood pressure in relation to the extent to which their organizational unit involved mostly administration, and higher blood pressure to the extent that it involved scientific engineering work (French & Caplan, 1970); presumably, the former setting better promotes friendship and support networks.

5. Among air traffic controllers, seeking out social contacts in time of stress buffered the effects of life stress on incidence of problems of clinically notable severity in five areas: subjective distress, lack of impulse control, alcohol abuse, work role, marital role (Jenkins, 1979).

Pearlin and Schooler (1978) have noted that effectiveness of coping (given their measures) is most limited in the occupational realm, and that self-reliance may be more effective than help seeking. If valid, such a conclusion would apply to social support effects in the work setting as well. However, an additional explanation of why the role of social support appears, in the existing literature, so limited is that measures have not yet been developed that are sensitive and appropriate for a variety of research questions. For example, Davidson and Veno (1980) have suggested that male police are an occupational group that is particularly in need of social support, especially from supervisors. The study of 23 occupations (Caplan *et al.*, 1975) does include data on male police; as a group they are quite ordinary on all three measures of social support and on the several indexes of psychological distress. But the social support measures may not be sensitive to the issue at hand. Do the measures reflect actual level of support, desired (needed) level, or some relation between the two that changes over time, depending on circumstances? For example, workers at the Three Mile Island nuclear power plant after the accident reported lower support from family and friends (but not lower co-worker or supervisor support) than nuclear workers at a control plant (Kasl, Chisholm, & Eskenazi, 1981); this difference was greatest for those in general management and operations, two groups considered by observers to be most affected by the accident (Chisholm & Kasl, 1982). However, it is not clear whether the accident created a greater need for support (hence the finding) or if the accident actually lowered supportive behavior by significant others because of the conflict it created between work role obligations and those to the family and the community. In the past, similar criticisms have been leveled at traditional job satisfaction indices, and measurement innovations in this area might be useful guides for developing additional support measures.

Work and the Family

In this section we wish to look at studies that consider the work role in a larger context: They include the impact on the respondent's family role and functioning, they explicitly include data on the spouse (i.e., the wife), and in general they provide a better picture of the work role–family role interplay and of social support in the family setting.

Research on work and the family has been quite segregated and it is not common to find a study focusing equally on both roles; the overviews have thus tended to be more speculative and less empirical than reviews of either area alone (Furstenberg, 1974; Handy, 1978; Kanter, 1979; Rainwater, 1974; Rapoport & Rapoport, 1965). It is likely that work is still seen as masculine and family responsibilities, including providing social support, as feminine (e.g., Belle, 1982; Gutek, Nakamura, & Nieva, 1981). Hence there are two separate streams of research. For example, it is astonishing to pick up a review of research on marital quality (Spanier & Lewis, 1980) and realize that highly relevant research and formulations have been taking place with no linkages to, or crossing of influence with, the research on work and social support.

One theme running through some of the research literature might be called the spillover effect from work to family: the extent to which stresses in the work setting influence or overwhelm family relationships so that the family's capacity for social support is diminished and the daily impact of the demanding job situation becomes cumulative. This effect is crucial for understanding the disease effects of stressful work conditions (Kasl, 1981). The spillover effect is apparently of greatest interest to European investigators, particularly the Swedes (e.g., Levi et al., 1982); the impact of repetitive work on family relationships is a special concern (Cox, 1980). Frankenhaeuser (1979) and Rissler (1977) have observed that female clerks working overtime show elevated catecholamine levels at work (during regular hours and overtime hours) and even in the evening at home away from work; such elevations are associated with greater fatigue and irritability. Similarly, saw mill workers—whose job is highly repetitive, machine paced and highly constricting, yet requires skilled judgments—show elevated levels of catecholamines that fail to decline at the end of the day; they report inability to relax after work (Gardell, 1976; Johansson, Aronson, & Lindstrom, 1978). In a major longitudinal survey of Swedish workers, it was observed that changes in jobs that represented richer job content and greater control were followed by greater participation in network relationships, such as voluntary associations, trade unions, and political groups (Levi *et al.*, 1982).

Spillover effects have also been suggested by correlational findings. For example, in a study of burnout among male police (Jackson & Maslach, 1982), the husband's report of emotional exhaustion was correlated with wife's reports of how much the husband brought police work home (upset, angry, complains about problems, comes home tense) and with her own assessments of quality of family life (*r* values between low .30s and .45). Being married to men (top level administrators) who score high on a measure of type A behavior appears to have broad consequences for the wife (Burke, Weir, & DuWors, 1979), including lower marital satisfaction, perception of a greater negative impact of husband's job demands on family; reporting fewer good friends, lower emotional support from neighbors, and a lesser sense of belonging to a supportive social network; showing a stronger preference for keeping problems to herself and being less likely to cope by talking to others; and being more depressed and feeling greater guilt and isolation. These are strongly suggestive correlational findings and would seem to contradict the generalization that, for social support, men turn to women but women turn to other women (Belle, 1982). Instead, they suggest that the high work commitment of the husbands isolates the wives socially and they are less likely to turn to anyone. And it was shown earlier (Menaghan, 1982) that selective ignoring and resignation are, in the marital setting, ineffective coping strategies.

The Burke *et al.* (1979) data, based on Canadian subjects, agree with observations on British middle-class managers (Cooper & Marshall, 1978). The majority of wives saw their roles in relation to husband's jobs as supportive and derived their sense of security from their husbands. The men, on the other hand, in the course of trying to build up their careers strove to maintain distance between their wives and the place of work. Clearly, current social support survey instruments and cross-sectional designs cannot capture the complex dynamics of career advancement among managers concomitantly with the development of supportive or nonsupportive relationships in the family (Burke & Weir, 1980; Cooper & Marshall, 1978).

These observations imply an asymmetry in work and family roles, and consequences for social support dynamics, that may be attributed to the family arrangement in which only the husband works. Does the wife's work status in fact affect these dynamics? Moos and colleagues (Billings & Moos,

1982a, 1982b; Holahan & Moos, 1981) have carried out a longitudinal study of 300 families providing some answers to this question. Certain findings suggested no impact of wife's working status. For example, stressful life events and supportive family relationships had an impact on depression and psychosomatic symptoms (controlling for initial levels) that was quite similar for both working and nonworking wives. However, there did seem to be a differential impact on the husbands. For example, the buffering effects of work resources and family resources on the relationship between stress and symptoms were reduced for men who had employed wives. Further, high stresses in the wives' work settings did have some negative impact on the husbands' symptoms. Vanfossen's (1981) analysis of the Chicago survey data also suggested differential dynamics attributable to wife's work status. For example, if the wife worked, then intimacy in the marriage became a less important influence on depression and inequity (nonreciprocity in the relationship) became a more important influence. For the employed wives, levels of depression were particularly influenced by husbands who did not express their appreciation of their wives, by inequity in marriage, and by disagreement over husband's help with domestic duties.

Social Support and Family and Work
Role Transitions

The health deficits of the divorced, compared to the married, have been adequately recognized and described (e.g., Bloom, Asher, & White, 1978; Gove, 1973; Verbrugge, 1979). However, specific studies of the divorce process in relation to social support are rare as well as rather informal from a methodological viewpoint. Because the spouse is such an important source of support (Belle, 1982; Lieberman, 1982; Lin, Light, & Woelfel, 1982; McFarlane, Neale, Norman, Roy, & Streiner, 1981), examining social support in relation to divorce is somewhat paradoxical and ironic. In fact, Chiriboga, Coho, Stein, and Roberts (1979) found that 27% of divorced men and 16% of divorced women named the former spouse as the person who potentially could be most helpful with the crisis of divorce. Notable also is the fact that the divorce studies predominantly deal with help seeking, which is not necessarily the same as social support (e.g., Gore, 1979; Pearlin & Schooler, 1979). Thus the finding of higher distress among divorced individuals who received help from family (Kitson, Moir, & Mason, 1982) could be both the negative effects of help when the source of help disapproves of the stressful event (divorce) and the self-selection of more distressed individuals seeking help.

Even though the size of networks does not show a sex difference, women are more likely to report larger numbers of people with whom they could discuss a variety of problems (McFarlane *et al.,* 1981). In the event of divorce, women do in fact seek out more contacts with a greater variety of helpers than do men (Chiriboga *et al.,* 1979). Characteristics of networks of divorced women have been examined in a few studies in relation to distress and unsuccessful adjustment (Hirsh, 1980, 1981; Wilcox, 1981). It appears that networks of higher density (proportion of actual to potential relationships that exist among the members of an individual's network), especially when this density is due to density of nuclear family, are associated with less frequent socializing and poorer mental health. On the other hand, multidimensional friendships (engaging in a variety of activities important to both individuals) seem to promote self-esteem and better mental health. Poorer mental health is also associated with a reduction in network size from before to after divorce. Economic hardships among single parents (mostly female) represent an overwhelming effect on distress (Pearlin & Johnson, 1977). However, when financial circumstances are tolerable, receiving only limited help may actually be associated with a stronger sense of independence and competence (Colletta, 1979).

We shall now turn to studies of unemployment and briefly consider the evidence in relation to social support. Many of the relevant studies had been done in the late 1930s and early 1940s and the methodology may not be up to present standards. Nevertheless, the overall impression is that the employment–unemployment–reemployment cycle was not associated with strong disruptions of family structure, personality, or attitudes, except perhaps in families or individuals who were allegedly unstable from the start (Kasl, 1979). A more recent report on engineers and scientists (Powell & Driscoll, 1973) documented informally the complex interplay: Support from family and friends is crucial in warding off depression and maintaining a consistent job search effort, but continued unemployment undermines family and friendship relations, which reduces the continued support that is needed. Somewhat different findings were reported in a German study of 1300 unemployed persons (Frohlich, 1983). Social contacts and activities with friends and acquaintances were more likely to intensify (41%) than be reduced (17%) after unemployment; however, higher work orientation and higher economic deprivation were more likely to lead to reduced contacts.

A report on unemployment among U.S. veterans of the Vietnam War and civilians (Vinokur, Caplan, & Williams, 1983) revealed a main effect of perceived social support on distress (anxiety, depression, resentment, and low self-esteem), even though it did not influence speed of reemployment. Veterans were more likely to be adversely affected by the unemployment experience than civilians, but buffer effects of social support were not reported. Pearlin *et al.* (1981) offered a detailed and searching analysis of longitudinal data on depression in relation to disruptions from work life (such as being laid off or fired). Presence of such disruptions was associated with increase in depression ($r = .34$) and changes in economic strain, mastery, and self-esteem were important intervening variables. Adding social support as a main effect or buffer did not improve the prediction of depression; social support did have small main effects on economic strain and mastery and some buffering effects on mastery and self-esteem.

The results of a prospective study of job loss from before a plant shutdown took place to 2 years later offer a particularly good glimpse of the complex role of social support (Cobb & Kasl, 1977). The findings have been reported in detail elsewhere (Kasl, 1982; Kasl & Cobb, 1979, 1980, 1982; Kasl, Gore, & Cobb, 1975). The Gore (1978) report represents preliminary analyses that did not take full advantage of the longitudinal nature of the data. Some illustrative findings follow.

1. Social support showed much evidence of a buffer function (among those with more severe unemployment, levels of social support had a greater impact on outcomes), but it was also necessary to pay attention to the full pattern of results including those from before the plant closing. Social support was a true buffer for some outcomes (e.g., perceived economic deprivation, insecurity about future), but not for others (e.g., depression, anomie), where apparent buffer effects in fact antedated plant closing (Kasl & Cobb, 1979).

2. The effects of social support were not always taking place at the same stage of adaptation. For example, initial changes in serum uric acid were only sensitive to employment status changes; later on, however, changes in uric acid ceased to be sensitive to employment status, but reflected levels of social support instead (Kasl & Cobb, 1982). Social support effects on blood pressure and serum cholesterol were seen primarily in the very early stages of the study (Kasl & Cobb, 1980).

3. Social support also showed reversals of effects. For example, phase-to-phase analysis of changes in anxiety–tension revealed that the benefits of prompt re-employment were seen primarily among those low in social support. However, later changes revealed that among those whose employment situation remained uncertain, high levels of social support were associated with reductions in anxiety–tension and low levels of support with increases. This pattern of findings suggests that social support as a buffer did not come into play until later, when it appeared that stable re-employment was not easily attained; on the other hand, the combination of prompt re-employment and low social support might have led to a sense of accomplishment and mastery by the unsupported individuals.

4. Many differences between urban and rural plants in the impact of

plant closing were observed. For example, in the urban setting the job loss had a larger impact on indicators of mental health; in the rural setting the impact was greater on indices of work role deprivation. Because the rural setting was one of higher levels of social support and of community cohesion and sharing of experience, such rural–urban differences are also presumptively linked to social support.

The speed with which stable employment was found was unrelated to social support. However, higher age and poorer health were much more strongly related to length of unemployment among the men high on indexes of social support. This seems to suggest that higher levels of social support acted as a selective deterrent to job-seeking efforts among older men in poorer health. This is consistent with a variety of studies showing that return from the sick role to normal functioning after severe illness may be impeded by high levels of support and concern and expressions of preferential treatment (e.g., Garrity, 1973; Hyman, 1975; Lewis, 1966).

Concluding Comments

Other chapters in this volume deal exclusively with various conceptual and methodological issues, and Chapter 5, on measuring social support, is written by House and Kahn—two investigators who have contributed much to the work and health literature. Therefore, our comments can be very brief. Three are specific research strategy comments and one is general.

1. There is a great need to conduct studies in very specific work settings where the objective work environment can be comprehensively described and its impact studied. There are too many general studies that ignore objective work settings and combine too great a variety of self-reported work conditions.
2. Investigators must look beyond studies that are merely longitudinal (Kasl, 1983). Unselected, slice-of-life longitudinal data usually produce well-correlated dependent variables, and covariance adjustments tend to leave researchers working mostly with measurement error. The longitudinal studies need to be set up around important transitions and need to be conducted at the point when greatest variance in adaptation can be observed.
3. If the central interest in social support studies is health outcomes, then investigators need to try to reconstruct as much of the causal network of other influences on the health outcome of interest as they can: prior health status, biological risk factors, health-related behaviors, and medical care data.

4. Social support effects must be viewed within the broader context of social influence processes. They do not generally come nicely packaged as "input, directly provided by an individual (or group), which moves the receiver of that input towards goals which the receiver desires" (Caplan, Robinson, French, Caldwell, & Shinn, 1976, p. 39). Rather, they are embedded in a large matrix of costs and benefits, constraints and facilitations, obligations and rewards. The literature betrays a subtle bias in favor of seeing the lights but not the shadows, the benefits but not the costs. We are reminded of the literature on smoking cessation (Schwartz & Dubitzky, 1968): Those interested in quitting prefer most a method that would provide them with instructions about how to quit on their own. They do not wish to enter into elaborate supportive relationships, but they may have to if they have failed to stop on their own several times. In short, social support may not be the most preferred, nor the most effective, nor the least costly method of coping in many circumstances. On the other hand, it may be the only method in other circumstances. Our social support theories must be complex enough to recognize this.

References

Andrews, G., Tenant, C., Hewson, D., & Schonell, M. (1978). The relation of social factors to physical and psychiatric illness. *American Journal of Epidemiology, 108,* 27–35.

Andrews, G., Tennant, C., Hewson, D. M., & Vaillant, G. E. (1978). Life event stress, social support, coping style, and risk of psychological impairment. *The Journal of Nervous and Mental Disease, 166,* 307–316.

Aneshensel, C. S., & Stone, J. D. (1982). Stress and depression: A test of the buffering model of social support. *Archives of General Psychiatry, 39,* 1392–1396.

Belle, D. (1982). The stress of caring: Women as providers of social support. In L. Goldberger & S. Breznitz (Eds.), *Handbook of stress.* New York: The Free Press.

Billings, A. G., & Moos, R. H. (1981). The role of coping responses and social resources in attenuating the stress of life events. *Journal of Behavioral Medicine, 4,* 139–159.

Billings, A. G., & Moos, R. H. (1982a). Social support and functioning among community and clinical groups: A panel mode. *Journal of Behavioral Medicine, 5,* 295–311.

Billings, A. G., & Moos, R. H. (1982b). Work stress and the stress-buffering roles of work and family resources. *Journal of Occupational Behavior, 3,* 215–232.

Blau, G. (1981). An empirical investigation of job stress, social support, service length, and job strain. *Organizational Behavior and Human Performance, 27,* 279–302.

Blazer, D. G. (1982). Social support and mortality in an elderly community population. *American Journal of Epidemiology, 115,* 684–694.

Bloom, B. L., Asher, S. J., & White, S. W. (1978). Marital disruption as a stressor: A review and analysis. *Psychological Bulletin, 85,* 867–894.

Boyce, W. T. (1981). Interaction between social variables in stress research. *Journal of Health and Social Behavior, 22,* 194–195.

Broadhead, W. E., Kaplan, B. H., James, S. A., Wagner, E. H., Schoenbach, V. J., Grimson, R.,

Heyden, S., Tibblin, G., & Gehlbach, S. H. (1983). The epidemiologic evidence for a relationship between social support and health. *American Journal of Epidemiology, 117,* 521–537.

Brown, G. W. (1979). A three-factor causal model of depression. In J. E. Barrett, R. M. Rose, & G. L. Klerman (Eds.), *Stress and mental disorders.* New York: Raven.

Burke, R. J., & Weir, T. (1980). Coping with the stress of managerial occupations. In C. L. Cooper & R. Payne (Eds.), *Current concerns in occupational stress.* Chichester: Wiley.

Burke, R. J., Weir, T., & DuWors, Jr., R. E. (1979). Type A behavior of administrators and wives' reports of marital satisfaction and well-being. *Journal of Applied Psychology, 64,* 57–65.

Caplan R. D. (1971). *Organizational stress and individual strain: A social psychological study of risk factors in coronary heart disease among administrators, engineers and scientists.* Unpublished Ph.D. dissertation, University of Michigan, Ann Arbor.

Caplan, R. D. (1979). Social support, person-environment fit, and coping. In L. A. Ferman & J. P. Gordus (Eds.), *Mental health and the economy.* Kalamazoo, MI: Upjohn Institute for Employment Research.

Caplan, R. D. (1983). Person-environment fit: Past, present and future. In C. L. Cooper (Ed.), *Stress research.* Chichester, England: Wiley.

Caplan, R. D., Cobb, S., French, Jr., J. R. P., Harrison, R. V., & Pinneau, Jr., S. R., (1975). *Job demands and worker health.* Washington, DC: HEW Publication No. (NIOSH) 75–160.

Caplan, R. D., Cobb, S., French, Jr., J. R. P., Caldwell, J. R., & Shinn, M. (1976). *Adhering to medical regimens: Pilot experiments in patient education and social support.* Ann Arbor: The Institute for Social Research.

Cassel, J. C. (1963). The use of medical records: Opportunity for epidemiologic studies. *Journal of Occupational Medicine, 5,* 185–190.

Chiriboga, D. A., Coho, A., Stein, J. A., & Roberts, J. (1979). Divorce, stress and social supports: A study in helpseeking behavior. *Journal of Divorce, 3,* 121–135.

Chisholm, R. F., & Kasl, S. V. (1982). The effects of work site, supervisory status, and job function on nuclear workers' responses to the TMI accident. *Journal of Occupational Behavior, 3,* 39–62.

Cleary, P. D., & Kessler, R. C. (1982). The estimation and interpretation of modifier effects. *Journal of Health and Social Behavior, 23,* 159–169.

Cobb, S. (1976). Social support as a moderator of life stress. *Psychosomatic Medicine, 38,* 300–314.

Cobb, S. (1979). Social support and health through the life course. In M. W. Riley (Ed.), *Aging from birth to death: Interdisciplinary perspectives.* Washington, DC: American Association for the Advancement of Science.

Cobb, S., & Kasl, S. V. (1977). *Termination: The consequences of job loss.* Cincinnati, OH: DHEW (NIOSH) Publication No. 77–224.

Colletta, N. D. (1979). Support systems after divorce: Incidence and impact. *Journal of Marriage and the Family, 41,* 837–846.

Cooper, C. L., & Marshall, J. (1978). Sources of managerial and white collar stress. In C. L. Cooper & R. Payne (Eds.), *Stress at work.* Chichester, England: Wiley.

Cooper, C. L., & Marshall, J. (Eds.). (1980). *White collar and professional stress.* Chichester, England: Wiley.

Cooper, C. L., & Payne, R. (Eds.). (1978). *Stress at work.* Chichester, England: Wiley.

Cooper, C. L., & Payne, R. (Eds.). (1980). *Current concerns in occupational stress.* Chichester: Wiley.

Cox, T. (1980). Repetitive work. In C. L. Cooper, & R. Payne (Eds.), *Current concerns in occupational stress.* Chichester, England: Wiley.

Davidson, M. J., & Veno, A. (1980). Stress and the policeman. In C. L. Cooper & J. Marshall (Eds.), *White collar and professional stress.* Chichester: Wiley.

Dean, A., & Lin, N. (1977). The stress-buffering role of social support: Problems and prospects for systematic investigation. *The Journal of Nervous and Mental Disease, 165,* 403–417.

DiMatteo, M. R., & Hays, R. (1981). Social support and serious illness. In B. H. Gottlieb (Ed.), *Social networks and social support.* Beverly Hills, CA: Sage.

Dohrenwend, B., Pearlin, L., Clayton, P., Hamburg, B., Riley, M., Rose, R. M., & Dohrenwend, B. (1982). Report on stress and life events. In G. R. Elliott, & C. Eisdorfer (Eds.), *Stress and human health.* New York: Springer.

Eaton, W. (1978). Life events, social supports, and psychiatric symptoms: A reanalysis of the New Haven data. *Journal of Health and Social Behavior, 19,* 230–234.

Eckenrode, J., & Gore, S. (1981). Stressful events and social supports: The significance of context. In B. H. Gottlieb (Ed.), *Social networks and social support.* Beverly Hills, CA: Sage.

Elliott, G. R., & Eisdorfer, C. (Eds.). (1982). *Stress and human health.* New York: Springer.

Folkman, S., & Lazarus, R. S. (1980). An analysis of coping in a middle-aged community sample. *Journal of Health and Social Behavior, 21,* 219–239.

Frankenhaeuser, M. (1979). Psychoneuroendocrine approaches to the study of emotion as related to stress and coping. In H. E. Howe & R. A. Dienstbier (Eds.), *Nebraska symposium on motivation.* Lincoln: University of Nebraska Press.

French, Jr., J. R. P. (1974). Person role fit. In A. A. McLean (Ed.), *Occupational stress.* Springfield, IL: Thomas.

French, Jr., J. R. P., & Caplan, R. D. (1970). Psychosocial factors in coronary heart disease. *Industrial Medicine and Surgery, 39,* 383–397.

French, Jr., J. R. P., Caplan, R. D., & Harrison, R. V. (1982). *The mechanisms of job stress and strain.* Chichester: Wiley.

Frohlich, D. (1983). Economic deprivation, work orientation and health: Conceptual ideas and some empirical findings. In J. John, D. Schwefel, & H. Zöller (Eds.), *Influence of economic instability on health.* Berlin: Springer-Verlag.

Frydman, M. I. (1981). Social support, life events and psychiatric symptoms: A study of direct, conditional and interaction effects. *Social Psychiatry, 16,* 69–78.

Furstenberg, Jr., F. F. (1974). Work experience and family life. In J. O'Toole (Ed.), *Work and the quality of life.* Cambridge: The MIT Press.

Gardell, B. (1976). *Job content and quality of life.* Stockholm: Prisma.

Garrity, T. F. (1973). Vocational adjustment after first myocardial infarction. *Social Science and Medicine, 7,* 705–717.

Gore, S. (1978). The effect of social support in moderating the health consequences of unemployment. *Journal of Health and Social Behavior, 19,* 157–165.

Gore, S. (1979). Does help-seeking increase psychological distress? *Journal of Health and Social Behavior, 20,* 201–202.

Gore, S. (1981). Stress-buffering functions of social supports: An appraisal and clarification of research models. In B. S. Dohrenwend & B. P. Dohrenwend (Eds.), *Stressful life events and their contexts.* New York: Prodist.

Gottlieb, B. H. (1983). Social support as a focus for integrative research in psychology. *American Psychologist, 38,* 278–287.

Gove, W. R. (1973). Sex, marital status, and mortality. *American Journal of Sociology, 79,* 45–67.

Gutek, B. A., Nakamura, C. Y., & Nieva, V. F. (1981). The interdependence of work and family roles. *Journal of Occupational Behavior, 2,* 1–16.

Habif, V. L., & Lahey, B. B. (1980). Assessment of the life stress-depression relationship: The use of social support as a moderator variable. *Journal of Behavioral Assessment, 2,* 167–173.

Handy, C. (1978). The family: Help or hindrance? In C. L. Cooper & R. Payne (Eds.), *Stress at work*. Chichester: Wiley.

Haw, M. A. (1982). Women, work and stress: A review and agenda for the future. *Journal of Health and Social Behavior, 23,* 132–144.

Haynes, S. G., & Feinleib, M. (1980). Women, work and coronary heart disease: Prospective findings from the Framingham Heart Study. *American Journal of Public Health, 70,* 133–141.

Henderson, S. (1980). A development in social psychiatry: The systematic study of social bonds. *The Journal of Nervous and Mental Disease, 168,* 63–69.

Hirsch, B. J. (1980). Natural support systems and coping with major life changes. *American Journal of Community Psychology, 8,* 159–172.

Hirsch, B. J. (1981). Social networks and the coping process: Creating personal communities. In B. H. Gottlieb (Ed.), *Social networks and social support*. Beverly Hills: Sage.

Holahan, C. J., & Moos, R. H. (1981). Social support and psychological distress: A longitudinal analysis. *Journal of Abnormal Psychology, 90,* 365–370.

Holt, R. R. (1982). Occupational stress. In L. Goldberger, & S. Breznitz (Eds.), *Handbook of Stress*. New York: The Free Press.

House, J. S., (1981). *Work stress and social support*. Reading, MA: Addison-Wesley.

House, J. S., McMichael, A. J., Wells, J. A., Kaplan, B. N., & Landerman, L. R. (1979). Occupational stress and health among factory workers. *Journal of Health and Social Behavior, 20,* 139–160.

House, J. S., & Wells, J. A. (1978). Occupational stress, social support, and health. In A. A. McLean, G. Black, & M. Colligan (Eds.), *Reducing occupational stress: Proceedings of a conference*. Cincinnati: DHEW (NIOSH) Publication No. 78–140.

Hyman, M. D. (1975). Social psychological factors affecting disability among ambulatory patients. *Journal of Chronic Diseases, 28,* 199–216.

Jackson, S. E., & Maslach, C. (1982). After-effects of job-related stress: Families as victims. *Journal of Occupational Behavior, 3,* 63–77.

Jenkins, C. D. (1979). Psychosocial modifiers of response to stress. In J. E. Barrett, R. M. Rose, & G. L. Klerman (Eds.), *Stress and mental disorder*. New York: Raven.

Johansson, G., Aronson, G., & Lindstrom, B. P. (1978). Social psychological and neuroendocrine stress reactions in highly mechanized work. *Ergonomics, 21,* 583–599.

Kahn, R. L. (1981). *Work and health*. New York: Wiley.

Kahn, R. L., Hein, K., House, J., Kasl, S. V., & McLean, A. A. (1982). Report on stress in organizational settings. In G. R. Elliott & C. Eisdorfer (Eds.), *Stress and human health*. New York: Springer.

Kahn, R. L., Wolfe, D. M., Quinn, R. P., Snoek, J. D., & Rosenthal, R. A. (1964). *Organizational stress: Studies in role conflict and ambiguity*. New York: Wiley.

Kanter, R. M. (1979). *Work and family in the United States: A critical review and agenda for research and policy*. New York: Russell Sage Foundation.

Kaplan, B. H., Cassel, J. C., & Gore, S. (1977). Social support and health. *Medical Care, 15* (5), supplement), 47–57.

Karasek, R. A., Triantis, K. P., & Chandhry, S. S. (1982). Coworker and supervisor support as moderators of associations between task characteristics and mental strain. *Journal of Occupational Behaviour, 3,* 181–200.

Kasl, S. V. (1974). Work and mental health. In J. O'Toole (Ed.), *Work and the quality of life*. Cambridge: The MIT Press.

Kasl, S. V. (1978). Epidemiological contributions to the study of work stress. In C. L. Cooper & R. Payne (Eds.), *Stress at work*. Chichester: Wiley.

Kasl, S. V. (1979). Changes in mental health status associated with job loss and retirement. In

J. E. Barrett, R. M. Rose, & G. L. Klerman (Eds.), *Stress and mental disorder*. New York: Raven Press.

Kasl, S. V. (1981). The challenge of studying the disease effects of stressful work conditions. *American Journal of Public Health, 71*, 682–684.

Kasl, S. V. (1982). Strategies of research on economic instability and health. *Psychological Medicine, 12*, 637–649.

Kasl, S. V., Chisholm, R. F., & Eskenazi, B. (1981). The impact of the accident at the Three Mile Island on the behavior and well-being of nuclear workers. *American Journal of Public Health, 71*, 472–495.

Kasl, S. V., & Cobb, S. (1979). Some mental health consequences of plant closing and job loss. In L. A. Ferman & J. P. Gordus (Eds.), *Mental health and the economy*. Kalamazoo, MI: Upjohn Institute for Employment Research.

Kasl, S. V., & Cobb, S. (1980). The experience of losing a job: Some effects on cardiovascular functioning. *Psychotherapy and Psychosomatics, 34*, 88–109.

Kasl, S. V., & Cobb, S. (1982). Variability of stress effects among men experiencing job loss. In L. Goldberger & S. Breznitz (Eds.), *Handbook of stress*. New York: The Free Press.

Kasl, S. V., Gore, S., & Cobb, S. (1975). The experience of losing a job: Reported changes in health, symptoms, and illness behavior. *Psychosomatic medicine, 37*, 106–122.

Kessler, R. C., & Essex, M. (1982). Marital status and depression: The importance of coping resources. *Social Forces, 61*, 484–507.

Kitson, G. C., Moir, R. N., & Mason, P. R. (1982). Family social support in crises: The special case of divorce. *American Journal of Orthopsychiatry, 52*, 161–165.

LaRocco, J. M., House, J. S., & French, Jr., J. R. P. (1980). Social support, occupational stress, and health. *Journal of Health and Social Behavior, 21*, 202–218.

LaRocco, J. M., & Jones, A. P. (1978). Co-worker and leader support as moderators of stress-strain relationships in work situations. *Journal of Applied Psychology, 63*, 629–634.

Levi, L. (1974). Stress, distress, and psychosocial stimuli. In A. A. McLean (Ed.), *Occupational stress*. Springfield: Thomas.

Levi, L., Frankenhaeuser, M., & Gardell, B. (1982). Report on work stress related to social structures and processes. In G. R. Elliott & C. Eisdorfer (Eds.), *Stress and human health*. New York: Springer.

Lewis, C. E. (1966). Factors influencing the return to work of men with congestive heart failure. *Journal of Chronic Diseases, 19*, 1193–1209.

Lieberman, M. A. (1982). The effects of social supports on responses to stress. In L. Goldberger & S. Breznitz (Eds.), *Handbook of stress*. New York: The Free Press.

Liem, R., & Liem, J. (1978). Social class and mental illness reconsidered: The role of economic stress and social support. *Journal of Health and Social Behavior, 19*, 139–156.

Liem, G. R., & Liem, J. H. (1979). Social support & stress: Some general issues and their application to the problem of unemployment. In L. A. Ferman, & J. P. Gordus (Eds.), *Mental health and the economy*. Kalamazoo, MI: Upjohn Institute for Employment Research.

Lin, N., Dean, A., & Ensel, W. M. (1981). Social support scales: A methodological note. *Schizophrenia Bulletin, 7*, 73–89.

Lin, N., Ensel, W. E., Simeone, R. S., & Kuo, W. (1979). Social support, stressful life events, and illness: A model and an empirical test. *Journal of Health and Social Behavior, 20*, 108–119.

Lin, N., Light, S. C., & Woelfel, M. (1982, October 11–12). *The buffering effects of social support: A theoretical framework and an empirical investigation*. Paper presented at the National Conference on Social Stress Research, University of New Hampshire.

Lipton, F. R., Cohen, C. I., Fischer, E., & Katz, S. E. (1981). Schizophrenia: A network crisis. *Schizophrenia Bulletin, 7*, 144–151.

McFarlane, A. H., Neale, K. A., Norman, G. R., Roy, R. G., & Streiner, D. L. (1981). Methodological issues in developing a scale to measure social support. *Schizophrenia Bulletin, 7,* 90–100.

McGrath, J. E. (1970). A conceptual formulation for research on stress. In J. E. McGrath (Ed.), *Social and psychological factors in stress.* New York: Holt.

McGrath, J. E. (1976). Stress and behavior in organizations. In M. D. Dunnette (Ed.), *Handbook of industrial and organizational psychology.* Chicago: Rand McNally.

Marsella, A. J., & Snyder, K. K. (1981). Stress, social supports, and schizophrenic disorders: Toward an interactional model. *Schizophrenia Bulletin, 7,* 152–163.

Medalie, J. H., & Goldbourt, U. (1976). Angina pectoris among 10,000 men. II. Psychosocial and other risk factors as evidenced by a multivariate analysis of a five year incidence study. *The American Journal of Medicine, 60,* 910–921.

Medalie, J. H., Snyder, M., Groen, J. J., Neufeld, H. N., Goldbourt, U., & Riss, E. (1973). Angina pectoris among 10,000 men: 5 year incidence and univariate analysis. *The American Journal of Medicine, 55,* 583–594.

Menaghan, E. (1982). Measuring coping effectiveness: A panel analysis of marital problems and coping efforts. *Journal of Health and Social Behavior, 23,* 220–234.

Miller, P. McC., Ingham, J. G., & Davidson, S. (1976). Life, events, symptoms and social support. *Journal of Psychosomatic Research, 20,* 515–522.

Mueller, D. P. (1980). Social networks: A promising direction for research on the relationship of the social environment to psychiatric disorder. *Social Science and Medicine, 14A,* 147–161.

Norbeck, J. S., & Tilden, V. P. (1983). Life stress, social support, and emotional disequilibrium in complications of pregnancy: A prospective, multivariate study. *Journal of Health and Social Behavior, 24,* 30–46.

Paykel, E. S., Emms, E. M., Fletcher, J., & Rassaby, E. S. (1982). Life events and social support in puerperal depression. *British Journal of Psychiatry, 136,* 339–346.

Payne, R. (1980). Organizational stress and social support. In C. L. Cooper & R. Payne (Eds.), *Current concerns in occupational stress.* Chichester, England: Wiley.

Pearlin, L. I., & Johnson, J. S. (1977). Marital status, life-strains, and depression. *American Sociological Review, 42,* 704–715.

Pearlin, L. I., Lieberman, M. A., Menaghan, E. G., & Mullan, J. T. (1981). The stress process. *Journal of Health and Social Behavior, 22,* 337–356.

Pearlin, L. I., & Schooler, C. (1978). The structure of coping. *Journal of Health and Social Behavior, 19,* 2–21.

Pearlin, L. I., & Schooler, C. (1979). Some extensions of "The structure of coping." *Journal of Health and Social Behavior, 20,* 202–204.

Pilisuk, M. (1982). Delivery of social support: The social inoculation. *American Journal of Orthopsychiatry, 52,* 20–31.

Powell, D. H., & Driscoll, P. J. (1973). Middle class professionals face unemployment. *Society, 10,* 18–26.

Rainwater, L. (1974). Work, well-being, and family life. In J. O'Toole (Ed.), *Work and the quality of life.* Cambridge, MA: The MIT Press.

Rapoport, R., & Rapoport, R. (1965). Work and family in contemporary society. *American Sociological Review, 30,* 381–394.

Rissler, A. (1977). Stress reactions at work and after work during a period of quantitative overload. *Ergonomics, 20,* 13–16.

Schaefer, C. (1982). Comment: Shoring up the "buffer" of social support. *Journal of Health and Social Behavior, 23,* 96–98.

Schaefer, C., Coyne, J. C., & Lazarus, R. S. (1981). The health-related functions of social support. *Journal of Behavioral Medicine, 4,* 381–406.

Schwartz, J. L., & Dubitzky, M. (1968). *Psychosocial factors involved in cigarette smoking and cessation.* Berkeley, CA: The Institute for Health Research.

Southwood, K. E. (1978). Substantive theory and statistical interaction: Five models. *American Journal of Sociology, 83,* 1154–1203.

Spanier, G. B., & Lewis, R. A. (1980). Marital quality: A review of the seventies. *Journal of Marriage and the Family, 42,* 825–839.

Thoits, P. A. (1982a). Conceptual, methodological and theoretical problems in studying social support as a buffer against life stress. *Journal of Health and Social Behavior, 23,* 145–159.

Thoits, P. A. (1982b). Life stress, social support, and psychological vulnerability: Epidemiological considerations. *Journal of Community Psychology, 10,* 341–362.

Thoits, P. A. (1982c, October 11–12). *Lack of social support in the face of life stress: Explaining epidemiological distributions of psychological vulnerability.* Paper presented at the National Conference on Social Stress Research, University of New Hampshire.

Timio, M., & Gentili, S. (1976). Adrenosympathetic overactivity under conditions of work stress. *British Journal of Preventive and Social Medicine, 30,* 262–265.

Tolsdorf, C. C. (1976). Social networks, support, and coping: An exploratory study. *Family Process, 15,* 407–417.

Turner, R. J. (1981). Social support as a contingency in psychological well-being. *Journal of Health and Social Behavior, 22,* 357–367.

Turner, R. J., & Noh, S. (1983). Class and psychological vulnerability among women: The significance of social support and personal control. *Journal of Health and Social Behavior, 24,* 2–15.

Vanfossen, B. E. (1981). Sex differences in the mental health effects of spouse support and equity. *Journal of Health and Social Behavior, 22,* 130–143.

Verbrugge, L. M. (1979). Marital status and health. *Journal of Marriage and the Family, 41,* 267–285.

Vinokur, A., Caplan, R. D., & Williams, C. C. (1983, January 3). *Work and unemployment: A comparative longitudinal study of stress and coping of Vietnam veterans and non-veterans.* Paper presented at the Third International Conference on Psychological Stress and Adjustment in Time of War and Peace, Israel.

Wells, J. A. (1982). Objective job conditions, social support and percieved stress among blue collar workers. *Journal of Occupational Behaviour, 3,* 79–94.

Wilcox, B. L. (1981). Social support in adjusting to marital disruption: A network analysis. In B. H. Gottlieb (Ed.), *Social networks and social support.* Beverly Hills, CA: Sage.

Williams, A. W., Ware, Jr., J. E. & Donald, C. A. (1981). A model of mental health, life events, and social supports applicable to general populations. *Journal of Health and Social Behavior, 22,* 324–336.

Winnbust, J. A. M., Marcelissen, F. H. G., & Kleber, R. J. (1982). Effects of social support in the stressor-strain relationship: A Dutch sample. *Social Science and Medicine, 16,* 475–482.

CHAPTER 10

Social Support and Health
of the Elderly

Meredith Minkler

Introduction

The notion that social support may play a particularly important role in
maintaining health and decreasing susceptibility to illness among the elderly has been suggested by a number of researchers (Kulys & Tobin, 1980;
Pilisuk, Montgomery & Parks, 1983; Treas, 1977). The aged, they have
pointed out, are at high risk both for illness and for disruptions in their
traditional sources of social support—for example, through the death of a
spouse, retirement, or a sudden geographic move. Yet the conclusion that
social support is of heightened importance to this age group may well be
premature. At minimum, such a conclusion assumes the homogeneity of a
large and heterogenous cohort, simply on the grounds that each of its members has survived his or her sixty-fifth birthday. Further, it assumes the
adequacy of a data base that is in reality small, methodologically flawed,
and hampered by the fact that few of the studies were originally designed
to measure social networks or social support.

As other contributors to this volume have discussed in detail, the conceptual confusion and the multiplicity of measures used to examine social
support have made it exceedingly difficult to understand the unique contributions of this phenomenon and to differentiate its effects from those of

199

other psychological and psychosocial variables. These difficulties take on added dimensions with a specific focus on the elderly.

This chapter begins with a broad look at social support and aging, with particular attention to analytical and related problems that must be considered when focusing on the social support needs and resources of the aged.

Two stressors prevalent among the elderly—bereavement and retirement—will be examined for the light they may shed on the relationship among social support, stressful life events, and health status. A third stressor, involuntary relocation, also will be examined with particular attention to the social meaning of the event and the extent to which its health effects may be mediated by social support.

Social Support and the Elderly: An Overview

In examining social support and the elderly, it is helpful to utilize Kahn's (1979) metaphor of the convoy to denote the movement of each individual through life surrounded by a set of others to whom he or she is related through the giving and receiving of social support.

As individuals age, people are added to or subtracted from their convoys through death, changes in job and family life, and geographic moves. With these changes, the potential of the social network for providing social support also varies over time.

Cross-sectional data suggest that the networks of older people are smaller than those of younger people, with significant changes around age 70 (Abeles, 1981, Kahn, 1979; Wan, 1982). The convoy characteristics of older persons additionally may include increasing asymmetry (receiving with less opportunity to give), increased instability, and changes in the type of interaction (relatively less receiving of affect and affirmation and increases in some forms of direct aid) (Kahn, 1979).

Despite a contracting social world (Rosow, 1974), as a consequence of the death of friends and relatives, geographic moves, and so forth, most of the elderly have the basic ingredients for social support. Approximately 56% of the elderly are married, and four out of five have at least one surviving child (Treas, 1977). Among the 95% of the elderly who are noninstitutionalized, approximately three-fourths see their children on a weekly basis (Shanas, 1979). For elderly parents living in in-law apartments or in the same neighborhood as their adult children, contacts may be of such frequency as to render the parents almost invisible. The latter often are so well integrated into the daily family routine that their adult children fail to report their almost daily contacts as visits (Stueve & Lien, 1979).

These statistics suggest a high degree of social contact for many of the elderly; however, other facts should not be overlooked. Of the population aged 65 and above in the 1970s and 1980s for example, greater proportions were women, widowed, and very old than in previous times. Indeed, the number of elderly women past age 85 doubled between 1900 and 1975, suggesting a greater number of frail elderly and of persons whose offspring are themselves in the period of past-prime adulthood (Pilisuk & Minkler, 1980).

Little evidence exists in support of the notion that the relationship among social networks, social support, and health status may be different for the elderly than for other age groups (House, Robbins, & Metzner, 1982; Kasl & Berkman, 1981). However, to the extent that social support may influence health status by leading to a more generalized sense of control (Antonovsky, 1979), the elderly—particularly if they are isolated or institutionalized—may be at a disadvantage. Schulz (1980) has reviewed an impressive array of studies suggesting that lack of personal autonomy may account for some of the negative effects observed among the elderly, particularly in institutional settings. In one such study, Langer and Rodin (1976) revealed that nursing home residents who were given a plant to care for and encouraged to participate more actively in their own care had an 18-month mortality rate only half that of the control group.

Both sense of control and social support are shown in this chapter to constitute key contextual variables that help determine the nature and intensity of the impact of major stressors on the health of the aged. In particular, the manner in which social support may work to mediate the effects of bereavement, retirement, and relocation on health status, without itself having a direct causal effect, will be discussed.

Special Research Problems

The difficulties inherent in examining the social support and health relationship are compounded by several factors in work with the elderly. As several researchers have noted (Satariano & Syme, 1981; Timiras, 1972) it is difficult to differentiate analytically among disease processes, the processes of normal aging, and the disease outcomes or exacerbations associated with a stressful life event or process (e.g., retirement or bereavement). Relatedly, traditional definitions of health, based on an absence of disease model, are particularly inappropriate with reference to those aged 65 and over, an estimated 86% of whom have at least one chronic illness (Shanas & Maddox, 1976).

Although gerontologists increasingly have urged the redefinition of health of the elderly in terms of functional ability and autonomy (Branch, 1980; Hickey, 1980), this perspective, for the most part, has yet to be operationalized and used by researchers in social epidemiology and related disciplines. Instead, the research on social support and health in older age groups has tended to focus on mortality rates and/or on morbidity measures and self-reported health status. With the partial exception of the latter, which carries its own set of biases and problematic elements, none of these measures is likely to capture the quality-of-life dimensions of health status of the elderly.

Problems in the definition and measurement of social support also become compounded in studies specifically of the elderly. Thus, excluded from most definitions of social support is the instrumental or tangible support that is of particular importance to many of the aged. Over one-third of the elderly require some degree of long-term supportive service, and an estimated 80–90% of this instrumental support is provided by family members (Brody, 1980); therefore, the need for expanding the definition of social support to include this often-neglected support dimension is clear.

Bereavement, retirement, and relocation are all situations characterized by a presumed loss of support. A final research problem in examining social support and aging involves the difficulty in determining whether the health outcomes witnessed are a function of the buffering effect of social support or of the presence or absence of some minimal level of support required for the maintenance of health and self-esteem. It is beyond the scope of this chapter to examine this problem in detail, but critical questions for researchers studying subgroups within the aged population at particular risk for major support losses will be discussed.

Bereavement

The notion that bereavement places the surviving spouse at elevated risk for mortality and/or morbidity has been widely and for the most part uncritically accepted by researchers. Several comprehensive reviews of the bereavement literature have been conducted (Jacobs & Ostfeld, 1977; Kasl, 1977; Klerman & Izen, 1977; Misczynski, 1982; Stroebe et al., 1982), and have been generally supportive of the thesis of a strong adverse relationship between death of a spouse and health status. At the same time, these reviews dramatically point up the fragile nature of the data base on which that thesis rests.

Misczynski (1982) thus has noted that, even considering only the 10–12 studies that met the criteria of adequate sample size and suitable comparison groups at that date, serious research problems are apparent in the areas of study design, methodology, field procedures, and data analysis.

The earliest bereavement studies of note (March, 1912; Kraus & Lilienfeld, 1959) thus demonstrated significantly higher age-specific mortality rates for widowed than for married and divorced persons, but failed to take into account the duration of widowhood. Because the effects of bereavement are believed to be most pronounced in the first 2 years, and probably in the first 6 months after the death, such analyses may be expected to reflect only diluted effects of bereavement (Kasl, 1977).

In a now-classic study, Parkes, Benjamin, and Fitzgerald (1969) corrected for this problem in a 9-year follow-up of 4,486 widowers aged 55 and over. A gradual decrease was observed in the mortality rate of widowers from 40% excess mortality in the first 6 months to the rate of the married controls by the fifth year. On examination of the disease-specific causes of mortality, Parkes further found that close to half of the deaths occurring in the first 6 months of bereavement were attributable to heart disease. The possibility of inflated rates of heart disease mortality due to inaccurate recording of the cause of death on death certificates was not ruled out by the investigators. However—and without dismissing other possible explanations, such as the effects of a joint unfavorable environment or of homogamy (unfit marrying unfit)—they did suggest that if either of the latter were the cause, a greater rate of both spouses dying of the same disease would have been observed.

The Parkes study suffered its own set of methodological problems, including lack of attention to loss by migration, slightly older subjects than controls, and the retention of remarried and hence possibly healthier widows in the cohort. At the same time, the Parkes "broken heart" study remains something of a landmark in the bereavement literature and perhaps more than any other work has helped draw attention to the relationship between death of a spouse and excess mortality in surviving mates.

Two additional studies confirming the finding of an elevated mortality rate in the first 6 months of bereavement (Rees & Lutkins, 1967; Ward, 1976) examined mortality rates of widows and widowers alike; both found the highest mortality among widowed men during the first 6 months of bereavement. Although these studies, too, had methodological weaknesses, the gender difference finding is an important one, particularly from the perspective of social support, and will be discussed later.

Of the small number of bereavement studies that have utilized health indexes other than mortality rates as the dependent variable, three are worthy of note. Maddison and Viola's (1968) study of approximately 500 widows and matched controls in Boston and Australia demonstrated significantly more psychological and physical symptoms among widows than among controls, but little change in the number or severity of major diseases. Clayton (1974) similarly found significantly higher reported symptoms among bereaved subjects in St. Louis, but no significant differences in mortality rates or in the number of physician visits or hospitalizations.

In a carefully controlled, albeit small, panel study of 41 elderly bereaved subjects, Heyman and Gianturco (1973) found no significant changes on any of a variety of indicators of health status. The high mean age at widowhood in their sample (74 years) was seen by the investigators as possibly meaning that subjects were psychologically prepared for the event.

Only a large-scale bereavement study conducted by Helsing, Comstock and Szklo in 1981 meets most of the criteria of strong research design, methodology, and analysis. That study examined the mortality rates of 4032 white adult residents of Washington County, Maryland, who were widowed between 1963 and 1974. Cases and matched married controls were followed until 1975, with controls introduced for such potential confounding variables as cigarette smoking and socioeconomic status.

Although findings indicated a significantly higher mortality rate for widowed than for married men in all age groups, no evidence was found to support the observation of earlier researchers (Parkes et al., 1969; Rees & Lutkins, 1967; Young, Benjamin, & Fitzgerald, 1963) of higher death rates in the first 2 years and particularly the first 6 months of bereavement.

Discussion

The findings of bereavement literature offer some interesting insights into social support and health. The observation in several studies of significant sex differences in relative risk associated with bereavement suggests that the marital relationship may well play differential supportive roles by gender (see also Depner & Ingersoll, 1982; Lopata, 1975).

Similarly, the observation that older bereaved individuals, and particularly older women, may be less at risk for adverse health outcomes of bereavement than their younger counterparts is of interest, and may relate in part to the "on-timing" of the event in older couples (Neugarten, 1979) and the anticipatory socialization enabling them to prepare for and rehearse the bereavement role as peers go through this experience.

A limitation of the bereavement literature to date lies in its tendency to ignore those events prior to and intimately connected with the death of the spouse that may themselves influence the health outcomes of the surviving mate. In our own research (Satariano, Minkler, & Langhauser, 1984) among 678 elderly residents of Alameda County, California, illness of a mate within the previous 6 months proved more strongly associated with self-rated health status than any other variable. Additional research is needed to determine whether a prebereavement period, particularly one characterized by extensive care giving and/or decreased social support from the spouse, may help to explain postbereavement declines in health status.

Social Support Interventions
and Postbereavement Morbidity

In the only major research study to examine the effectiveness of intentional supportive interventions in lowering postbereavement morbidity and/or mortality, Raphael (1977) followed 200 recently bereaved widows at risk for postbereavement morbidity and randomly allocated them to treatment and control groups. Members of the treatment group received specific support for grief and the encouragement of mourning over a 3-month period, and control group members received no intervention.

Results of the 13-month follow-up revealed a significant lowering of morbidity in the treatment group, with the most significant impact occurring in those subjects who reported having received little support from their social networks through the bereavement crisis.

The small number of subjects in this study and the restriction of the sample to widows under age 60 severely limit the generalizability of findings. In addition, the brevity of the follow-up period prevented the analysis of long-term morbidity and mortality trends. Raphael's study is important, however, in pointing up the potential role of intentional social support interventions as a buffer for negative health outcomes of bereavement and in suggesting a promising avenue for further research and practice.

Retirement

As Kasl noted, "retirement can be associated with so many important changes in one's life situation that the potential for adverse health effects should be overwhelming." At the same time, however, it is "so richly embedded in a network of individual and social influences . . . that any hope of being able to trace health changes to retirement *per se* appears small" (Kasl, 1977, p. 202).

In fact, there appears to be a general consensus among researchers that retirement itself does not adversely affect health (Eisdorfer & Wilkie, 1977; Kasl, 1980; Sheppard, 1976; Wan, 1982). Yet the problems implicit in studying this relationship and the methodological limitations of most of the existing research warrant caution in making such judgments.

Debate over the validity of viewing retirement as a major stress inducer or life event has pointed up the importance of taking into account such issues as the person's *degree of control* over the event (i.e., mandatory versus voluntary retirement), the *timing* of its occurrence in the life cycle, and the *stage* of the retirement process in which the phenomenon is being examined (Kasl, 1980; Minkler, 1981; Wan, 1982).

The latter concern has given rise to a process approach to retirement, which enables the researcher to differentiate among the individual's responses to the retirement event prior to, during, and at different intervals following its occurrence. It is beyond the scope of this chapter to examine and critique the process approach to retirement (see Atchley, 1977; Minkler, 1981); the usefulness of such a perspective is suggested, however, in empirical studies demonstrating differential morbidity and/or mortality at different points in the retirement process (Haynes, McMichael, & Tyroler, 1977; Martin & Doran, 1966).

In the most frequently cited such study, Haynes and colleagues (1977) examined longitudinally the patterns and correlates of mortality among upper- and lower-status blue-collar workers near compulsory retirement (age 65) in two U.S. rubber tire companies.

Elevated mortality rates were observed 3–4 years after retirement, and lower-status workers were more likely to die within 3 years of retirement than higher-status workers. This finding was compatible with Martin and Doran's (1966) observation of serious illness peaking 4–6 years following the retirement event. Moreover, the results of both studies appeared to support Stokes and Maddox's (1967) finding of a marked decrease in life satisfaction among blue-collar workers 3–5 years after retirement. Burgess (1958) and others also have shown poorer postretirement adjustment among blue-collar workers, and Palmore (1971) has suggested a possible link among retirement, social support, and longevity. In his view, when retirement involves the relinquishing of a person's most meaningful social contacts—as is more frequently the case among blue-collar than among white-collar workers—the resultant diminished involvement and activity may contribute to the shortening of the life span.

A few studies have suggested that, rather than shortening the life span, retirement may in fact result in improved health status (Ryser & Sheldon, 1969; Shanas, 1962; Thompson & Streib, 1959). The more frequent and well-substantiated finding, however, is of no significant association between retirement and health status (Ekerdt, Bosse, & Goldie, 1983; Kasl, 1980; Wan, 1982; Streib & Schneider, 1971).

The strongest evidence for this position is provided in Wan's (1982) prospective study utilizing four waves of data from the U.S. Social Security Administration's Longitudinal Retirement History Study (LRHS). Retirement *per se* was found to have no significant effect on health status in this six-year study of 5884 men and women aged 58 and over. However, a syn-ergistic effect of retirement in combination with other life events was ob-served, pointing up the importance of viewing retirement and other major stressors at least partially in terms of their joint effects on health status. Social networks were not found to have a direct effect on health, but they *did* appear to have a direct negative effect on the amount of life change experienced. These findings led Wan to conclude that social support is most appropriately viewed as a contextual factor that mediates the impacts of life events on health, principally by reducing the amount of change expe-rienced in the first place. Although Wan's carefully controlled prospective study makes a major contribution to the literature on retirement and health status, the sample selection methods used may have introduced important biases, particularly in the area of socioeconomic status, which may limit the generalizability of findings.

With the exception of the Wan study, little of the research on retirement and health sheds much light on the relationship among retirement, social support, and health status. At the same time, several findings are suggestive of avenues for further research.

Palmore's (1971) hypothesis that retirement may lead to increased mor-tality rates when it involves the relinquishing of a person's most valued social contacts suggests one such research direction. If, as several studies (Burgess, 1958; Haynes *et al.,* 1977; Martin & Doran, 1966) have suggested, a significant difference exists in the health outcomes and postretirement adjustment of blue- versus white-collar workers, an investigation of the role of differentially disruptive social networks in influencing these retirement outcomes would be informative.

Gore's (1978) study of social support and involuntary job loss may suggest a useful avenue for retirement research. In that study, recently unem-ployed men characterized as high on indexes of social support were found to have fewer physiological illness symptoms and to suffer less depression and self-blame than their counterparts who had little perceived social sup-port. Important differences exist, of course, between sudden job loss and retirement at the end of a career. However, the findings of Gore's study suggest the utility of research aimed at discovering whether social support may play a similar role in buffering the negative consequences of invol-untary retirement.

Lowenthal and Haven's (1968) widely quoted study of intimacy and adap-tion among the elderly also suggests useful research directions with respect to the potential role of social support in buffering the effects of stressful life changes, such as retirement. Among their sample of 280 elderly resi-dents of San Francisco, California, decreases in social interaction were sig-nificantly linked to depression in those lacking a confidant. Among those reporting that they did have someone to confide in, no such association was observed. Although this study did not focus specifically on retirement, the investigators noted that retired persons in their sample who had a confidant ranked as high in morale as those who were still working. In contrast, retired persons without confidants were almost twice as likely to be depressed as to be satisfied. Further research should be undertaken to look specifically at the influence of presence or absence of a confidant on health outcomes of retirement and to determine whether depression precedes or follows lack of social support.

Another area worthy of investigation derives from the finding of significant gender differences in retirement outcomes. Jacobson (1974) and others (Levy, 1980; Prentis, 1980) have reported that retirement is a more stressful event for both married and unmarried women than for men, primarily because of the greater importance attached by women to work-based social ties. This finding is a curious one, particularly given the fact that women tend to have a broader web of social relationships and more diverse set of confidants (Depner & Ingersoll, 1982). One possible factor contributing to the observed increased stressfulness of retirement for women may involve the fact that they are far more likely than men to experience two major losses—widowhood and retirement—within a short time of each other. This negative synergistic effect of retirement and widowhood applies to only a small proportion of retired women, however, and other factors that might contribute to the observed gender differences should be explored.

Studies on women and retirement have focused almost exclusively on women's adjustment to this event, and hence shed little light on health outcomes and the extent to which they may be related to or mediated by social network variables. These studies further have tended to underestimate the importance of class differences among women in influencing the retirement experience (Atchley, 1982). Further research taking into account class and cohort differences, possible synergistic effects of retirement and other life events, and the role of social supports in influencing health outcomes are needed to help clarify the actual extent of gender differences in the retirement experience and the extent to which such differences may in fact reflect different social support needs and resources.

Relocation

Unlike bereavement and retirement, geographic relocation occurs less frequently among the elderly than among younger adults. At the same time, the social meaning of this phenomenon and indications that unplanned or unintended moves may have negative health effects in the elderly warrant its investigation.

Several comprehensive reviews of the literature on relocation and the elderly (Carp, 1976; Kasl & Rosenfield, 1980; Lawton, 1980; Lawton & Nahemow, 1973) provide a good overview of this subject. In this chapter highlights of that literature will be used to examine the health effects of involuntary residential moves among the elderly.

Two forms of involuntary relocation—moves within the community and transfers from one institutional residence to another—will be examined separately. As will be shown, contextual variables including social support and perceived degree of control over the event appear to play a significant role in both types of moves, influencing the likelihood of adverse health effects. (It should be noted that the little empirical work available in the area of voluntary moves of the elderly also has demonstrated the importance of such variables as social support and sense of control in mitigating possible negative health effects [Schooler, 1980].)

Involuntary Moves within the Community

As Lawton (1980) has pointed out, the research on forced community relocation has, with a single exception, been done after the fact on those subjected to mass relocation, usually as a consequence of urban renewal. Fried's (1963) classic work, "Grieving for a Lost Home," and early studies by Neibanck (1968) on relocation of the elderly underscored the psychological distress of relocatees as a consequence of these moves, but failed to examine the possibility of changes in physical health status.

In the only carefully controlled longitudinal study in this area, Kasl and Rosenfield (1980), followed 225 elderly relocatees and 175 matched neighborhood controls in Connecticut and found no significant differences in 2-year mortality rates between cases and controls. However, some evidence of adverse health outcomes among the relocatees was suggested on a diversity of indicators, including self-rated health status, nursing home and hospital admissions, and physician visits.

Of particular relevance is the finding that although some cases experienced some decline in contact with friends, they were also more likely to report that their closest friend or confidant lived in the new building. Additionally, they reported knowing their neighbors in the new building better than in the old. The latter findings are in keeping with Wan's (1982) observation that social ties disrupted as a consequence of relocation or retirement frequently are renegotiated among the elderly, and thus these life changes do not result in an overall diminishing of social support.

A final and important observation from Kasl's study involved the finding that despite the *de facto* involuntary nature of the relocation, 63% of the cases perceived themselves as having chosen to move, and only 14% reported feeling that they had no choice in the decision. This high degree of perceived choice and a marked increase in environmental satisfaction among relocatees suggest again the importance of contextual factors in mediating potentially adverse health effects of the move itself.

In an effort to look specifically at the role of social networks in mediating relocation stress, Eckert (1983) followed 82 forced relocatees in five single-room occupancy (SRO) hotels in San Diego, California, and a comparison group of 75 SRO residents not subject to relocation. With the exception of those who were in poor health before the move and whose health continued to deteriorate afterward, little change was observed among relocatees in pre- and postmove health status. This finding was attributed in part to the facts that relocatees were given the choice of remaining within the SRO neighborhood and that most consequently did stay in the area. The social network characteristics of the SRO elderly (e.g., widely dispersed contacts within the neighborhood) were seen as highly adaptive to such moves and as serving an important role in mediating potential relocation stress.

Institutional Relocation

In contrast to the dearth of research on relocation of the elderly within the community, a large body of literature exists on the effects of moves out of, into, or between institutional environments. Interinstitutional relocation provides a particularly good natural experiment because such confounding variables as self-selection are largely controlled for.

In one of the earliest and best-known of these studies, Aldrich and Mendkoff (1963) followed the transfer to several institutions of 182 residents of a nursing home that was being closed down; 32% of the residents died in the year following relocation, with the highest death rate occurring in the first 3 months. This figure contrasted with an average annual death rate of 19% within the institution over the preceding 10-year period.

The findings of Aldrich and Mendkoff's study were typical of those reported in other early studies in this area (see Blenkner, 1967; Kasl, 1972; Lawton & Nahemow, 1973 for excellent reviews of this literature). More recent studies, however, have consistently failed to find a significant association between such interinstitutional transfers and mortality (Kasl & Rosenfield, 1980).

In discussing this phenomenon, Kasl and Berkman (1981) suggested that variations in the way the transfer process was handled may account for much of this discrepancy. Although other factors (e.g., differences in the quality of the new environment and problems in the comparability of cases and their nonrelocated controls) also must be considered, it is noteworthy that the literature increasingly has focused on the role of pretransfer preparation, social support, and other factors believed to moderate the potential effects of the move (Lebowitz, 1975; Novick, 1967; Pastalan, 1973).

Schultz and Brenner (1977) have suggested that carefully planned transfers and prerelocation preparation programs may decrease posttransfer mortality rates by increasing control or perceived sense of control among prospective relocatees. Additional studies (e.g., Marlowe, 1973) have suggested that to the extent that the new environment provides greater independence and opportunities for richer relationships, positive health outcomes and improved functional independence may be observed.

Research on relocation and the elderly, particularly Kasl's well-designed longitudinal study, has increased the understanding of some of the complexities involved in this life change. As with bereavement and retirement, however, there is a great need for carefully controlled prospective studies utilizing a process approach in examining adaptation to and impacts of involuntary residential moves. Research on the potential synergistic effects of relocation and such other stressors as retirement and bereavement would provide an important supplement to existing studies, which have tended to view these events in isolation. Finally, research is needed that focuses more specifically on the social network characteristics of relocatees and on the potential role of social networks and social support in mediating the health outcomes of relocation among the aged. The translation of research findings into policy and practice, particularly in the area of relocation preparation, should help minimize the potential adverse effects of relocation on the elderly.

Conclusion

The evidence presented in this chapter suggests that it is indeed premature to conclude that social support may play a particularly important or unique role in influencing the health of the elderly. Rather, what uniqueness there is about social support and health in aging appears to lie primarily in the special research problems inherent in studying the social support and health relationship in this age group.

The difficulty in differentiating analytically between disease processes, the processes of normal aging, and disease outcomes or exacerbations linked to such phenomena as retirement and bereavement hence were seen as only one of several special research problems complicating the study of social support and health in older adults. Major methodological weaknesses in research to date on the effects of bereavement, retirement, and relocation further suggest the need for caution in the interpretation of findings.

The extant literature does appear to support Wan's (1982) contention that social support is perhaps best viewed as a contextual variable that may mediate the health effects of major life stressors. Yet even this conclusion must be drawn tentatively because the bulk of the research examined was not designed to measure social networks or social support.

Although the findings of several studies have important implications for policymakers and practitioners (e.g., in pointing up the usefulness of relocation preparation for the elderly), the translation of such research findings into policy and practice must be accompanied by continued research attention to the outcomes of such implementation efforts.

Finally, of particular importance to a discussion of social support and health is a consideration of the potential for the political misuse of findings to rationalize cutbacks in major domestic programs for the elderly, the poor, and other groups in society. As early as 1978, the Report of the President's Commission on Mental Health cautioned that efforts to strengthen personal and community support systems carry with them the possibility that such supports may be used to "justify public policies which would withhold from various communities and individuals the resources they need to obtain professional and formal institutional services" (Snow & Gordon, 1980, p. 464).

Such justifications were utilized in the early 1980s to support the dismantling of major health and social service accomplishments of the preceding half-century. They present an important example of the potential for misuse of research findings on social support and health and one that researchers in this field have an ethical obligation to confront.

References

Abeles, R. P. (1981, July 11–18). *Social support, health and aging.* Paper presented at the International Congress of Gerontology, Hamburg, Germany.

Aldrich, C. K., & Mendkoff, L. (1963). Relocation of the aged and disabled: A mortality study. *Journal of American Geriatrics Society, 11,* 183–194.

Antonovsky, A. (1979). *Health, stress and coping.* San Francisco: Jossey Bass.

Atchley, R. (1977). *The social forces in later life* (2nd ed.) Monterey, CA: Wadsworth.

Atchley, R. (1982). The process of retirement: Comparing women and men. In M. Szinovacz (Ed.), *Women's retirement* (pp. 153–168). Beverly Hills, CA: Sage.

Blenkner, M. (1967). Environmental change and the aging individual. *The Gerontologist, 7,* 101–105.

Branch, L. (1980). Functional abilities of the elderly: An update on the Massachusetts Health Care panel study. In S. G. Haynes & M. Feinleib (Eds.), *Second conference on the epidemiology of aging* (pp. 737–768). Washington, DC: U.S. Department of Health and Human Services, National Institutes of Health Publication No. 80-969.

Brody, E. M. (1980). Women's changing roles and care of the aging family. In J. P. Hubbard (Ed.), *Aging: Agenda for the Eighties* (pp. 11–16). Washington, DC: Government Research Corporation.

Burgess, E. W. (1958). Occupational differences in attitudes toward retirement. *Journal of Gerontology, 13.*

Carp, F. (1976). Housing and living environments of older people. In R. H. Binstock & E. Shanas (Eds.), *Handbook of aging and the social sciences* (pp. 244–271). New York: Van Nostrand.

Clayton, P. J. (1974). Mortality and morbidity in the first year of widowhood. *Archives of General Psychiatry, 30,* 747–750.

Depner, C., & Ingersoll, B. (1982). Employment status and social support: The experience of mature women. In M. Szinovacz (Ed.), *Women's retirement: Policy implications of recent research* (pp. 61–76). Beverly Hills, CA: Sage.

Eckert, J. K. (1983). Dislocation and relocation of the urban elderly: Social networks as mediators of relocation stress. *Human Organization, 42,* 39–45.

Eisdorfer, C., & Wilkie, F. (1977). Stress, disease, aging and behavior. In J. Birren & K. W. Schaie (Eds.), *Handbook of the psychology of aging* (pp. 251–275). New York: Van Nostrand.

Ekerdt, D., Bosse, R., & Goldie, C. (1983). The effects of retirement on somatic complaints. *Journal of Psychosomatic Research, 27,* 61–67.

Fried, M. (1963). Grieving for a lost home. In L. H. Duhl (ed.) *The urban condition* (pp. 151–171). New York: Basic Books.

Gore, S. (1978). The effect of social support in moderating the health consequences of unemployment. *Journal of Health and Social Behavior, 19* (June), 157–165.

Haynes, S., McMichael, A., & Tyroler, H. (1977). The relationship of normal involuntary retirement to early mortality among U.S. rubber workers. *Social Science and Medicine, 11,* 105–114.

Helsing, K., Comstock, G. W., & Szklo, M. (1981). Mortality after bereavement. *American Journal of Epidemiology, 114*(1), 41–52.

Heyman, D., & Gianturco, D. (1973). Long-term adaptation by the elderly to bereavement. *Journal of Gerontology, 28*(3), 359–362.

Hickey, T. (1980). *Health and aging.* Monterey, CA: Brooks/Cole.

House, J. S., Robbins, C., & Metzner, H. L. (1982). The association of social relationships and activities with mortality: Prospective evidence from the Tecumseh Community Health Study. *American Journal of Epidemiology, 116*(1), 123–140.

Jacobs, S., & Ostfeld, A. An epidemiological review of the mortality of bereavement. *Psychosomatic Medicine,* 1977, *39*(5), 344–357.

Jacobson, C. J. (1974). Rejection of the retiree role: A study of female industrial workers in their 50's. *Human Relations, 27,* 477–492.

Kahn, R. L. (1979). Aging and social support. In M. W. Riley (Ed.), *Aging from birth to death: Interdisciplinary perspectives* (pp. 77–92). Boulder, CO: Westview Press.

Kasl, S. V. (1972). Physical and mental health effects of involuntary relocation and institutionalization on the elderly: A review. *American Journal of Public Health, 62,* 379–384.

Kasl, S. V. (1977). Contributions of social epidemiology to study in psychosomatic medicine. In S. V. Kasl & F. Reichsman (Eds.), *Advances in psychosomatic medicine: Epidemiologic studies in psychosomatic medicine* (pp. 106–223). Basel, Switzerland: Karger.

Kasl, S. V. (1980). The impact of retirement. In C. L. Cooper & R. Payne (Eds.), *Current concerns in occupational stress* (pp. 137–186). London: Wiley.

Kasl, S. V., & Berkman, L. (1981). Psychosocial influences on health status of the elderly: The perspective of social epidemiology. In J. L. McGaugh & S. B. Kiesler (Eds.), *Aging: Biology and behavior* (pp. 345–385). New York: Academic Press.

Kasl, S. V., & Rosenfield, S. (1980). The residential environment and its impact on the mental health of the aged. In J. Birren & B. Sloane (Eds.), *Handbook of mental health and aging* (pp. 468–498). Englewood Cliffs, NJ: Prentice Hall.

Klerman, G. L., & Izen, J. (1977). The effects of bereavement and grief on physical health and general wellbeing. In S. Kasl & F. Reichsman (Eds.), *Advances in psychosomatic medicine: Epidemiologic studies in psychosomatic medicine* (pp. 64–104). Basel, Switzerland: Karger.

Kraus, A. S., & Lilienfeld, A. (1959). Some epidemiologic aspects of the high mortality rate in the young widowed group. *Journal of Chronic Disease, 10,* 207–217.

Kulys, R., & Tobin, S. S. (1980). Older people and their responsible others. *Social Work,* March, 138–145.

Langer, E. J., & Rodin, J. (1976). The effects of choice and enhanced personal responsibility for the aged: A field experiment in an institutional setting. *Journal of Personality and Social Psychology, 34*(2), 191–198.

Lawton, M. P. (1980). *Environment and aging.* Monterey, CA: Brooks/Cole.

Lawton, M. P., & Nahemow, L. (1973). Ecology and the aging process. In C. Eisdorfer & M. P. Lawton (Eds.), *The psychology of adult development and aging* (pp. 619–674). Washington, DC: American Psychological Association.

Lawton, M. Powell. (1980). The impact of the environment on aging and behavior. In J. Birren & B. Sloane (Eds.), *Handbook of mental health and aging* (pp. 276–301). Englewood Cliffs, NJ: Prentice Hall.

Lebowitz, B. D. (1975). Age and fearfulness: Personal and situational factors, *Journal of Gerontology, 30,* 696–700.

Levy, S. M. (1980). The adjustment of older women: Effects of chronic ill health and attitudes toward retirement. *International Journal of Aging and Human Development, 12,* 93–110.

Lopata, H. Z. (1975). Widowhood: Societal factors in life-span disruption and alternatives. In N. Datan & L. H. Gindsberg (Eds.), *Life span developmental psychology.* New York: Academic Books.

Lowenthal, M. F., & Haven, C. (1968). Interaction and adaptation: Intimacy as a critical variable. In B. L. Neugarten (Ed.), *Middle age and aging* (pp. 390–400). Chicago: University of Chicago Press.

Maddison, D., & Viola, A. (1968). The health of widows in the year following retirement. *Journal of Psychosomatic Research, 12*(4), 297–306.

March, L. (1912). Some researches concerning the factors of mortality. *Journal of the Statistical Society, London Journal Series A, 75*(5), 505–538.

Marlowe, R. A. (1973, May). *Effects of environment on elderly state hospital relocatees.* Paper presented at the Annual Meeting of the Pacific Sociological Association, Scottsdale, AZ.

Martin, J., & Doran, A. (1966). Evidence concerning the relationship between health and retirement, *Sociological Review, 14,* 329.

Minkler, M. (1981). Research on the health effects of retirement: An uncertain legacy, *Journal of Health and Social Behavior, 22*(June), 117–130.

Misczynski, M. (1982, October). *Study of the effects of bereavement on morbidity and mortality among the elderly.* Excerpts from a grant proposal submitted to NIA.

Neugarten, B. (1979). Time, age and the life cycle. *The American Journal of Psychiatry, 136,* 887–894.

Niebanck, P. L. (1968). *Relocation and urban planning: From obstacle to opportunity,* Philadelphia: University of Pennsylvania Press.

Novick, L. J. (1967). Easing the stress of moving day. *Hospitals, 41,* 64–74.

Palmore, E. (1971). The relative importance of social factors in predicting longevity. In E. Palmore & F. Jeffers (Eds.), *Prediction of life span* (pp. 237–248). Lexington, MA: Lexington Books.

Parkes, C. M., Benjamin, B., & Fitzgerald, R. G. (1969). Broken hearts: A statistical study of increased mortality among widowers. *British Medical Journal, 1*, 740–743.

Pastalan, L. A. (1973). Involuntary environmental relocation. In W. F. E. Preiser (Ed.), *Environmental design research* (Vol. 2), Stroudsburg, PA: Dowden.

Pilisuk, M., & Minkler, M. (1980). Supportive networks: Life ties for the elderly, *Journal of Social Issues, 36*(2), 95–116.

Pilisuk, M., Montgomery, M., & Parks, S. H. (1983, September). *Health status and supportive relationships among older adults.* Paper presented at the Annual Meeting of the Gerontological Society of America, San Francisco, CA.

Prentis, R. S. (1980). White-collar working women's perceptions of retirement. *The Gerontologist, 20*, 90–95.

Raphael, B. (1977). Preventive intervention with the recently bereaved. *Archives of General Psychiatry, 34*, 1450–1454.

Rees, W. D., & Lutkins, S. G. (1967). Mortality of bereavement. *British Medical Journal, 4*, 13–16.

Rosow, I. (1974). *Socialization to old age.* Berkeley: University of California Press.

Ryser, C., & Sheldon, A. (1969). Retirement and health. *Journal of the American Geriatrics Society, 17*, 180–190.

Satariano, W., Minkler, M., & Langhauser, C. (1984). The significance of an ill spouse for assessing health differences in an elderly population. *Journal of the American Geriatrics Society, 32*, 187–190.

Satariano, W., & Syme, S. L. (1981). Life changes and disease in elderly populations. In J. L. McGaugh & S. B. Kiesler (Eds.), *Aging: Biology and behavior* (pp. 311–324). New York: Academic Press.

Schooler, K. K. (1980). Response of the elderly to the environment: A stress-theoretic perspective. In M. P. Lawton, P. G. Windley, & T. O. Byerts (Eds.), *Aging and the environment: Directions and perspectives.* New York: Garland STPM Press.

Schulz, R. (1980). Aging and Control. In J. Garber & M. Seligman (Eds.), *Human helplessness: Theory and applications* (pp. 261–277). New York: Academic Press.

Schulz, R., & Brenner, G. (1977). Relocation of the aged: A review and theoretical analysis. *Journal of Gerontology, 32*, 323–333.

Shanas, E. (1962). *The health of older people, a social survey.* Cambridge, MA: Harvard University Press.

Shanas, E. (1979). The family as a social support system in old age. *The Gerontologist, 18*, 169–174.

Shanas, E., & Maddox, G. L. (1976). Aging health and the organization of health resources. In R. H. Binstock & E. Shanas (Eds.), *Handbook of aging and the social sciences* (pp. 592–618). New York: Van Nostrand.

Sheppard, H. L. (1976). Work and retirement. In R. H. Binstock & E. Shanas (Eds.), *Handbook of aging and the social sciences* (pp. 386–406). New York: Van Nostrand.

Snow, D. L., and Gordon, J. B. (1980). Social network analysis and intervention with the elderly. *The Gerontologist, 20*, 463–467.

Stokes, R. G., & Maddox, G. L. (1967). Some social factors on retirement adaptation. *Journal of Gerontology, 22*, 329–333.

Streib, G., & Schneider, C. J. (1971). *Retirement in American society,* Ithaca, NY: Cornell University Press.

Stroebe, W., Stroebe, M. S., Gergen, K. J., & Gergen, M. (1982). The effects of bereavement on mortality: A sociopsychological analysis. In J. R. Eiser (Ed.), *Social psychology and behavioral medicine.* New York: Wiley.

Stueve, A., & Lein, L. (1979, October). *Problems in network analysis: The case of a missing person.* Paper presented at the 32nd Annual Meeting of the Gerontological Society of America, Washington, DC.

Thompson, W. E., & Streib, G. (1959). Situational determinants, health and economic deprivation in retirement. *Journal of Social Issues*, 14(2), 18–34.

Timiras, P. (1972). *Developmental physiology and aging.* New York: MacMillan.

Treas, J. (1977). Family support systems for the aged: Some social and demographic considerations. *The Gerontologist, 17.*

Wan, T. T. (1982). *Stressful life events, social support networks and gerontological health.* Lexington, MA: Lexington Books.

Ward, A. M. (1976). Mortality of bereavement. *British Medical Journal, 1,* 700–702.

Young, M., Benjamin, B., & Fitzgerald, R. G. (1963). Broken heart: A statistical study of increased mortality among widowers. *British Medical Journal, 1,* 740–743.

PART III

Social Support and Disease Etiology

Social Support and Mental Health in Community Samples*

Ronald C. Kessler and Jane D. McLeod

Introduction

In this chapter we review evidence for an effect of social support on mental health. As the review makes clear, there is compelling evidence that support is significantly associated with well-being and with the absence of psychological distress in normal population samples. Most researchers have interpreted this association as indicative of an influence of support on mental health. However, others have noted that mental illness can reduce access to support (Strack & Coyne, 1983) and that social competence might be responsible for some aspects of both support and emotional functioning (Henderson, Byrne, & Duncan-Jones, 1981). There is no clear way to adjudicate among these alternative interpretations with the data available from normal population surveys.

Several commentators have nonetheless concluded that support is consequential for mental health on the basis of evidence from other sources (House, 1981; Turner, 1983). They have cited animal studies of stress responses as a function of isolation from a mother or from litter mates, social

*This research was supported, in part, by NIMH Grants 37706 and 16806 and by the National Institutes of Health Biomedical Research Support Grant to the Vice President for Research at the University of Michigan. We would like to thank Sheldon Cohen and James House for comments on an earlier version of the chapter.

219

psychological analogue experiments in which subjects were placed under conditions of stress either in the presence or absence of a confederate, intervention experiments for people who are in the midst of a life crisis, and longitudinal surveys of change in support and mental health over time. All of these paradigms yield some evidence for a health-promoting effect of human companionship.

This convergence of evidence, combined with knowledge that support has been linked to a broad array of physical and mental health outcomes in a wide range of stress situations, has led to optimism about the potential for designing experimental public health interventions around the concept of social support. Experiments of this sort could document causal influences rigorously while demonstrating the effectiveness of programs to reduce risk of illness in target populations.

As Gottlieb (Chapter 15 in this volume) has argued, intervention experiments should be grounded in knowledge, or at least strong inferences, about which specific aspects of support are likely to be consequential for health. This knowledge will build upon itself through successive evaluation, refinement, and retesting as evidence from these experiments begins to accumulate. This knowledge has not yet become available and hence the design of interventions has been based, in part, on nonexperimental normal population research.

Unfortunately, normal population research has generated scant evidence about which specific aspects of support are linked to mental health and under what conditions. Only a small number of published studies have used multidimensional support inventories of the sort advocated by House and Kahn (Chapter 5 in this volume), and the extant studies have not been summarized in a way that highlights the different influences of these various dimensions.

In the following analysis we review and summarize the available evidence comprehensively. As we shall demonstrate, there is consistent evidence about which aspects of support are associated with mental health and which are not.

The Sample of Studies Reviewed

The review is based on normal population surveys that consider support in relation to stressful life experiences and that focus on mental health outcomes. Studies including individuals who have experienced one specific type of event (e.g., birth of a child) and those sampling a specific segment of the population (e.g., the elderly) are excluded. We located 23 studies that fit these inclusion criteria; 14 of these used life events as the stress measure, 4 used chronic strains, and 5 used both. The studies are described in Table 11.1.

Analysis is limited to normal population studies because we consider the two other most commonly studied populations—students and victims of particular crises—too restrictive for making inferences about general patterns. Much can be learned from a comparative analysis of the relationship between support and adjustment in different crisis situations, but there are too few studies available for this sort of systematic comparison.

Most of the studies reviewed assessed mental health with symptom-screening scales that give information about diagnostically nonspecific psychological distress. A few studies are based on clinically specific measures of depression or anxiety or on transformed screening scales that make inferences about psychiatric caseness.

Early research on social support and mental health documented simple zero-order associations without investigating possible processes. These studies were important in calling attention to social support but they served more to raise questions than to answer them. It is quite clear from the accumulated results of this early work that a broad range of support indicators are positively related to mental health in the normal population and that the same array of measures discriminate psychiatric cases from normal population controls. Several comprehensive reviews of this literature have been reported (Heller & Swindle, in press; House, 1981; Leavy, 1983; Mitchell, Billings, & Moos, 1982; Mueller, 1980; Turner, 1983).

Our review begins where the others left off, and focuses on studies that examine support in the context of stress. In the absence of a simultaneous consideration of support and stress it is difficult to get beyond a simple statement that support is related to health in some way, because there is no way to determine if this relationship is confined to those who are exposed to stressful life events or if it is present among all people irrespective of stress exposure. This limitation of focus is critical, as the part played by support is intimately entangled with its role in relation to stress.

Three questions are asked of these studies: First, is there evidence of stress buffering—that the relationship between support and mental health is stronger under conditions of high stress than those of low stress? Second, in those cases where stress buffering exists, does support influence mental health under conditions of low stress? Third, in the absence of stress buffering is there an association between support and mental health independent of stress?[1]

---

[1]Some reviews have also considered the effect of support on stress prevention (Mitchell *et al.*, 1982; Wheaton, 1983). We have not considered this effect, although it is useful to note that if support prevents the occurrence of stresses that are secondary to a serious life crisis, this will appear as a buffer on the crisis impact.

Table 11.1

Studies Reviewed

Study number and citation	Sample	Stress measure	Mental health measure
IA. Cross-sectional life event studies			
1. Andrews *et al.*, 1978	n = 863, aged 20–69, in suburban Sydney	63-item weighted life event inventory[a]	General Health Questionnaire, dichotomized at a cutpoint of 4
2. Lin *et al.*, 1979	n = 170, Chinese–Americans in Washington, DC	20-item weighted life event inventory	24-item nonspecific distress scale
3. Schaefer *et al.*, 1981	n = 100, aged 45–65, white, in Alameda County, California, interviewed monthly for one year[b]	24-item undesirable event inventory, divided into loss and nonloss subinventories	Hopkins Symptom Check-List, Bradburn Negative Morale Scale
4. Wilcox, 1981	n = 320, aged 18 and over, in a large southwestern community	60-item weighted life event inventory	Langner Scale, Profile of Mood States, Tension subscale
5. Bell *et al.*, 1982	n = 2029, aged 16 and over, in southeastern United States	30-item undesirable life event inventory	18-item depression scale
6. Husaini *et al.*, 1982	n = 965, aged 18–75, white, married persons in rural counties in southeastern United States	52-item life event inventory	Center for Epidemiologic Studies Depression scale
7. Cleary and Mechanic, 1983	n = 1026, aged 18 and over, married persons in central Wisconsin	15-item undesirable life event inventory	9-item depression scale
IB. Cross-sectional chronic strain studies			
1. House and Wells, 1978	n = 1809, white men, hourly work force of a manufacturing plant in a small northeastern city	7 separate items for occupational stress	Health Opinion Survey
2. LaRocco *et al.*, 1980	n = 636, men employed in 23 different occupations in eastern, southern, and midwestern United States	5 separate items for perceived job stress, 3 scales for job-related strain: job dissatisfaction (4 items), work load dissatisfaction (3 items), boredom (3 items)	6-item depression scale, 4-item anxiety scale

222

3. Cohen *et al.*, 1982	$n = 602$, aged 18 and over, in New York City	5-item fear scale, 6-item social problems scale, 5-item violent crimes scale, 1 chronic illness item	8-item nonspecific distress scale
4. Kessler and Essex, 1982	$n = 2300$, aged 18–65, in Chicago	3-item economic strain scale, 7-item housework strain scale, number of preschoolers in the home	11-item depression scale
IC. Cross-sectional life event and chronic strain studies			
1. Brown and Harris, 1978	$n = 458$, women in Camberwell, England	Presence of severe event or major difficulty	Caseness designation for depression based on the Present State Examination
2. Aneshensel and Stone, 1982	$n = 1003$, in Los Angeles	12-item loss event inventory, perceived strain measure, coded 1–4 on the basis of scores on three scales of chronic strains (financial, marital, work-related)	Center for Epidemiologic Studies Depression scale, dichotomized at cutpoint of 16
3. Mitchell *et al.*, in press	$n = 318$, 159 community resident–spouse pairs	15-item undesirable life event inventory, 4-item chronic strain scale (medical condition, childrens' health problems, work stress, negative home environment)	18-item depression scale
IIA. Panel life-event studies			
1. Eaton, 1978	$n = 720$, two-wave panel (2-year interval) in New Haven	62-item life event inventory	Gurin Scale
2. Warheit, 1979	$n = 517$, two-wave panel (3-year interval) in southeastern United States	23-item weighted loss event inventory	18-item depresssion scale
3. Williams *et al.*, 1981	$n = 2234$, aged 14–61, two-wave panel (12-month interval) in Seattle	20-item weighted undesirable life event inventory	38-item General Well-Being Scale

(Continued)

Table 11.1 (*Continued*)

Study number and citation	Sample	Stress measure	Mental health measure
4. Dean and Ensel, 1982	n = 871, aged 17–70, two-wave panel (12-month interval) in northern New York State	118-item life event inventory	Center for Epidemiologic Studies Depression Scale
5. Thoits, 1982	See IIA1	26-item undesirable life event inventory, 2-item undesirable health-related events inventory	Gurin Scale
6. McFarlane et al., 1983	n = 428, subjects from practices of 10 family physicians, three-wave panel (6-month interval) in Hamilton, Ontario	Life events, neutral or undesirable no-control events, all other events, and total events	Langner Scale
7. Thoits, in press	n = 1106, aged 18–65, two-wave panel (4-year interval) in Chicago	19-item undesirable life event inventory, 2-item undesirable health-related events inventory	12-item anxiety scale, 11-item depression scale
IIB. Panel life event and chronic strain studies			
1. Henderson et al., 1981	n = 231, four-wave panel (4-month interval)	73-item list of recent experiences, acute and chronic, weighted	General Health Questionnaire
2. Pearlin et al., 1981	See IIA7	Presence of any of three work disruption events, 9-item economic strain scale	10-item depression scale

[a]Unless explicitly stated to be otherwise, life event scales are unweighted and include desirable, ambiguous, and undesirable events.
[b]Although these data are from a panel study, the analysis is cross-sectional.

We consider how the answers to these questions differ across three aspects of support: membership in affiliative networks, feelings of being emotionally supported, and perceived availability of support. These three are the only aspects of support that appear enough times in the studies reviewed to allow summary statements to be made about them. These aspects and the studies in which they were measured are presented in Table 11.2.

Membership in affiliative networks encompasses all measures related to the number of members in the respondent's social network, the number and types of organizations to which the respondent belongs, and the frequency of contact with these people and organizations. We conceptualize measures in this category as defining the extent to which the respondents are integrated into the social world around them. Emotional support includes measures of intimacy, confiding, and feeling esteemed by closest associates. These measures are intended to reflect general feelings of being loved and cared for as opposed to perceptions of access to specific types of supportive actions. The latter comprise the third category, perceived availability of support. This category includes measures of the respondents' perceptions of the availability of tangible, informational, or crisis emotional support. It differs from emotional support in that its measures ask about specific actions that can be provided to the respondent.

Information about three other types of support measures that have not figured prominently in our review also appear in Table 11.2: measures of recent use of support, measures of the adequacy of support, and measures that we classified invalid. The recent-use measures were excluded from the analysis because they confound stress with support, as shown by Cohen and Hoberman (1983).[2] The adequacy measures were also excluded because, in a similar way, they confound need for support with access.

Although it is obvious why we would want to discard invalid measures, it might not be obvious why we classify marital status as invalid in Table 11.2. The main reason is that although married people have higher levels of support than their never-married or previously married counterparts, it is unclear in the absence of more explicit support measures whether a relationship between marital status and mental health is evidence of a support effect. Married persons enjoy a well-established mental health advan-

---

[2]Several studies have looked at recent support in a different framework by questioning respondents about use of support after learning that they have experienced a recent life event (Husaini & Neff, 1980; Lieberman, 1982; Lin, Woefel, & Light, 1982). All three studies then examined the relationship between use of support and distress *among those who reported an event*. In two of the three, use of support was associated with reduced distress, whereas in the third support was unrelated to mental health outcome. More work along this line needs to be done to examine explicitly the dimensions of support use that are influential on mental health in the face of a stressful life event.

Table 11.2

Summary of Support Scales

Study number[a]	Scale

Membership in affiliative networks: number of friends and relatives, membership in clubs and church, frequency of interaction

IA1	6-item scale
IA1	5-item scale concerned exlusively with church and clubs
IA2	9-item scale
IA3	9-item scale including marital status as one item
IA6	3 separate items
IB3	1 item, frequency of visits with friends and relatives
IB3	6-item scale
IB4	9-item scale
IC2	1 item: number of close relatives, friends
IIA1	7 separate items
IIA2	1 item: number of close relatives nearby
IIA3	9-item scale
IIA5	4 separate items
IIB1	16-item scale: integration and perceived access

Emotional support: presence of an intimate, perception that others care for you, hold you in esteem, and consider you a part of a network of mutual obligation

IA3	4-item scale: each item a weighted count of the number of supporters enumerated in a network inventory
IA6	1 item: spouse being understanding
IB4	3-item scale
IC1	Coded from open-ended interview data
IIA4	2-item scale: lack of close companion and too few close friends (items reverse-coded)
IIA7	2-item scale: confidant and integration
IIB1	8-item scale
IIB2	2-item scale

Perceived availability of support: emotional, tangible, informational, or some combination

IA1	5-item scale
IA3	9-item scale: tangible only
IA4	Count of potential supporters
IA4	18-item: 6 items each for emotional, tangible, and informational
IA7	5-item scale
IB1	4 multi-item scales: for supervisor, co-worker, spouse, and other family and friends
IB2	3 multi-item scales: for supervisor, co-worker, and family and friends
IIA2	2 separate items

Recent use of support

IA3	1 item: frequency of recent use summed over all supporters enumerated in a network inventory

[a]The study numbers listed correspond to study numbers in Table 11.1.

Table 11.2 (*Continued*)

Study number[a]	Scale
IC2	6-item scale
IIA6	6-item scale: each item created by averaging over all supporters enumerated in a network inventory
Adequacy of support	
IIB1	12-item scale: intimacy
IIB1	17-item scale: integration
Invalid measures	
IA5	8-item scale: married (1 item), integration (2 items), perceived access (4 items), confidant (1 item)
IA6	4 separate items: marital satisfaction, spouse satisfaction, self-reliance versus help-seeking orientation with respect to relatives and to friends
IB3	Married
IC3	27-item subscale of the Family Environment Scale: cohesion, expressiveness, and conflict in the family
IIA1	Married
IIA2	Married
IIB1	1 item: recent arguments in network

tage, consistent with the hypothesis that support influences mental health. However, marital status is too highly associated with other coping resources (Kessler & Essex, 1982) to make it a valid indicator of support for our purposes. It might be thought that a similar argument applied to measures of membership in affiliative networks. We feel, however, that the affiliation measures are purer indicators than marital status in that they reflect little more than interactions, whereas marital status is associated with a great many things other than support.

Table 11.2 also shows how great the variability is in the complexity with which support has been measured. Some studies use simple 2-item measures, whereas others use sophisticated 18-item scales. Logically, the strength of the evidence for an effect of support might be expected to vary with this complexity, but previous reviews have not taken this and other methodological differences into account in assessing the consistency of findings. As a result, they have seen more diversity in results than actually exists. As we shall demonstrate, almost all of the inconsistencies in results can be traced to weaknesses in conceptualization, measurement, sample size, or analysis method—differences that are largely methodological.

Our ultimate concern is with the effects of conceptually different measures in determining whether some aspects of support have greater health-promoting effects than others. To determine this, though, it is necessary to take methodological differences among the studies into consideration.

We did this by reviewing each study and noting the existence of weak measures, small samples, or low-power analysis techniques. The substantive results are summarized with these methodological differences in mind. We find that the strongest studies consistently show particular aspects of support to have a buffer effect and others to have a main effect. Inconsistent results only appear among the methodologically weak studies.

As our results hinge so centrally on methodological strength it is important to discuss each factor we considered important in this determination. We briefly mentioned measurement earlier. Several studies have failed to find statistically significant evidence for stress buffering with a measure of support that is conceptually similar to one that has significant buffer effects in methodologically stronger studies but that is either a single-item fixed-choice measurement of support (Thoits, 1982; Warheit, 1979) or a highly skewed measure (Dean & Ensel, 1982). There is no reason to expect that a significant interaction will emerge when attenuated measures of this sort are used.

Small samples have the same effect on the ability to detect associations; several studies that failed to find a significant buffer effect can be criticized on this point. Schaefer, Coyne, & Lazarus (1981), for example, concluded that there was no buffer effect in their data, based on the fact that the R^2 increment associated with the interaction between life events and support was not significant; however, it is unlikely that a buffer could be detected in a sample as small as theirs ($n = 100$) even if it existed in the population from which the sample was drawn. A population R^2 increment as substantial as .05, in fact, could be detected with only about .4 power in their sample; that is, a population association of this magnitude has only a 40% chance of turning up as significant at the .05 level.

Several studies that failed to find significant evidence of buffering used low-power data analysis techniques. Bell, LeRoy, & Stephenson (1982), for example, used an analysis of covariance approach that classified life events into four categories (0, 1, 2, and 3 or more events) and support into three categories (high, medium, and low). The six degree of freedom interaction test is insignificant even though there is clear evidence in their tabular presentation of average distress scores that a meaningful buffer effect exists in the data.

Other studies failed to detect significant interactions because they collapsed continuous measures of stress and support into dichotomies and analyzed the tabular data with log-linear methods (Andrews, Tennant, Hewson, & Vaillant, 1978; Aneshensel & Stone, 1982).[3] Not only does col-

---

[3] The Andrews *et al.* study also used a life event inventory that failed to distinguish undesirable events from desirable or ambiguous ones. This almost certainly attenuates the estimate of the buffer effect.

lapsing reduce the sensitivity of measures, but log-linear analysis absorbs additive interactions into the main effects and so fails to detect interactions that are uncovered with linear modeling (Kessler, 1983).

On the basis of these methodological considerations, each of the 23 studies was classified as confirming, disconfirming, or unclear with respect to whether there is a stress-buffering effect of social support, a marginal effect of support under conditions of low stress, or an influence of support independent of stress.[4] A detailed classification of the results for each study is presented in Table 11.3. This table is the basis for all summary statements made in subsequent sections of the chapter.

Results

Throughout this section, we discuss only those studies that document clear confirming or disconfirming results. Results are considered unclear if we found methodological problems in the study, such as those discussed in the previous section. Table 11.3 lists, for each study, whether the results do or do not document the existence of a marginal or buffering effect of social support; it also indicates the level of stress at which the marginal effect was estimated. If results for the study differ across subsamples or for different stress or support measures, they are listed as a range of values and the specification is clarified in a footnote. Whenever available, standardized regression coefficients or phi coefficients are presented. Unclear results are discussed in footnotes 3, 5, and 6 and in the text.

After discarding unclear results, strong evidence for stress buffering was found. Evidence for a marginal effect under conditions of low stress was found in one-third of the studies where the buffering effect was significant. Almost all of the studies in which buffering was not documented contain evidence for significant main effects of support.

These results differ from those presented in several reviews of this literature in yielding stronger evidence for buffering. This is primarily because we classified weak studies as unclear in their results, whereas previous reviews have counted weak studies as evidence against buffering.

---

[4]The methodological problems reviewed here do not exhaust those that appear in these studies, but merely describe those that differentiate among the stronger and weaker studies. Some of the more serious common problems shared by most of the studies are (1) failure to control for demographic variables known to be related to mental health and to social support (for example, age, sex, socioeconomic status), (2) failure to discriminate the effects of marital status from those of support, and (3) use of a support measure that is potentially confounded with the life events whose impact on mental health it presumably buffers.

Table 11.3

Detailed Summary of Results across All Studies Reviewed[a]

Support factor	Study number[b]	Marginal effects			Where marginal effect was evaluated	Buffer effects		
		Yes[c]	No[c]	NA[c]		Yes	No	UC
Membership in affiliative networks	IA1		x		LE = below mean			x
	IA2	-.36			Total sample			x
	IA3				Total sample			x
	IA6		-.03 to .06		LE = 0			
	IB3		x		Total sample		x	
	IB4			x		-.12	.00	
	IC2	-.16			(LE, CS) = 0			-.12
	IIA1			x			x	
	IIA2		x		LE = low		x	
	IIA3	-.12			LE = 0		-.03 to -.02	
	IIA5[d]			x			x	
	IIB1	x			(LE, CS) = 0	x		
Emotional support	IA3	-.31			Total sample			x
	IA6	-.16			LE = 0	-.07		
	IB4			x		-.24 to -.63		
	IC1		x		(LE, CS) = 0	x		
	IIA4	-.32 to -.57			LE = 0		x	
	IIA7	x			LE = 0		x	
	IIB1		x		(LE, CS) = 0	x		
	IIB2		x		LE = 0, CS = 0	x		

Perceived availability of support					
IA1[c]	−.07		Total sample		x
IA3	−.20		Total sample		x
IA4	x	x	LE = 0	x	
IA7[f]	−.12	x	LE = 0	x	x
IB1	x	x	CS = 0	x	
IB2	x			x	
IIA2	x	x	LE = low	x	

[a] All coefficients reported in this table are standardized partial regression coefficients or subgroup phi coefficients. When an X appears in the entry it means either that the author did not report the regression coefficient or that some other analysis method was used. When an X appears in an entry that is described in Table 11.2 as consisting of several different separate items it means that the result applies to each item analyzed one at a time. In those cases where results differ across separate items a note describes the nature of the discrepancy.

[b] The study numbers in this column correspond to the study numbers in Table 11.1

[c] YES = the effect is significant (usually at the .05 level); NO = the effect is not significant and we judge the study to be strong enough that a meaningful effect in the population is likely to have been detected in the sample with the measures and analysis methods used; UC = it is unclear whether there is support for the effect's existence or not, due to a weakness in the study; NA = data were not reported; LE = life events; CS = chronic strains.

[d] Health events interact with one of four network measures, church attendance, and other events are involved in no significant interactions. Because health events are not weighted for seriousness, the significant interaction could be a seriousness weight: that is, being able to attend church could indicate that the illness is not so serious that it leads to confinement at home and so is associated with better mental health.

[e] In this study stress and support are both dichotomized at their means and the data are analyzed with tabular methods. The power to detect an interaction is reduced by these procedures. Stress is defined in terms of total life events rather than undesirable life events. This also attenuates buffer effects. Nonetheless, published data show that the probability of extreme distress due to event exposure is .19 in the low-support condition and .10 in the high-support condition, a pattern consistent with buffering. The marginal effect reported is a subgroup phi coefficient calculated from published tabular data.

[f] A buffer effect was found among homemakers but not among either men in the labor force or women in the labor force. The marginal effects happened to equal the same value (−.12) in all three subsamples.

In further analysis we went beyond previous reviews in looking for patterns separately within three different aspects of support.

Buffer Effects

The traditional buffering hypothesis states that the impact of stress on mental health is stronger under conditions of low support than of high support. This interaction can be interpreted in another way that is equivalent to the traditional statement, which is that support and mental health are more strongly related under conditions of high stress than of low stress. This alternative way of thinking of a buffer emphasizes that an assessment of a buffer effect inherently requires a comparison of support's predictive power across at least two different situations defined by the level of stress that characterizes them.

When investigators work with community survey data and operationalize stress in a life event inventory, the buffer effect is assessed by comparing support's predictive power across heterogeneous stress groups. Whether or not support has a buffer effect in the sample hinges on whether the importance of support among the heterogeneous subsample of people exposed to some undesirable event differs significantly from that among people who have been free of any such event in the recent past. It is important to recognize that this sort of evaluation is concerned with the existence of a *pervasive* buffer effect that cuts across a range of stressful life situations.

Because evidence for a pervasive buffer effect of this sort is precisely what we shall review, it is important to note that this evidence is completely independent of evidence for buffer effects that are *specific* to particular stress situations. Based on our reading of the literature on crisis coping we believe that there can be little doubt that specific buffer effects do exist, and that certain aspects of support are more influential in some situations than others (Lowenthal & Haven, 1968). The question we address, then, is whether there are any buffers that are pervasive.

Our summary data show clearly that membership in affiliative networks does not have a pervasive effect of this sort and equally clearly that emotional support does. The evidence is more mixed for perceived availability of support. We consider each set of findings separately.

Eight studies examined interactions between membership in affiliative networks and a life event inventory in predicting psychological distress. Only two of these (Henderson *et al.*, 1981; Kessler & Essex, 1982) documented a significant buffer effect. In one of these (Henderson *et al.*, 1981) the interaction disappeared when perceived adequacy of affiliation was controlled and the other study showed a significant interaction for only one of three subsamples. It is quite clear, then, that affiliation does not have a buffer effect.[5]

Of the seven studies that examined interactions between emotional support and a life event inventory, five documented significant buffer effects. The two exceptions (Dean & Ensel, 1982; Thoits, in press) used two-item support measures. As mentioned earlier, it is not surprising that these attenuated measures did not show significant interactions. We consequently consider the available evidence perfectly consistent in documenting a pervasive buffer effect of emotional support.

Interactions between perceived availability of support and a life event inventory are examined in five studies. Four of these documented a significant buffer effect (one of them in a subgroup). The exception is a weaker test of the buffer effect based on a single-item fixed-choice measure of support (Warheit, 1979), so failure to detect a significant effect is not surprising. On the basis of the evidence from all five studies we argue that there is a pervasive underlying buffer process.

Main and Marginal Effects

Even when there is no buffer effect it is possible that support will influence health, independent of stress. There is some evidence, although by no means uniform, that this is true for membership in affiliative networks. The main effect of support is significant in three of the eight studies that did not find a significant buffer effect and did contain measures of network membership. We believe that there might be a small effect here. Most of the studies that failed to document a main effect are weak. The three significant effects appear in strong studies (Aneshensel & Stone, 1982;[6] Lin *et al.*, 1979; Williams *et al.*, 1981), one of which is a panel that shows Time 1

---

[5]Suggestive evidence that network membership has a buffer effect comes from the results of Lin, Simeone, Ensel, and Kuo (1979) as reinterpreted by Boyce (1981). In this sample of Chinese–Americans, life events were to some extent ameliorated by an integration into the ethnic community. Leavy (1983, p. 10) reviewed unpublished results that Southern- and Eastern-European–Americans in an urban sample were influenced by neighborhood attachments in much the same way.

[6]Although the Aneshensel and Stone (1982) study was based on dichotomous support and stress measures and so provides a weak test of buffering, it yields very strong evidence for the existence of a marginal support effect both because the association between the dichotomous support and depression measures in the low-stress subgroup would presumably be a good deal larger if full-range scales had been used and because low stress was defined in a very rigorous fashion (as the absence of any recent stressor events and any chronic difficulties). On the importance of this second feature, see the following section of this chapter.

network membership to predict continued mental health over time (Williams *et al.*, 1981). Furthermore, once the conclusion has been reached that stress is irrelevant for an understanding of network membership, a much larger literature than the 23 studies reviewed here can be considered (Mueller, 1980). In this literature there is consistent evidence that attachment to affiliative networks—indicated by such things as number of friends, frequency of going out with friends, frequency of church attendance, and number of club memberships—is modestly associated with mental health.

When there is a buffer effect, as is true generally of emotional support and perceived availability of support, it makes no sense to ask if support has a main effect. Its effect varies with stress and so has to be evaluated at a specific level of stress to be meaningful. This is possible in most of the studies that documented buffer effects, although they differ in how they defined low stress. As we shall discuss, this difference has important implications for evidence of marginal effects.

Of the five studies documenting a buffer effect of emotional support, a marginal effect under low-stress conditions was found in only one (Husaini *et al.*, 1982). In three of the five studies the low-stress marginal association was very close to zero and in one the effect was not estimated. For reasons we discuss in the next section, we discounted the study that found a marginal effect, and we believe that emotional support does not have a general influence on mental health in the absence of high stress.

Evidence for a marginal effect of perceived availability of support is inconsistent. A significant marginal effect is found in one of the four studies that documented a buffer effect (Cleary & Mechanic, 1983) and in two that gave unclear results for buffering (Andrews, *et al.*, 1978; Schaefer *et al.*, 1981). Two of the other three significant buffer studies found perceived availability unrelated to mental health under conditions of low stress.[7]

Chronic Strains

We have so far only discussed studies measuring acute stresses—life events. In four others that measured chronic strains, all but the weakest showed clear evidence of stress buffering. Additionally, in the one study that measured both life events and chronic strain and reported results separately for the two (Aneshensel & Stone, 1982), there is evidence that social

---

[7]In one of these studies (House & Wells, 1978), wife support interacted significantly with distress five of seven times (there are seven types of job stress and strain). In four of these the marginal effect of wife support was not meaningfully different from zero. The LaRocco *et al.* (1980) study has similar results.

support buffers the impact of chronic strains even in the absence of life events.

These results are important for two reasons. First, they point to the fact that buffering might be more pronounced for chronic than acute strains, a possibility that has been argued by Wheaton (1983). Second, they have implications for the interpretation of marginal effects in studies defining low stress as the absence of stressful events.

We have very little to say about the first of these two points. With only three strong studies of chronic strain, two of which focused on job strains in samples of working men, there is little basis for generalization. We feel that the analysis of coping with chronic strains has been sorely neglected in the epidemiologic literature and that this is the single most important avenue of development open to those who work with normal population surveys of stress and health. Yet the available evidence provides little more than a hint of what might be found if this topic were pursued in a rigorous fashion.

There is more to be said about the second point. If support can buffer the impact of chronic strain, the marginal effects documented in studies defining low support as the absence of life events could represent buffer effects associated with unmeasured chronic strains. It is significant in this context to note that the three studies controlling simultaneously for both life events and chronic strains (Brown & Harris, 1978; Henderson *et al.*, 1981; Pearlin, Lieberman, Meneghan, & Mullen, 1981) found least evidence for a marginal effect of emotional support. We noted earlier that two of the five significant buffer studies also documented a significant marginal effect of support under conditions of low stress. Both of these studies, though, defined low stress as the absence of recent stressful events. In the studies that defined low stress as the absence of either events or ongoing chronic difficulties there is consistent evidence that emotional support does not have a marginal effect on emotional functioning. Although not definitive, this specification highlights the importance of assessing chronic strain when studying the marginal effects of support.

It is instructive to note that the study finding the strongest evidence of a marginal effect used an *absence* of support scale, defined in terms of the frequency with which problems are experienced due to lack of an intimate relationship or to having too few friends (Dean & Ensel, 1982). It might be that support has a marginal influence only when the absence of support becomes so extreme that it is experienced as a stress in itself. This is a conventional notion in the support literature, but it is not conventional to suggest highlighting the negative in order to find a marginal influence of support. By asking people how much they can count on their friends, how frequently they see their relatives, and other standard questions in support inventories, investigators are examining variation among those with at least some social contact. For a marginal influence, information about the extreme low end of the distribution might be more important. This possibility implies the need for a more complex statistical model than has been estimated to date, one in which the marginal effect of support has a different functional form than the buffer effect. It may prove fruitful to evaluate a model of this sort in future research.

Summary

Our analysis leads us to conclude that membership in affiliative networks does not, in general, buffer the impact of stressful life events on mental health but that it may have a small influence on mental health independent of stress. Emotional support and perceived availability of support both have general buffer effects, but they do not have marginal effects in the absence of high stress. Taken as a whole, these results show that several different aspects of social support are associated with mental health and that the character of these associations varies from one aspect to another. It is likely that discrimination of other support characteristics would show an even greater variety of general effects.

Two caveats are important to make about the results reported here. The first is that although our discussion of findings has been couched in the language of cause and effect, we have very little evidence that support is consequential for mental health. It might be that mental health is the causal variable and support the outcome or, more likely, that mental health and social support are connected in a complex web of mutual influence. We have also noted that the published studies have a number of methodological flaws that limit our ability to trust the findings completely. A respecification to highlight extreme support deprivation might turn up more evidence of marginal effects than we found. Or the introduction of more complete controls for both chronic and acute stress might make some of the marginal effects we found disappear.

Second, even if we could have faith in the specifications found for different aspects of support we could not be sure that they are independent, because only a handful of studies have examined more than one aspect of support at a time. The separate buffer effects of emotional support and perceived availability of support might turn out to be a single effect if they were examined simultaneously. Only one study in the entire set did this (Henderson *et al.,* 1981), and found that perceptual adequacy of support is much more important than actual attachment to emotional supporters—a result that led the authors of the study to suggest that some determinant of perceptual variation, such as social competence, accounts for the putative buffering effect of emotional support. Although their data are consistent with this interpretation, the results of our review suggest caution in reading too much into the findings of a single study. As we have shown, it is quite common in this literature to find results that do not replicate.

Discussion

Now that we have presented the evidence, what can we make of it? Several general conclusions are in order. The first is one that has already been stated: Evidence for a causal influence of support is not likely to come from normal population surveys of the type reviewed here. Intervention experiments hold out the greatest promise for this sort of evidence. Is it possible that the evidence assembled here might be useful in facilitating the design and implementation of effective interventions? This is certainly a hope of others who have reviewed the literature before us (Mitchell *et al.,* 1982). In our view the answer is a qualified no. The sorts of evidence that can be generated from such studies are limited to inferences about *general* exposure to stress. If there were serious thought of designing general population preventive interventions aimed at ameliorating the distress that can be caused by any number of inadvertent life crises, then we would see the results presented here as more useful. However, no such initiative is likely in the near future, nor would one be appropriate before solid evidence was offered that support has health-promoting effects in a number of specific high-risk crisis situations. Such evidence requires targeted interventions, and for these the results reviewed here are of only the most limited relevance. For this purpose studies of people coping with one particular life crisis are necessary.

This is not to say there is nothing left to be done in normal population surveys. We already argued that stress buffering is nothing more than support being consequential to different degrees in different situations. One important class of situations is made up of normal people living under normal conditions. Even if they are not in the midst of any special crisis, most people face chronic difficulties that have implications for their health. Indeed, there is evidence suggesting that chronic stresses (Pearlin & Schooler, 1978) and daily hassles (Kanner, Coyne, Schaefer, & Lazarus, 1981) are more consequential for emotional functioning than crisis events. These sorts of ongoing situations can be uniquely studied in normal population surveys.

As results begin to accumulate from prospective crisis coping studies and from intervention experiments, a whole host of questions about normal social support networks will invariably arise. To make sense of crisis situations comparative evidence about normal control groups is needed. To construct interventions aimed at manipulating support more complete information than is currently available about how networks are created and change over time is also needed. These are other ways in which normal population surveys will continue to be useful.

Large-scale normal population surveys also have a part to play in the analysis of stressful life events, but to address the increasingly more specific research questions posed to the literature on social support it will be necessary to abandon the use of highly aggregated life event inventories. Pearlin *et al.* (1981) have demonstrated that this can be done by working with clusters of a small number of events that share some common characteristic, such as income losses, health problems, or serious interpersonal difficulties. Their analysis of job disruptions, although combining some events that would be considered separately in crisis-coping studies, nonetheless yielded results that were a great deal richer than those that could be obtained from analyses of an overall life event inventory. Kessler, McLeod, and Wethington (in press) have shown that this approach can be generalized to consider a variety of life event clusters simultaneously. This partially disaggregated approach, which investigators have only begun to explore, opens up the possibility of a truly comparative analysis of the influence of support and other coping resources across a number of generic stress situations. This approach is probably the most appealing way to begin bridging the gap between epidemiologic research on general stress processes and interventions in particular populations.

References

Andrews, G., Tennant, C., Hewson, D. M., & Vaillant, G. E. (1978). Live event stress, social support, coping style, and risk of psychological impairment. *The Journal of Nervous and Mental Disease, 166,* 307–316.

Aneshensel, C. S., & Stone, J. D. (1982). Stress and depression: A test of the buffering model of social support. *Archives of General Psychiatry, 39,* 1392–1396.

Bell, R. A., LeRoy, J. B., & Stephenson, J. J. (1982). Evaluating the mediating effects of social supports upon life events and depressive symptoms. *Journal of Community Psychology, 10,* 325–340.

Boyce, W. T. (1981). Interaction between social variables in stress research. *Journal of Health and Social Behavior, 22,* 194–195.

Brown, G. W., & Harris, T. (1978). *Social origins of depression: A study of psychiatric disorder in women.* New York: Free Press.

Cleary, P. D., & Mechanic, D. (1983). Sex differences in psychological distress among married women. *Journal of Health and Social Behavior, 24,* 111–121.

Cohen, P., Struening, E. L., Muhlin, G. L., Genevie, L. E., Kaplan, S. R., & Peck H. B. (1982). Community stressors, mediating conditions, and well being in urban neighborhoods. *Journal of Community Psychology, 10,* 377–391.

Cohen, S., & Hoberman, H. M. (1983). Positive events and social supporters as buffers of life change stress. *Journal of Applied Social Psychology, 13*, 99–125.

Dean, A., & Ensel, W. M. (1982). Modelling social support, life events, competence, and depression in the context of age and sex. *Journal of Community Psychology, 10*, 392–408.

Eaton, W. W. (1978). Life events, social supports, and psychiatric symptoms: A reanalysis of the New Haven data. *Journal of Health and Social Behavior, 19*, 230–234.

Heller, K., & Swindle, R. W. (in press). Social networks, perceived social support and coping with stress. In R. D. Felner, L. A. Jason, J. Moritsuga, & S. S. Farber (Eds.), *Preventive psychology: Theory, research and practice in community intervention*. Elmsford, N.Y.: Pergamon.

Henderson, S., Byrne, D. G., Duncan-Jones, P. (1981). *Neurosis and the social environment*. New York: Academic Press.

House, J. S. (1981). *Work stress and social support*. Reading, MA: Addison-Wesley.

House, J. S., & Wells, J. A. (1978). Occupational stress, social support and health. In A. McLean, G. Black, & M. Colligan (Eds.), *Reducing occupational stress: Proceedings of a conference*. Washington, DC: U.S. Department of Health, Education and Welfare (NIOSH). (Publication No. 78–140).

Husaini, B. A., & Neff, J. A. (1980). Characteristics of life events and psychiatric impairment in rural communities. *The Journal of Nervous and Mental Disease, 168*, 159–166.

Husaini, B. A., Neff, J. A., Newbrough, J. R., & Moore, M. C. (1982). The stress-buffering role of social support and personal competence among the rural married. *Journal of Community Psychology, 10*, 409–426.

Kanner, A. D., Coyne, J. C., Schaefer, C., & Lazarus, R. S. (1981). Comparison of two modes of stress measurement: Daily hassles and uplifts versus major life events. *Journal of Behavioral Medicine, 4*, 1–39.

Kessler, R. C. (1982). Life events, social supports, and mental health. In W. R. Gove (Ed.), *Deviance and mental illness*. Beverly Hills, CA: Sage.

Kessler, R. C. (1983). Methodological issues in the study of psychosocial stress. In H. B. Kaplan (Ed.), *Psychosocial stress: Trends in theory and research*. New York: Academic Press.

Kessler, R. C., & Essex, M. (1982). Marital status and depression: The role of coping resources. *Social Forces, 61*, 484–507.

Kessler, R. C., McLeod, J. D., & Wethington, E. (in press). The costs of caring. In I. G. Sarason & B. R. Sarason (Eds.), *Social support: Theory, research, and applications*. The Hague: Martinus Nijhof.

LaRocco, J. M., House, J. S., & French, J. R. P. Jr. (1980). Social support, occupational stress, and health. *Journal of Health and Social Behavior, 21*, 202–218.

Leavy, R. L. (1983). Social support and psychological disorder: A review. *Journal of Community Psychology, 11*, 3–21.

Lieberman, M. A. (1982). The effects of social support on responses to stress. In L. Goldberger & S. Breznitz (Eds.), *Handbook of stress: Theoretical and clinical aspects*. New York: Free Press.

Lin, N., Simeone, R. S., Ensel, W. M., & Kuo, W. (1979). Social support, stressful life events, and illness: A model and an empirical test. *Journal of Health and Social Behavior, 20*, 108–119.

Lin, N., Woefel, M. W., & Light, S. C. (1982, October). *The buffering effect of social support subsequent to an important life event*. Paper presented at the National Conference on Social Stress Research, University of New Hampshire.

Lowenthal, M. F. & Haven, C. (1968). Interaction and adaptation: Intimacy as a criterion variable. *American Sociological Review, 33*, 20–30.

McFarlane, A. H., Norman, G. R., Streiner, D. L., & Roy, R. G. (1983). The process of social stress: Stable, reciprocal and mediating relationships. *Journal of Health and Social Behavior, 24,* 160–173.

Mitchell, R. E., Billings, A. G., & Moos, R. F. (1982). Social support and well-being: Implications for prevention programs. *Journal of Primary Prevention, 3,* 77–97.

Mitchell, R. E., Cronkite, R. C., & Moos, R. H. (in press). Stress, coping and depression among married couples. *Journal of Abnormal Psychology.*

Mueller, D. P. (1980). Social networks: A promising direction for research on the relationship of the social environment to psychiatric disorder. *Social Science and Medicine, 14A,* 147–161.

Pearlin, L. I., Lieberman, M. A., Meneghan, E. G., & Mullen, J. T. (1981). The stress process. *Journal of Health and Social Behavior, 22,* 337–356.

Pearlin, L. I., & Schooler, C. (1978). The structure of coping. *Journal of Health and Social Behavior, 19,* 2–21.

Schaefer, C., Coyne, J. C., & Lazarus, R. S. (1981). The health-related functions of social support. *Journal of Behavioral Medicine, 4,* 381–406.

Strack, S., & Coyne, J. C. (1983). Social confirmation of dysphoria: Shared and private reactions to depression. *Journal of Personality and Social Psychology, 44,* 798–806.

Thoits, P. A. (1982). Life stress, social support, and psychological vulnerability: Epidemiological considerations. *Journal of Community Psychology, 10,* 341–362.

Thoits, P. A. (in press). Explaining distributions of psychological vulnerability: Lack of social support in the face of life stress. *Social Forces.*

Turner, R. J. (1983). Direct, indirect, and moderating effects of social support on psychological distress and associated conditions. In H. B. Kaplan (Ed.), *Psychosocial stress: Trends in theory and research.* New York: Academic Press.

Warheit, G. J. (1979). Life events, coping, stress, and depressive symptomatology. *American Journal of Psychiatry, 136,* 502–507.

Wheaton, B. (1983, August-September). *Models for the stress-buffering functions of coping resources.* Paper presented at the Annual Meetings of the American Sociological Association in Detroit.

Wilcox, B. L. (1981). Social support, life stress, and psychological adjustment: A test of the buffering hypothesis. *American Journal of Community Psychology, 9,* 371–386.

Williams, A. W., Ware, J. E., Jr., & Donald, C. A. (1981). A model of mental health, life events and social supports applicable to general populations. *Journal of Health and Social Behavior, 22,* 324–336.

CHAPTER 12

The Relationship of Social Networks and Social Support to Morbidity and Mortality*

Lisa F. Berkman

Introduction

With all the concern that has been devoted to the issue of social networks and social support, it might be helpful to ask what *led* to the suspicion that social networks and support influence health status? In epidemiology, understanding this historical perspective is particularly important because it has played a critical role in shaping the causal models used and types of questions asked on surveys.

Before the early 1970s, barely a word was published in the epidemiologic literature on the topic of social networks or support (although by that time there was a growing amount of social–epidemiologic work under way on the effect of mobility, social disorganization, and rapid social change). In the early to middle 1970s, several papers were published suggesting that some people were apparently protected from these social upheavals. The things that protected people were labeled resistance resources (Antonovsky, 1974), psychosocial assets (Nuckolls, Cassel, & Kaplan, 1972) and social

---

*Parts of this chapter have appeared in Berkman, L. F., Assessing the physical health effects of social networks and social support. *Annual Review of Public Health*, 1984, *5*, 413–432.

241

support (Cassel, 1976; Kaplan, Cassel, & Gore, 1977). In all cases important elements of these protective factors were social and community ties. However, the measures did not exclusively tap social ties, but frequently included items on economic resources and psychological strengths. This conceptualization led to a series of studies in which stressors were generally viewed as acute, discrete life events (typified by the Schedule of Recent Experience [SRE], developed by Holmes and Rahe, 1967), and resistance resources or supports were seen as an amalgamation of many social, economic, and psychological conditions or states. Social support was viewed primarily as a buffer, having no effects under conditions of low stress, in these studies.

At the same time, a number of investigators grew increasingly dissatisfied with the ambiguity involved in the measures and results of studies of social change, urbanization, industrialization, poverty, and mobility (Jenkins, 1976; Syme & Berkman, 1976) and sought to determine more precisely what features of these macrosocial phenomena might be disease producing. In exploring this hypothesis, they sought characteristics that were held in common by these conditions and that in themselves were thought to have deleterious health consequences. One of the characteristics common to these conditions was that the people experiencing them were frequently found to lack certain social connections to others. In one way or another, these people had become isolated or untied from important social relationships. Such phenomena as migration, poverty, mobility, social change, and urbanization had been shown to exert powerful influences on the ability to maintain enduring and effective social ties (Bell & Boat, 1957; Bell & Force, 1965; Berkman, 1977; Litwak, 1960). Thus, it was possible that what was stressful about these phenomena was the disconnectedness and isolation in which people found themselves. According to this perspective, social ties (or the lack of them) were not buffers but actually stressors themselves. They were what made social change or mobility stressful experiences. When the health data on widows (viewed as having experienced a profound social loss) and members of certain religious and ethnic groups known to maintain very extensive and supportive social ties (Mormons, Seventh Day Adventists, Japanese, Italian–Americans) were viewed from this perspective, the hypothesis became even more enticing. In fact, it was possible to view many life events included in the Holmes and Rahe SRE as breaks or disruptions in social ties.

From this perspective it was fundamentally relationships, or the lack of them, that were either stress producing or health promoting. Searching for methods in which characteristics of social ties might be measured and described as direct, independent predictors of declines in physical health became the next important step in this research process. It was in this context that social network analysis became particularly attactive.

The two models of disease causation, one in which social networks and supports are seen as buffers and the other in which they are seen as stressors, are not necessarily mutually exclusive. It may well turn out that some aspects of relationships are buffering and others are capable of having direct health consequences. In the long run, a model of disease causation that takes both of these possibilities into account is needed.

Social Networks, Social Support, and Health: The Evidence

Most studies of morbidity and mortality have examined social networks and support as having either direct *or* buffer effects. Although this situation may have occurred because investigators were guided by one perspective or another, there is a more pragmatic reason. Because prospective studies take so many years to complete (most have at least 5 years of follow-up), epidemiologists interested in this issue have had to rely on secondary analyses of data collected for entirely different purposes. This has meant that the choice of network measures and life event or change measures has, in most cases, been limited. This is not the case for studies of pregnancy complications, which obviously have a very short and defined follow-up period of 9 months, these studies have used more sophisticated and up-to-date measures.

In this chapter the data on the relationship of social ties to physical health are reviewed. The large body of research linking social ties to mental health or self-reported symptoms of illness or recovery from illness will not be dealt with in this chapter. Studies will be reviewed in fine enough detail that the reader will be able to evaluate why discrepancies among findings exist and what factors might contribute to these discrepencies. This has meant that particular attention is paid to identifying questionnaire items.

Mortality

There have been three studies indicating that particular network or support characteristics are associated with mortality risk. One of these is an analysis of 9-year mortality data from 6928 adult residents of Alameda County, California (Berkman & Breslow, 1983; Berkman & Syme, 1979). In the survey, basic information on several essential aspects of an individual's personal network was collected. A Social Network Index was developed based on four types of social connection: (1) marriage, (2) contacts with extended family and close friends, (3) church group membership, and (4) other group affiliations. Contacts with friends and relatives were measured by the number of close friends and relatives a respondent reported and the frequency with which he or she saw them. Another index of marital satisfaction was created from nine items, such as spouse gives as much understanding and affection as needed, regretted marriage, considered divorce, and problems getting along.

The age- and sex-specific mortality rates from all causes in relation to the Social Network Index reveal a consistent pattern of increased mortality rates associated with each decrease in social connection. The age-adjusted relative risks were 2.3 for men and 2.8 for women ($p < .001$). When the Social Network Index was examined in relation to the separate causes of death, people with few connections were found to be at increased risk of dying from many separate causes of death: ischemic heart disease, cancer, cerebrovascular and circulatory disease, and a final category of all other causes of death. The index of marital satisfaction was not associated with mortality risk.

In subsequent multivariate analyses using a multiple logistic risk model, the Social Network Index was found to be associated with mortality risk independent of initial physical health status, socioeconomic status, cigarette smoking, alcohol consumption, level of physical activity, obesity, race, life satisfaction, and use of preventive health services. In the multivariate analyses, when all variables were considered simultaneously the approximate relative mortality risk was reduced but still remained over 2.

When each of the four components were considered individually in the multiple logistic analyses, three of the four remained statistically significant in predicting mortality risk. Only the risk associated with group membership was reduced to nonsignificance. In univariate analyses, this variable was significant for women but not for men.

A prospective community study of adults in Tecumseh, Michigan, by House, Robbins, and Metzner (1982) has both extended and, in part, replicated the findings of the Alameda County study. In this analysis, 2754 men and women who were interviewed and medically examined during the third round of the Tecumseh Community Health Study in 1967–1969 and who were 35–69 years old at that time were included in a 10-year mortality follow-up.

Measures of social relationships and activities fell into four major categories: (1) intimate social relationships (marital status, visits with friends and relatives, going on pleasure drives and picnics), (2) formal organizational involvements outside of work (going to church or meetings or voluntary associations), (3) active and relatively social leisure (going to classes, movies, affairs, museums, etc.), and (4) passive and relatively solitary leisure (watching television, listening to radio, reading). Confounding variables considered in the analyses were age, cigarette smoking, alcohol consumption, education, employment status, occupation, weight and height, and a variety of morbidity measures assessed from physical examination. One of the major strengths of the study was the ability of the investigators to control for such factors as coronary heart disease (CHD) (defined as probable history of myocardial infarction [MI], or angina, or electrocardiographic evidence of MI), chronic bronchitis or persistent cough or phlegm, probable hypertension, levels of serum cholesterol and blood glucose, and forced expiratory volume.

Among seven individual components of social integration and activities, four were statistically significant for men in multiple logistic analyses after adjusting for age and other risk factors: marital status, attendance at voluntary associations, spectator events, and classes and lectures. For women, only church attendance was significant. Frequency of visits with friends and relatives and going out on pleasure drives and picnics were not significant for either men or women. In two cumulative indexes of social integration using the same seven factors, multiple logistic analyses revealed that among men the indexes were related to mortality when confounding variables were considered. Among women, the relationships of both indexes to mortality were significant independent of age, but became nonsignificant when all risk factors were covariates. Additionally, in these data there was no evidence that satisfaction with relationships and activities had any significant association with mortality once the intensity or frequency of an activity or relationship was controlled.

A third study of mortality risk was conducted in Durham County, North Carolina, by Blazer (1982) on 331 men and women 65 years of age and older. Eleven items tapping social support were included in the original survey. These items from the Older Americans Resources and Sources Community Survey (OARS) Questionnaire were divided into three dimensions: (1) roles and attachments available (marital status, number of living children and siblings), (2) frequency of interaction (telephone calls and visits with friends and relatives during the past week), and (3) perception of social support (lonely even with people, someone cares what happens to you, difficulty speaking to new people, enough contact with confidant, seems like no one understands, someone would help if you were ill or disabled). Control variables considered in analyses were age, sex, race, economic resources, physical health, activities of daily living, stressful life events, symptoms of major depressive episode, cognitive dysfunction, and cigarette smoking.

In several types of analyses, the three parameters of impaired social support were significant risk factors for 30-month mortality independent of the 10 covariates. Using three binary regression analyses, the estimates of relative mortality risk were found to be 3.40 for impaired perceived social support, 2.04 for impaired roles and attachments, and 1.88 for impaired frequency of social interaction. Impaired perceived support and roles and attachments predicted mortality when the other two support parameters were controlled for. This was not the case for the third measure, tapping frequency of interaction. Thus, in this survey of older men and women, the parameter with the highest predictive value was perceived social support, a measure Blazer correctly pointed out is a subjective appraisal of the adequacy of support rather than a more objective characteristic of a social network.

The three cohort studies reviewed have provided some evidence that social networks or social support predict mortality risk among adults of all ages. However, there is little consistency in the network measures, and in several instances similar measures predicted differently in different studies. For instance, contacts with friends and relatives is a highly significant factor in the Alameda County data, but not very important in either the Tecumseh or the Durham County studies. Satisfaction with marriage and satisfaction with relationships and activities is not associated with mortality in the Alameda and Tecumseh County studies, but is the strongest network–support predictor of mortality in the Durham County data.

Morbidity

Studies of mortality alone do not tell where along the spectrum of disease social networks have their greatest impact. For instance, it is not known if they influence disease incidence, recovery, or case fatality, or how they are intertwined with other important biological risk factors, such as high blood pressure or serum cholesterol levels. The only specific disease for which there are some data on networks and incidence or prevalence is CHD. Oddly, with one exception, the only studies in which the CHD–network relationship has been explored in detail are of immigrants: Japanese immigrants or first-generation Japanese–Americans in California and Hawaii and immigrants to Israel. This is particularly disappointing because it is well known that these groups of immigrants may have unique patterns of networks, and thus the degree to which these findings may be generalized to other groups is unclear.

The Japanese–American Studies

The prevalence of CHD among Japanese–Americans in California has been examined in relation to social affiliation and social disconnection by Joseph (1980) and Joseph and Syme (1981). The sample of 3809 Japanese–American men aged 30–74 living in the San Francisco Bay Area had been examined previously to study acculturation, biological risk factors, and CHD

(Marmot & Syme, 1976; Marmot *et al.*, 1975; Worth *et al.*, 1975). This time, the data were analyzed looking at the cross-sectional association among social affiliation, social disconnection, biologic risk factors, and prevalence of CHD as defined by electrocardiographic findings and scores on the London School of Hygiene Cardiovascular Questionnaire. Definite and probable (mild) CHD cases (n = 394) were included in this study. Because severe illness or disability might cause people to cut back on social contacts, the authors decided to include mild cases in their analyses and reduce the risk that any cross-sectional associations between CHD prevalence and networks were the result of ill people being unable to maintain extensive ties.

Risk factors examined were high serum cholesterol level, high systolic blood pressure, cigarette smoking, family history of heart attack, and lack of physical activity. Social affiliation was assessed by marital status, attendence at religious services, and membership in either formal or informal organizations. Attitudinal components of affiliation assessed the importance placed on group-oriented, nonindividual behavior. Social disconnection was based on a history of events that disrupt social ties (i.e., bereavement, occupational and geographical mobility, and acculturation into U.S. society from traditional Japanese culture).

The results of multiple logistic risk analysis of these factors show that social affiliation, age, physical inactivity, and family history of heart attack were independently associated with the prevalence of CHD in this cohort. When the extreme categories of the social affiliation measure are compared, the odds ratio (an approximate relative risk measure) of low to high risk calculated from the logistic equation is 1.94 (p = .002).

Following this study, Reed, McGee, Yano, and Feinleib (1983) examined the impact of social networks on CHD in the Hawaii cohort of Japanese–Americans. In 1971, 7639 men who had completed the initial examination between 1965 and 1968 and who were thought to be alive and residing in Hawaii were given a psychosocial questionnaire; 61% of these people returned the questionnaire (n = 4653). Nonresponse, although high, does not seem to reflect any systematic nonresponse bias (Reed *et al.*, 1982). Prevalent cases were defined as those CHD cases existing at the time of the survey; incident cases were new ones occuring during the follow-up period. At the time of the survey, 264 prevalent CHD cases were identified. In the subsequent time through 1978, 218 men developed new coronary heart disease.

In this study, nine questions were used in two network scales. The first included all nine items: (1) geographic proximity of parents, (2) geographic proximity of parents-in-law, (3) marital status, (4) number of living children, (5) number of people in household, (6) frequency of social activities with co-workers, (7) frequency of discussing serious personal problems with co-workers, (8) frequency of attendance at religious services, and (9) number of social organizations attended regularly. The second scale included the first five of these items, which involve more intimate contacts. Among individual items, men who were never married and/or were living alone had a particularly high risk of both prevalent and incident heart disease, although these risks were not statistically significant.

In logistic analyses of the prevalence data, both scores predicted total CHD (an outcome measure including cases of myocardial infarction and angina pectoris) independent of such standard biologic risk factors as high blood pressure, serum cholesterol and serum glucose levels, as well as cigarette smoking, alcohol consumption, physical inactivity, and body mass. The set of five items tapping family contacts and household composition predicted angina pectoris; however, neither score predicted MI alone.

Different findings emerged from the analyses of incidence or prospective data. In logistic analyses with all potentially confounding variables there was no significant association of either score with total CHD, fatal myocardial infarction, or angina. The second network score of more intimate contacts was of borderline significance ($p = .08$) in predicting nonfatal myocardial infarction. Although of borderline significance, the standardized logistic coefficient was of the same magnitude as the coefficient for systolic blood pressure in this group (a coefficient that was also nonsignificant). These findings must lead to the question of what might be responsible for the differences in prevalence and incidence data.

The most obvious possibility is that the experience of disease is antecedent to and influences a person's ability or desire to maintain social ties, thereby causing an association to appear in the prevalence data but not in the prospective incidence data. Some variables in this analysis are more likely to be influenced by health status than others (e.g., attendance at social activities and religious services as well as membership in and regular attendance at organizations). In fact, the scales including these items were more predictive of CHD prevalence than of incidence. Other variables are much less likely to be influenced by concurrent health status (e.g., never being married, geographic location of parents and in-laws, number of children, and household composition). If these variables predicted prevalence, then other explanations must be examined. In fact, these items were found exclusive of the others in the second scale. This second scale of marital status, contacts with relatives, and household composition predicted CHD prevalence and angina prevalence, and was of borderline significance in predicting nonfatal MI incidence.

Is there another explanation for these associations? Because prevalence data obviously do not include fatal cases, there is a suggestion in this cohort that the network variables may have been more predictive of nonfatal CHD than of fatalities. The authors noted that the MI case fatality rate was *higher* in the group with most connections than in the group with fewer contacts (43% compared to 34%). In the univariate analyses of incident cases, the network scales showed no association or clear pattern with fatal MI. However, the scale of intimate contacts was significantly associated with non-fatal MI; the relative risk was 1.5 ($p = .04$). The possibility that more isolated people would be more sensitive to their illness and be more likely to be diagnosed as having MI should also be considered. This possibility would most likely occur when diagnosis was dependent on an individual's discretion to *seek* care, as in ordinary medical care settings but not as in the standardized research setting of this study. Thus, although the association of the network variables to prevalence data and nonfatal MI cannot fully be explained, they also cannot be dismissed lightly as being artifactual. In the long run, developing more substantive hypotheses to explain these findings will be useful.

The Israeli Ischemic Heart Disease Study

In the Israeli Ischemic Heart Disease Study, a prospective cohort study of almost 10,000 Israeli adult male civil service and municipal employees, psychosocial problems (particularly family ones) and wife's love and support were found to be important predictors of the development of angina pectoris over a 5-year follow-up period (Medalie & Goldbourt, 1976). Incidence cases were subjects at risk for angina pectoris (excluding known angina and MI cases in 1963) who in 1968 were diagnosed as having definite angina on the basis of a pretested chest pain questionnaire designed for the study (Medalie *et al.,* 1973).

In this study family problems were measured by responses to four questions: (1) Did you have any problems (conflicts) with your family (wife, children) in the past? (2) Do you have any problems with your family at present? (3) How does it affect you when your wife or children do not listen to you or even oppose you? (4) Does your wife show you her love? Other variables found to be statistically significant and included in the final logistic analyses were higher age level, high blood pressure, anxiety, high serum cholesterol levels, diabetes, and electrocardiographic abnormalities. In an analysis of 5-year angina incidence rates, family problems emerged as strong predictors after controlling for the six covariates. In another analysis, wife's love and support were shown to buffer the effects of anxiety. When anxiety was low, wife's love and support were not associated with angina. When anxiety was high, men who did not have the love and support of their wives were 1.8 times as likely to develop angina during the follow-up period as those with support ($p < .05$). In this study, these same variables did not predict myocardial infarction in multivariate analyses (Goldbourt, Medalie, & Neufeld, 1975).

Can these findings be explained on the basis of the disease process influencing a person's family situation? Because the data were prospective and included none of the prevalent angina cases, this seems unlikely. Medalie and Goldbourt noted, however, that when a condition is dependent on subjective symptoms (as in the case of chest pain) it may be a product of cultural conditioning, coping, or utilization of the advantages of the sick role (Mechanic, 1972). For the most part, however, these studies used on patients in their usual care system where the advantages of registering such complaints are clearer. Whether subjects utilized such responses in systematically conducted surveys where the advantages are unclear is impossible to say. However, it is important to keep in mind that these are incidence cases, none of whom registered feeling chest pain at the time they were interviewed concerning their family problems.

The Framingham Heart Disease Study

In the Framingham cohort of women, clerical workers ($n = 142$) who had a nonsupportive supervisor were found to be at increased risk of developing CHD over an 8-year follow-up period (Haynes & Feinleib 1980). Incidence of CHD was defined as diagnosis of MI, coronary insufficiency syndrome, angina pectoris, or CHD death. Nonsupport from supervisor predicted CHD incidence independent of other standard risk factors (high systolic blood pressure, high serum cholesterol levels, and number of cigarettes smoked) and other psychosocial scales (anger, job changes, and family responsibilities). This factor was not a significant CHD predictor for other working women or for men (Haynes, Feinleib, & Kannel, 1980). Framingham working women with the highest CHD risk were those in clerical jobs. Thus, women in this position may experience stress from several sources including lack of autonomy and control over the work environment, under-utilization of skills, and lack of recognition of accomplishment.

The results of these studies are inconsistent. In only the Israeli study did social support appear to be strongly related to incidence of angina pectoris, although other studies showed it to be related to angina prevalence (Joseph, 1980; Reed et al., 1983). With regard to the incidence of MI, the Japanese–Hawaii cohort showed only a modest relationship with incidence of nonfatal MI, the Israeli study showed no significant associations, and incidence data in the California–Japanese cohort have not been examined. Prevalence data of total CHD show stronger relationships to social ties in both the Hawaii and California cohorts. The Framingham study showed total CHD incidence to be related to support from supervisor in one group of female clerical employees. It is unfortunate that there are no other studies available with strong outcome measures and appropriate statistical control of relevent variables with which to examine this issue. The studies to date have been weak in terms of adequately assessing dimensions of social networks and social support and, in most cases, have been secondary analyses of data collected for different purposes.

Complications in Pregnancy

Three studies have focused on the effects of social support and companionship during pregnancy. One of the first of these studies was conducted by Nuckolls, Cassel, and Kaplan (1972) on 170 caucasian, primaparous U.S. Army wives who were followed through the delivery of their babies at a military hospital. A questionnaire tapping psychosocial resources was administered at the time of their prenatal registration prior to the 24th week of pregnancy. The psychosocial asset scale measured five dimensions: ego strength, qualities of marriage, relationships with extended family, social resources including friendship patterns, and feelings about the pregnancy. Thus, this scale did not reveal the individual impact of social ties as distinct from other assets. A questionnaire assessing life events was administered in the 32d week of pregnancy.

Neither psychosocial assets nor life events were independently associated with complications. When interactions were examined in stratified analyses, however, psychosocial assets were found to have a buffering effect on life events. In the small group of women ($n = 26$) who reported many life changes both during pregnancy and in the years preceding pregnancy, those with low psychosocial assets had a complication rate of 91% compared to 33% for women with many psychosocial assets. The weaknesses of this study are mainly in the analyses, which did not distinguish among different aspects of the psychosocial assets score nor take full advantage of the continuous nature of the independent variables.

In a more recent study, many of these variables were examined in an analytically more rigorous fashion in a sample of 117 women attending an obstetric clinic in a large, urban, university medical center. Norbeck and Tilden (1983) looked at the effects of life stresses, social support, and emotional disequilibrium on complications of pregnancy on a group of women from various racial, marital, and socioeconomic groups. Social support was measured by two factors: emotional support and tangible support. Other variables were life stress, anxiety, depression, low self-esteem, parity, age, marital status, education, and race. Pregnancy complications were scored from a chart review and were similar to those of Nuckolls *et al.* (1972). Following this procedure, 48.7% of the cases were classified as complicated.

They were divided into three categories: gestation complications; labor, delivery and postpartum complications, and infant condition complications. Questionnaires were administered to women between the ages of 20 and 39 without pre-existing medical risk factors at 12–20 weeks of gestation.

With regard to the social support variables, when tangible support and emotional support were combined they were not independent predictors of total complication rates nor of any of three subgroups. However, the interaction of tangible support and life change *during* pregnancy was significant for each type of complication. For both gestation and infant complications, subjects with many life changes and low support had the highest rate of complications. For labor and delivery complications, low support was surprisingly related to higher rates of complications only among those with little life change. Because life change is negatively correlated with one outcome and positively correlated with two, it is not surprising that neither life change nor the interaction term is significantly associated with overall complications. Whether tangible support would be directly associated with overall complications or any particular one is unclear from the analyses described, because it always seems to have been combined with emotional support in predictions. Emotional support is not as highly correlated with pregnancy outcome in pairwise correlations as tangible support is ($-.05$ compared to $-.19$). However, assuming that tangible support by itself is not a significant predictor (which does not seem to have been tested), these findings are consistent with the stress-buffering effect found for psychosocial assets in the Nuckolls *et al.* study.

In a third study, Sosa, Kennel, and Klaus (1980) took an experimental approach, studying the effects of a supportive companion on perinatal problems, length of labor, and mother–infant interaction in a social security hospital in Guatamala City where it was routine hospital policy for women to undergo labor alone, without spouse, family, friends, or constant nurse care taker. In addition to routine care, mothers in an experimental group received constant support from an untrained lay woman from admission to delivery. The support provided by the woman consisted of physical contact, conversation, and the presence of a friendly companion whom the mother had not met before.

Twenty primigravid women with uncomplicated labors and normal vaginal deliveries were to be enrolled randomly in each the experimental and control groups. A woman was removed from study if labor or delivery was complicated. For the 40 mothers retained in the study, length of labor was 19.3 hours for the control group and 8.7 hours for the experimental group.

Mothers in the experimental group were awake more in the hour following delivery and were more likely to stroke, smile, and talk to their infants than the controls even with adjustment for time spent awake. No differences were found for amount of simple touching, handling, or time spent in body-to-body contact.

The elimination of women with problems requiring intervention during labor and delivery prevents the calculation of an approximate relative risk of the development of such conditions in this study. This is unfortunate because the increased number of women needed to fill the control group (103 compared to 33) indicates a substantial relationship between such complications and the presence or absence of a supportive companion. However, this study, consistent with the other two discussed, indicates that social support appears to have an effect on pregnancy outcomes and mother–infant interactions.

Marriage: A Special Kind of Tie

Marriage is one of the most fundamental and intimate ties among people. Those who are not married, whether single, separated, widowed, or divorced, experience higher mortality rates than married people (Carter & Glick, 1970; Ortmeyer, 1974; Thiel, Parker, & Bruce, 1973). These differences cannot be explained by an increase in any one cause of death. However, the cause-specific ratios are not as great for women as they are for men (Ortmeyer, 1974).

Widowhood seems to have a profound effect on physical well-being, especially for men (Cox & Ford, 1964; Kraus & Lilienfeld, 1959; McNeil, 1973; Parkes, 1964; Rees & Lutkins, 1967). (See Minkler, Chapter 10 in this volume, for a discussion of this issue.) To date, the most comprehensive and well-controlled analysis of widowhood is by Helsing, Szklo, and Comstock (1981), who found that being a widow or widower carried an increased mortality risk among men but not among women. Their 10-year retrospective cohort study of men and women in Washington County, Maryland, showed that the excessive risk in men persisted when age, education, age at first marriage, cigarette smoking, church attendance, and a proxy economic status measure were controlled. In contrast to other investigators, Helsing and co-workers reported that the increased mortality risk among widowers was not confined to the first 6 months of the bereavement but persisted throughout a 10-year follow-up period. If further studies confirm this finding, viewing widowhood as a chronically stressful situation, rather than attributing the increased mortality to the acute effects of the spouse's death, would seem reasonable (Helsing & Szklo, 1981; Susser, 1981). In addition, the increased risks were not observed in only one or two causes of death but were spread across many causes. Notable increases were found for infectious diseases, accidents, and suicide for males and cirrhosis of the liver for females (Helsing, Comstock, & Szklo, 1981).

Socioeconomic status conceivably might account for mortality rate differences between married and unmarried people; however, three studies (Helsing, Szklo, & Comstock, 1981; Koskenvuo, Kaprio, Kesaniem, & Sarna, 1980; Parkes, Benjamin, & Fitzgerald, 1969) have reported this relationship to be independent of socioeconomic status.

Attempting to understand what might account for the increased risk of dying from CHD among unmarried people, Weiss (1973) examined the relationship among marital status, CHD, serum cholesterol levels, systolic and diastolic blood pressure, and ponderal index in a sample of 6672 adults interviewed in the U.S. Health Examination Survey. He found substantial CHD risks associated with being single, widowed, or divorced, independent of all these risk factors. Some evidence to the contrary, however, has come from Finland where Aromaa reported that married men smoke less than other men and have lower systolic and diastolic blood pressure than widowed men, and that divorced women smoke more than married women (unpublished data reviewed in Koskenvuo *et al.,* 1980).

What We Need to Know

What is known about the relationship between social ties and physical health has been reviewed in the previous section. The focus of this section is on what we *need* to know, because it is clear that the studies produced so far raise many more issues than they resolve. For instance, they do little to inform us about which network characteristics are important or how such a social phenomenon "enters" the body to influence disease processes. The remainder of this chapter is devoted to a discussion of four issues raised by these studies: (1) specificity of social network and support measures, (2) determination of whether social networks are stressors or buffers, (3) clarification of the role of cultural expectations, and (4) discovery of the pathways linking support and health status.

Specificity of Social Network and Support Measures

Perhaps the greatest problem with the studies reviewed is the inadequacy of the social network and support measures. With few exceptions, the measures used in these studies have been developed post hoc from a few items included in questionnaires for other reasons. Thus, many studies purporting to measure social networks and support do not in fact do so, or do so in a very limited way. This is understandable in early studies when preliminary relationships are being uncovered; however, it is now necessary to move on and take full advantage of the more sophisticated measures currently available, which allow the measurement of specific network and support characteristics. For instance, many studies have intermingled measures of support with measures of networks. Other authors in this volume address this issue in detail. Briefly, social networks might be seen as the web of social relationships that surround an individual and the characteristics of those social ties—that is, their size, composition, geographic dispersion, density, homogeniety, level of reciprocity, intimacy, frequency of contact, and so forth (Fischer, Jackson, Stueve, Gerson, & Jones, 1977; Laumann, 1973; Mitchell, 1969). Social support might then be viewed as the aid (emotional, instrumental, and financial) that is transmitted among network members (House, 1981; Kaplan, Cassel, & Gore, 1977; Mitchell & Trickett, 1980). Thus, social networks and social support are two different concepts. As Wellman (1981) has so cogently argued, networks may or may not be supportive; that is an empirical question. It must be determined specifically which network and support characteristics are related to morbidity and mortality, with the understanding that certain characteristics may even increase risk of one type of outcome and decrease risk of another. For example, some evidence indicates that individuals with large networks may increase their utilization of health services and independently decrease their risk of disease. This may come about because large networks may be stress reducing but at the same time consist of cosmopolitan members who have pro-medical care orientations. It is important to know if dispersed networks are as effective as networks of equal size in which members are geographically proximate. Most of all, it is necessary to move beyond measures of household composition, presence of kin, or group affiliation as adequate measures of social networks and support.

Social Networks: Buffers or Stressors?

Whether social networks and support are considered buffers or stressors is not only dependent, in part, on statistical tests and model building, but also on the conceptualization and measurement of social networks and support. Whether death of a spouse or divorce are seen as breaks in networks or as acute life events is dependent on conceptualization, not on statistical manipulation. It has now been discussed by several investigators (Mueller, 1980; Thoits, 1982; Gore, 1981; Berkman, 1982) that stress and support are neither operationally nor conceptually independent variables. Many life changes are actually losses or breaks in social ties; others are not really life events at all but reflect ongoing poor or deteriorating social relationships. Many other events "may seriously disrupt, distort, reduce, or otherwise change existing network relationships" (Mueller, 1980, p. 151). Moving, changing jobs, and retiring almost inevitably cause changes in networks. Mueller has hypothesized that much of the impact of life events may result from the profound disturbances they introduce into social networks, as discussed at the beginning of this chapter. The extent to which life events and networks are overlapping and redundant severely hampers the ability to assess their relative impacts on health status.

The findings reviewed in this chapter indicate the existence of both main effects and buffer effects. It may well turn out that certain network or support characteristics have buffer effects (perhaps emotional support buffers certain occupational stresses) and others have main effects (network size may influence mortality). In either case, investigators must examine these relationships empirically and not assume a priori the greater validity of one model over another.

Cultural Expectations and Well-Integrated Communities

It is a cliché that responses to survey questions are influenced by cultural attitudes and expectations, but this obvious fact has been ignored in most research. The reason it is so important to pay attention to this possible influence is the suggestion in the findings reviewed that in some populations known to be very socially cohesive and well integrated (i.e., women in Tecumseh, Japanese–Americans in Hawaii) differences in risks between isolated and nonisolated people are not great. One possible explanation for these findings is that these communities have such overall high levels of social contact and support that very few people are isolated in severe enough ways to reveal significant increases in risk. For instance, only about 2% of Japanese men in Hawaii live alone (Reed *et al.,* 1983). Another possibility is that social contacts are so much a part of routine in the lives of these people that they go unnoticed and unreported. As a result, the measures of social activities do not differentiate well in these groups (House *et al.,* 1982). For instance, there is some evidence that in studies of older people, the daily visits to parents who live in in-law apartments or nearby commonly go unreported by their children as visits. This seems to occur because they are so much a part of daily life that they are not seen as formal occasions worthy of reporting (Stueve &. Lein, 1979). Similar experiences have been reported for women in Tecumseh (House *et al.,* 1982) and for the Japanese. In a cross-cultural study comparing the experiences of older Japanese in Japan with Americans in the United States, 42% of Japanese and 78% of Americans reported feeling rooted; they felt that they belonged and were part of things (Hashimoto, personal communication, 1983). This is in contrast to the fact that 69% of Japanese had lived in their town for 50 years or more compared to only 24% of older Americans. Even comparing only those who lived in their town since before World War II, 46% of Japanese and 86% of Americans reported feeling they belonged and were rooted (Hashimoto, personal communication, 1983). Reporting those kinds of feelings may be very foreign to the Japanese in spite of the belief of U.S. investigators that this sense of fit is a common theme of Japanese culture.

Questions that tap discussion of personal or financial problems may be culturally unacceptable to different groups. For instance, it appears to be very difficult for Japanese men to discuss personal problems with co-workers; only about 1.5% reported they do so in the Japanese–American study in Hawaii (Reed *et al.,* 1983). Studies designed to tap networks and support must take this into consideration in the future by probing more fully and developing more culturally sensitive questions.

Pathways Leading to Disease

Social networks seem to be related to disease states in a remarkably nonspecific way. It would be premature at this time to say that social ties are related to one category of disease and not to another. In fact, they may turn out to influence biologic mechanisms that increase an individual's vulnerability to a host of conditions. With regard to the spectrum of disease, the most consistent findings that have emerged are those relating network variables to mortality. In all mortality studies reviewed, including those on bereavement, various aspects of networks predicted mortality risk. Results are more mixed in morbidity studies. Certainly the results of the few CHD studies are most confusing and contradictory; however, in these immigrant studies the measures of social networks are by far the weakest and in some ways may not be tapping dimensions of networks at all. Studies of pregnancy complications designed with social network characteristics as major predictor variables have shown clearer and stronger effects.

The next question is how social networks and the functions they serve might influence physical health status; that is, what are the biologic pathways linking these two phenomena? Although there has not been much work in this area and space limitations preclude a lengthy discussion of this issue, several potential pathways leading from social networks to morbidity and mortality can be described.

The first is that through the provision of advice, services, and access to new social contacts, individuals with particular network ties obtain better medical care than others. Through the transmission of certain pro-medical care values, knowledge of how to obtain those services, subsequent access to and utilization of them, people simply get superior health care, which in turn influences their physical health.

A second possible pathway is by the direct provision of aid, services, and tangible or economic assistance to individuals. According to this hypothesis, some networks take better care of their members than others—independent of professional medical services—and it is this factor that influences a member's health status.

A third mechanism related to social integration has to do with social control and peer pressure. That is, individuals in a network frequently feel constrained to behave like other network members. Thus, people who have ties with people who smoke cigarettes, drink alcohol, are physically active, or maintain certain dietary practices may follow the patterns set forth by their group simply to maintain their group identity (not because of the health value of the behavior.) Therefore, groups or networks have the potential to be either health promoting or not, and this may influence the health status of individuals.

A final mechanism is a more direct physiologic pathway. People who are lacking ties that provide for intimacy, a sense of belonging, opportunities for nurturance, and reassurance of worth may experience this situation as stressful. Some individuals may then respond with a changing psychological state (becoming depressed or fatalistic, for example) and the psychological state may lead to alterations in physiologic functioning. In this instance, the psychological state is viewed as a mediating factor. The stressful condition may also directly alter physiologic patterns, without notable changes in psychological states. Social networks may well turn out to influence generalized susceptibility to illness as has been hypothesized (Antonovsky, 1972; Berkman & Syme, 1979; Cassel, 1976), or they may affect the course of many diseases through multiple mechanisms. In any of these cases, the biologic responses to this stressful condition may lead to alterations in both known biologic risk factors (e.g. blood pressure, serum cholesterol) and in as yet unidentified processes. If they function, in part, by altering known risk factors, it will be a mistake in analyses to treat such risk factors as simple confounders of the relationship instead of more properly considering them as potential mediators or pathways leading from a social experience to a health outcome.[1]

Cassel (1976), guided by the stress theory of disease originally formulated by Cannon (1935), Selye (1956), and Wolff (1953), described a pathway by which social factors could increase susceptibility to disease in general. According to this hypothesis, psychosocial factors influence physiological reactions by acting as signs and symbols of danger. In Cassel's view, signs and symbols exert their influence by altering the neuroendocrine system, thereby increasing susceptibility to disease agents.

Animal experiments have shown that stressful social circumstances alter neural, hormonal and immunologic control systems and lead to disease consequences (Ader, Kreutner, & Jacobs, 1963; Calhoun, 1962; Gross, 1972;

---

[1] I wish to thank Hal Morgenstern for his insight into this issue.

Ratcliffe, 1968). In human populations this series of links has not been established in any single study, though depressed lymphocyte function has been reported after bereavement (Bartrop, Luckhurst, Lazarus, Kiloh, & Penny, 1977). In cancer patients, both cell-mediated and humoral immunity are frequently depressed. Furthermore, different hormonal patterns have been reported in patients with cancer of the breast and prostate, and it is possible that some estrogens and androgens are responsive to stress (Lemon, 1969).

There is more animal, laboratory, and clinical evidence correlating social attachments (or the lack of them) with cardiovascular disease (Bovard, 1959; Buell & Eliot, 1979; Engel, 1971; Herd, 1979; Lown *et al.*, 1980; Raab, 1966; Ratcliffe, 1968). The pathways most often invoked as links are sympathetic–adrenomedullary responses and a more slowly acting and hormonally mediated adrenocortical response (Bovard, 1980; Buell & Eliot, 1979). In some cases, the role that social networks or social support may play is to inhibit a physiological response to stress. For example, individuals with extended social networks might have significantly lower resting pulse rates because of sympathetic inhibition than individuals without such support. On the other hand, individuals faced with a loss, particularly a sudden one, may experience increased sympathetic–andrenomedullary activity.

The pathways outlined are not meant to be definitive but only illustrative of potential mechanisms linking social ties to disease processes. Social relationships have the potential to influence health status in profound ways—in ways that investigators have just started to uncover. The findings from completed studies justify a more refined and purposeful search into the causes of diseases related to social connectedness or the lack of it.

References

Ader, R., Kreutner, A., & Jacobs, H. L. (1963). Social environment, emotionality and alloxan diabetes in the rat. *Psychosomatic Medicine, 25*, 60–68.

Antonovsky, A. (1972). Breakdown: A needed fourth step in the conceptual armamentarium of modern medicine. *Social Science and Medicine, 6*, 537–544.

Antonovsky, A. (1974). Conceptual, methodological problems in the study of resistance resources and stressful life events. In B. S. Dohrenwend & B. P. Dohrenwend (Eds.), *Stressful life events: Their nature and effects.* New York: Wiley.

Bartrop, R. W., Luckhurst, E., Lazarus, R., Kiloh, L. G., & Penny, R. (1977). Depressed lymphocyte function after bereavement. *Lancet, 1*, 834–836.

Bell, W., & Boat, M. D. (1957). Urban neighborhoods and informal social relations. *American Journal of Sociology, 62*, 391–398.

Bell, W., & Force, M. (1965). Urban neighborhood types and participation in formal associations. *American Sociological Review, 21*, 25–34.

Berkman, L. F. (1977). *Social networks, host resistance, and mortality: A follow-up study of Alameda County residents.* Ph.D. thesis, University of California, Berkeley.

Berkman, L. F. (1982). Social networks and analysis and coronary heart disease. *Advances in Cardiology, 29,* 37–49.

Berkman, L., & Breslow, L. (1983). *Health and ways of living: Findings from the Alameda County Study.* New York: Oxford University Press.

Berkman, L., & Syme, S. L. (1979). Social networks, host resistance, and mortality: A nine-year follow-up study of Alameda County residents. *American Journal Epidemiology, 109,* 186–204.

Blazer, D. (1982). Social support and mortality in an elderly community population. *American Journal of Epidemiology, 115,* 684–694.

Bovard, E. (1959). The effects of social stimuli on the response to stress. *Psychology Reviews, 66,* 267–277.

Bovard, E. (1980). *Brain mechanisms in effects of social networks on viability.* Unpublished manuscript.

Buell, J., & Eliot, R. S. (1979). The role of emotional stress in the development of heart disease. *Journal of the American Medical Association, 242,* 365–368.

Calhoun, J. B. (1962). Population density and social pathology. *Scientific American, 206,* 139–148.

Cannon, W. B. (1935). Stresses and strains of homeostates. *American Journal Medical Science 189,* 1–14.

Carter, H., & Glick, P. C. (1970). *Marriage and divorce: A social and economic study* (American Public Health Association, Vital and Health Statistics). Cambridge, MA: Harvard University Press.

Cassel, J. (1976). The contribution of the social environment to host resistance. *American Journal Epidemiology, 104,* 107–123.

Cox, P. R., & Ford, J. R. (1964). The mortality of widows shortly after widowhood. *Lancet, 1,* 163–164.

Engel, G. (1971). Sudden and rapid death during psychological stress. *Annals Internal Medicine, 74,* 771–782.

Fischer, A., Jackson, R., Stueve, C., Gerson, K., & Jones, L. (1977). *Networks and places: Social relations in the urban setting.* New York: The Free Press.

Goldbourt, U., Medalie, J., & Neufeld, H. (1975). Clinical myocardial infarction over a five year period. III. A multivariate analysis of incidence. *Journal Chronic Disease, 28,* 217–237.

Gore, S. (1981). Stress-buffering functions of social supports: An appraisal and clarification of research models. In B. S. Dohrenwend & B. P. Dohrenwend (Eds.), *Stressful life events and their contexts.* New York: Prodist.

Gross, W. B. (1972). Effect of social stress on occurrence of Marek's disease in chickens. *American Journal of Veterinarian Research, 33,* 2275–2279.

Haynes, S., & Feinleib, M. (1980). Women, work and coronary heart disease: prospective findings from the Framingham Heart Study. *American Journal Public Health, 70,* 133–141.

Haynes, S., Feinleib, M., & Kannel, W. (1980). The relationship of psychosocial factors to coronary heart disease in the Framingham Study. III Eight year incidence of coronary heart disease. *American Journal of Epidemiology, 111,* 37–58.

Helsing, K., Comstock, G., & Szklo, M. (1982). Causes of death in a widowed population. *American Journal of Epidemiology, 116,* 524–532.

Helsing, K., & Szklo, M. (1981). Mortality after bereavement. *American Journal of Epidemiology, 114,* 41–52.

Helsing, K., Szklo, M., & Comstock, G. (1981). Factors associated with mortality after widowhood. *American Journal of Public Health, 71,* 802–809.

Herd, A. (1979). *Behavioral factors in the physiological mechanisms of cardiovascular disease.* Paper presented at First Annual Meeting on Behavioral Medicine Research, Snowbird, Utah.

Holmes, T. H., & Rahe, R. H. (1967). The Social Readjustment Rating Scale. *Journal of Psychological Research, 11,* 213–218.

House, J. (1981). *Work, stress, and social support.* Reading, MA: Addison-Wesley.

House, J., Robbins, C., & Metzner, H. (1982). The association of social relationships and activities with mortality: Prospective evidence from the Tecumseh Community Health Study. *American Journal Epidemiology, 116,* 123–140.

Jenkins, C. D. (1971). Psychological and social precursors of coronary disease. *New England Journal of Medicine, 284,* 244–255, 307–317.

Joseph, J. (1980). *Social affiliation, risk factor status, and coronary heart disease: A cross-sectional study of Japanese–American men.* Unpublished Ph.D. thesis, University of California, Berkeley.

Joseph, J. G., & Syme, S. L. (1981, March). *Risk factor status, social isolation, and CHD.* Presented at 21st Conference on Cardiovascular Disease Epidemiology, American Heart Association, San Antonio, Texas.

Kaplan, B. H., Cassel, J. C., & Gore, S. (1977). Social support and health. *Medical Care, 15,* 47–58.

Koskenvuo, M., Kaprio, J., Kesaniemi, A., & Sarna, S. (1980). Differences in mortality from ischemic heart disease by marital status and social class. *Journal of Chronic Disease, 33,* 95–106.

Kraus, S., & Lilienfeld, A. M. (1959). Some epidemiologic aspects of the high mortality rates in the young widowed group. *Journal of Chronic Disease, 10,* 207–217.

Laumann, E. (1973). *Bonds of pluralism: The form and substance of urban social networks.* New York: Wiley.

Lemon, H. M. (1969). Endocrine influences on human mammary cancer formation. *Cancer, 23,* 781–790.

Litwak, E. (1960). Occupational mobility and extended family cohesion. *American Sociologic Review, 25,* 9–21.

Lown, B., Desilva, R., Reich, P., & Murawski, B. (1980). Psychophysiologic factors in sudden cardiac death. *American Journal of Psychiatry, 127,* 1325–1335.

McNeil, D. (1973). *Mortality among the widows in Connecticut.* MPH Essay, Yale University, New Haven, CT.

Marmot, M., & Syme, S. L. (1976). Acculturation and coronary heart disease in Japanese-Americans. *American Journal of Epidemiology, 104,* 225–246.

Marmot, M., Syme, S. L., Kagan, A., Kato, H., Cohen, J. B., & Belsky, J. (1975). Epidemiologic studies of coronary heart disease and stroke in Japanese men living in Japan, Hawaii and California: Prevalence of coronary and hypertensive heart disease and associated risk factors. *American Journal of Epidemiology, 102,* 514–525.

Mechanic, D. (1972). Social psychological factors affecting the presentation of bodily complaints. *New England Journal of Medicine, 286,* 1132–1135.

Medalie, J., & Goldbourt, V. (1976). Angina pectoris among 10,000 men: II. Psychosocial and other risk factors as evidenced by a multivariate analyses of a five year incidence study. *American Journal of Medicine, 60,* 910–921.

Medalie, J., Snyder, M., Groen, J. J., Neufeld, H. N., Goldbourt, Y. & Riss, E. (1973). Angina pectoris among 10,000 men: 5 year incidence and univariate analysis. *American Journal of Medicine 55,* 583–594.

Mitchell, J. C. (1969). The concept and use of social networks. In J. C. Mitchell (Ed.), *Social networks in urban situations.* Manchester, England: Manchester University Press.

Mitchell, R., & Trickett, E. (1980). Task force report: Social networks as mediators of social support. An analysis of the effects and determinants of social networks. *Community Mental Health Journal, 16,* 27–43.

Mueller, D. (1980). Social networks: A promising direction for research of the relationship of the social environment to psychiatric disorder. *Social Science and Medicine, 14,* 147–161.

Norbeck, J., & Tilden, V. (1983). Life stress, social support and emotional disequilibrium in complications of pregnancy: A prospective, multivariate study. *Journal of Health and Social Behavior, 24,* 30–46.

Nuckolls, K. B., Cassel, J. C., & Kaplan, B. H. (1972). Psychosocial assets, life crisis, and prognosis of pregnancy. *American Journal of Epidemiology, 95,* 431–441.

Ortmeyer, C. F. (1974). Variations in mortality, morbidity, and health care by marital status. In L. L. Erhardt & J. E. Berlin (Eds.), *Mortality and morbidity in the United States.* Cambridge, MA: Harvard University Press.

Parkes, C. M. (1964). The effects of bereavement on physical and mental health—A study of medical records of widows. *British Medical Journal, 2,* 274–279.

Parkes, C. M., Benjamin, B., & Fitzgerald, B. G. (1969). A broken heart: A statistical study of increased mortality among widows. *British Medical Journal, 1,* 740–743.

Raab, W. (1966). Emotional and sensory stress factors in myocardial pathology. *American Heart Journal, 72,* 538–564.

Ratcliffe, H. L. (1968). Environment, behavior and disease. In E. Stellar & J. M. Sprague (Eds.), *Progress in physiological psychology.* New York: Academic Press.

Reed, D., McGee, D., Cohen, J., Yano, K., Syme, S. L., & Feinleib, M. (1982). Acculturation and coronary heart disease among Japanese men in Hawaii. *American Journal of Epidemiology, 115,* 894–905.

Reed, D., McGee, D., Yano, K., & Feinleib, M. (1983). Social networks and coronary heart disease among Japanese men in Hawaii. *American Journal of Epidemiology 117,* 384–396.

Rees, W. P., & Lutkins, S. G. (1967). Mortality of bereavement. *British Medical Journal, 4,* 13–16.

Selye, H. (1956). *The stress of life.* New York: McGraw-Hill.

Sosa, R., Kennel, J., & Klaus, M. (1980). The effect of a supportive companion on perinatal problems, length of labor and mother-infant interactions. *New England Journal of Medicine, 305,* 597–600.

Stueve, A., & Lein, L. (1979). *Problems in network analysis: The case of the missing person.* Paper presented at the 32nd Annual Meeting of the Gerontological Society.

Susser, M. (1981). Widowhood: A statistical life stress or a stressful life event. *American Journal of Public Health, 71,* 793–795.

Thiel, H. G., Parker, D., & Bruce, T. (1973). Stress factors and the risk of myocardial infarction. *Psychology Research, 17,* 43–57.

Thoits, P. (1982). Conceptual, methodological, and theoretical problems in studying social supports as a buffer against life stress. *Journal of Health and Social Behavior, 23,* 145–159.

Weiss, N. S. (1973). Marital status and risk factors for coronary heart disease: The United States Health Examination Survey of Adults. *British Journal Preventative and Social Medicine, 27,* 41–43.

Weiss, R. (1969, July-August). The fund of sociability. *Transaction,* pp. 36–43.

Wellman, B. (1981). Applying network analyses to the study of support. In B. H. Gottlieb (Ed.), *Social networks and social support.* Beverly Hills, CA: Sage.

Wolff, C. H. (1953). *Stress and disease.* Springfield, IL: Thomas.

Worth, R., Rhoads, G., Kagan, A. *et al.* (1975). Epidemiologic studies of coronary heart disease and stroke in Japanese men living in Japan, Hawaii and California: Mortality. *American Journal of Epidemiology, 102,* 481–490.

CHAPTER 13

Social Support and Styles of Coping with Stress*

Susan Gore

Introduction

Models of the stress process recognize the influence of personal and situational variables in mitigating or exacerbating stress and its health effects. To date, the point of departure for most research in this area has been what is known as the stress-buffering function of social supports. Briefly, the idea of buffering supposes a model in which increases in level of life stress place all people at risk for illness, but the impact of exposure to high levels of stress should be offset or buffered in the presence of adequate social supports. What, then, is adequate support, how does it come to be given, and how does it function to reduce stress? These are the practical questions that underlie all research on stress buffering. Some of the difficulties in doing research to answer these questions are the subject of this chapter.

*The preparation of this chapter was supported in part by NIMH Grant MH35648. I would like to thank Mary Ellen Colten, John Eckenrode, Nan Lin, and Blair Wheaton for engaging in helpful discussions about the issues considered herein.

263

New Emphases in Stress-Buffering Research

To begin, it is important to recognize that researchers have been preoccupied with issues of measurement since the early 1970s. Measurement here specifically means the method of assessing the presence and magnitude of life stress on one hand and the presence and nature of social supports on the other. Because of the diffuseness of these two concepts, stress and support, there have been understandable difficulties in making them operational.

Although these issues are by no means resolved (see House & Kahn, Chapter 5 in this volume), other complexities pertaining to models of stress buffering have surfaced. In fact, it might be argued that issues of measurement have not been resolved precisely because these broader concerns must first be addressed. Two of these concerns will be the focus of this chapter.

1. How do social support and other more personal coping characteristics fit into a larger picture of coping with stress?
2. What are the expected relationships among variables in stress-buffering models and what type of statistical evidence is required to document stress buffering?

Social Support and Personal Coping Variables

Interestingly, research on the function of social supports in buffering the impact of stressful experiences progressed for a number of years quite independently of the work on more personal, rather than interpersonal, coping styles. In fact, the idea of coping, which pertains to all types of individual efforts to alter or control stressful circumstances and reduce the negative emotions attendant to these situations, has come to be identified with individual activities and styles of behavior. Some types of coping, for example, might include making a plan of activity and following it, standing one's ground, and trying to look on the bright side of things (Folkman & Lazarus, 1980). Although, conceptually, the myriad of coping strategies and activities in which people engage when confronting crisis would certainly include eliciting the help of others, the research as a whole has not reflected this. Instead, there appear to be parallel but distinct research traditions, one focusing on the stress-buffering function of social support and the other dealing similarly with individual means of coping. This schism, which seems artificial and cumbersome, in part reflects disciplinary boundaries. It also stems from the view of social supports as a fairly stable supply of environmental resources. From this perspective the relationship between these support resources and individual coping efforts, which are the crux of coping, is not easily conceptualized.

The point of departure for most discussions of this issue is the small body of evidence that has shown an apparent harmful health impact of seeking help from others to deal with problems, in contrast to the beneficial effects of working things through by oneself (Pearlin & Schooler, 1978; Warheit, Vega, Shimizu, & Meinhardt, 1982). Most researchers agree that knowledge about the context in which help seeking takes place should provide important clues to why help seeking seems to be a dysfunctional coping behavior. For example, Husaini and colleagues (Husaini, Newbrough, Neff, & Moore, 1982) argue that help seeking is a means of last resort for individuals who are otherwise unable to cope. Pearlin and Schooler (1979) have argued, similarly, that quality support is only likely to be obtained from more spontaneous help giving. Like Husaini *et al.*, they view the act of engaging in help seeking as an indicator of underlying coping ineffectiveness. This interpretation, according to Gottlieb (1983), receives some support from the body of research documenting the impoverished social networks of clinical populations. Like other researchers (Heller, 1979; Henderson, 1980) Gottlieb believes that a personality trait of social competence might be at the root of findings pertaining to the stress-buffering effects of social support. If this is true, excessive help seekers, like the impaired, may lack the social competence required to maintain potentially helpful relationships and to mobilize them successfully.

Finally, in a different vein, Brickman and associates (Brickman, Rabinowitz, Karuza, Coates, Cohn, & Kidder, 1982) have focused on the question of what constitutes effective and ineffective help. The act of helping, they argue, is victimizing rather than helpful when it is not compatible with the understandings that people have about themselves, the nature of the problems they face, and the solutions that are needed.

> The very label *help* implies that recipients are not responsible for solving a problem . . . and that help givers are. When people say that someone deserves help, they may mean only that this individual is not to be blamed for their problems. . . . But, unwittingly or not, they also imply that this individual is not in control of and cannot be held responsible for solutions. (p. 376).

This dilemma of helping describes the problems that are often generated by the well-intentioned friends of accident victims, as described by Bulman and Wortman (1977) in their study of paraplegics. The paraplegics' repeated affirmation that their crippling accident resulted from activities in which they genuinely wished to engage, and would do so again, is interpreted by friends as the victims' need to blame themselves for the accident.

This is not the case; for victims, a solution to the loss is to regain control of their lives, which is achieved by seeing themselves as having chosen the fateful course of activity.

Discussions such as these concerning the role of giving and seeking help in the coping process are a first step toward more systematic investigation of the relationship between interpersonal and intra-individual coping variables in the stress process. One schema central to understanding how measures of these moderators actually relate to each other is a classification of coping variables as reflecting either a latent or active dimension of coping. This, it must be emphasized, pertains both to social support and to personal coping variables. In addition, this view of coping variables provides more than a typology. Distinguishing between the latent and active components of the coping process addresses some of the ambiguity in the conceptualization and empirical tests for stress-buffering processes. Thus, the two themes of this chapter, as noted earlier, are in fact components of the same problem—that is, how to model the stress-buffering process.

Coping Resources and Coping Activity

Most research on the topic of stress buffering has utilized measures of coping resources, whether these resources are defined as social support variables or as personal styles or traits. *Resources,* such as being married, having a confidant, or having an active orientation toward problem solving, *reflect a latent dimension of coping because they define a potential for action, but not action itself.*

With respect to social support variables, the presence of support resources is usually indicated by measures of structural interconnectedness or aloneness. Some of the more popular measures of support potential have included marital status; number of friends, relatives and neighbors; living alone or with others; and other relatively objectively measured features of social context such as membership in formal groups. Measures of network structure, such as size, density, reciprocity, and multiplexity, also reflect the idea of social support resource because they define features of the actor's social environment at a particular moment in time and in a nontransactional sense.

Internal coping resources include aspects of personality, such as flexibility and fatalism (Wheaton, 1982), and values concerning the appropriateness or efficacy of seeking help from others (Eckenrode, 1983). Drawing on the work of Kohn (1972), Wheaton (1982), has outlined the role of fatalism and inflexibility in the stress process. He argues that these predispositions should not be interpreted as the equivalent to coping activity.

Instead, they are expected to affect illness outcomes indirectly through their influence on two important features of coping *activity*: ability and effort. Whereas inflexibility implies a tendency to narrow the range of coping strategies and thus affects ability, a fatalist perspective does this and more; it "puts in doubt the *point* of coping" (p. 296) at all.

Resources may be seen as background variables in the coping process in two respects. First, they affect the definition of stressful stimuli as threatening or not—an evaluation that Lazarus and Launier (1978) have called primary appraisal and that House (1981) and colleagues (French, Rogers, & Cobb, 1974) have called perceived stress. Second, resource variables set constraints on what can and will be done in the way of coping once the individual judges a situation to be threatening. According to Lazarus and Launier (1978), the individual's appraisal of the possibilities for dealing with the stress situation is a secondary appraisal of threat that *sets in motion the coping process.*

The idea of a coping resource, then, contrasts with that of coping activity because the latter pertains to the ways in which people actually respond to stressful situations, the extent and ways in which they draw upon the various individual and social resources that are potentially available.

The study of coping activities is a more recent research emphasis and it has brought with it major changes in research design and the modeling of stress buffering because it is necessarily situation oriented. Basically, a situational approach means that coping strategies must be linked to the specific stressors they are presumed to affect (Pearlin, Lieberman, Menaghan, & Mullan, 1981). For example, Pearlin and Schooler (1978) investigated the effectiveness of different cognitive and behavioral coping strategies (e.g., controlled reflectiveness, negotiation, and selective ignoring) in alleviating the distress associated with problems that are usually encountered in the marital, work, and parenting spheres of life. The approach is decidedly situational because it involves consideration of the different sources of stress and the differential relevance of the coping strategies to the problems that arise in each domain of activity. This contrasts with the analytic strategies associated with the measurement of life stress through use of the Holmes and Rahe (1967) instrument. In this case, because the occurrence and magnitude of stress is indicated by a tally of recent events, assessments of coping are generally not linked to the specific problems or challenges posed by the stressful events.

Clearly, whether a research approach is situation-oriented is a matter of degree. Whereas Pearlin and Schooler focused on what people *usually* do when stresses arise, Folkman and Lazarus (1980) studied what people do and think in specific stressful encounters. In studying these coping repertoires, Folkman and Lazarus and other researchers (Billings & Moos, 1981;

Pearlin *et al.*, 1981; Pearlin & Schooler, 1978) have assessed psychological, behavioral and social support-related actions.[1] All have emphasized the importance of cognitive strategies such as optimistic comparison, for reducing emotional distress. With respect to the social support concept, these and other investigators (Carveth & Gottlieb, 1979; Eckenrode, 1983) have focused on contacts with others and on seeking and receiving help. As noted earlier, the use of help seeking and receiving as an indicator of coping has led to counterintuitive findings: Supportive interventions seem to increase rather than decrease psychological distress.

Finding the unexpected, however, should not be surprising because certain activities, such as help seeking, looking on the bright side, and talking things out, are used as markers for more complex coping sequences. Selection of any single indicator of coping, be it a measure of resources or of activity, necessarily results in a snapshot of events, perceptions, and responses. It is for this reason that advocates of process study (e.g., Eckenrode & Gore, 1981; Lazarus & Launier, 1978) have called for a consideration of many snapshots—actually, the multiple linkages that interpret the relationship between stress and its health impacts.

The Stress-Buffering Model and the Mobilization of Coping Resources

The distinction between coping resource variables and activity variables (i.e., the latent and active dimensions of coping) provides direction for this interpretive work. First, although there are many ways in which coping resources and activities can offset the health impact of stress (Dohrenwend & Dohrenwend, 1981; Wheaton, 1983a) the buffering hypothesis entails some rather specific assumptions about the model of stress-reduction. With respect to social support for example, it is hypothesized that adequate support will offset or moderate the health effects of stress. Conversely, the effect of exposure to stress will be most pronounced in the absence of sup-

---

[1] Wheaton's research (1982, 1983b) also can be called situational, but it differs in two respects. First, stressors were differentiated not in terms of the specific problems that arise, but rather in terms of an acute–chronic dimension. "Acute stressors typically have a more clearly delimited time referent; they refer to discrete events that occur and then are over. Chronic stressors tend to persist over longer periods of time and do not reach a noticeable peak or higher point before they fade" (1982, p. 210). Second, his investigations utilized variables more properly understood as coping resources than as coping strategies because of their rather stable nature. Although the missing ingredient is actual coping behavior, his analyses demonstrate the importance of linking coping resources as well as coping activities to particular stress contexts.

ports. Additionally, in this model social support is defined as a vulnerability factor because it is understood to operate *only* in conjunction with stress; that is, it alleviates the burden of the highly stressed but is irrelevant to the situation of those at relatively low levels of stress. Why is it that social support should be effective only in the face of high levels of stress? Stress-buffering models assume an active coping function of the vulnerability factor that causes increases in perceived stress to be met by a mobilization of resources to reduce or manage the level of threat. For example, Lin (personal communication, 1983) hypothesizes that individuals high in support resources prior to stressful experiences will succeed in mobilizing members of their social network in response to the threat. Conversely, individuals low in resources will fail to do so. Thus, although the stress-buffering process is often described in terms of the strength of initial and subsequent (to the stress) levels of coping resources (Thoits, 1982a), it is more accurate to speak of the initial level of *coping resources,* which is the potential of a *still-latent support system,* and the subsequent extent of *coping activity* (for example, making coping contacts).

In sum, the question of a stress-buffering effect of social support, strictly speaking, is contingent upon evidence that support is mobilized, not that it exists as a potential. This model, therefore, suggests the importance of investigating how resource type and level influence coping effort and activity. Some work of this nature is under way. Eckenrode (1983), for example, has studied the relationship among personal coping resources, social network resources (number of physically proximate network members), and extent of interpersonal contact to deal with specific problem situations. As an indicator of personal resources he used a measure of internal (versus external) locus of control predisposition. This, basically, is an assessment of an individual's beliefs regarding the amount of control people have in shaping or responding to environmental events and personal experiences. He found that locus of control predisposition was not associated with the total number of potential network supporters. However, having an internal locus of control (being "internal") was associated with making more coping contacts; these data suggest that internals may be more effective in mobilizing available supporters in response to stress than externals. The findings, according to Eckenrode, are consistent with those of Sandler and Lakey (1982), who found that persons having internal locus of control beliefs were less affected by high levels of stress, although externals reported more friendships. Interestingly, it appears from the Eckenrode research that problem-solving contacts are an extension of personal resourcefulness, whereas findings from several studies noted earlier indicate that help seeking is a hallmark of the poor coper. Subtleties in conceptualization and operationalization are clearly involved: Eckenrode operationalized social support as a social contact variable, not as a help-seeking variable.

A number of other research questions are suggested by this classification of resource and activity dimensions of coping. The path between resource and activity, exemplified in Eckenrode's findings concerning the influence of psychological resources on use of social contacts for problem-solving efforts, has been emphasized. An alternative question concerns the influence of social support resources on coping strategies and behaviors. In other words, do social support resources affect health status indirectly through individual coping efforts? Some research suggests the significance of this line of thinking. Pearlin *et al.* (1981), for example, found that emotional support seemed to mitigate depression indirectly through its effects on self-esteem and mastery. This pattern of data suggests the importance of social support for sustaining coping activity. Finally, attention should be given to how episodes of coping in turn influence resource levels. For example, if social network resources diminish in number subsequent to a coping episode, this might say something about the network's effectiveness in that particular situation and its potential in the longer run (i.e., when resource mobilization is next initiated).

How Is Resource Mobilization Evidenced?

The idea of resource mobilization, which hinges on a distinction between latent and active coping variables, also underscores the importance of stressors as stimuli in the resource mobilization process. In early representations of the stress-buffering model the relationship between the occurrence and appraisal of stress and the initiation of coping activity was not a subject of investigation. It was probably assumed that a significant association between measures of stress and support would refute the notion of stress buffering. For example, if an inverse relationship between these variables were evidenced, a stress-prevention role of support would be suggested—an idea at odds with stress buffering, because the latter requires individuals at all levels of support to be exposed to identical stress experiences. Thus, most researchers hoped to find measures of stress and social support to be orthogonal. With stress characterized as fortuitous and social support as a stable feature of the social environment, the central question was simply whether the stress–illness relationship differed by level of support resources.

This classic stress-buffering model differs from more recent models (e.g., Lin, Simeone, Ensel, & Kuo, 1979, p. 111; Wheaton, 1983a) in which the relationship between stress and coping activity is an explicit feature. In describing such models of stress reduction, Wheaton has underscored the fact that empirical documentation of stress buffering calls for a positive relationship between the stress and coping variables, a negative relationship between the coping variables and distress, and a positive direct effect of stress on distress. Under these circumstances, the total causal effect of stress will be less than its direct effect alone, a pattern of evidence suggesting that coping functions to attenuate the impact of stress on health.

Some consideration should be given to the question of whether a positive relationship between exposure to or perceptions of stress and the coping measure is counterintuitive. This would seem to be the case only because most coping measures do not assess coping activities, such as making coping contacts; such behavior would be expected to increase in response to stress. Rather, investigators have relied largely on a class of resource variables that are not clear-cut with respect to their temporal location and function in the coping process. For this reason the earlier discussion of resource variables did not mention the many different measures of the quality of social relationships (Billings & Moos, 1981) and perceived supportiveness of significant others (Andrews, Tennant, Hewson, & Vaillant, 1978; Aneshensel & Frerichs, 1982; Brown & Harris, 1968; Cohen & Hoberman, 1983; Cohen, Struening, Muhlin, Genevie, Kaplan, & Peck, 1982; Gore, 1978; Lin, et al., 1979; Lowenthal & Haven, 1968; Turner, 1981; and others too numerous to mention). Whether these indicators focus on the anticipated reliability of significant others or on current feelings of being supported versus experiencing conflict, they differ from the structural measures of support resource because they call for conclusions about how good (e.g., caring, effective, or reliable) people really are. In some cases, these perceptions come dangerously close to indicating the more global feelings of well-being or distress that are seen as the consequence of coping efforts. Similarly, there are personal resource variables that also tap some combination of coping potential and long-term coping success. These include mastery or competence (Caplan, 1981), self-esteem (Pearlin et al., 1981), and hardiness (Kobasa, Maddi, & Courington, 1981).

It is known, of course, that the availability of coping resources is itself the consequence of prior coping episodes and that, over time, these experiences become traitlike characteristics of personality.[2] Thus, the analytic distinctions among coping resource, coping activity, and coping results are

[2]If the distinction between coping resource and coping activity is to be useful there must be some limitations on what is classified as a resource variable. There is good reason to draw the line with these more global social support and personality variables. Interestingly, because evidence indicates that measures of perceived support are likely to be highly stable over time (Aneshensel & Frerichs, 1982) and probably reflect fairly long-term social processes, the sense of support or of being able to elicit support could be conceived of as a personal characteristic, not unlike other coping-related variables such as self-esteem and mastery.

not easily investigated. The problem, however, is that models of stress buffering call for attention to these distinctions. Resource variables, and especially these more global resource variables, will probably be negatively associated with measures of exposure to stress and perceived stress, suggesting a type of more long-term and generalized coping activity in limiting exposure to stress and in dealing with the threats and challenges that regularly occur. This idea of chronic coping is consistent with Wheaton's model (1983a) of a stress-counteracting process.

The Search for Stress-Buffering Effects

With respect to such alternative formulations of stress reduction, most discussion has focused on whether different statistical patterns of evidence confirm or refute the idea of stress buffering. As noted earlier, the model of stress buffering has been defined as interactive: Social support is seen to benefit health only through its influence in cushioning or short-circuiting the risk associated with high levels of stress. This vulnerability model is distinguished from the additive burden model (Dohrenwend & Dohrenwend, 1981), under which stress and social support variables are *each* seen to contribute to health outcomes. In this latter case, the coping variable, such as social support, also affects the health status of individuals who are exposed to very low levels of stress.

This would seem incompatible with the stress-buffering framework, because only increasing levels of stress should lead to the initiation of coping activity (La Rocco, 1983). However, as noted earlier, most of the coping variables that are studied (e.g., perceived support and social interaction versus isolation) are not measures of specific coping activities; nor are they indicators of personal and interpersonal strengths that are only relevant in the face of considerable stress.[3]

How, then, should additive effects be interpreted? It might be argued that even when exposure to stress is relatively low, coping continues as an ongoing process, enhancing the health even of individuals who are not at risk by virtue of stressful conditions (Wheaton, 1983a). The social situation of these copers should be contrasted with that of those who also report low levels of recent stressful occurrences, and in addition a low sense of

---

[3]House (1981, Appendix B) has alluded to this problem in his discussions of the conditions under which evidence would not support an interactive model of stress buffering. He noted that additive rather than interactive statistical effects will be observed in any study in which the period of observation does not allow for the identification of *distinct coping episodes*. This is certainly the case in most research on stress buffering.

social support, mastery, or competence. *Because these characteristics would certainly be debilitative over the long run, having little coping capacity even in the absence of major life events might be viewed as a type of constitutional risk factor that operates independently of stress.*

The distinction between an additive and interactive model of stress reduction, therefore, may be reduced to the question of whether low social support or certain personal coping styles or strategies are in fact stressors that may directly impact mental health.[4] Such an interpretation will necessarily be contingent on the facet of coping that is measured. With respect to the support concept, for example, it is likely that individuals who report a low sense of support from others also have experienced interpersonal disappointments over a period of time. These individuals might be expected to be more highly distressed than others with more positive relationships. On the other hand, low affiliative frequency may reflect an absence of active coping activity or a long-term modest level of sociability to which an individual has become accustomed. In either case, low affiliative values would not necessarily reflect stress or threaten health.

Whatever the implications for health of these different coping-related variables, the more general and important point is that much research has not really been attentive to the design and measurement requirements of an interactive model of stress buffering. With respect to design and analytic issues, House (1981, Appendix B) has explained why evidence of additive effects is so likely. The appropriateness of coping measures, as discussed earlier, is another significant issue.

New Research Directions

Before concluding, it is important to call attention to some of the strategies that have been used to provide more insight into the stress-buffering process. Basically, what these approaches have in common is formulations of stress-buffering problems that are situation-specific. This is true in two respects. First, as Cohen and McKay (1984) also have noted, aspects of coping resources and behavior should be linked to particular stressors or challenges. Second, the dynamics of stress reduction may vary for different segments of the populations. A few illustrative approaches are summarized next.

---

[4]Thoits (1982a) also has discussed this issue, but with a different purpose. This discussion focuses on the meaning of low values on coping variables for persons exposed to minimal stress, whereas she was concerned with decrements of support among those under maximal stress.

In regard to the first aspect of specificity, a number of investigators (House & Wells, 1978; La Rocco, House, & French, 1980; Pearlin et al., 1981; Wheaton, 1982, 1983b) have consistently pursued a differentiated view of coping resources and stress. For example, La Rocco and colleagues have studied the effects of co-worker, supervisor, and family supportiveness on relationships involving job stress (e.g., underutilization of skills), job-related strains (e.g., job dissatisfaction), and more general symptoms of psychological distress. This approach yielded different patterns of findings depending on the relationships that were investigated. Where job-related strain was high, for instance, co-worker support was generally found to be more effective in offsetting symptoms of anxiety and depression than were other types of support. However, where more general somatic symptoms were involved, the wider range of supports was found to be relevant. Analyses of this nature demonstrate the importance of examining stress and support processes within specific life roles. In the case of work roles, it is evident that spouse support is not as important as is generally accepted in the wider research literature.

Whereas much of the work on life stress has been based on simple models consisting of stress, coping, and outcome measures, Pearlin and colleagues (Pearlin et al., 1981) have examined how coping alters a series of negative outcomes that are likely to intervene in the relationship between a single major stressor—in this case job loss—and subsequent changes in depression. In their theory, life events are understood to intensify existing role strains, such as those in marriage. To the extent that these strains persist, they are seen to threaten self-concept and self-esteem, with the obvious implications for depressive disorder. On the basis of this model, Pearlin and colleagues were able to test for the effects of coping variables in preventing depression directly or indirectly by "neutralizing any or all of its antecedent conditions" (p. 348). In general, they found cognitive coping strategies to ameliorate strain at several points in the causal chain. Social support had a more specific function in maintaining self-esteem and a sense of mastery.

Working with the concepts of fatalism and inflexibility, Wheaton (1982, 1983b) also has attempted to specify the conditions under which stress more or less surely leads to disorder. Whereas Pearlin and colleagues achieved this through examining how coping style alters a series of relationships intervening between an event and disorder, Wheaton, in contrast, has examined the relevance of different coping resources for acute versus chronic stressors. According to his stability-matching framework, variability in coping *effort* should have a strong moderating impact on the effects of *acute stressors* on symptoms, because effort can be increased or decreased to meet changing environmental demands. Variability in coping *ability* will also influence outcome from acute stress; however, it should be more relevant to reducing the impact of *chronic stressors*. To operationalize these concepts, Wheaton reasoned that coping effort is implied by a predisposition of fatalism and that coping ability is implied by one of inflexibility. Thus, through its effects on ability or effort, the impact of each coping resource should be contingent on the nature of the stressor (i.e., whether acute or chronic). His analyses confirm the expectation that these coping variables will function differently for each type of stress stimuli.

Other researchers have attempted to gain a better understanding of the nature of the stressors to which people are exposed. In their research on the stress-buffering function of social support, Aneshensel and Stone (1982) have considered whether the magnitude of the relationship between loss events and depression differs by level of social support, *within categories defined by the extent of longer-term life strain.* They found that at high levels of life strain there was a buffering effect of support; that is, social support offset the impact of having one or more personal loss events on subsequent levels of depressive symtomotology. This stress-buffering effect was not observed for persons in the low life strain category.

A somewhat different approach to gaining a better appreciation of stress context has been evidenced in research on explanations for differential vulnerability to stress (Kessler, 1979; Kessler &. Essex, 1982; Thoits, 1982b; Turner &. Noh, 1983). The point of departure of these studies is the observation that although there may be little difference in *exposure* to stress among some sociodemographic groups, such as the married and the unmarried, there appear to be significant differences in psychological and health *response* to similar life stresses. Thoits (1982b) refers to this group vulnerability as the applied buffering hypothesis. Studies that address this issue provide a needed conceptual bridge between stress research and more descriptive epidemiological research on the prevalence of disorder in significant categories of the population. For example, Thoits (1982b) has tested for differential vulnerability and stress buffering for a number of groups (including the elderly, female, unmarried, and persons of lower socioeconomic status) that have been understood to be at high risk for psychological distress. In general, she found very weak support for the explanation that group differences in coping with stress account for differences in vulnerability to stress. This, she noted, may be due to the indirectness of the coping variable utilized, a measure of neighborhood integration. Although Thoits concluded that the overall pattern of findings for differential coping is unimpressive, several of her findings are important. First, females were not found to be significantly more vulnerable to the impact of stressful events than males. Because this probability has been discussed in epidemiological research on gender differences (Kessler, 1979), a negative finding in this area should be noted. Thoits also found, as did Kessler and Essex

(1982) in a similar analysis, that without the resources for dealing with stress married persons would have evidenced higher distress levels than the unmarried. Findings such as these say something important about the coping of the married, again an epidemiological topic about which there has been considerable speculation.

Conclusion

The purpose of this chapter has been to underscore some of the conceptual and methodological issues that must be tackled if further headway is to be made into understanding the relationship between stress and health. Researchers seem to be recognizing that the requirements for testing the stress-buffering model are in fact very constraining. This, no doubt, will have positive effects on the field because it will encourage researchers to define better and to meet the requirements for this model, and to broaden the scope of inquiries by applying new models of stress reduction to a wider range of empirical problems.

References

Andrews, G., Tennant, C., Hewson, D. H., & Vaillant, G. E. (1979). Life event stress, social support, coping style, and risk of psychological impairment. *Journal of Nervous and Mental Disease. 166*, 307–316.

Aneshensel, C., & Frerichs, R. R. (1982). Stress, support and depression: A longitudinal causal model. *Journal of Community Psychology, 10,* 363–376.

Aneshensel, C., & Stone, J. (1982). Stress and depression: A test of the buffering model of social support, *Archives of General Psychiatry, 39,* 1392–1396.

Billings, A. G., & Moos, R. H. (1981). The role of coping responses and social resources in attenuating the stress of life events. *Journal of Behavioral Medicine, 4,* 139–157.

Brickman, P., Rabinowitz, V. C., Karuza, J., Coates, D., Cohn, E., & Kidder, L. (1982). Models of helping and coping. *American Psychologist, 37,* 368–384.

Brown, G. N., & Harris, T. (1968). *Social origins of depression: A study of psychiatric disorders in women.* London: Tavistock.

Bulman, R. J., & Wortman, C. (1977). Attributions of blame and coping in the "real world": Severe accident victims react to their lot. *Journal of Personality and Social Psychology, 35,* 351–363.

Caplan, G. (1981). Mastery of stress: Psychosocial aspects. *American Journal of Psychiatry, 138,* 413–420.

Carveth, W. B., & Gottlieb, B. H. (1979). The measurement of social support and its relation to stress. *Canadian Journal of Behavioral Science. 11,* 179–186.

Cohen, P., Struening, E. L., Muhlin, G. L., Genevie, L. E., Kaplan, S. R., & Peck, H. B. (1982). Community stressors, mediating conditions, and wellbeing in urban neighborhoods. *Journal of Community Psychology, 10,* 377–391.

Cohen, S., & Hoberman, H. M. (1983). Positive events and social supports as buffers of life change stress. *Journal of Applied Social Psychology, 13,* 99–125.

Cohen, S., & McKay, G. (1984). Social support, stress and the buffering hypothesis: a theoretical analysis. In A. Baum, J. E. Singer, & S. E. Taylor (Eds.), *Handbook of psychology and health* (Vol. IV). Hillsdale, NJ: Erlbaum.

Dohrenwend, B. S., & Dohrenwend, B. P. (1981). Life stress and illness: Formulation of the issues. In B. S. Dohrenwend & B. P. Dohrenwend (Eds.), *Stressful life events and their contexts.* New York: Prodist.

Eckenrode, J. (1983). The mobilization of social support: Some individual constraints. *American Journal of Community Psychology, 11,* 509–528.

Eckenrode, J., & Gore, S. (1981). Stressful events and social supports: The significance of context. In B. H. Gottlieb (Ed.), *Social networks and social support in community mental health.* Beverly Hills, CA: Sage.

Folkman, S., & Lazarus, R. (1980). An analysis of coping in a middle-aged community sample. *Journal of Health and Social Behavior, 21,* 219–239.

French, J. R. P., Jr., Rogers, W., & Cobb, S. (1974). Adjustment as person-environment fit. In G. V. Coehlo, D. A. Hamburg, & J. E. Adams, (Eds.), *Coping and adaptation.* New York: Basic.

Gore, S. (1978). The effect of social support in moderating the health consequences of unemployment. *Journal of Health and Social Behavior, 19,* 157–165.

Gottlieb, B. (1983). Social support as a focus for integrative research in psychology. *American Psychologist, 38,* 278–287.

Heller, K. (1979). The effects of social support: Prevention and treatment implications. In A. P. Goldstein & F. H. Kaufos (Eds.), *Maximizing treatment gains.* New York: Academic Press.

Henderson, S. (1980). A development in social psychiatry: The systematic study of social bonds. *Journal of Nervous and Mental Disease, 168,* 63–69.

Holmes, T. H., & Rahe, R. H. (1967). The social readjustment rating scale. *Journal of Psychosomatic Research, 11,* 213–218.

House, J. (1981). *Work stress and social support.* Reading, MA.: Addison-Wesley.

House, J. S., & Wells, J. A. (1978). Occupational stress, social support and health. In A. McLean, G. Black, & M. Zolligan, (Eds.), *Reducing occupational stress: Proceedings of a conference.* Washington, DC: U.S. Department of Health, Education and Welfare, HEW (NIOSH). (Publication No. 78–140)

Husaini, B. A., Newbrough, J. R., Neff, J. A., & Moore, M. C. (1982). The stress-buffering role of social support and personal competence among the rural married. *Journal of Community Psychology, 10,* 409–423.

Kessler, R. C. (1979). A strategy for studying differential vulnerability to the psychological consequences of stress. *Journal of Health and Social Behavior, 20,* 100–108.

Kessler, R., & Essex, M. (1982). Marital status and depression: The importance of coping resources. *Social Forces, 61,* 485–507.

Kobasa, S. C., Maddi, S. R., & Courington, S. (1981). Personality and constitution as mediators in the stress-illness relationship. *Journal of Health and Social Behavior, 22,* 368–378.

Kohn, M. L. (1972). Class, family and schizophrenia. *Social Forces, 50,* 295–302.

La Rocco, J. M. (1983). Theoretical distinctions between causal and interaction effects of social support. *Journal of Health and Social Behavior, 24,* 91–92.

La Rocco, J. M., House, J. S., & French, J. R. P., Jr. (1980). Social support, occupational stress, and health. *Journal of Health and Social Behavior, 21,* 202–218.

Lazarus, R. S., & Launier, R. (1978). Stress-related transactions between person and environment. In L. A. Pervin & M. Lewis (Eds.), *Internal and external determinants of behavior.* New York: Plenum.

Lin, N., Simeone, R. S., Ensel, W. M., & Kuo, W. (1979). Social support, stressful life events, and illness: A model and empirical test. *Journal of Health and Social Behavior, 20,* 108–119.

Lowenthal, M. F., & Haven, C. (1968). Interaction and adaptation: Intimacy as a critical variable. *American Sociological Review, 33,* 20–30.

Pearlin, L. I., Lieberman, M. A., Menaghan, E., & Mullan, J. E. (1981). The stress process. *Journal of Health and Social Behavior, 22,* 337–356.

Pearlin, L. I., & Schooler, C. (1978). The structure of coping. *Journal of Health and Social Behavior, 19,* 2–21.

Pearlin, L. I., & Schooler, C. (1979). Some extensions of "The structure of coping." *Journal of Health and Social Behavior, 20,* 202–205.

Sandler, I. N., & Lakey, B. (1982). Locus of control as a stress moderator: The role of control perceptions and social support. *American Journal of Community Psychology, 10,* 65–80.

Thoits, P. (1982a). Problems in the study of social support. *Journal of Health and Social Behavior, 23,* 145–159.

Thoits, P. (1982b). Life stress, social support, and psychological vulnerability: Epidemiological considerations. *Journal of Community Psychology, 10,* 341–363.

Turner, R. J. (1981). Experienced social support as a contingency in emotional well being. *Journal of Health and Social Behavior, 22,* 357–67.

Turner, R. J., & Noh, S. (1983). Class and psychological vulnerability among women: The significance of social support and personal control. *Journal of Health and Social Behavior, 24,* 2–15.

Warheit, G., Vega, W., Shimizu, D., & Meinhardt, K. (1982). Interpersonal coping networks and mental health problems among four race/ethnic groups. *Journal of Community Psychology, 10,* 312–325.

Wheaton, B. (1982). A comparison of the moderating effects of personal coping resources on the impact of exposure to stress in two groups. *Journal of Community Psychology, 10,* 293–311.

Wheaton, B. (1983a, September). Models for the stress-buffering functions of coping resources. Paper presented at the meeting of the American Sociological Association, Detroit, Michigan.

Wheaton, B. (1983b). Stress, personal coping resources and psychiatric symptoms: An investigation of interactive models. *Journal of Health and Social Behavior, 24,* 208–229.

PART IV

Social Support Interventions and Health Policy

The Role of Social Support in Adaptation and Recovery from Physical Illness*

Camille B. Wortman and Terry L. Conway

Introduction

During the 1970s, investigators in the health field began to show a great deal of interest in the construct of social support. Drawing from a diverse group of studies in many fields of inquiry, a number of early review papers concluded that social support has beneficial effects on a wide range of health outcomes (Caplan, 1974; Cassel, 1974, 1976; Cobb, 1976). These papers generated excitement among researchers as well as practitioners interested in enhancing the support available to distressed individuals. Although more recent literature has been critical of the earlier claims, social support continues to be regarded as a central psychosocial issue in health research (for reviews, see Broadhead, Kaplan, James, Wagner, Schoenbach, Grimson, Heyden, Tibblin, & Gehlbach, 1983; DiMatteo & Hays, 1981; Wortman, 1984; and Wallston, Alagna, DeVellis, & DeVellis, 1983).

*This work was supported in part by Bureau of Community Health Services Grant MC–J–220 to Dr. Wortman. The authors are grateful to Jim House, Ronald Kessler, and the editors of this volume for helpful comments on an earlier version of this chapter. Sequence of authors' names was determined randomly.

The purpose of this chapter is to examine theoretical and empirical work on social support as it relates to recovery from serious physical illness. Because several comprehensive reviews of this literature are available (see the reviews just cited), we do not provide a review of empirical studies. Instead, we focus on conceptual and methodological issues that confront investigators studying the impact of social support on the physically ill. We begin with a brief examination of current research on social support and physical recovery to determine how well the early, enthusiastic claims about the benefits of support have been substantiated. Next, we examine research exploring the unique needs for support and problems in obtaining support that may be faced by the physically ill. Drawing from this work, we identify several aspects of supportive interactions that may have implications for extending theory and research in this area. We conclude by summarizing the implications of the current research for intervention and public policy.

Social Support and Physical Recovery: Prior Research and Methodological Concerns

Although there has been broad acceptance of the claim that social support influences health outcomes, most of the early studies demonstrating a relationship between support and health have employed cross-sectional, retrospective, or case-control designs. As other investigators have noted, the majority of these early studies are flawed by their inability to address the issue of causality (Broadhead *et al.*, 1983; Heller, 1979; House, 1981; Thoits, 1982). For example, a simple correlation between low social support and poor health might reflect a causal sequence in which illness has an impact on perceived or actual support, rather than vice versa (see Heller, 1979). Poor health might contribute to a negative outlook on life which leads to harsher judgments of social relationships. People who are seriously ill might also drive support away by placing high demands on and engendering a sense of vulnerability in others.

Many investigators have noted that these problems in interpretation could be reduced by longitudinal research examining social support as a predictor of subsequent health status while controlling for other variables also likely to have an impact on health—for example, prior health status or stressful life events (see e.g., Broadhead *et al.*, 1983; House, 1981). In fact, three longitudinal studies of large community samples have demonstrated a relationship between social ties and subsequent mortality, even after statistically controlling for potentially relevant mortality risk factors (Berkman & Syme, 1979; Blazer, 1982; House, Robbins, & Metzner, 1982). In the more specific area of recovery from physical illness, the results from longitudinal studies have been less clear-cut. Some investigators have found evidence for a relationship between social support and subsequent recovery (e.g., Berle, Pinsky, & Wolff, 1952; Funch & Marshall, 1983; Vachon, 1979), whereas others have found no evidence for such a relationship (e.g., Revenson, Wollman, & Felton, 1983). Still other studies have produced mixed results (e.g., Funch & Mettlin, 1982; Garrity, 1973; Norbeck & Tilden, 1983). In one study, for example, support from one's doctor and family influenced psychological adjustment to breast cancer, but had no effect on physical recovery. However, financial support (i.e., insurance coverage for breast surgery) did appear to influence physical recovery (Funch & Mettlin, 1982).

A second methodological concern that can cloud the interpretation of results, even in prospective longitudinal studies, is the so-called "third variable" problem that can produce spurious associations between social support and health (see Reis, in press). For example, social competence (Heller, 1979) and neuroticism (Costa, Zonderman, & McCrae, 1983) may be such underlying variables. Socially competent and nonneurotic individuals may have easier access to social support and may also be more effective at negotiating the health care system to receive optimal treatment and care. Thus, associations between social support and recovery may actually be the result of other variables having the true causal impact. Research designed to measure variables potentially related both to the availability and perception of social support and to the recovery and adaptation to physical illness—along with use of statistical procedures such as structural equation modeling techniques (see Reis, in press)—could be used to deal with the third variable problem. However, few studies have done this.

Problems in establishing a causal relationship between support and recovery can also be addressed by conducting intervention studies in which participants are assigned to treatments that mobilize or supplement the support available to them. Perhaps because of the enthusiasm generated from early correlational studies on support, a large number of such intervention studies have appeared in the literature. The majority of these studies have focused on respondents who were hospitalized for physical illness (e.g., Gruen, 1975) or injury (e.g., Bordow & Porritt, 1979; Porritt, 1979). For example, supportive interventions have been developed to reduce preoperative anxiety or to facilitate recovery from surgery (see Mumford, Schlesinger, & Glass, 1982, for a review.) Some studies have been conducted with populations, such as the recently bereaved, who are at risk for the development of health problems (e.g., Raphael, 1977; Vachon, 1979). Still others have examined respondents with a specific health problem, such as hypertension (e.g., Earp & Ory, 1979) and have assessed the impact of support on compliance with a medical regimen designed to control the problem (Caplan, 1979a; or see Levy, 1983, for a review). Almost all of the studies to date have involved interventions delivered by health care professionals (e.g., Gruen, 1975; Porritt, 1979), although some examined interventions provided by support groups (e.g., Barrett, 1978; Caplan, Harrison, Wellins, & French, 1976; Spiegel et al., 1981), or by lay persons who have had similar experiences (e.g., Bloom et al., 1978; Spiegel et al., 1981; Vachon et al., 1980). Surprisingly, few supportive interventions have been designed to enhance the support available from members of the naturally occurring support network, that is, family and friends (see Levy, 1983).

Although there are exceptions (e.g., Caplan, Harrison, Wellins, & French, 1976; Spiegel, Bloom, & Yalom, 1981), the majority of these intervention studies provide clear evidence that support facilitates recovery from health problems (see Broadhead et al., 1983; DiMatteo & Hays, 1981; Mumford et al., 1982; or Wallston et al., 1983, for reviews). In a study of patients suffering a first heart attack, for example, Gruen (1975) found that patients given supportive "psychotherapy" (i.e., development of a genuine interest in the patient, reassurance, positive feedback, and encouragement) spent fewer days in the intensive care unit, on a heart monitor, and in the hospital; showed less evidence of congestive heart failure and supraventricular arrhythmias; and were rated as having less anxiety and less retarded activity at a 4-month follow-up interview. Positive results were also obtained in an intervention study designed to examine the effects of a supportive companion on physical health complications of childbirth (Sosa et al., 1980). Women in the group assigned a supportive companion were significantly less likely to develop complications during labor and delivery than were women in the control group. Also, length of time from admission to delivery was shorter for the treatment group mothers compared to control mothers (8.8 versus 19.3 hours). Taken as a whole, evidence regarding the impact of social support on recovery from surgery is impressive, with patients who received supportive interventions averaging a hospital stay two days shorter than that of control respondents (see Mumford et al., 1982, for a review).

The majority of intervention studies have focused on outcome measures indicative of physical health. However, the literature also provides clear evidence that supportive interventions may lessen the likelihood of subsequent mental distress among those recovering from physical illness (e.g., Gruen, 1975; Spiegel et al., 1981) or injury (e.g., Bordow & Porritt, 1979). Supportive interventions also appear to reduce the likelihood of long-term distress among the bereaved, a group at risk for mental and physical health problems (Raphael, 1977; Vachon et al., 1980).

Although past studies suggest that social support may be an important variable in promoting recovery from physical illness, they provide little insight into the mechanisms through which support may influence recovery. In some of these studies, a family member, health care provider, or lay person was instructed to be supportive to the respondent, but it is not clear exactly how the support provider chose to operationalize this manipulation.

As Levy (1983) has noted with regard to many studies on social support and compliance, actual supportive behaviors are generally not monitored. Without such information it is unclear whether supportive "reminders, systematic reinforcement, or something else" (p. 1332) is responsible for the effect.

In still other studies, the supportive treatment has been better specified but multifaceted. For example, Kirscht, Kirscht, and Rosenstock (1981) used a support intervention involving phone calls and home visits by a nurse, selection of a home support person to help the patient with problems in following the medical regimens, and reinforcement and information from the nurse. This intervention did increase adherence to hypertensive medication regimens, but it is difficult to determine which aspects of the support intervention produced the impact.

In a few studies, investigators have manipulated several different types of supportive interventions to determine which are most efficacious (see, e.g., Earp & Ory, 1979; Levine, Green, Deeds, Chualow, Russell, & Finlay, 1979). Even in these studies, however, the interventions compared are often multifaceted. In the study by Earp and Ory (1979), for example, five different supportive interventions were compared, one of which involved home monitoring of blood pressure by a significant other. Earp and Ory found home monitoring to be superior to a variety of other treatments. Yet, because this treatment combined family support with the use of monitoring equipment, it is not clear which part of the intervention was actually effective. Such problems in interpretation could be resolved by conducting systematic follow-up studies that examine various components of treatments shown to be effective. However, few investigators have done this.

Taken as a whole, this research suggests social support may be a variable worthy of serious consideration among researchers interested in physical illness. However, previous studies have provided little insight into the processes through which social support may influence health outcomes. Clearly, if the goal is to advance theoretical understanding of the social support construct, studies are needed that will clarify how social support influences the recovery process.

Social Support Needs and Problems
of the Physically Ill

In our judgment, the conceptualization and measurement of social support among the physically ill requires a careful consideration of this population's special needs and problems. The following section attempts to provide some background on the unique needs for support that are frequently experienced by the physically ill as well as the problems they may encounter in obtaining effective support.

The Need for Support

Physical illness is often accompanied by a host of fears and problems such as severe pain, progressive deterioration, disfigurement, recurrence, energy loss, dependency on others, changes in self-concept, and numerous other potential changes that can be terrifying (Dunkel-Schetter & Wortman, 1982). To cope with these problems, the physically ill person may have greater than average needs for various forms of social support. For example, a person who is no longer able to meet family responsibilities may need outside help with household tasks (e.g., tangible support). The variety of uncertainties and fears that the ill person is experiencing may intensify needs for clarification of what is happening (e.g., informational support) and reassurance that the feelings and fears are a normal consequence of the illness (e.g., validation). The resultant threat to self-concept may intensify needs for reassurance that others will still love and not abandon the ill person (e.g., emotional support). These various forms of support can be especially important for easing the burdens encountered by the seriously ill at a time when they have less emotional and physical strength to deal with them.

Problems in Obtaining Support

Ironically, although the physically ill may experience needs for many kinds of support, they may encounter problems obtaining adequate support from others. Numerous authors have suggested that such problems may occur in interactions with health care providers (e.g., Cobb, 1976), family members (e.g., Meyerowitz, Sparks, & Spears, 1979), and friends (e.g., Silberfarb, Maurer, & Crouthalem, 1980). In a study of breast cancer patients, for example, approximately three-fourths of the respondents agreed that people treated them differently after learning that they had cancer (Peters-Golden, 1982). Of these, 72% reported that they were misunderstood by others, and over 50% indicated that they were avoided or feared. Similarly, in a study examining the social relationships of hemodialysis patients, the quality of patients' interactions was found to decrease over time while their feelings of alienation and estrangement increased (O'Brien, 1980).

Some of the unsupportive negative responses to the physically ill may occur for reasons specific to a particular disease. The disease of cancer, for example, can evoke physical aversion and repulsion if others are fearful of catching the disease or if they see previously healthy individuals become radically changed by surgery, chemotherapy, or general deterioration (Kleiman, Mantell, & Alexander, 1977). Other negative reactions may be more general, and may occur whenever a person is confronted with someone who is in distress. According to some social psychological theories, people are motivated to maintain certain beliefs about the world (see Wortman, 1976, for a review). Exposure to someone who is suffering may challenge these beliefs and lead to unsupportive behaviors. For example, Lerner and associates (1970; Lerner, Miller & Holmes, 1976) have suggested that people are motivated to believe that they live in a "just world" where people "get what they deserve and deserve what they get." Encounters with those who are ill can make people feel threatened and uncomfortable. Attributing the illness to another's undesirable personal characteristics or past behavior can provide one with a sense of protection. However, such beliefs may result in behavior towards the ill person that is insensitive and uncaring.

Aside from the physical repulsion and fear that a serious disease can engender, simply trying to deal with a person who is in pain or feeling depressed can be a stressful experience for potential supporters. Interacting with a seriously ill person may result in feelings of awkwardness, inadequacy, and frustration because there seems to be little that one can say or do. People may also become demoralized if they notice little improvement in the patient after providing support or reassurance. Finally, those closest to the patient may feel sadness because the ill person is suffering as well as anger and resentment that the disease has disrupted their own lives (Dunkel-Schetter & Wortman, 1982).

There is evidence that, against the backdrop of these negative feelings about the patient's illness, others believe that they should remain optimistic and cheerful in their interactions with the patient (see Dunkel-Schetter & Wortman, 1982, or Wortman & Lehman, in press, for a more detailed discussion). Although the supporters of physically ill people undoubtedly want to be helpful, their feelings and beliefs may result in behaviors that are unintentionally damaging to the patient. Such behaviors may include avoidance of the patient, avoidance of open discussion about the illness, and strained and uncomfortable interactions. Unfortunately, the ill person may interpret these behaviors as evidence of rejection at the very time when support from others is especially important. For all of these reasons, people who are physically ill may find that their social relationships not only fail to buffer them from the stress of the illness, but constitute an additional source of distress.

Social Support Research: Issues for Further
Theoretical and Empirical Work

The previous section emphasized that subsequent research should be grounded in a full understanding of the unique needs for support that are experienced by the physically ill. The discussion also highlighted the importance of conducting studies that would clarify the process through which support may influence health outcomes. Ideally, studies should be designed to provide specific information about which types of support satisfy which needs and influence which physical health outcomes in each phase of the illness recovery process—and why. This section draws from the previous discussion to identify several issues that may help to refine our knowledge of the impact of social support on the physically ill.

Components of Support

Much of the criticism of early social support research has focused on the lack of a good definition of the construct (see House, 1981; Thoits, 1982). In previous studies, such diverse indicators as frequency of social contact, marital status, presence of a confidant, participation in clubs and organizations, the provision of information, and involvement in self-help groups have all been conceptualized as social support. In fact, many studies have combined a variety of these variables into a single measure of support. More recently, investigators have come to appreciate the complex and multifaceted nature of social support and the need for more systematic and precise conceptualization of the construct. Toward this end, attempts have been made to identify several distinct types or components of support. These include structural indexes of relationships such as marital status, participation in community organizations, or involvement in a social network as well as measures of the functions that support may provide (e.g., information, love, and tangible aid). Which types or components of support are most critical in research with the physically ill?

It is probably wise for investigators in this area to include structural measures of support such as frequency of social contact and involvement in social activities, although House and Kahn (Chapter 5 in this volume) have emphasized that these measures are more accurately described as the existence or quantity of social relationships than as social support. All four of the prospective longitudinal studies described earlier (Berkman & Syme, 1979; Blazer, 1982; Funch & Marshall, 1983; House et al., 1982) provide evidence that the existence of social relationships reduces the risk of mortality. However, it probably is not advisable to measure social support exclusively in terms of structural variables because such data provide little information about the process through which social ties influence health. Are social ties beneficial because they provide support, or because those with such ties are simply motivated "to manage their lives more effectively and to take explicit steps to protect their health" (Schaefer, Coyne, & Lazarus, 1983, p. 383)?

Another approach to examining the structural properties of relationships involves studying a person's social network or the set of relationships among a particular group of people (e.g., Fischer, 1982; Hirsch, 1979; Mitchell & Trickett, 1980). Social networks are commonly defined in terms of such variables as size, density (the extent to which members are in contact with one another), and reciprocity. With the exception of network size, there is little consistent evidence that network characteristics are related to health outcomes (see Israel, 1982). However, there are several reasons why it may be worthwhile to examine some properties of a person's network in studies of the physically ill. It would be interesting to study the extent to which physical illness alters network structure. Do cancer patients' social networks shrink or contract over time, as some investigators have suggested? It may also be important to determine whether networks characterized by high density (members who know one another) are more capable of coordinating the support that is necessary to ensure that all of the patient's needs are met (Wortman, 1984). Again, however, it should not be assumed that structural indicators such as the size of the network are equivalent to social support. Clearly, network members may make demands and exercise constraints over people's choices in addition to providing support (Hirsch, 1979; Schaefer *et al.,* 1983).

Regarding the functions that support may provide, investigators have also identified several conceptually distinct components (see Wortman, 1984, for a more detailed discussion): (1) the expression of positive affect, which may include information that a person is cared for, loved, or esteemed (see Cobb, 1976, 1979; Weiss, 1974); (2) expressing agreement with or acknowledging the appropriateness of a person's beliefs, interpretations, or feelings (see House, 1981; Kahn & Antonucci, 1980; Walker, MacBride, & Vachon, 1977); (3) encouraging the open expression or ventilation of feelings and beliefs (see Wortman & Dunkel-Schetter, 1979); (4) the offering of advice or information or providing access to new sources of information (see Barrera, 1981; Cobb, 1976, 1979; Caplan, 1974; House, 1981; Mitchell & Trickett, 1980); (5) the provision of material aid (see House, 1981; Caplan, 1974; Kahn & Antonucci, 1980); and (6) providing information that the person is part of a network or support system of mutual obligation or reciprocal help (see Cobb, 1976, 1979; Caplan, Robinson, French, Caldwell, & Shinn, 1976; Kahn & Antonucci, 1980; Walker *et al.,* 1977). In research on recovery from physical illness it may be useful to assess these various types of support, because there is some evidence to suggest that different types may have different effects on particular health outcomes (see Funch & Mettlin, 1982; House, 1981).

Providing separate measures of these types of support may also help to elucidate what it is about support that is particularly beneficial to people with certain illnesses at certain times. Cohen and McKay (1984) have suggested that all stress experiences can be categorized in terms of the particular adaptive tasks with which the person is confronted. They have argued that social support may influence subsequent health outcomes only when these tasks are taken into account and when the type of support received is relevant for resolving the coping task in question. In the case of recovery from physical illness, the nature of the coping tasks faced may change over time. Shortly after the illness has been diagnosed, the major adaptive task required of the patient is to appraise symptoms and initiate treatment. At this time the provision of information may be more important than other types of support. Among patients hospitalized for a long period of time, the illness may begin to interfere with the adaptive task of meeting their responsibilities to their family. For these patients, tangible help with chores like shopping, cooking and meal preparation may be most important. Cohen and McKay's analysis might be very useful in studies of the physically ill, especially when it is not possible to assess all of the types of support that have been distinguished in the literature. By carefully considering the adaptive tasks facing the patient population, a researcher may be able to make a good guess about the types of support most likely to be important.

For example, emotional support may be especially important among people who are extremely ill or who are experiencing distressing physical changes. In a study examining cancer patients' perceptions of the effectiveness of various types of support, Dunkel-Schetter (1981) found that emotional support was more likely than other types of support to be identified as most helpful. Over 90% of the sample mentioned some form of emotional support as one of the most helpful things anyone had done. Drawing from a wide range of studies on the impact of social support on subsequent health, House and Kahn (Chapter 5 in this volume) concluded that emotional support has been found to be a more important predictor of health outcomes than other types of support. They recommend giving priority to measures of emotional support in studies where time is limited and a full assessment of various types of support is impossible.

In studies conducted on support in health settings or with health care providers, it may be beneficial to conceptualize the provision of information as social support. In a study assessing physician behaviors perceived as most helpful and unhelpful by breast and colo-rectal cancer patients, Dunkel-Schetter (1981) found that provision of information was mentioned as valuable with about the same frequency as was emotional support.

Sources of Support

In assessing social support, investigators must decide whether to ask about the adequacy of support from the network as a whole or to ask specific questions about particular sources of support, such as partner, relatives, friends, or physicians. Assessing the support provided by different sources might be particularly advantageous for research on the physically ill (see Meyerowitz, 1980; Peck & Boland, 1977), because the perception of particular behaviors as supportive may well depend on who provides them. For example, there is some evidence that advice might be perceived as helpful and appreciated when provided by a physician, but regarded as unhelpful and interfering when given by friends or relatives (see Dunkel-Schetter, 1981). Similarly, a patient with a serious illness might feel supported by an empathetic comment such as "I know how you feel" if that statement is made by a person with a similar problem; however, the same statement might engender hostility and resentment if made by a healthy friend or acquaintance (Wortman & Lehman, in press).

Although it is desirable to assess several different types of support provided by several different sources, such a comprehensive assessment may not always be possible. If the investigator is able to focus on just a few sources of support, which ones should be selected? There is considerable evidence that the spouse's and family's reaction to cancer patients are critical in adjustment (see Lindsey, Norbeck, Carrieri, & Perry, 1981; Meyerowitz, 1980). The assessment of support provided by others who have had similar experiences (Dunkel-Schetter & Wortman, 1982) might also be worthwhile. Finally, it may be very important to measure the support provided by physicians and other health care providers. In a study of cancer patients conducted by Bloom (1981), the physician was ranked higher than family and friends as an important provider of support.

Recipient versus Provider Perspectives on Social Support

There has been a growing awareness that some well-intentioned efforts by others to provide support may be regarded as unhelpful, may have long-term consequences that are negative, or both (DiMatteo & Hays, 1981; Dunkel-Schetter & Wortman, 1982; Silver & Wortman, 1980; Thoits, 1982; Wortman & Lehman, in press). In many cases, people seem to have misconceptions about how those in distress should behave and how they should be treated by others (see Wortman & Lehman, in press, for a more detailed discussion). For example, it is commonly believed that the physically ill should remain as optimistic about their condition as possible. In a study by Peters-Golden (1982), a majority of healthy individuals reported that they would go out of their way to cheer up a person with cancer. Yet a majority of the cancer patients studied perceived the "unrelenting optimism" of others as unauthentic and disturbing.

A related misconception is that it is harmful for people in distress to discuss their feelings about what is happening. In the study by Peters-Golden (1982), healthy individuals not only assumed that such discussions would be detrimental to the patients but also regarded those who wanted to discuss their illness as less adjusted to their situation. There is evidence that because of these beliefs others often prevent the physically ill from discussing their disease or its implications (Silver & Wortman, 1980). Nonetheless, the cancer patients studied by Peters-Golden reported that they were "disturbed by this ban on communication and confused by the assumption that avoiding the subject would actually be better for them" (p. 489). Similarly, Dunkel-Schetter (1981) found that "being told not to worry because things will work out" or "minimizing the patient's problems and feelings about cancer" were commonly judged as unhelpful by the cancer patients studied.

Potential supporters may also have misconceptions about the most important issues or adaptive tasks facing the patient, and may fail to provide appropriate support for this reason. In the study by Peters-Golden (1982), for example, healthy people felt that the most salient concerns of a mastectomized woman center on the loss of her breast. In fact, women with breast cancer were much more concerned about such factors as fear of recurrence, death, and treatment side effects.

Brickman and his associates (Brickman, Rabinowitz, Karuza, Cohn, & Kidder, 1982) have identified another factor that may lead recipients and providers of support to draw different conclusions about the helpfulness of particular behaviors. As these investigators have noted, receiving help carries the implicit assumption that a person is incapable of solving his or her own problems (Brickman *et al.*, 1982). For this reason, receiving social support could undermine self-esteem if it makes the sick person perceive his or her status as an impaired person (DiMatteo & Hays, 1981). Consistent with this view, the patients in Peters-Golden's (1982) study reported that others' oversolicitous attitudes made them feel incompetent to perform ordinary tasks. Patients felt that by preventing or discouraging them from carrying out their usual chores, others were "forcing incapacitation on them."

Of course, this does not mean that the recipient's judgment about supportiveness of behaviors is necessarily accurate. Some behaviors, such as encouraging false hopes or maladaptive denial, may be appreciated and regarded as highly supportive but have negative consequences for physical or mental health. On the other hand, some behaviors that might be judged as unsupportive because they are painful (such as honest feedback forcing the patient to face certain realities) might be beneficial in the long run (see House, 1981). Certainly, whether intended supportive behaviors are ultimately associated with positive or negative outcomes is an empirical question. However, the potential complexities considered here point to the usefulness of obtaining judgments from both providers and recipients of support as to the perceived helpfulness of various behavioral exchanges (Wortman, 1984).

Assessing Negative Aspects of Social Interaction

In most scales designed to measure social support (see House & Kahn, Chapter 5 in this volume, for a review), the items have focused solely on the adequacy of positive behaviors such as providing love, understanding, or aid. However, there are several reasons why it might be worthwhile to ask parallel questions about negative behaviors which produce "disaffirmation of a person's thoughts, beliefs, and feelings, the impression of negative regard and disaffection, and certain kinds of direct withholding of aid or erection of barriers" (Caplan, Abbey, Abramis, Andrews, Conway, & French, 1984, p. 34). There is evidence that such negative interactions constitute an important share of the stresses people experience in their daily lives (Pearlin, 1982). In fact, in at least two studies comparing positive and negative elements of social interaction, negative elements were more strongly and consistently related to mental health outcomes than were positive elements of social relationships (Fiore, Becker, & Coppel, 1983; Rook, in press).

Drawing from the previous discussion, it is possible to identify several reasons why it may be especially important to assess the negative elements of social interaction in studies on the physically ill. First, support providers appear to hold misconceptions about the process of coping with illness (see Wortman & Lehman, in press, for a more detailed discussion). These misconceptions can result in behaviors that are perceived as inappropriate and unsupportive, such as telling patients to cheer up or minimizing their problems or concerns. Second, it was pointed out earlier that potential supporters often lack understanding of the patient's illness. This might lead support providers to make well-intentioned but ill-advised suggestions, such as encouraging a person who has had a heart attack to "be ever so careful" or "take it easy." Such comments may not only be annoying to the patient, but may also constitute bad medical advice, because the resumption of former activities is in many cases desirable and feasible (Finlayson, 1976). Third, unlike healthy individuals who can terminate relationships that fail to satisfy their needs, the physically ill are often thrust into relationships that are not egalitarian or reciprocal. Clearly, individuals receiving care in a particular medical setting have little choice about the nurses or physicians with whom they interact. It may be difficult for the patient to control or terminate professional relationships that are distressing.

Fourth, because illness often evokes negative feelings in others, the physically ill are likely to find that their closest and most important relationships are characterized by both positive and negative elements. In a study of breast cancer patients, Bloom (1981) reported that the physician was rated as the greatest source of stress as well as the most important source of support. Dunkel-Schetter and Wortman (1982) have reviewed evidence indicating that health care providers, family members, and friends have conflicting feelings about cancer, which may lead them to behave in contradictory ways when dealing with patients. Seriously ill patients may receive mixed messages as supporters try to be reassuring and comforting on the surface, yet exhibit negative nonverbal behaviors. Furthermore, the positive behaviors evidenced by care providers are likely to be mixed with signs of strain and occasional negative outbursts as the stress of caring for an ill person takes its toll.

For all of these reasons, we believe that measuring behaviors perceived as negative along with those judged as positive will provide a much fuller picture of the kinds of social relationships that are likely to influence recovery among the physically ill.

Assessing Specific Supportive Behaviors

Most research on social support has relied either on structural assessments of social networks (e.g., frequency of contact with family members and friends) or very general measures of perceived support—that is, measures that probe whether various types of support are provided *in the abstract.* For example, respondents might be asked to indicate how much their support network makes them feel loved, cared for, and so forth. An alternative approach is to measure more precise natural helping behaviors that people engage in when they are trying to assist others (Barrera, 1981). However, very few studies have examined such supportive behaviors.

Although it did not deal specifically with recovery from illness, one study that did focus on natural supportive behaviors was conducted by Gottlieb (1978). Single mothers were asked to indicate what kinds of problems they were having and to describe the specific ways that others had been helpful in dealing with the problem(s). Content analysis of these behaviors identified many of the types of support frequently included in taxonomies of support such as listening, providing reassurance, giving information, or providing material aid. But the mothers also mentioned other specific behaviors of supporters that were helpful, such as taking the time to accompany them when they had to face a stressful situation, providing testimony from the supporter's own experiences, or modeling appropriate behavior such as by remaining calm and confident.

Identifying such behaviors might help enhance our understanding of which specific types of emotional support or tangible aid are especially likely to be perceived as helpful. Such information would not only shed light on the mechanisms through which support may influence health, but might also be useful to health care professionals in developing interventions to enhance the support available to the patient. For example, family members might be encouraged to adopt those specific behaviors that have been identified as supportive, such as accompanying the patient during stressful medical procedures. Such recommendations might be more effective in generating social support than simply exhorting the family to be more supportive in general. Moreover, since others' perceptions about which behaviors are most useful to the patient are frequently wrong, it would be very worthwhile to study natural helping behaviors from the perspective of both the support providers and the patient. Both could be asked to identify natural helping behaviors that occurred and to make judgments regarding the helpfulness of these. Both could also be asked to identify instances in which natural helping behaviors were perceived as unhelpful or unsupportive.

Determinants of Support

Most conceptual development and empirical research on social support has focused on the consequences of receiving social support. Relatively little concern has been given to identifying the factors that may determine whether social support will be available, offered, or utilized effectively (see Broadhead *et al.,* 1983; House, 1981; Wortman, 1984). For example, environmental determinants of the availability of support might include community size and resources, socioeconomic status, ethnic group customs, and cultural norms. Personal factors might include values and beliefs about when it is appropriate to ask others for help (Eckenrode, 1983) as well as skills such as sociability, assertiveness, comfort with intimacy, and ability to emphathize with others (Heller & Swindle, 1983). As Mitchell and Trickett

(1980) have noted, there has been a surprising lack of discussion of the role people play in influencing the quality of their support networks.

Earlier in this chapter it was suggested that people often feel threatened and uncomfortable when they interact with others who are suffering or in pain. This suggests that among the physically ill such factors as the severity of the illness, or the amount of pain the respondent is suffering, may be important determinants of support (DiMatteo & Hays, 1981). There is some empirical evidence to suggest that patients with a poor prognosis may receive less social support than those with better physical health (Peters-Golden, 1982). The recipient's ability to cope successfully with illness may also be a powerful determinant of support. Research by Wortman and associates (e.g., Coates, Wortman, & Abbey, 1979) has suggested that those who indicate that they are coping well with a crisis are regarded as more attractive by others and are less likely to be avoided than those who indicate that they are having some difficulties in coping. Taken as a whole, these data suggest that those in greatest need of social support may be least likely to receive it.

Costs and Consequences of Providing Support

In the past, there has been considerably more research on the consequences of receiving support than on the consequences of providing it (see Belle, 1982; Dunkel-Schetter & Wortman, 1982; Kessler, McLeod, & Wethington, in press). Yet the deleterious consequences for the provider may be substantial when provision of sustained high levels of support are required but the recipient is unwilling or unable to reciprocate (Belle, 1982; Caplan, 1979b). Such a lack of reciprocity in giving and receiving support is quite likely to characterize relationships in which one party is seriously ill. In future research, it would be very worthwhile to examine such issues as what types of behaviors from the patient are most sustaining to family members, how family members and health professionals might support each other, and what other sources of support are particularly effective in alleviating the distress and frustration experienced by those who provide support to the seriously ill (Wortman, 1984).

The one-sided giving of support may not only become overburdening for the provider, but may also do a disservice to the recipient by fostering dependency and discouraging active efforts toward self-help (Brickman *et al.*, 1982). We need to know more about what types of social support will be most helpful to the seriously ill in garnering the coping skills and social resources necessary to regain health or adapt to illness (Broadhead *et al.*, 1983). Supportive interventions should also be designed with the explicit goal of avoiding dependency on the provider and encouraging self-reliance (Janis, 1983).

Conclusions and Implications

In writing about implications of social support for prevention and treatment, Heller (1979) said that "the level of research in this field is such that detailing the ingredients in a social support treatment package would be premature at this time" (p. 375). Heller's statement still applies to the general state of knowledge about the specific ingredients that would be most beneficially applied in supportive interventions. More recent reviewers of research on the relationship between social support and physical health seem to agree. For example, DiMatteo and Hays (1981) stated that, "based on this review, we suggest that, although intervention may be important, not enough is yet understood about how social support operates to warrant liberal implementation of social support programs" (p. 142).

From the previous discussion it is possible to draw several conclusions about possible directions for subsequent work. First, there is clearly a need for both manipulations and measures of support that are more well-defined and more specific. In intervention studies, it is important that the interactions between support providers and recipients be monitored closely to determine whether the manipulation was delivered as designated by the investigator and perceived as intended by the recipient (see Levy, 1983). Second, there is a need for more research on transactions between support providers and recipients in natural settings. When people are attempting to provide various forms of support, what do they actually do and how is this perceived by the recipient? For example, specifically how do family members attempt to encourage the patient to adhere to a difficult treatment regimen? When are reminders regarded as supportive, and when are they perceived as nagging, patronizing, or overprotective? When are others' calming, minimizing appraisals of the illness effective in reducing the recipient's distress, and when do they increase distress because they make the recipient feel that his or her concerns are not being heard?

Third, it is important that subsequent studies be designed to explicate the mechanisms and active ingredients through which support may help people to adapt or recover from serious illness. A number of such mechanisms have been discussed in the literature (see Caplan, 1979b; Cohen & Wills, 1983; House, 1981; Lieberman, 1982; or Wortman, 1984). For example, social support may influence recovery by enhancing motivation to adhere to difficult treatment regimens. Alternatively, individuals who receive support may develop greater self-confidence and feelings of autonomy, and may therefore be more likely to initiate successful coping efforts. Social support might also protect people from the deleterious effects of stress by altering their mood, which may contribute to positive outcomes by influencing neuroendocrine pathways or by facilitating constructive coping efforts. Although these and other mechanisms have been discussed in the literature, few studies have been designed to discriminate among different mechanisms. Including measures of such variables as respondents' motivation to comply with treatment, actual compliance, mood, self-esteem, coping behavior, and possibly physiological or biochemical measures may shed light on how support influences health outcomes.

Some of the support processes described in this chapter may influence compliance behavior; others may have an impact only on psychological well-being or social functioning, and still others may have a direct impact on physiological functioning only. In fact, a particular type of supportive transaction may influence different outcome variables at different phases in a cycle of illness onset and recovery. In designing studies to clarify the mechanisms that underlie support effects, it is therefore desirable to assess multiple outcomes, preferably at more than one point in time.

In conclusion, investigators in the social support area agree that it is time to move beyond demonstrations of a relationship between support and health outcomes to a more careful explication of the processes underlying support. In addition to enhancing theoretical understanding and development in this important area, such information is likely to be critical in the development of effective interventions to promote support among the physically ill.

References

Barrera, M. (1981). Social support in the adjustment of pregnant adolescents: Assessment issues. In B. Gottlieb (Ed.), *Social networks and social support* (pp. 69–96). Beverly Hills, CA: Sage.

Barrett, C. J. (1978). Effectiveness of widows' groups in facilitating change. *Journal of Consulting and Clinical Psychology, 46*(1), 20–31.

Belle, D. (1982). The stress of caring: Women as providers of social support. In L. Goldberger & S. Breznitz (Eds.), *Handbook of stress: Theoretical and clinical aspects.* New York: The Free Press.

Berkman, L., & Syme, S. (1979). Social networks, host resistance, and mortality: A nine-year follow-up study of Alameda County residents. *American Journal of Epidemiology, 2,* 186–204.

Berle, B. B., Pinsky, R. H., Wolf, S., & Wolff, H. G. (1952). A clinical guide to prognosis in stress diseases. *Journal of the American Medical Association, 149,* 1624–1628.

Blazer, D. G. (1982). Social support and mortality in an elderly community population. *American Journal of Epidemiology, 115,* 684–694.

Bloom, J. (1981). Cancer-care providers and the medical care system: Facilitators or inhibitors of patient coping responses. In Elsenier (Ed.), *Coping with cancer.* New York: North Holland Press.

Bloom, J., Ross, R., & Burnell, G. (1978). The effect of social support on patient adjustment after breast surgery. *Patient Counseling and Health Education, 1*(2), 50–59.

Bordow, S., & Porritt, D. (1979). An experimental evaluation of crisis intervention. *Social Science and Medicine, 13A,* 251–256.

Brickman, P., Rabinowitz, B. C., Karuza, J., Jr., Cohn, E., & Kidder, L. (1982). Models of helping and coping. *American Psychologist, 37* (49), 368–384.

Broadhead, W. E., Kaplan, B. H., James, S. A., Wagner, E. H., Schoenbach, V. J., Grimson, R., Heyden, S., Tibblin, G., & Gehlbach, S. H. (1983). The epidemiologic evidence for a relationship between social support and health. *American Journal of Epidemiology, 117,* 521–537.

Caplan, G. (1974). *Support systems and community mental health.* New York: Behavioral Publications.

Caplan, R. D. (1979a). Social support, person-environment fit and loving. In L. A. Ferman & J. P. Gordus (Eds.), *Mental health and the economy.* Kalamazoo, MI: Upjohn Institute.

Caplan, R. D. (1979b). Patient, provider, and organization: Hypothesized determinants of adherence. In S. J. Cohen (Ed.), *New directions in patient compliance* (pp. 75–110). Lexington, MA: Heath.

Caplan, R. D., Abbey, A., Abramis, D. A., Andrews, F. M., Conway, T. L., & French, J. R. P., Jr. (1984). *Tranquilizer use and well-being: A longitudinal study of social and psychological effects.* Ann Arbor, MI: Institute for Social Research.

Caplan, R. D., Harrison, R. V., Wellins, R. V., & French, J. R. P. (1976). Social support and patient adherence: Experimental and survey findings. Ann Arbor, MI: Institute for Social Research.

Caplan, R. D., Robinson, E. A. R., French, J. R. P., Jr., Caldwell, J. R., & Shinn, M. (1976). *Adhering medical regimens: Pilot experiments in patient education and social support.* Ann Arbor: University of Michigan.

Cassel, J. (1974). Psychosocial processes and "stress": Theoretical formulations. *International Journal of Health Services, 4,* 471–482.

Cassel, J. (1976). The contribution of the social environment to host resistance. *American Journal of Epidemiology, 104,* 107–123.

Coates, D., Wortman, C. B., & Abbey A. (1979). Reactions to victims. In I. H. Frieze, D. Bartal, & J. S. Carroll (Eds.), *New approaches to social problems.* San Francisco: Jossey-Bass.

Cobb, S. (1976). Social support as a moderator of life stress. *Psychosomatic Medicine, 38* (5), 300–314.

Cobb, S. (1979). Social support and health through the life course. In M. Riley White (Ed.), *Aging from birth to death: Interdisciplinary perspectives.* Boulder, CO: Westview Press.

Cohen, S., & McKay, G. (1984). Social support, stress and the buffering hypothesis: A theoretical analysis. In A. Baum, J. E. Singer, & S. E. Taylor, (Eds.), *Handbook of psychology and health* (Vol. 4). Hillsdale, NJ: Erlbaum.

Cohen, S., & Wills, T. (1983). *Social support, stress and the buffering hypothesis: An empirical review.* Unpublished manuscript, Carnegie-Mellon University.

Costa, P. T., Jr., Zonderman, A. B., & McCrae, R. R. (1983 September). Longitudinal course of social support among men in the Baltimore Longitudinal Study of Aging. Paper presented at the NATO Advanced Research Workshop: Social Support—Theory, Research and Application, Chateau de Bonas, France.

DiMatteo, M., & Hays, R. (1981). Social support and serious illness. In B. Gottlieb (Ed.), *Social networks and social support.* Beverly Hills, CA: Sage.

Dunkel-Schetter, C. (1981). *Social support and coping with cancer.* Unpublished doctoral dissertation, Northwestern University.

Dunkel-Schetter, C., & Wortman, C. (1982). The interpersonal dynamics of cancer: Problems in social relationships and their impact on the patient. In H. S. Friedman & M. R. DiMatteo (Eds.), *Interpersonal issues in health care.* New York: Academic Press.

Earp, J. L., & Ory, M. G. (1979). The effects of social support and health professionals' home visits on patient adherence to hypertensive regimens. *Preventive Medicine, 8,* 155.

Eckenrode, J. (1983). The mobilization of social supports: Some individual constraints. *American Journal of Community Psychology, 2* (5), 509–528.

Finlayson, A. (1976). Social networks as coping resources: Lay help and consultation patterns used in husband's post infarcation cancer. *Social Science and Medicine, 10,* 97–103.

Fiore, J., Becker, J., & Coppel, D. (1983). Social network interactions: A buffer or a stress. *American Journal of Community Psychology.*

Fischer, C. (1982). *To dwell among friends.* Chicago: University of Chicago Press.

Funch, D. P., & Marshall, J. (1983). The role of stress, social support and age in survival from breast cancer. *Journal of Psychosomatic Research, 27,* 77–83.

Funch, D. P., & Mettlin, C. (1982). The role of support in relation to recovery from breast surgery. *Social Science and Medicine, 16,* 91–98.

Garrity, T. F. (1973). Social involvement and activeness as predictors of morale six months after first myocardial infarction. *Social Science and Medicine, 7,* 199.

Gottlieb, B. H. (1978). Development and application of a classification scheme of informal helping behavior. *Canadian Journal of Behavioral Science, 10,* 105–115.

Gruen, W. (1975). Effects of brief psychotherapy during the hospitalization period on the recovery process in heart attacks. *Journal of Consulting and Clinical Psychology, 43,* 223–232.

Heller K. (1979). The effects of social support: Prevention and treatment implications. In A. P. Goldstein & F. H. Kanfer (Eds), *Maximizing treatment gains: Transfer enhancement in psychotherapy.* New York: Academic Press.

Heller, K. & Swindle, R. (1983). Social networks, perceived social support and coping with stress. In R. D. Felner, L. A. Jason, J. Moritsugu, & S. S. Farber (Eds.), *Prevention psychology: Theory, research and practice in community intervention.* New York: Pergamon Press.

Hirsch, B. J. (1979). Social networks and the coping process. In B. Gottlieb (Ed.), *Social networks and social support.* Beverly Hills, CA: Sage.

House, J. S. (1981). *Work, stress and social support.* Reading, MA: Addison-Wesley.

House, J. S., Robbins, C., & Metzner, H. L. (1982). The association of social relationships with mortality: Prospective evidence from the Tecumseh Community Health Study. *American Journal of Epidemiology, 116* (1), 123–140.

Israel, B. A. (1982). Social networks and health status: Linking theory, research and practice. *Patient Counseling and Health Education, 4,* 65–79.

Janis, I. L. (1983). The role of social support in adherence to stressful decisions. *American Psychologist, 38* (2), 143–160.

Kahn, R., & Antonucci, T. (1980). Convoys over the life course: Attachment, roles and social support. In P. B. Baltes & O. G. Brim, Jr. (Eds.), *Life-span development and behavior.* (Vol. 3) New York: Academic Press.

Kessler, R. C., McLeod, J. D., & Wethington, E. (in press). The costs of caring. In I. G. Sarason & B. R. Sarason (Eds.), *Social support: Theory, research, and applications.* The Hague: Martinus Nijhof.

Kirscht, J. P., Kirscht, J. L., & Rosenstock, I. M. (1981). A test of interventions to increase adherence to hypertensive medical regimens. *Health Education Quarterly, 8*(3), 261–272.

Kleiman, M. A., Mantell, J. E., & Alexander, E. S. (1977). Collaboration and its discontents: The perils of partnership. *Journal of Applied Behavioral Science, 13*, 403–410.

Lerner, M. J. (1970). The desire for justice and reaction to victims. In J. R. Macaulay & L. Berkowitz (Eds.), *Altruism and helping behavior.* New York: Academic Press.

Lerner, M. J., Miller, D. T., & Holmes, J. (1976). Deserving and the emergence of justice. In L. Berkowitz & E. Walster (Eds.), *Advances in experimental social psychology.* New York: Academic Press.

Levine, D. M., Green, L. W., Deeds, S. G., Chualow, J., Russell, R. P., & Finlay, J. (1979). Health education for hypertensive patients. *Journal of the American Medical Association, 241,* 1700–1703.

Levy, R. L. (1983). Social support and compliance: A selective review and critique of treatment integrity and outcome measurement. *Social Science and Medicine, 17*(18), 1329–1338.

Lieberman, M. (1982). The effects of social support on response to stress. In. L. Goldberger & S. Breznitz (Eds.), *Handbook of stress: Theoretical and clinical aspects.* (pp. 764–783). New York: The Free Press.

Lindsey, A. M., Norbeck, J. S., Carrieri, V. L., & Perry, E. (1981). Social support and health outcomes in post-mastectomy women: A review. *Cancer Nursing, 4,* 377–384.

Meyerowitz, B. (1980). Psychosocial correlates of breast cancer and its treatment. *Psychological Bulletin, 87*(1), 108–131.

Meyerowitz, B., Sparks, F., & Spears, I. (1979). Adjuvant chemotherapy for breast carcinoma. *Cancer, 43,* 1613–1618.

Mitchell, R. E., & Trickett, E. J. (1980). Task force report: Social networks as mediators of social support (An analysis of the effects and determinants of social networks). *Community Mental Health Journal, 16*(1), 27–44.

Mumford, E., Schlesinger, H. J., & Glass, G. V. (1982). The effects of psychological intervention on recovery from surgery and heart attacks: An analysis of the literature. *American Journal of Public Health, 72*(2), 141–151.

Norbeck, J. S., & Tilden, V. P. (1983). Life stress, social support, and emotional disequilibrium in complications of pregnancy: A prospective, multivariate study. *Journal of Health and Social Behavior, 24,* 30–46.

O'Brien, M. E. (1980). Effective social environment and hemodialysis adaptation: A panel analysis. *Journal of Health and Social Behavior, 21,* 360–370.

Pearlin, L. (1982). The social contents of stress. In L. Goldberger & S. Breznitz (Eds.), *Handbook of stress: Theoretical and clinical aspects.* (pp. 367–379). New York: The Free Press.

Peck, A., & Boland, J. (1977). Emotional reactions to radiation treatment. *Cancer, 40,* 180–184.

Peters-Golden, H. (1982). Breast cancer: Varied perceptions of social support in the illness experience. *Social Science and Medicine, 16,* 483–491.

Porritt, D. (1979). Social support in crisis: Quantity or quality? *Social Science and Medicine, 12A,* 715–721.

Raphael, B. (1977). Preventive intervention with the recent bereaved. *Archives of General Psychiatry, 34,* 1450–1454.

Reis, H. T. (in press). Social interaction and well-being. In S. Duck (Ed.), *Personal relationships V: Repairing personal relationships.* London: Academic Press.

Revenson, T. A., Wollman, C. A., & Felton, B. J. (1983). Social supports as stress buffers for adult cancer patients. *Psychosomatic Medicine, 45*(4), 321–331.

Rook, K. S. (in press). The negative side of social interaction: Impact on psychological well-being. *Journal of Personality and Social Psychology.*

Schaefer, C., Coyne, J., & Lazarus, R. (1981). The health-related functions of social support. *Journal of Behavioral Medicine, 4*(4), 381–406.

Silberfarb, P. M., Maurer, H., & Crouthalem, C. (1980). Psychological aspects of neoplastic disease: I. Functional status of breast cancer patients during different treatment regimens. *American Journal of Psychiatry, 137*(4), 450–455.

Silver, R., & Wortman, C. (1980). Coping with undesirable life events. In J. Garber & M. E. P. Seligman (Eds.), *Human helplessness* (pp. 279–375). New York: Academic Press.

Sosa, R., Kennell, J. Klaus, M., Robertson, I., & Urrutia, J. (1980). The effect of a supportive companion on perinatal problems, length of labor, and mother-infant interaction. *New England Journal of Medicine, 303,* 597–600.

Spiegel, D., Bloom, J. R., & Yalom, I. (1981). Group support for patients with metastatic cancer. A randomized prospective outcome study. *Archives of General Psychiatry, 38,* 527–533.

Thoits, P. (1982). Conceptual, methodological and theoretical problems in studying social support as a buffer against life stress. *Journal of Health and Social Behavior, 23,* 145–159.

Vachon, M. L. S. (1979, September). *The importance of social support in the longitudinal adaptation to bereavement and breast cancer.* Paper presented at the Annual American Psychological Association meetings, New York.

Vachon, M. L. S., Lyall, W., Rogers, J., Freedman-Letofsky, K., & Freeman, S. J. (1980). A controlled study of self-help intervention for widows. *American Journal of Psychiatry, 137*(11), 1380–1384.

Walker, K. N., MacBride, A., & Vachon M. L. S. (1977). Social support networks and the crisis of bereavement. *Social Science and Medicine, 11,* 35–41.

Wallston, B. S., Alagna, S. W., DeVellis, B. M., & DeVellis, R. F. (1983). Social support and physical health. *Health Psychology, 2*(4), 367–391.

Weiss, R. (1974). The provisions of social relationships. In Z. Rubin (Ed.), *Doing unto others.* Englewood Cliffs, NJ: Prentice Hall.

Wortman, C. B. (1976). Causal attributions and personal control. In J. H. Harvey, W. J. Ickes, & R. F. Kidd (Eds.), *New directions in attribution research* (Vol. 1, pp. 23–52). Hillsdale, NJ: Erlbaum.

Wortman, C. B. (1984). Social support and cancer: Conceptual and methodologic issues. *Cancer, 53*(10), 2339–2360.

Wortman, C., & Dunkel-Schetter, C. (1979). Interpersonal relationships and cancer: A theoretical analysis. *Journal of Social Issues, 35*(1), 120–155.

Wortman, C., & Lehman, D. (in press). Reactions to victims of life crises: Support that doesn't help. In I. G. Sarason & B. R. Sarason (Eds.), *Social support: Theory, research, and application.* The Hague: Martinus Nijhof.

CHAPTER 15

Social Support and Community Mental Health

Benjamin H. Gottlieb

Introduction and Overview

In Ann Arbor, Michigan, an organization called Intervention Associates tried a unique—if somewhat controversial—approach to prod resistant alcoholics into treatment (Logan, 1983). Initial contact was made with a family member or close friend of the alcoholic, who provided information about the latter's drinking history, social relations, and financial affairs. Next, the staff contacted 8–12 additional members of the alcoholic's social network, requesting each to compile a list of the occasions on which they witnessed the alcoholic's self-destructiveness. To prepare them further for their roles in the main intervention, these social intimates were asked to read the volume *I'll Quit Tomorrow* (Johnson, 1980). Shortly thereafter, this small social network was convened and participants read aloud from their prepared lists. Their collective observations formed the basis for a diagnostic judgment of alcoholism, which, if confirmed, led to the main intervention. The network was reassembled in the workplace, at home, or in a hospital conference room (this time in the alcoholic's presence), typically including the alcoholic's employer, close relatives, family members, a member of the clergy, neighbors, and other significant peers. After an introductory ex-

303

planation of the meeting's purpose, network members presented their testimony, followed by a collective recommendation that the alcoholic enter treatment. In the face of the alcoholic's continued resistance or outright refusal, network members described such adverse consequences of continued drinking as marital separation, job loss, and social rejection. Treatment entailed a month's attendance at a program designed along the principles of Alcoholics Anonymous (AA), followed by participation in AA meetings and adjunctive counseling.

The results of this coercive referral strategy are very promising: 54 of the 60 alcoholics participating in this intervention entered treatment. Of the 45 who had completed treatment by the time the published report was written, 37 could be reached. Of these, 26, or 70%, had maintained abstinence and were actively participating in AA.

Another intervention program, mounted by Berkowitz, Kuipers, Eberlein-Frief, and Leff (1981), was directed toward modifying the quality of the support offered by a segment of patients' networks that is of greatest significance for their affective well-being. This program exemplified a method of optimizing the supportive provisions of the patient's network rather than mobilizing the network to prompt utilization of treatment services. It was based on evidence that schizophrenics are more likely to relapse with florid symptomatology when they have frequent contact with a close relative who expresses highly critical or emotionally overinvolved attitudes toward them (Brown, Birley, & Wing, 1972; Vaughn & Leff, 1976). In contrast, patients living with relatives who show low levels of such expressed emotion (EE) are much less likely to relapse in the 9 months following discharge from the hospital. Accordingly, Berkowitz and her colleagues designed a program of education and group support attempting to lower the level of EE among the schizophrenic's family members. In the experimental design, high EE relatives were randomly assigned to a "treatment" group or to a control group receiving routine clinical care. The treatment consisted of three elements: (1) a joint interview held shortly after discharge with the patient's key relative, concentrating on ways of reducing contact and conflict between the two; (2) four short educational lectures followed by discussion, covering the etiology, diagnosis, course, and prognosis of schizophrenia; and (3) participation in a relative's group aimed at shifting high-EE families toward a calmer, more accepting, and tolerant style of interacting with the patient. Because the groups are composed of both high- and low-EE relatives, the latter serve as models for the former; for the group as a whole, the expression of support, catharsis, and problem solving is critical. Preliminary results were that more patients from the high-EE experimental group than from the control group were well at follow-up, and more of their relatives shifted from high to low levels of EE.

A third example highlights the marshaling of peer support in a brief, preventive intervention designed for children coping with the transitional tensions surrounding their parents' separation and divorce. Through a workshop approach combining mutual aid and structured group exercises that encourage ventilation of feelings and problem solving, participants can begin to deal more constructively with their anxieties and communicate more assertively with family members. Kessler and Bostwick's (1977) workshop was attended by 10 children between the ages of 10 and 16 whose families represented all stages of divorce, from immediately after parental separation to remarriage 6 years after separation. Although the leaders preferred to conduct a series of group sessions over several weeks, the childrens' geographic distance from one another precluded this format. Consequently, a one-day workshop was held featuring a series of structured activities, films, and vignettes intended to encourage the participants to compare notes about their feelings, coping strategies, fearful fantasies, and hopes. Evaluation of the program was not conducted in a rigorous manner, relying instead on a direct measure of consumer satisfaction in the form of a 10-point rating scale. All participants gave the highest possible rating to the workshop, emphasizing gains they had made in understanding their feelings and those of their parents. Subsequent anecdotal evidence gleaned from parents' telephone calls confirmed changes in the participants' communication content and style.

Each of the interventions described was predicated on a recognition that the primary social context in which individuals are embedded has a critical direct and indirect impact on their health and well-being. The first intervention spotlighted the social network's indirect influence on health. Here, family members and close friends first provided important diagnostic information about their associate's pattern of behavior in the natural environment and then mobilized themselves to force the individual into treatment. Capitalizing on the network's lay diagnostic and lay referral functions (Gottlieb, 1982b), the intervention was powered by the explicit threat of a loss or withdrawal of support from family members, friends, and workmates if treatment was not obtained. In contrast, the second intervention was aimed at optimizing the quality of the support given to patients during their rehabilitation from mental illness. In order to prevent a recrudescence of symptoms, the patients' interactions with critical family members were carefully modulated in accordance with empirical evidence about the kind of support most conducive to their stabilization. It is noteworthy that the lay treatment extended by a key relative was modified through participation in a supportive milieu composed of other family members with a mentally ill relative. The third intervention was also predicated on the assumption that the support inherent in the process of social comparison among similar peers can improve coping and foster adaptation. However, it involved the creation of a temporary support system addressing the participants' needs for ventilation of the feelings precipitated by a critical life transition and for planning ways of reassuming their family roles under very different conditions. This approach exemplifies preventive interventions that alter the trajectory of coping with life crises and transitions by marshaling the supportive provisions of peers facing similar stressful circumstances.

In this chapter I will elaborate on these and other applications of social network and social support concepts to the field of community mental health practice. Specifically, I will selectively review both prevention and treatment strategies that mobilize or modify the support available to high-risk groups and diagnosed populations in the community or that attempt to alter the structure of the enveloping social network. I will highlight interventions that can be undertaken by clinicians in out-patient practice as well as programs that can be implemented by mental health workers charged with the task of promoting more durable community support systems for the chronically mentally ill. In addition, I will touch on primary preventive outreach activities in which support development figures prominently, and I will offer a set of guidelines for professional collaboration with mutual aid groups, the most highly organized and visible type of lay helping network. Before addressing these topics, I will begin with a brief overview of the historic significance of social support in the field of community mental health.

Social Support: A Recurrent Theme
in Community Mental Health

In 1974 the social psychiatrist Gerald Caplan wrote a highly influential paper outlining his ideas on the nature of informal support systems in the community and the roles that mental health workers could assume in fostering their development. On the latter score, he emphasized ways in which professionals could help to create mutual aid groups among persons experiencing similar life crises and lend their expertise to existing groups. He also extended his earlier ideas about mental health consultation with community caregivers to contexts in which the consultee was at the center of a neighborhood-based network of informal service delivery. Moreover, he drew on his knowledge of crisis intervention in formulating his thoughts about the fundamental role of the kith and kin network in responding to stressful life events and transitions:

> The results of some of my studies (1964), of individual responses during crisis . . . repeatedly demonstrate that the outcome is influenced not only by the nature and vicissitudes of the stress and by the current ego strength of the individual, but, most important, by the quality of the emotional support and task-oriented

Caplan's ideas were widely embraced by community mental health workers and psychiatric epidemiologists because they integrated prior developments in research and practice pointing to the significance of social support for public mental health. In particular, his disquisition on the nature and functions of support systems can be traced to certain historic themes in community mental health inquiry and practice.

First, Caplan (1974) acknowledged the legacy of the epidemiologist John Cassel, who had recently reviewed a great deal of evidence revealing that both humans and animals suffered adverse health consequences when exposed to social upheavals or placed in a context characterized by social disorganization. However, those who had access to psychosocial processes entailing feedback from "the primary groups of most importance to the individual" (Cassel, 1974, p. 478) were unaffected by stressful conditions, signifying the health-protective power of social support. Moreover, Cassel's (1974) proposition echoed the results of a series of classic epidemiological studies of mental disorder, beginning with the keystone inquiries of Faris and Dunham (1939), Leighton (1959), and Langner and Michael (1963), and extending to Hinkle and Wolff's (Hinkle, 1974) intensive ecological investigations linking abrupt life changes to psychopathology. Whereas these early studies testified to the increased health risk posed by absent or deficient support from the social environment, Cassel's and Caplan's later treatises spotlighted the need "to improve and strengthen the social supports rather than reduce the exposure to the stressors" (Cassel, 1974, p. 479).

Additional historic themes reflected in Caplan's writing can be traced to the seminal work of the Joint Commission on Mental Illness and Health (1961). One theme concerns the important role that lay persons play in fielding the public's mental health problems, and the other concerns the introduction of nonprofessionals in the delivery and interpretation of services to potential consumers. In the book *Americans View Their Mental Health,* Gurin, Veroff, and Feld (1960) documented widespread public reliance on kith, kin, and community caregivers such as teachers, physicians, and members of the clergy during periods of emotional distress. This research launched programs of mental health consultation in schools, religious organizations, and other primary institutions of the community. Recognizing that citizens with little training in mental health could be effective treatment agents (Cowen, Gardner, & Zax, 1967; Durlak, 1979; Karlsruher, 1974) and that in ethnic and minority-group areas they could help to bridge the gap between the professional and the local culture (Levine, Tulkin, Intagliata, Perry, & Whitson, 1979), community mental health centers drew volunteers, paraprofessionals, college student companions, and indigenous helpers into a variety of direct practice and educative roles. Hence, Caplan's thesis on the contribution of ordinary citizens to mental health, as well as his recommendations for consultation programs to community gatekeepers and natural helpers, had been clearly foreshadowed by earlier developments that invited new forms of collaboration between professional and lay helpers.

Finally, the main thrust of Caplan's message dovetailed with the aims of the deinstitutionalization-of-treatment movement. Mental health center staff, actively involved in engineering strategies of diverting mental patients from state hospitals and providing community-based alternative treatment and aftercare programs, found a blueprint for action in Caplan's ideas. He emphasized the importance of weaving patients into a social fabric composed of professionals and lay persons capable of sustaining effective functioning in the open community. Although Caplan did not specifically prescribe avenues for creating durable support systems on behalf of the mentally ill, he outlined a set of supportive provisions that have figured centrally in the design of many psychosocial rehabilitation programs serving the mentally ill. Moreover, he fully recognized the need to tailor support systems for vulnerable populations:

> In an unorganized or disorganized society such spontaneous support systems may be inadequate, especially for marginal people. And it is particularly in such situations and for such people that community-based feedback is likely to be insufficient and the need for individual-oriented support systems greatest. So in these cases the risk of illness will be highest unless someone takes special steps to organize a planned support system to fill the gap. (Caplan, 1974, p. 7) [Copyright © 1974 by Human Sciences Press Inc, 72 Fifth Avenue, New York, NY 10011.]

In the decade following Caplan's appeal, numerous initiatives were taken by community mental health workers interested in fostering more effective support systems. I will review types of preventive interventions involving the mobilization and optimization of support among populations at risk and then consider some of the ways that social support has been extended to mental patients in psychosocial rehabilitation programs.

Preventive Interventions Involving the Optimization of Social Support Groups

A small working conference called "Family Support Programs: The State of the Art" was organized by the Bush Center in Child Development and Social Policy at Yale University in 1983. The conference report included descriptions of 39 community programs, including information about each's goals, services, target populations, and funding sources (*Programs to*

Strengthen Families, 1984). The titles of many of these programs made evident their focus on informal support: Family Support Center, Neighborhood Support Systems for Infants, Parent-to-Parent Family Support Program, Parents Place, New Parents as Teachers, Family Clusters, Inc., Jewish Family Daycare Network, Caring Connection. Their targeted families include teenaged parents, parents of chronically ill children, abusive parents or families at risk of abuse, single parents, low-income families, rural Hispanic and American Indian families that are seasonally employed, and parents of retarded or otherwise handicapped children. Moreover, all but three listed one of the following activities among the services they offer to families: networking, parent support groups, and peer support groups. These terms signify that the programs shared a commitment to a mutual aid approach and to a consumer-intensive approach to service delivery (Gartner & Riessman, 1977).

Equally important, these family support programs represent a type of preventive intervention that has been widely adopted by community mental health workers, involving the creation of social aggregates composed of people in common stressful predicaments or anticipating stressful life events or transitions. Essentially, they supplement or substitute for the network of ongoing social contacts that people maintain in their daily life, thus augmenting the supportive provisions to which they have access. In short, interventions involving the creation of support groups accomplish two goals. First, they alter the structure of people's social networks, populating them with similar peers who are facing similar developmental challenges or situational crises. Second, they set into motion a process of social comparison that facilitates the ventilation of fearful feelings, offers validation for new social identities (Dunkel-Schetter & Wortman, 1981; Hirsch, 1981), and minimizes threatening appraisals of both present and future stressors. This process of social comparison lies at the heart of social support's stress-mediating role, and is chiefly responsible for producing its various salutary effects on cognitive, affective, behavioral, and physiological functioning (Epley, 1974). However, as Cohen and McKay (1984) have pointed out, there are certain conditions that inhibit people from engaging spontaneously in social comparisons (e.g., when people feel guilty about or ashamed of their feelings) or that minimize the likelihood they will benefit from such comparisons (e.g., when associates do not react relatively calmly to their common predicament).

The support group format has been used most widely by community mental health workers in crisis intervention. Practically, it is a cost-effective approach not only because many clients receive service simultaneously, but also because the groups need not be led by a highly trained professional. Indeed, the professional is most active in the initial stage of identifying clients experiencing common life changes or transitions, and can then transfer responsibility to an agency volunteer, a paraprofessional, a veteran of a past group, or to a community caregiver such as a member of the clergy or a public health nurse. Such "event-centered support groups" (Gottlieb, 1981, 1983) have been formed among the bereaved (Barrett, 1978; Silverman, 1976), couples making the transition to parenthood (McGuire &. Gottlieb, 1979; Wandersman, 1982), children coping with parental separation (Kessler &. Bostwick, 1977), and couples preparing for remarriage (Messinger, Walker, &. Freeman, 1978). It is noteworthy that each of these events entails a major change in the parties' social fields, including disruptions of ongoing close relationships and additions to and departures from the family. Moreover, each of these social entrances and exits can have ripple effects throughout the parties' personal networks, shifting social patterns and causing secondary rends in the social fabric. The impact of marital disruption on the family's wider network vividly illustrates these social–ecological reverberations (Wilcox, 1981). It follows that support groups offer both compensatory social ties (thus counteracting feelings of loneliness and uniqueness) and a safe context for planning ways of regaining equilibrium and resuming life under very different social circumstances. Through the group's normalizing, supportive, and modeling functions, members gain a "psychological sense of community" (Sarason, 1974) that is not available in traditional, individual crisis intervention.

Support groups can offer participants a temporary personal community or they can continue indefinitely. In many cases, groups that are germinated by professionals are later transplanted in the open community, meeting without professional guidance. Some transitions, such as school entrance, job change, and new parenthood, are clearly time-limited, characterized by an intensive period of adjustment. Other life changes and critical events engender chronic burdens that continuously tax the adaptive resources of the affected parties. For example, the birth of a child with Down's syndrome or the move of an aged parent with Alzheimer's disease into the younger generation's home are events that pose long-term challenges for the caregivers. Indeed, support groups for those who live with a chronically ill, dependent relative have increased in proportion to the growing prevalence of chronic disease and as a result of the emphasis on community, rather than institutionally-based, treatment. Citizens have taken the lead in forming mutual aid associations among the relatives of the mentally ill (e.g., Association of Relatives and Friends of the Mentally Ill, Parents of Adult Schizophrenics), the alcoholic's family members (e.g., Al-Anon, Al-Ateen), and the children of prison inmates (Prison Children Anonymous).

The preceding discussion suggests that support groups have a salutary impact on the mental health of participants and that they place participants in a more supportive social field. Unfortunately, only a handful of studies evaluating these outcomes in a rigorous way have been reported in the literature. Studies involving the use of an experimental or quasi-experimental design have shown promising results. For example, Roskin (1982) divided a sample of 45 adults who had recently experienced two or more stressful life changes into two support groups that met during two consecutive 6-week periods, thus allowing him to compare the groups' health status before and after the intervention. During each group session a social worker made a short presentation about different aspects of the stress management process; the remaining time was devoted to "concentrating on mutual aid among members and fostering warm, supportive, nonconfrontive participant interactions" (p. 334). Pooled scores on five health dimensions revealed that the support groups succeeded in cushioning the impact of the stressful life events. Specifically, he found a significant reduction in interpersonal over sensitivity and decreased somatic complaints, anxiety, and obsessive–compulsive and depressive symptomatology. Further, he observed that some members contacted each other outside the group meetings and many were eager to continue meeting after the last formal group session.

Evidence that support groups hasten the process of adjusting to stressful life changes has been reported by Vachon, Lyall, Rogers, Freedman-Letofsky, and Freeman (1980), who organized such groups on behalf of a sample of recent widows. To examine changes over time in postbereavement adaptation, the authors interviewed the entire sample initially and again 6, 12, and 24 months after their spouses' deaths. Those randomly assigned to the experimental condition, consisting of both one-to-one supportive counseling with a widow who had successfully resolved her own bereavement as well as participation in support groups, were compared to an untreated control group in terms of their scores on the Goldberg General Health Questionnaire (Goldberg, 1972). At 6 months, the former achieved a higher level of emotional integration than the latter, experiencing less depressive symptomatology and preoccupying themselves less with the past. By 12 months, they attained a greater measure of social reintegration, making new friends and engaging in new activities. The authors concluded that the supportive intervention speeded the widows along a pathway of adaptation following bereavement.

Two additional interventions bear spotlighting because they address the primary preventive impact of support groups. Both deal with the transition to parenthood and both were designed along experimental lines. The first was undertaken in collaboration with two family physicians who hoped that a psychoeducational group experience would instill greater confidence in first-time parents and reduce their use of the physicians' services for problems that were self-limiting in nature (McGuire & Gottlieb, 1979). Accordingly, couples who had recently had their first child were randomly assigned to two groups, each convened by one of the physicians and his wife, and to two comparison groups that received educational material in the mail. Pre- and postexperimental measures were taken of parenting strain, feelings of well-being, health status, and confidence in parenting skills. In addition, out of an interest in gauging the extent to which the support group experience encouraged the new parents to rely more strongly on their natural social networks for help, measures tapping nine aspects of the couples' use of and satisfaction with their ongoing parenting support were included. After six biweekly group sessions, the results showed that the intervention had its greatest impact on the latter (social) dimension, not on the former (health-related) measures. Five weeks after the last session, couples in both support groups discussed child-rearing matters with people in their own social networks more frequently than did control couples, and participants in one of the groups also increased the number of network members with whom they discussed these matters. In short, the group experience taught them the value of the social comparison process, prompting them to tap the informal resources to which they had access. Continued use of peer ties to mitigate or avert the stressful byproducts of life events would provide convincing evidence of the intervention's primary preventive impact.

A second illustration of the application of support groups to parental competence provides clearer testimony of their health-protective effects. Minde, Shosenberg, Marton, Thompson, Ripley, and Burns (1980) evaluated the groups' impact on the attitudes and behaviors of mothers of premature infants. Specifically, they randomly assigned 16 couples to 5 support groups that met for 1½–2 hours weekly for from 7 to 12 weeks. A nurse–counselor and a veteran mother of a premature infant attended each group session. Evaluation centered on the parents' attitudes toward hospital personnel and practices, their parenting competence, and the actual quality of interaction between mother and infant in the nursery, measured by twice-weekly observation of 12 infant and 10 caretaker behaviors. Results showed impressive differences between the experimental and control group parents in respect to the latter infant and maternal behaviors. Mothers who had attended the support groups touched their babies more, looked at the faces of and spoke to their infants more frequently, and visited them more often in the hospital. This trend toward greater maternal involvement was accompanied by more favorable attitudes toward their ability to care for their newborns at home, and a greater understanding of their babies' conditions. Commenting on the primary preventive significance of these findings, Minde *et al.* (1980) concluded: "If . . . there exists a 'critical period' during which contact between the mother and her infant has implications for their later relationships, such group meetings may indeed be highly relevant for the later development of these children" (p. 938).

Optimizing the Network's Supportive Provisions

Another strategy of preventive intervention concentrates on upgrading the supportive provisions available from people's ongoing social networks. It is not timed to coincide with exposure to imminent or actual stressors, but aims to strengthen the capacity of social networks or central figures therein to provide ongoing and crisis support. It is predicated on research (touched on earlier) revealing that family members, close friends, and informal community caregivers are extensively involved in fielding the public's mental health problems.

Three interventions exemplify this strategy of support development. The first is described in a series of papers by D'Augelli and his colleagues who implemented the Community Helpers Project in two rural areas of Pennsylvania (D'Augelli & Ehrlich, 1982; D'Augelli, Vallance, Danish, Young, & Gerdes, 1981; Ehrlich, D'Augelli, & Conter, 1981). Briefly, they aimed to enhance the helping skills of self-selected local informal helpers such as ministers, agricultural extention agents, and small shop owners by offering them a training program and subsequently teaching them how to train other local residents in these helping skills. The training was fundamentally directed toward shifting the participants' style of helping from a directive to a nondirective stance—a decision based on both the classical counseling literature and the expressed preferences of local residents for this type of help. Ehrlich *et al.* (1981) showed that, once refinements were made in the training procedure, videotaped recordings of discussions of actual problems revealed that this shift in the kind of help expressed by both trainers and their trainees was achieved, and that self-rated helping skills improved. However, despite these positive results regarding the project's proximal goal, data comparing the participants' pretraining and posttraining helping activities in the community revealed significant changes on only three of eight helping dimensions: (1) Following training, a greater proportion of helping transactions involved the helper's spouse; (2) more helping took place in the helpee's own home; and (3) helpers reported greater confidence in their helping. Trainees did not significantly change their reported use of types of helping behaviors, a result that D'Augelli and Ehrlich (1982) felt "could be a serious problem if it reflects a failure of the training to generalize to natural settings." (p. 455). Nevertheless, this study provides rich details of the frequency, scope, and duration of informal helping activities in rural areas. For example, in a single week the 37 helpers reported assisting more than 150 different people, friends and relatives being the most common recipients of aid.

A second intervention program bears a strong resemblance to the first, but was targeted at a unique segment of the community's informal caregivers. Wiesenfeld and Weis (1979) offered a 10-week helping skills training program to a group of hairdressers who had expressed interest in upgrading this aspect of their interactions with clients. Here, too, an effort was made to shift the participants' modal helping behaviors toward a nondirective style, increasing their use of empathic responses and decreasing the frequency with which they offered specific advice. In contrast, a group of control hairdressers—who were equally motivated to receive training but had insufficient time to participate—did not change their manner of responding to hypothetical vignettes. Although the authors of the study did not go as far as D'Augelli and Ehrlich (1982) in assessing the effects of the training on those actually helped by their trainees, they expressed concern about its potential adverse impact: that the hairdressers' new approach might alienate clients who were accustomed to their former style of helping. For this reason, Wiesenfeld and Weis (1979) advised that "steps must be taken to ensure that any type of training can be easily and constructively integrated into any existing support network" (p. 792). More generally, interventions directed toward changing the helping strategies practiced by lay persons can only proceed following study and appreciation of the meaning and impact of the supportive provisions exchanged among citizens. Once it is recognized that universally accepted and valued forms of help do not exist but that such forms differ from one local culture to another, deliberate efforts can be made to promote and optimize the fund of support that has the greatest ecological validity.

Todd's (Gottlieb & Todd, 1979) Support Development Workshops offer a model for intervention that is far less prescriptive than the preceding strategies and that can be adapted by community mental health workers for use with numerous citizen groups. Bearing in mind Miller's (1969) dictum to give psychology away to the public, Todd conceived a workshop in which the participants were introduced to the topic of social support and taught about the structural properties of social networks. Once they gained an appreciation of the protean character of social support and learned to map their own personal network, they were in a position to consider changes that might improve their access to support. Moreover, the process of planning such changes illuminated how prior situational factors, personal preferences for different sources and types of support, and dispositional factors influenced the structure and supportive provisions of their networks. In short, the virtue of Todd's approach to primary prevention is that it conditions an appreciation of the interplay of personality, social structural, and processual variables affecting the expression of social support, without forcing the participants to conform to a single set of values about helping.

From Todd's perspective, the workshop can be of particular value as a preventive–developmental intervention for people facing life transitions entailing changes in the structure of their social field. Originally, he convened a workshop on behalf of first-year college students who were actively involved in forming a new network of social ties following their recent transition. However, other populations entering new settings and assuming new roles could also benefit from the workshop. Community mental health workers could offer it to employees recently relocated to branch offices, to workers who have lost their jobs and been forced to move to another city, to those facing retirement or who have sustained work injuries necessitating withdrawal from the workplace , and to people returning to full-time work following a lengthy absence. Divorced couples and their children also could profit from an opportunity to consider ways of reconstituting a fragmented social network and finding compensatory social ties that meet their special needs for support at a time when their feelings about close relationships are in flux.

Collaboration with Self-Help Groups

While I have emphasized the ways that community mental health workers can initiate support groups and cultivate the supportive provisions available in the natural environment, I wish to call attention to the roles they can assume in relation to existing self-help groups, the most organized and visible type of lay helping arrangement. My purpose is not to review the nature and scope of mutual aid groups in North America, because this task has already been undertaken by numerous chroniclers (e.g., Borman, Borck, Hess, & Pasquale, 1982; Gartner & Riessman, 1977; Katz, 1981; Spiegel, 1980), but to highlight both the tensions and the opportunities for collaboration between professionals and self-help groups. The President's Commission on Mental Health signaled its recogniton of the potential for conflict and for cooperation between the two systems of service delivery in the following terms:

> Linkages need to be developed between these social and community support systems, including mutual help groups, and the professional and formal institutional caregiving systems. They should be established on a basis of cooperation and collaboration, not cooptation and control, and without disturbing the potency of their very different helping processes. (1978, p. 208)

In fact, antagonistic relationships between professionals and mutual help groups have been relatively rare. Kleiman, Mantell, and Alexander (1976) have described "the perils of partnership" between the staff of a chapter of the American Cancer Society and Cancervive, a mutual aid group initiated by the agency. Here, "professional preciousness" manifested itself in the imposition of values and a heirarchical structure that were antithetical to the egalitarian ethos of the Cancervive volunteers. Acrimonious feelings toward professionals have also been documented by Lamb and Oliphant (1978), who worked with a mutual aid group called Parents of Adult Schizophrenics. This organization was founded, in part, out of the resentment of its members toward the blame that professionals have assigned to them for causing their relatives' mental illness, communicated in such terms as "the schizophrenogenic mother" and "the identified patient," the latter phrase suggesting that certain family members other than the patient are equally in need of treatment. Other mental patients' rights groups, such as the Mental Patients' Association in Vancouver and On Our Own in Toronto, have been strident in their quest to create what Chamberlin (1978) has called "patient-controlled alternatives to the mental health system." Chiefly, they have sought ways of counteracting the iatrogenic consequences of psychiatric labeling, compulsory treatment, and psychoactive medications. Instead they have been establishing voluntary, peer-helping systems, patient education programs, and a variety of housing and employment services owned and managed by consumers.

Professionals' attitudes toward self-help groups differ according to the degree of contact they have had with specific groups and participants. Although the creation of regional and local clearinghouses that provide referral information and educational workshops has increased professionals' knowledge of the range and nature of self-help groups (Borck & Aronowitz, 1982), some skepticism has remained about the effectiveness of the approach and a good deal of uncertainty about the most suitable roles for professionals to assume in relation to mutual aid groups. Indeed, only a handful of studies have examined the efficacy of self-help groups (e.g., Behavior Associates, 1978; Grosz, 1973; Katz, 1981, pp. 148–150; Lieberman *et al.*, 1979; Videka-Sherman, 1982) and typically experimental designs have not been used. As Katz (1981) and Knight, Wollert, Levy, Frame, and Padgett (1980) have observed, the voluntary and intermittent nature of self-help group participation, the diversity of members, and their concurrent involvement with other mental health services confound rigorous evaluative research.

Two Canadian studies explored the mutual perceptions of professionals and self-help group members. Todres (1982) surveyed 308 professionals in

Toronto, inquiring about their knowledge of local self-help groups and their referral relations with them. He found widespread familiarity and strong referral practices with the longer-established, more visible organizations such as Parents Without Partners, Alcoholics Anonymous, and Women for Sobriety, 43% of the sample adding that they had been involved with one or more groups as speakers or consultants. Gottlieb (1982a) asked 87 members of three types of self-help groups in Montreal and Toronto about their present and prior use of professionals for help with the same problem addressed by their groups, as well as about the appropriateness of several alternative roles for professionals to assume regarding mutual aid groups. Almost two-thirds of his sample had used professionals prior to attending their groups, and 29% were concurrently involved with both types of help. Moreover, group members expressed a preference for professionals assuming the more indirect roles, such as consultant and referral agent, rather than taking a more active role in leadership or training activities. Generally, group members perceived little conflict between mutual aid and professional methods of helping.

With the establishment of several self-help clearinghouses (in New Jersey, Chicago, New York City, and Long Island and Westchester County in New York), experience has shown that collaboration between professionals and self-help groups can be mutually instructive. The two parties have participated in numerous workshops to educate professionals about the work of local groups, clarifying the latter's criteria for accepting members while improving the former's referral accuracy. Detailed guidelines for the initiation of self-help groups have been spelled out, and both sides have compared notes about differences in the helping processes and group facilitation skills of therapy and mutual aid groups. New partnerships between professionals and mutual aid groups have led to innovative service delivery arrangements that ensure comprehensive treatment for a variety of target populations. For example, the introduction of self-help groups in the health care field has meant that patients recovering from heart ailments, mastectomy, and serious burns are not left on their own to deal with the psychosocial aftermath of their medical conditions. Moreover, persons diagnosed with such chronic diseases as multiple sclerosis, diabetes, and Hodgkin's disease are routinely referred by physicians to local chapters of the self-help groups serving these diseases' victims; their relatives and caregivers are also given access to family support groups. These groups fill gaps in the continuum of care that patients require, and they hold out the promise of improving patient adherence to medical regimens involving medication, dietary restrictions, and exercise. In the mental health and addictions fields, organizations like Recovery, Inc., Alcoholics Anonymous, Gamblers

Anonymous, and the Alzheimer's Association of America have developed strong links to professionally dominated treatment agencies and mental health centers.

Short of actually leading or directly intervening in the helping processes of mutual aid groups, community mental health agents can further animate their development and extend their reach by counsulting with members about referral processes, ways of identifying the most suitable candidates for the groups, and ways to heighten the groups' impact on members. The latter entails evaluative research into the characteristics of those who benefit most and least and the formulation of reliable outcome measures. Professionals can also advocate on behalf of local groups, helping to educate their colleagues about group processes and ideologies, and they can sponsor health fairs jointly with representatives of self-help organizations. A meaningful exchange of resources would also entail consultation *by* mutual help group members *to* professionals wherein the latter learn about the nature of informal helping behaviors (Gottlieb, 1978), the groups' impact on the structure of members' ongoing social networks, and about organizational structures for delivering human services designed along egalitarian lines. At the University of Toronto, self-help group members contribute to the training of medical students by describing the ways their groups can be used as adjunct treatment resources and by offering their insights into methods of improving physician–patient rapport. These and other instances of productive collaboration (e.g., Borman, Pasquale, & Davies, 1982; Raiff, 1982; Wollert, Barron, & Bob M., 1982) testify to the benefits accruing to both parties so long as neither imposes hegemony on the other.

Designing Support Systems for the Chronically Mentally Ill

With the establishment of the National Institute of Mental Health's Community Support Program (CSP), a pilot approach to the treatment of the chronically mentally ill, a variety of new initiatives have been taken to ensure that patients have access to "a network of caring and responsible people committed to assisting a vulnerable population to meet their needs and develop their potential without being unnecessarily isolated or excluded from the community" (National Institute of Mental Health, 1977, p. 1). Included among the 10 functions of a CSP are psychosocial rehabilitation services that offer opportunities to develop social skills and a sense of participation and worth, as well as support to families, friends, and community members. Unfortunately, early findings, based on data collected from 1471 clients participating in 15 demonstration sites, have suggested that the CSP has not yet found ways of providing patients with a meaningful network of supportive social ties. Tessler and Goldman (1982) showed that 16.9% of clients never engaged in any scheduled daytime activity, 23.5% did so only once a week, 12% never socialized with friends, and 30.2% did so no more than once a week. They concluded that "many of the clients appear to lead very lonely lives" (p. 114). These data gain greater importance in light of findings reported by Lehman and his colleagues (Lehman, 1983; Lehman, Ward, & Linn, 1982) that the quality of life of mental patients living in 30 urban board-and-care homes is perceived largely in terms of the adequacy of their social relations, particularly their satisfaction with social relationships in the home.

Several intensive inquiries have shed more light on the structural properties of mental patients' social networks (Froland, Brodsky, Olson, & Stewart, 1979; Hammer, Makiesky-Barrow, & Gutwirth, 1978; Sokolovsky, Cohen, Berger, & Geiger, 1978), and comparisons have been made with the networks of undiagnosed community samples (Baker, 1979; Kleiner & Parker, 1974; Pattison, Llamas, & Hurd, 1979; Silberfeld, 1978). Generally, they have found that, in comparison to nonpsychotic control groups of patients or to general population samples, the networks of psychiatric patients are smaller and are characterized by less interpersonal intimacy, greater asymmetry in helping exchanges, and less stability (see Gottlieb, 1983, for a detailed review of these studies). Henderson, Duncan-Jones, McAuley, and Ritchie (1978) have concentrated on the quality of psychiatric outpatients' close relationships, finding that they have access to fewer principal attachment figures than do members of a demographically matched community sample and that they receive deficient support from these attachment figures. Although these studies identify the structural deficiencies of the social orbits in which mental patients participate, they do not provide a basis for decisions about intervention: Should efforts be made to improve the patients' social skills or to restructure their networks?

The Community Lodge Society

In the absence of a single coherent ideology about ways of structuring the social field to optimize the support available to the chronically mentally ill, numerous psychosocial rehabilitation programs have experimented with alternative designs. Perhaps the best known of these programs is the Community Lodge, pioneered by Fairweather, Sanders, Maynard, and Cressler (1969). It demonstrates how a cohesive social system, developed among patients in the hospital, can be transplanted to and take root in the community.

To accomplish this, patients first form small, autonomous problem-solving groups whose members are mutually accountable, and are then transplanted to the community lodge, progressively taking over its administration and maintenance and developing a patient-controlled small business. Members are collectively responsible for monitoring work performance, adherence to medication regimens, and maintenance of the social system as a whole. Although patients who display psychiatric symptomotology in the lodge are tolerated, they are notified by the group that deviant behavior in the community is unacceptable. Evaluative research, 40 months after discharge, comparing the lodge group with a control group of patients who received routine aftercare services and medication revealed that the former spent about 80% of the time in the community and the latter 20%. More impressive, the lodge residents were employed full time 40% of the time, compared to virtually no full-time employment among the controls (Rappaport, 1977). However, the fact remains that the program did not reduce the rate of hospital recidivism but postponed the patients' return; it failed to offer a better "cure" for psychiatric illness, instead effecting a longer and more productive adjustment to community life at a cost that was approximately one-third that of traditional community mental health programs (Fairweather, 1979).

Berkeley House

Budson and Jolley's (1978) approach to the development of a social support network among psychiatric patients in the community shares the lodge society's emphasis on patient self-government while also concentrating on ways of promoting an extended psychosocial kinship system among the halfway house residents. Here, paraprofessional house managers play a much more active role than in the lodge, helping to germinate a network of close ties that is suited to each patient's needs and composed of relationships with co-residents who have "affinities of interest and temperament" (Budson & Jolley, 1978, p. 612), nearby family members, and other work, neighborhood, and day center contacts. The staff is especially active in promoting reciprocal helping exchanges in these networks, modulating the intensity of relationships with family members, and involving ex-residents in the process of aiding the next generation of patients to make a smooth transition from the halfway house to the open community. The success of the psychosocial kinship model is attested to by evaluative research revealing that almost 60% of 78 ex-residents maintained contact with one another 1 year after leaving (Budson, Grob, & Singer, 1977), and that almost three-fourths of the 182 residents served over a 7-year period continued to affiliate with the house (Lynch, Budson, & Jolley, 1977).

Fountain House and Fellowship House

Two final examples of psychiatric rehabilitation programs that foster the development of peer support networks while also providing a more comprehensive array of services than the preceding programs are Fountain House in New York City (Beard, 1978) and Fellowship House in South Miami, Florida. These programs incorporate the four basic elements of Test's (1981) formulation of effective community treatment: individualized treatment plans, continuity of care, an assertive style of service delivery, and ongoing, rather than time-limited, service provision. Moreover, these programmatic components are introduced within a social matrix that rewards interdependence and mutual aid. For example, a team approach is taken to employment preparation, on-the-job skill development, and independent living arrangements in the 40 apartments and the halfway house owned by Fountain House. Roommates hold regular group meetings to discuss housekeeping problems and to forestall interpersonal tensions. Once again, evaluation research reveals that participation in the full range of Fountain House programming delayed, but did not prevent, rehospitalization (Beard, Malamud, & Rossman, 1978).

Test's (1981) review of research on the community treatment of the chronically mentally ill prompted the conclusion that comprehensive psychosocial treatments like those just described yield "substantially lower recidivism rates" (p. 77), improved instrumental functioning, and a higher quality of life than less intensive programs by providing direct assistance to clients and "an enveloping system of social supports" (p. 77). Although diverse in structure, they share an emphasis on peer support, including the utilization of paraprofessionals either as primary care managers or as house staff. This is also true of other community treatment programs, such as Weinman and Kleiner's (1978) Enabler Program in Philadelphia and Mosher and Menn's (1978) Soteria House. Yet, for the most part, these programs have not incorporated mental patients' family members within the support systems they have created, thus failing to meet one of the critical functions of a CSP; to provide support to the immediate relatives of the mentally ill. Granted, in some instances the patient's family ties have atrophied due to lengthy hospital stays, and in other cases family members have become too psychologically or geographically distant to be included in the patient's reconstituted network. However, for those family members who are accessible to the rehabilitation program serving their relatives and for the large number who carry the burden of caring for a severely psychiatrically disabled relative at home, support and guidance are desperately needed. They too need a support system capable of sustaining their informal caregiving activities. Two sorts of initiatives touched on earlier in this chapter are providing promising evidence that such support is forthcoming.

On the one hand, professionals have taken the lead, providing family support and education programs aimed at lowering the elements of expressed emotion among the schizophrenic's relatives. In the preface to a (1981) volume describing several intervention strategies of this sort, Goldstein wrote that the programs' designers

> see beyond these acrimonious relationships to latent strengths in the families of patients—strengths that can be mobilized under the right circumstances as a constructive force for change. Rather than isolating or rejecting relatives of schizophrenics, [they] try to involve them as allies in the aftercare of the patient. (p. 2)

On the other hand, the relatives and close associates of the mentally ill have formed self-help groups and mutual-aid associations such as the National Alliance for the Mentally Ill, Parents of Adult Schizophrenics, and Association of Relatives and Friends of the Mentally Ill, using these forums both to shore up their caregiving efforts and to advocate for legislative, financial, and service-related improvements in the lot of the mentally ill and their relatives. These groups offer an antidote to the isolation and stigma that compound the day-to-day tensions of caring for a mentally ill person. Moreover, their exponential growth in membership is likely to force professionals to recognize the power of citizens as constituents, not consumers, of mental health services. Indeed, these associations are putting professionals on notice regarding the network-rending consequences of deinstitutionalization, signaling to them the responsibility they share with the community for safeguarding public well-being.

Conclusion

Progress has been made in translating early ideas about the nature and role of social support into practical approaches to clinical and preventive interventions in the field of community mental health. By creating support groups among similar peers and by optimizing the supportive provisions available in people's ongoing social networks, professionals can directly buttress the lay system of helping. Moreover, by concentrating more intensely on the social ecology in which patients are embedded, they can fashion support systems that are more capable of sustaining community tenure precisely because they meet basic human needs for a sense of belonging, self-worth, and reliable interdependence. Professionals can also indirectly promote lay helping initiatives by advocating on behalf of self-help groups, establishing more active and reciprocal referral relations with them, and lending them their expertise when invited to do so. Yet, in all of these activities mental health workers must be careful not to dictate their own standards of practice and values about helping to the lay network, and they should not attempt to absorb natural helping systems or to impose a system of credentials on their members.

References

Baker, L. H. (1979). *Natural support systems and the previously hospitalized mental patient.* Paper presented at the meeting of the American Psychological Association, New York.

Barrett, C. J. (1978). Effectiveness of widows' groups in facilitating change. *Journal of Consulting and Clinical Psychology, 46,* 20–31.

Beard, J. H . (1978). The rehabilitation services of Fountain House. In L. I. Stein & M. A. Test (Eds.), *Alternatives to mental hospital treatment.* New York: Plenum.

Beard, J. H., Malamud, T. J., & Rossman, E. (1978). Psychiatric rehabilitation and long-term rehospitalization rates: The findings of two research studies. *Schizophrenia Bulletin, 4,* 622–635.

Behavior Associates. (1978). *Overview of the Parents Anonymous self-help for child abusing parents project evaluation study for 1974–1976.* Tucson, AZ: Behavior Associates.

Berkowitz, R., Kuipers, L., Eberlein-Frief, R., & Leff, J. (1981). Lowering expressed emotion in relatives of schizophrenics. In M. Goldstein (Ed.), *New directions for mental health services: New developments in interventions with families of schizophrenics,* No. 12. San Francisco: Jossey-Bass.

Borck, L., & Aronowitz, E. (1982). The role of the self-help clearinghouse. *Prevention in Human Services, 1,* 121–129.

Borman, L. D., Borck, L. E., Hess, R. , & Pasquale, F. L. (Eds.). (1982). *Helping people to help themselves.* New York: Haworth.

Borman, L. D., Pasquale, F. L., & Davies, J. (1982). Epilepsy self-help groups: Collaboration with professionals. *Prevention in Human Services, 1,* 111–120.

Brown, G. W., Birley, J. L., & Wing, J. K. (1972). Influence of family life on the course of schizophrenic disorders: A replication. *British Journal of Psychiatry, 121,* 241–258.

Budson, R. D., Grob, M. C., & Singer, J. E. (1977). A follow-up study of Berkeley House—A psychiatric halfway house. *International Journal of Social Psychiatry, 23,* 120–131.

Budson, R. D., & Jolley, R. E. (1978). A crucial factor in community program success: The extended psychosocial kinship system. *Schizophrenia Bulletin, 4,* 609–620.

Caplan, G. (1974). Support systems. In G. Caplan (Ed.), *Support systems and community mental health.* New York: Human Sciences Press.

Cassell, J. (1974). Psychosocial processes and stress: Theoretical formulations. *International Journal of Health Services, 4,* 471–482.

Chamberlin, J. (1978). *On our own.* New York: McGraw-Hill.

Cohen, S., & McKay, G. (1984). Social support, stress and the buffering hypothesis: A theoretical analysis. In A. Baum, J. E. Singer, & S. E. Taylor (Eds.), *Handbook of Psychology and Health* (Vol. 4). Hillsdale, NJ: Erlbaum

Cowen, E. L., Gardner, E. A., & Zax, M. (Eds.). (1967). *Emergent approaches to mental health problems.* New York: Appleton-Century-Crofts.

D'Augelli, A. R., & Ehrlich, R. P. (1982). Evaluation of a community-based system for training natural helpers. II. Effects on informal helping activities. *American Journal of Community Psychology, 10,* 447–456.

D'Augelli, A. R., Vallance, T. R., Danish, S. J., Young, C. E., & Gerdes, J. L. (1981). The community helpers project: A description of a prevention strategy for rural communities. *Journal of Prevention, 1,* 209–224.

Dunkel-Schetter, C., & Wortman, C. B. (1981). Dilemmas of social support: Parallels between victimization and aging. In S. Kiesler, J. Morgan, & V. K. Oppenheimer (Eds.), *Aging: Social change.* New York: Academic Press.

Durlak, J. A. (1979). Comparative effectiveness of paraprofessional and professional helpers. *Psychological Bulletin, 86,* 80–92.

Ehrlich, R. P., D'Augelli, A. R., & Conter, K. R. (1981). Evaluation of a community-based system for training natural helpers. I. Effects on verbal helping skills. *American Journal of Community Psychology, 9,* 321–338.

Epley, S. W. (1974). Reduction of the behavioral effects of aversive stimulation by the presence of companions. *Psychological Bulletin, 81,* 271–283.

Fairweather, G. W. (1979). Experimental development and dissemination of an alternative to psychiatric hospitalization: Scientific methods for social change. In R. F. Munoz, L. R. Snowden, & J. G. Kelly (Eds.), *Social and psychological research in community settings.* San Francisco: Jossey-Bass.

Fairweather, G. W., Sanders, D. H., Maynard, H., & Cressler, D. L. (1969). *Community life for the mentally ill: An alternative to institutional care.* Chicago: Aldine.

Faris, R. E., & Dunham, H. W. (1939). *Mental disorders in urban areas.* Chicago: University of Chicago Press.

Froland, C., Brodsky, G., Olson, M., & Stewart, L. (1979). Social support and social adjustment: Implications for mental health professionals. *Community Mental Health Journal, 15,* 82–93.

Gartner, A., & Riessman, F. (1977). *Self-help and the human services.* San Francisco: Jossey-Bass.

Goldberg, P. P. (1972). *The detection of psychiatric illness by questionnaire* (Maudsley Monograph 21). London: Oxford University Press.

Goldstein, M. J. (Ed.). (1981). *New developments in interventions with families of schizophrenics.* San Francisco: Jossey-Bass.

Gottlieb, B. H. (1978). The development and application of a classification scheme of informal helping behaviors. *Canadian Journal of Behavioral Science, 10,* 105–115.

Gottlieb, B. H., (1982a). Mutual-help groups: Members' views of their benefits and of roles for professionals. *Prevention in Human Services, 1,* 55–67

Gottlieb, B. H. (1981). Preventive interventions involving social networks and social support. In B. H. Gottlieb (Ed.), *Social networks and social support.* Beverly Hills, CA: Sage.

Gottlieb, B. H. (1982b). Social support in the workplace. In D. E. Biegel & A. J. Naparstek (Eds.), *Community support systems and mental health.* New York: Springer.

Gottlieb, B. H. (1983). *Social support strategies: Guidelines for mental health practice.* Beverly Hills, CA: Sage.

Gottlieb, B. H., & Todd, D. M. (1979). Characterizing and promoting social support in natural settings. In R. F. Munoz, L. R. Snowden, & J. G. Kelly (Eds.), *Social and psychological research in community settings.* San Francisco: Jossey-Bass.

Grosz, H. J. (1973). *Recovery Inc. survey, second report.* Chicago: Recovery, Inc.

Gurin, G., Veroff, J., & Feld, S. (1960). *Americans view their mental health.* New York: Basic Books.

Hammer, M., Makiesky-Barrow, S., & Gutwirth, L. (1978). Social networks and schizophrenia. *Schizophrenia Bulletin, 4,* 522–545.

Henderson, S., Duncan-Jones, P., McAuley, H., & Ritchie, K. (1978). The patient's primary group. *British Journal of Psychiatry, 132,* 74–86.

Hinkle, L. E., Jr. (1974). The effect of exposure to culture change, social change, and changes in interpersonal relationships on health. In B. S. Dohrenwend & B. P. Dohrenwend (Eds.), *Stressful life events.* New York: Wiley.

Hirsch, B. J. (1981). Social networks and the coping process: Creating personal communities. In B. H. Gottlieb (Ed.), *Social networks and social support.* Beverly Hills, CA: Sage.

Johnson, V. (1980). *I'll Quit Tomorrow* (rev. ed.). New York: Harper & Row.

Joint Commission on Mental Illness and Health. (1961). *Action for mental health.* New York: Basic Books.

Karlsruher, A. E. (1974). The nonprofessional as a psychotherapeutic agent: A review of the empirical evidence pertaining to his effectiveness. *American Journal of Community Psychology, 2,* 61–77.

Katz, A. H. (1981). Self-help and mutual aid: An emerging social movement. *Annual Review of Sociology, 7,* 129–155.

Kessler, S., & Bostwick, S. H. (1977). Beyond divorce: Coping skills for children. *Journal of Clinical Child Psychology, 6,* 38–41.

Kleiman, M. A., Mantell, J. E., & Alexander, E. S. (1976). Collaboration and its discontents: The perils of partnership. *Journal of Applied Behavioral Science, 12,* 403–410.

Kleiner, R. J., & Parker, S. (1974). *Network participation and psychosocial impairment in an urban environment.* U. S. Department of Health, Education and Welfare, National Institute of Mental Health.

Knight, B., Wollert, R., Levy, L., Frame, C., & Padgett, V. (1980). Self-help groups: The members' perspectives. *American Journal of Community Psychology, 8,* 53–65.

Lamb, H. R., & Oliphant, E. (1978). Schizophrenia through the eyes of families. *Hospital and Community Psychiatry, 29,* 803–806.

Langer, T. S., & Michael, S. T. (1963). *Life stress and mental health.* New York: Macmillan.

Lehman, A. F., (1983). The well-being of chronic mental patients. *Archives of General Psychiatry, 40,* 369–373.

Lehman, A. F., Ward, N. C., & Linn, L. S. (1982). Chronic mental patients: The quality of life issue. *American Journal of Psychiatry, 139,* 1271–1276.

Leighton, A. H. (1959). *My name is legion.* New York: Basic Books.

Levine, M., Tulkin, S., Intagliata, J., Perry, J., & Whitson, E. (1979). The paraprofessional: A brief social history. In S. Alley, J. Blanton, & R. E. Feldman (Eds.), *Paraprofessionals in mental health: Theory and practice.* New York: Human Sciences.

Lieberman, M. A., & Borman, L. D. and Associates. (1979). *Self-help groups for coping with crisis.* San Francisco: Jossey-Bass.

Logan, D. G. (1983). Getting alcoholics to treatment by social network intervention. *Hospital and Community Psychiatry, 34,* 360–361.

Lynch, V. J., Budson, R. D., & Jolley, R. E. (1977). Meeting the needs of former residents of a halfway house. *Hospital and Community Psychiatry, 28,* 585.

McGuire, J. C., & Gottlieb, B. H. (1979). Social support groups among new parents: An experimental study in primary prevention. *Journal of Child Clinical Psychology, 8,* 111–116.

Messinger, L., Walker, K., & Freeman, S. (1978). Preparation for remarriage following divorce: The use of group techniques. *American Journal of Orthopsychiatry, 48,* 263–272.

Miller, G. (1969). Psychology as a means of promoting human welfare. *American Psychologist, 24,* 1063–1075.

Minde, K., Shosenberg, N., Marton, P., Thompson, J., Ripley, J., & Burns, S. (1980). Self-help groups in a premature nursery—A controlled evaluation. *Journal of Pediatrics, 96,* 933–940.

Mosher, L. R., & Menn, A. Z. (1978). Lowered barriers in the community: The Soteria model. In L. I. Stein & M. A. Test (Eds.), *Alternatives to mental hospital treatment.* New York: Plenum.

National Institute of Mental Health—Community Support Section. (1977, July). *Request for proposals* (No. NIMH–MH–77–0080–0081). (Mimeo)

Pattison, E. M., Llamas, R., & Hurd, G. (1979). Social network mediation of anxiety. *Psychiatric Annals, 9,* 56–57.

President's Commission on Mental Health. (1978, February). *Task Panel Report: Community Support Systems.* (NTIS No. PB–279801)

Programs to strengthen Families: A resource guide. (1984). New Haven, CT: Yale Bush Center in Child Development and Social Policy.

Raiff, N. R. (1982). Self-help participation and quality of life: A study of the staff of Recovery, Inc. *Prevention in Human Services, 1,* 79–90.

Rappaport, J. (1977). *Community psychology.* New York: Holt, Rinehart & Winston.

Roskin, M. (1982). Coping with life changes—A preventive social work approach. *American Journal of Community Psychology, 10,* 331–340.

Sarason, S. B. (1974). *The psychological sense of community: Prospects for a community psychology.* San Francisco: Jossey-Bass.

Silberfeld, M. (1978). Psychological symptoms and social supports. *Social Psychiatry, 13,* 11–17.

Silverman, P. R. (1976). *If you will lift the load I will lift it too.* New York: Jewish Funeral Directors of America.

Sokolovsky, J., Cohen, C., Berger, D., & Geiger, J. (1978). Personal networks of ex-mental patients in a Manhattan SRO hotel. *Human Organization, 37,* 5–15.

Spiegel, D. (1980). The recent literature: Self-help and mutual support groups. *Community Mental Health Review, 5,* 1, 15–22.

Tessler, R. C., & Goldman, H. H. (1982). *The chronically mentally ill: Assessing community support programs.* New York: Ballinger.

Test, M. A. (1981). Effective community treatment of the chronically mentally ill: What is necessary? *Journal of Social Issues, 37,* 71–86.

Todres, R. (1982). Professional attitudes, awareness and use of self-help groups. *Prevention in Human Services, 1,* 91–98.

Vachon, M., Lyall, W., Rogers, J., Freedman-Letofsky, K., & Freeman, S. (1980). A controlled study of a self-help intervention for widows. *American Journal of Psychiatry, 137,* 1380–1384.

Vaughn, C. E., & Leff, J. P. (1976). The measurement of expressed emotion in the families of psychiatric patients. *British Journal of Social and Clinical Psychology, 15,* 157–165.

Videka-Sherman, L. (1982). Effects of participation in a self-help group for bereaved parents: Compassionate Friends. *Prevention in Human Services, 1,* 69–78.

Wandersman, L. P. (1982). An analysis of the effectiveness of parent-infant support groups. *Journal of Primary Prevention, 3,* 99–115.

Weinman, B., & Kleiner, R. J. (1978). The impact of community living and community member intervention on the adjustment of the chronic psychotic patient. In L. I. Stein & M. A. Test (Eds.), *Alternatives to mental hospital treatment.* New York: Plenum.

Wiesenfeld, A. R., & Weis, H. M. (1979). A mental health consultation program for beauticians. *Professional Psychology, 10,* 786–792.

Wilcox, B. L. (1981). Social support in adjusting to marital disruption: A network analysis. In B. H. Gottlieb (Ed.), *Social networks and social support* Beverly Hills, CA: Sage.

Wollert, R. W., Barron, N., & Bob, M. (1982). Parents United of Oregon: A natural history of a self-help group for sexually abusive families. *Prevention in Human Services, 1,* 99–110.

CHAPTER 16

Social Support and the Physical Environment*

Raymond Fleming, Andrew Baum, and Jerome E. Singer

Introduction

Since the early 1950s, behavioral scientists have become increasingly aware of the importance of social relationships and support in determining health. Paralleling this development, but rarely intersecting it, has been a growth of interest in the effects of the physical environment on mood and behavior. Theoretical perspectives have ranged from the mechanisms of determinism through various levels of possibilism and positivism, but the one clear finding is that the environment exerts powerful influences over social behavior, emotion, and motivation. This finding is important for a number of reasons, including its implications for efforts at improving the quality of life. Just as it is possible to build oppressive environments that stifle social activity, it is also possible to design them to promote social activity and support. This chapter considers such a possible enhancement of social support in light of research on environmental influences on social behavior. Because there are no data directly relating environmental variables to social support, the tone of the discussion is sometimes speculative.

*Preparation of this chapter was facilitated by Research Grant C07205 from the Uniformed Services University of the Health Sciences. The opinions presented are those of the authors and do not necessarily reflect those of the sponsoring agency.

Many of these hypotheses are testable, however, and examination of them may ultimately facilitate design of more supportive environments.

Some basic assumptions were made in writing this chapter. First, we assumed that group formation and friendship formation are related to social support. This makes sense, and is supported by the many definitions and measures of social support that tap these processes (see Cohen & McKay, 1984). However, to consider the possibility that features of the environment can affect social support it is necessary to make a jump from group development to support; available data do not address the question directly. We have also assumed that local social interactions and support derived from those nearby are important. Few would dispute that, for at least some people, having friends in the neighborhood is highly valued. However, social support derives from a number of sources, ranging far beyond the neighborhood or residential building. The importance of local ties and support will determine the effects of features of a setting on social support.

Environmental Determinants
of Social Experience

The basic premise of this chapter is the notion that environmental variables affect the frequency and quality of social contacts, which, in turn, influence social support. Ultimately, this suggests a search for variables that increase positively regarded contact (thereby facilitating social involvement and support). Shunned would be those characteristics of environments that make social experience more aversive. Of course, this is an oversimplification of the process by which research tends to develop, but, for the most part, relationships between environmental and social variables appear to follow this pattern.

The simplest way to demonstrate relationships between social support and the physical environment would be to test the notion directly. This has not been done, and reliable measurement of such a relationship would pose several methodological problems. Social variables are likely to covary with a number of environmental and demographic variables, and the simple demonstration of a correlational relationship between settings and support would not greatly advance understanding. An alternate way of showing that social support is related to environmental variables would be to demonstrate relationships between the environment and processes that affect social support. This section considers evidence of relationships between environmental and social variables. Because there are relevant data on architectural influences on social behavior, we have concentrated primarily on architectural design of interior and exterior space. Although research on social support has not typically examined environmental determinants of group membership and friendship networks, there has been interest in other areas that is pertinent. Social psychologists, sociologists, and others interested in the influence of the physical environment on behavior have examined how people use space in their social encounters and how the arrangement of space affects social experience and the use of this space.

The first question that must be addressed reflects a definitional dilemma. In order to demonstrate relationships involving social processes that are associated with social support, these processes must be specified. However, definitions of social support have varied widely, and there is no obvious set of criteria on which to base such a decision. Central to the concept of social support, however, is the notion of groups of people. Cobb (1976), for example, referred to feelings of belonging to a group—feelings of being cared about by other people—in defining social support. Similarly, some of the mechanisms used to explain the effects of social support are based on phenomena observed in groups. Appraisal support, for example, is partly based on research showing that one of the primary functions of group membership is to provide opinion validation and a reference for construction of individuals' social reality (e.g., Schachter, 1959).

If the assertion that groups are basic to social support is accepted, then it should be possible to specify variables that affect social support by addressing group formation as a mediator. Variables and processes that foster group development should be associated with enhanced social support. The converse, that factors inhibiting group formation inhibit support, should also be true.

Research in naturalistic settings has suggested that group formation is enhanced by at least three variables. First, the opportunity for *passive social contact* appears to be important. In many instances, people get to know one another gradually, often through a succession of casual interactions that grow longer and more involved over time. This process of familiarization requires frequent opportunities for such contact. In a setting where neighbors are never seen, these incidental interactions never occur.

Second, *proximity* appears to be influential in group development. Passive contacts are more frequent among people living close to one another, and the face-to-face interaction that characterizes groups is also facilitated by closeness. However, research has suggested that proximity can be modified by architectural features such as how space is arranged. A related issue is the requirement that groups have a place to meet. In naturalistic settings, group meetings are informal and more or less continuous. Therefore, *appropriate space* for a group to use as its own appears to be an important factor in group development. A neighborhood that provides spaces between or near homes that can be used by neighborhood groups should be associated with more advanced group development than a neighborhood that does not furnish such space.

Space can be central to social activity and the basic functioning of groups. The distances between people, the ease of reaching them, and the use of shared spaces (i.e., areas governed by a group rather than by an individual) are important to groups. In fact, the opportunity for regular face-to-face contact is part of what makes a group "a group," and if space does not permit this regular contact, groups cannot form or survive. People use space in ways that satisfy needs for contact, privacy, and intimacy. When people are unable to do so, normal social activity may be truncated and group formation can be slowed or prevented.

The arrangement of space and the degree to which it facilitates passive contact appear to affect group development and may therefore affect social support as well. A number of factors that appear to contribute to group formation and social support—including the opportunity to meet people under benign conditions, see friends and other group members regularly, and use shared spaces for group-based activities—are affected by the design or layout of the environment in which people live or work. It is reasonable to argue that environmental factors that inhibit certain kinds of social activity can affect support. Friends with whom one has little contact because of distance or inconvenience may be less likely to contribute in a major way to social support. The potency of local support networks, however, has not been demonstrated.

The notion that the arrangement of space can influence social support is based on research showing links between environmental factors and social behavior. Studies have indicated that architectural arrangement of space can affect the development of small groups, the use of semiprivate or group-controlled areas, and the development of friendship networks (Baum & Valins 1977; Festinger, Schachter, & Back, 1950; Newman, 1972; Yancey, 1972). Because these aspects of social experience should be related to support, this research should be useful in understanding relationships between the physical environment and social support.

Architecture and Social Behavior

Several studies have addressed architectural variables related to social contact, friendship formation, and group development. Some design features, such as shared access to residences or common areas, have been associated with high levels of comfortable social contacts and friendship formation. Other features, such as the lack of space for groups to use, have been associated with frequent but unwanted social contact and low levels of friendship. These design features appear to affect group development by influencing the frequency and quality of passive social contact, the proximity of potential group members, and the availability of usable group space, which is consistent with the earlier discussion.

The first systematic investigation of environmental influences on social behavior was a study of student housing by Festinger, Schachter, and Back (1950). Before this, research had not typically considered the importance of ecological determinants of friendship and group formation. Implicit in those studies that were done was the notion that ecological variables (such as distance) could play an important role in determining who people choose as friends, what groups they join, and who they choose as mates. More subtle environmental influences were not tapped, and it remained for Festinger and colleagues to recognize that environmental determinants could play a dramatic role in social experience, even when the existence of these determinants was barely noticeable. They suggested, among other things, that small differences in the placement of an entrance to a dwelling might have dramatic effects on who becomes friends with whom. In fact, they stated that "when our data had been assembled, the most striking item was the dependence of friendship formation on the mere physical arrangement of the houses" (p. 10).

Festinger *et al.* focused on environmental variables affecting passive social contact. Their analyses revealed that the ease of interacting with neighbors, influenced by such variables as the placement of access paths or stairways, was a strong determinant of friendship formation. Social networks appeared to be determined by variables affecting passive contact.

Friendship Formation and Passive Social Contact

Festinger *et al.* studied these variables in housing facilities for married university students. One, called Westgate, consisted of single-story dwellings (2½–4 rooms) laid out in U-shaped courts. Each court grouped 9–13 units around a central access area. The other housing project, Westgate West, consisted of 17 two-story buildings, each containing 10 apartment units. The housing projects were adjacent to one another, and were filled on a first-come, first-served basis. The resident populations were homogeneous, and the residents of the two projects were comparable to one another.

In interviews with persons living in Westgate, Festinger *et al.* (1950) found that approximately 75% of developing friendships were among Westgate neighbors. This finding gave them the unique opportunity to study the formation of informal groups within a relatively closed system. They reasoned that in communities such as Westgate and Westgate West, friendships were likely to develop out of a series of brief and passive contacts between residents. Therefore, two ecological factors that might prove important in the development of friendships were physical proximity and functional proximity.

Physical proximity refers to *measured distance.* People who live nearer to one another are more likely to meet each other and at least experience passive contact. Functional distance is dependent on the features of the design of building or series of buildings that influence the *likelihood of coming into contact with neighbors.* Thus, the placement of stairwells may influence whose door a resident passes or does not pass. This factor proved to be important in both Westgate neighborhoods.

Physical distance should be influential in determining friendship networks. Figure 16.1 depicts the design of the buildings in the Westgate West complex. Assuming equal distance between doors, people living in Apartment 7 should have been much more likely to pass or meet neighbors in Apartment 6 or Apartment 8 than they would have been to encounter neighbors in Apartment 10. Because Apartment 6 and Apartment 8 were so much closer, chance contact with these people was much more likely. If chance contact eventually leads to friendship, then persons in Apartment 7 should have been more likely to designate closer neighbors as friends. Festinger *et al.* (1950) found precisely this; when they asked residents to list the three people that they spent time with, those living in adjacent apartments were four times as likely to be listed as were neighbors living four units away.

Although physical distance was important, functional distance also emerged as a major determinant of friendship formation. It also can be seen in Figure 16.1 that Apartments 1 and 5 were located at the foot of stairways leading to the second floor. The presence and position of these stairs should have increased incidental contact between those who needed to use the

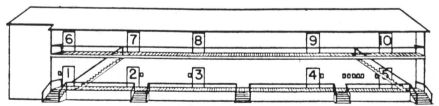

Figure 16.1. Schematic diagram of the arrangement of a Westgate West building. Numbers are apartment numbers. Reprinted from *Social Pressures in Informal Groups* by Leon Festinger, Stanley Schachter, and Kurt Back with the permission of the publishers, Stanford University Press. Copyright © 1950 by Leon Festinger, Stanley Schachter, and Kurt Back.

stairs and those who lived near them. Residents of these apartments reported a greater number of passive contacts with neighbors than did other residents, and contact was particularly frequent with neighbors using the stairs near their dwelling. Thus, residents of Apartment 8, though physically closer to Unit 3 than to Unit 1, would have been more likely to encounter residents of Unit 1 because the functional distance between them was reduced by placement of access routes.

This same pattern was found in the courts. As can be seen in Figure 16.2, access to housing was determined by a pattern of paths, and most units were reached by two or three shared routes. Units a and m, however, were angled away from the court and either had a separate path or did not share very much of the central paths. This increased their functional distance from the other units, and Festinger *et al.* (1950) found that residents of these units were less likely to encounter neighbors from other units and were less frequently identified by neighbors as being social acquaintances. Passive contact and friendship formation were influenced by access-authored functional distances.

Use of Space by Groups

Subsequent research has considered similar instances of the effects of the arrangement of space on the ways in which it is used and on the nature of social experience of people using it. Some structures or designs appear to promote contact between individuals, either by increasing passive contact or by making the context of these contacts more positive. Others seem to inhibit contact by making contact less frequent or more aversive. Thus far, however, we have considered only design variables that affect passive contact and functional proximity. The presence of appropriate space for passive contact may be as important as whether the contact occurs at all.

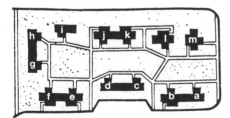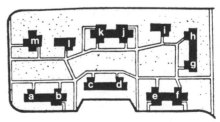

Figure 16.2. Schematic diagram of the arrangement of the Westgate Court. Letters refer to the housing units. Reprinted from *Social Pressures in Informal Groups* by Leon Festinger, Stanley Schachter, and Kurt Back with the permission of the publishers, Stanford University Press. Copyright © 1950 by Leon Festinger, Stanley Schachter, and Kurt Back.

Architectural design of space can affect group development in other ways as well. Yancey (1972) described an instance of atomization of social networks and inhibition of group development as a function of design in a low-cost housing project. The Pruitt-Igoe housing project consisted of a number of high-rise buildings. Because of the high-rise design, residents did not live close enough to exterior spaces that could be used for social contact. In addition, the design of space within the apartment buildings did not provide any areas outside the private apartment that neighbors could share other than the corridors connecting the individual apartment units. As a result, Yancey argued, social contacts were infrequent, proximal space that could serve a group function remained unused, and local groups did not form.

Yancey (1972) made this clearer by distinguishing between life in the Pruitt-Igoe project and in an adjacent slum area. He argued that in slums the cluttered streets and alleyways provided places for individuals to gather and conduct informal social contacts, both supporting the development of a social network and providing residents with informal social control over these areas in their neighborhood. In typical slums, semiprivate space conducive to group use and control is readily available. However, the no-waste design of the Pruitt-Igoe project had reduced the availability of semiprivate space in these buildings. Passive contact was infrequent, social networks were atomized, and residents retreated into their apartments. Yancey (1972) provided an interesting illustration of these effects in his description of the experiences of the research team studying the two areas. While interviewing people in the slum neighborhoods, they often encountered people on the street who questioned them as to where they were going. After an introduction, residents often told interviewers instructions where a family could be found, when they might return home, or how to get through an alley to their apartment. Later, when the interviewers returned and approached the intended participant, they often received responses such as, "Oh yes, you were here earlier." Neighbors had given the message that someone had been there to see them. During the 3 years of intensive research in the Pruitt-Igoe project, this never occurred; because groups did not form and come to exert control over space, residents and nonresidents were not treated differently.

One explanation of this difference in surveillance between the project and the nearby slum has to do with the kind of space available in each. Pruitt-Igoe provided private apartment space, which ended at the apartment door, and public access space. Residents could congregate in someone's apartment or in narrow hallways. In contrast, most of the buildings in the slum had stoops that extended private space beyond the building and created a semiprivate buffer zone between private residences and public urban space. Residents could thus congregate in public space around semiprivate space or in the semiprivate space itself.

One further point of contrast is relevant here. Yancey reported that typical slum dwellers were generally dissatisfied with their internal dwellings (many with very poor plumbing and heating) but generally satisfied with their surrounding neighborhood. With the Pruitt-Igoe residents, just the opposite was true. Residents were generally dissatisfied with the surrounding neighborhood, often complaining of fears of being assaulted, robbed, or raped, but were generally satisfied with their private dwellings.

Semiprivate and Defensible Space

Yancey's findings suggest that semiprivate space is necessary for the development of social networks and groups as well as for residential satisfaction. The ill-fated (demolished) Pruitt-Igoe project is a stark reminder of the consequences of designs that do not meet behavioral as well as biological needs. The arrangement of space reduced passive contact, resulting in inhibited group formation, failure to exert group-based control over nearby spaces, and a number of social problems.

Newman (1972), in research on crime rates in various buildings and parts of buildings, discussed shared group-controlled space in terms of its defensibility. Defensible space is similar to semiprivate space; it is shared by a small group of neighbors who use it regularly and control it (e.g., regulate who may use it or how it may be used). The key to this is the idea of a space where residents can see all the interactions that occur and can exert some control over these interactions. Areas where surveillance and control were possible were found to have lower crime rates than were areas not under the informal control of residents.

A good illustration of defensible space is provided by an occurrence at the Pruitt-Igoe housing project. One building was scheduled to have maintenance done and also to have some recreational equipment refurbished for children living in the building. In order to protect people from injury and equipment from theft, a fence was installed around the entire building. Keys to the gates were given only to residents and to some construction workers. The construction lasted about 6 months, during which residents of the building began to sweep their hallways and pick up the litter surrounding the apartments. When the construction ended, several residents petitioned to have the fence remain—residents had found that crime rates and vandalism had been dramatically reduced while the fence had been there. Apparently, the fence increased the appropriateness of space around

the building to serve as defensible space. Two years following the construction, the fence remained and the crime rate for that building was 80%
below the Pruitt-Igoe norm. Also, the vacancy rate of this building averaged
2–5%, while the rate for the rest of Pruitt-Igoe was approximately 70%
(Newman, 1972).

Control of Social Contact

The importance of control over passive contacts is suggested by these
studies, but is not clearly addressed. Control again refers to the ability to
regulate social experience by determining when, where, and with whom
one may interact. Passive contact is crucial to friendship and group formation, but most studies of this relationship have focused on settings that
are more likely to provide inadequate or infrequent contact than excessive
contact among neighbors. Baum and Valins (1977) studied two architecturally different dormitory designs that were most notably distinct in the degree to which excessive social contact led to the same kinds of responses
associated with the lack of encounters in other settings.

The principal difference between the dormitory types was architectural—the ways in which residential space was arranged. One type of building, using a corridor design, housed students in groups of about 34 per
floor. Each floor consisted of a long hallway with bedroom units off to
either side along the hallway. Each bedroom was shared by two residents.
A large bathroom area and a lounge area, shared by all 34 residents of the
floor, were also provided along the hallway. Because access was provided
by the hallway, it was also used by all floor residents.

The second design, a suite design, housed equal numbers of residents on
a floor but broke the shared spaces on the floor into smaller units. Several
suites were arranged along a central hallway, again shared by all floor residents. However, lounge and bathroom areas were provided within each
suite, which consisted of two or three double-occupancy bedrooms grouped
around a central lounge area and a small bathroom used by suite residents.

These designs resulted in a number of different conditions. First, the
group size or social density of the corridor-design buildings was high—34
people shared all living space outside the bedroom. In the suite-style housing most living space was shared by 4 or 6 residents. This factor appeared
to be related to both frequency and location of passive contact. Corridor
dormitory residents reported frequent passive contact, usually in the hallways, and were more likely to feel that contact was excessive than were
suite residents (who experienced most contact in the suite lounge). Corridor
residents complained of unwanted social encounters, again usually in the

hallway, and reported less control over when, where, or with whom an interaction might occur. The architecturally derived social density in the corridor dormitories was apparently responsible for promoting excessive, unwanted, and uncontrollable interaction among neighbors.

The design of interior dormitory space also influenced group formation. Because of the excessive contact in the dormitory, corridor-building residents exhibited withdrawal and attempted to avoid contact with neighbors. This strategy persisted despite the fact that encounters could not be eliminated. In addition, the design of the corridor dormitories forced passive social contact into the hallway, an area not well suited to conversion to semiprivate space. Group formation in these dormitories was inhibited and control over hallway space never achieved. Unwanted interactions, then, occurred in uncontrolled areas.

Withdrawal from interaction is reminiscent of the conditions generated in Pruitt-Igoe. In fact, some of the processes involved are probably quite similar. Residents of the Pruitt-Igoe housing project faced a situation in which interactions outside of their apartments were largely uncontrollable. Group space was not available and groups did not form. Fear of assault, robbery, and rape were prominent in these residents. The magnitude of the consequences of unfortunate designs at Pruitt-Igoe are clearly on a different order than those observed by Baum and Valins (1977), but in many ways the same problems were responsible for resident distress.

The influence of the arrangement of space on social experience is potent. Social interaction or passive contact may lead to familiarity and eventually to group formation, depending on whether social experience is positive or negative. If negative (i.e., excessive contacts, uncontrollable contacts), social interaction may be viewed as aversive and may not be wanted, but when positive, interaction should facilitate group function. Several studies have revealed consistent, and sometimes major, consequences of architectural design on the evolution of social networks. This is clearly related to social support; if residents have less contact with neighbors or actively withdraw or avoid contact with them, they will be less likely to derive any social support from them. We will discuss this further in the next section.

The findings we have reviewed suggest that the quality of social experience is affected by environmental variables such as architectural design. The arrangement of both exterior and interior space can affect social experience. Further, the social conditions associated with layout of space (e.g., access routes or group size) can affect the social value of people, friendships, and so on. The pertinent and unanswered question, however, remains. The extent to which these kinds of effects are influential in the development of social support is still a matter of speculation.

Social Support in the Environment

The findings discussed in the preceding section provide some bases for speculation about environmental influences on the extent or effectiveness of social support. Clearly, social interactions occur in an environmental context, and this context affects several dynamics that common sense tells us are related to social support. Friendship, group formation, and the use of shared space all seem central to the milieu out of which support is derived.

Distance is a factor in social support. If individuals are alone in a place far from friends and family, their level of support should be low. Technological compensation for distance has moderated this somewhat. Modern telecommunications and transportation often put distant relatives and friends only seconds or hours away. These devices have changed the nature of family and social relations and have made interaction with neighbors or co-workers less central than they once were. However, these interactions are still important, and environmental variables that affect the arrangement of local space should primarily affect social support derived from local sources.

The Importance of Local Social Support

As noted at the outset of this chapter, there are a number of sources of social support beyond the neighborhood or building. The implications of the research that we have discussed are limited to locally based social support, and their significance will depend on the relative importance of having social support from people in the immediate environment. In all likelihood, the importance of local support will usually be a joint function of the situation and people involved. Those who live near an extended family may be less dependent on local support from neighbors or co-workers; transient or highly mobile people may be more dependent on these sources of support. More research on relative benefits of different sources of support is needed because research suggests that different sources are more or less important to different people at different times (Holahan & Moos, 1981). As a general rule, however, it is reasonable to assume that social ties with neighbors or co-workers are important for many people.

Another way to consider the importance of local sources of support is to consider the different functions of social support and how they may be affected by the extent of local, as opposed to more distant, support. For example, instrumental support—that aspect of social support having to do with the availability of actual, physical assistance (such as giving a ride to the airport or watching someone's children)—should be greatly affected by local sources. Distant friends are less often able to lend instrumental support than are nearby friends. Appraisal support, or help from friends in interpreting events and making decisions, may not be as dependent on local sources. Distant friends can provide advice and opinions, although local friends may have more opportunity to do so.

A good example of a situation in which local support networks may be of particular importance is provided by research on mass psychogenic illness (MPI) (e.g., Colligan, Pennebaker, & Murphy, 1982). MPI refers to unexplained, spontaneous outbreaks of illness or illness symptoms, usually in a work setting, that follow a pattern beginning with the presence of an initial *index* case of the illness or symptoms. Outbreaks usually occur in settings that are characterized by the presence of stressors such as noise, boredom, pressures toward increased production, strained labor–management relationships, and a lack of interaction among workers (Singer, Baum, Baum, & Thew, 1982). Of interest is that the lack of contact among workers suggests that local social networks are curtailed and the opportunity for normal social comparison is not available. In the absence of this appraisal support (which would normally be supplied by a local network), symptoms experienced because of stress or pressure may be attributed to illness if the opportunity for comparison with another is possible. On the contrary, if more people were present and accessible, this would tend to increase accurate assessment of symptoms as opposed to the inaccurate assessments seen in MPI. In the case of MPI, this is furnished when a worker attributes symptoms to a new stimulus or irritant (such as a strange odor) and develops an index case of illness. Singer *et al.* (1982) argued that the lack of opportunities to discuss this new stimulus in settings characterized by MPI outbreaks is an important determinant of the outbreaks.

Architecture and Social Support

Architectural variables are among the many that appear to affect social relationships and support. The impact that these variables have on passive contact and social networks as well as the importance of locally based social support highlight their potential significance. However, most research has given only lip service to physical features of the environment in studies of social support.

One finding of Festinger *et al.* (1950) of particular interest is that those people who reported the greatest number of friendships within the housing development also reported the greatest number of friendships outside of their complexes. It seems as though the greater numbers of informal social contacts for residents in the project may have also facilitated friendship formation outside of the housing area. In this case, the architectural design of the housing may have indirectly influenced social outcomes beyond the housing environment.

Determinants of Support

In a review of the literature on social support and health, Broadhead, Kaplan, James, Wagner, Schoenbach, Grimson, Heyden, Tibblin, and Gehlbach (1983) noted that "much of social support may be environmentally determined" (p. 530). However, the environment to which they referred is often the social rather than the physical. The influences they suggested include those of social class, community, and culture. The presence of opportunities for comfortable social interaction and friendship formation should also reflect determinants of support.

Personal characteristics affect social support as well. Age, gender, race, and marital status all appear to be important in determining support levels (Broadhead *et al.*, 1983). Research has indicated an average support network size of 9 or 10 people (Ingersoll & Depner, 1980) and has suggested that the composition of these networks is typically weighted toward friends and co-workers (McFarlane *et al.*, 1981). Women tend to maintain slightly larger networks than do men but do not appear to garner more overall support (McFarlane *et al.*, 1981; Stephens *et al.*, 1978). Being married is associated with higher levels of support, and being older tends to reduce support levels somewhat (Ingersoll & Depner, 1980; Stephens *et al.*, 1978).

Beyond these determinants of support, a number of social conditions are important. For example, family size helps to shape support. The more children a person has, the greater support he or she is likely to have; more people living in the household is also associated with greater social support (Broadhead *et al.*, 1983). Similarly, the availability of people with whom comfortable interactions have been worked out, places where casual contact can occur, and a community where the sheer load of interactions do not overwhelm residents can determine level of social support. The bottom line is an untested one—that friendship networks and the development of small groups are central to social support. It is probably untested because it is so obvious. However, the links between environmental variables and support appear necessarily based in these conditions.

Sources of Environmental Stress

Our position, then, rests on the hypothesized links between social conditions (e.g., friendship patterns, passive contact, semiprivate space) and social support. It makes sense to argue that the more friends people have, the more controllable their social experiences are, or that the more suitable an environment is for passive contact and group interaction, the more support would be available. Despite the intuitive appeal of these arguments, no data are available reflecting on the role of environmental variables in determining level of social support; there is a similar lack of data about how environments contribute to stress directly by posing threats and indirectly by suppressing social support.

Preliminary results from studies of urban stress provide some information. In one study, the presence of small local markets, convenience stores, and so on at the ends of residential streets was associated with higher social density, more frequent unwanted social contact, less group use of shared space, and inhibited group formation on the streets (Baum, Aiello, & Davis, 1979). This was apparently caused by the increased pedestrian traffic (relative to areas without stores) and by the fact that the people walking to and from the stores were often strangers to residents. The space that neighbors might normally use for interaction was now subject to use by strangers. Residents complained of lack of control over social experience and withdrew from neighborhood interactions. This was mediated by social support levels in that those who reported higher levels of social support exhibited fewer symptoms of stress than did those reporting lower levels of support (Baum, Davis, & Aiello, 1978). There were no effects of social support in low-stress comparison neighborhood areas. There was, however, a trend suggesting that residents of streets without stores reported more social support than did residents of streets with stores.

This is an interesting finding because it suggests that environments may cause stress indirectly by suppressing social support, as well as directly by posing threats. Research already reviewed has shown that architectural arrangement of interior and exterior space influences friendship networks, group development and control of space, and overall residential satisfaction. Because social support is at least partly derived from group membership and networks of friends, it is probable that support is also affected by these spatial variables. In fact, research suggests that the same environmental variables that inhibit friendships and group development are also associated with stress (Baum, Singer, & Baum, 1981). We have also observed changes in social support over time, and preliminary analyses suggest that control and perceived health both fluctuate with social support changes over time. Most interestingly, social support ratings appear to be lower in the winter than at any other time; decreases in support may be due to inhibition of neighborhood social interaction by the colder weather. Curtailment of interaction, which may reduce perceived support, may also cause increases in stress symptoms and loss of personal control.

A study by Miller and Ingham (1976) provided some evidence of this phenomenon. They found that people reporting having fewer acquaintances reported more troubling symptoms than did people reporting some acquaintances. In addition, people reporting having many acquaintances showed higher symptom profiles than did those with some acquaintances. Social dynamics may be a source of stress as well as of support, and too much social contact (or inappropriate conditions for social contact) may produce environmental demands that cannot be met.

Also, Cassel (1972, 1976) asserted, characteristics inherent in the social environment have been overlooked for their importance in the susceptibility to disease. He reviewed a large group of studies showing that the people most susceptible to a broad group of diseases are those persons whose social networks are truncated (Christenson & Hinkle, 1961; Holmes, 1956; Mishler & Scotch, 1963; Tillman & Hobbs, 1949). Cassel argued that research should be focused on interventions that will increase the positive aspects of the physical environment and decrease the negative. The construction of a fence around one of the Pruitt-Igoe buildings provided a glimpse of the effects of such interventions. The fence provided control over the space surrounding the building (converting it from public space to semiprivate, defensible space) and positive social interaction was facilitated (e.g., neighbors began sweeping hallways and interacting) while negative social occurrences (e.g., vandalism and vacancy rates) were decreased.

Design Implications

Because differences in architecture may affect the development and maintenance of social support, it may be inferred that whatever benefits may be derived from having support will be accentuated by design facilitating group formation and use of space. Health and well-being are affected by the environment within which people live. Although most of the data already presented concerning architectural influences on behavior focused on crime rates and observations of social behavior, research has shown emotional changes, behavioral performance deficits, withdrawal, and greater use of health facilities for residents of environments where there was a minimum of semiprivate or controllable living space (e.g., Baum & Paulus, in press). If architecture has an impact on not only who people choose as friends but also upon their moods, social behavior, and even health in general, what must be the rallying cry of social support intervention researchers?

Surely, if any of this information is to provide positive change, it is not necessary to call for widespread renovation of the architecture that is presently occupied. This is especially true in metropolitan areas, where "wasted space" has often been eliminated. Even if the benefits were found to outweigh the many costs, it does not seem necessary to mandate large-scale demolition of "bad" architecture in favor of construction of better living spaces, as suggested by the dramatic impact of a construction fence on the Pruitt-Igoe residents using that space. Also, Baum and Davis (1980) have shown that bisecting long-corridor style dormitories with the addition of an interior door and lounge halfway down one of the hallways was sufficient to reverse the effects previously associated with the unmodified environment. Essentially, this interior design modification created two "better" short-corridor dorms from one long-corridor design.

All 43 11-story buildings of the Pruitt-Igoe housing project had been demolished by 1972. Approximately 2800 apartments were destroyed because the costs of continued use of the housing project were greater than the perceived benefits. There may have been an alternative to this destruction. Of course, architecture still in the planning stage should be designed with considerations given to the viability of its living space; it is much better to change blueprints than to create living space that is at best useless and at worst occupied by persons subjected to its "bad" influence on their lives. Plans toward eliminating wasted space that might be useful as semiprivate space should consider the effects of even small concessions to social needs. Although a good goal may be to create positive, supportive environments in which people may live, many less desirable architectural achievements may be quite a way from being more supportive living space.

Policy Implications

The distinction between design and policy implications is somewhat artificial. If general policy mandates maximizing the habitability of environments as they are built, then design changes based on links between design and health are policy as well. However, the policy implications of our analysis extend beyond design change and environmental planning. As Lindheim and Syme (1983) have argued, whereas physical aspects of environments, such as sanitation, were the focus of earlier attempts at improving living conditions, modern concerns should be social and psychological aspects of these settings.

Gans (1962) documented the destructive effects of breaking up neighborhoods, with consequent reduction in social support and group interaction. However, this research also highlighted the positive and powerful effects of such neighborhoods. It is possible that such positive neighborhoods could be renovated while maintaining an environment permissive of such positive contact. Ultimately, the cost of housing must include its effects on its residents, even in an economic sense. High ideals are sufficient to demand consideration of mental and physical health in building homes and apartments or, for that matter, in making any environmental changes.

However, the economic implications of future Pruitt-Igoes are probably more effective in shaping policy. A construction savings based on an inhospitable but efficient architectural design may quickly disappear if social service and health care costs increase as a result. Emphasis on preventive health care lends credibility to seeing prevention by environmental design as a viable approach.

At another level, this analysis suggests an important level for policy input. Although physical health is consistently accepted as a valid input into environmental impact decisions, psychosocial variables are less consistently considered. Assessments of the effects of airport noise and prison crowding, for example, have considered psychological reports, but have often weighed health data more heavily. A Supreme Court decision (People Against Energy v. U.S. Nuclear Regulatory Commission), however, suggested that only physical health may be considered in decisions regarding the nuclear reactor at Three Mile Island. Thus, psychosocial *outcomes* are not always given appropriate consideration.

The demonstration of links between environmental change and social support, given the well-documented health effects of support, suggest that credence be given to psychosocial variables as *mediators* of health. Impact assessments may more readily include psychosocial factors if they can be shown to have reliable effects on the health outcomes already considered to be important.

References

Baum, A., Aiello, J., & Davis, G. (1979, September). *Neighborhood determinants of stress symptom perception.* Paper presented at the meeting of the American Psychological Association, New York City.

Baum, A., & Davis, G. E. (1980). Reducing the stress of high-density living: An architectural intervention. *Journal of Personality and Social Psychology, 38,* 471–481.

Baum, A., Davis, G., & Aiello, J. R. (1978). Crowding and neighborhood mediation of urban density. *Journal of Population, 1,* 266–279.

Baum, A., & Paulus, P. (in press). Crowding. In I. Altman & D. Stokols (Eds.), *Handbook of environmental psychology.* New York: Wiley.

Baum, A., Singer, J. E., & Baum, C. S. (1981). Stress and the environment. *Journal of Social Issues, 37,* 4–35.

Baum, A., & Valins, S. (1977). *Architecture and social behavior: Psychological studies in social density.* Hillsdale, NJ: Erlbaum.

Baum, A., & Valins, S. (1979). Architectural mediation of residential density and control: Crowding and the regulation of social contact. In L. Berkowitz (Ed.), *Advances in experimental social psychology* (Vol. 12, pp. 131–175). New York: Academic Press.

Broadhead, W. E., Kaplan, B. H., James, S. A., Wagner, E. H., Schoenback, V. J., Grimson, R., Heyden, S., Tibblin, B., & Gehlbach, S. H. (1983). The epidemiologic evidence for a relationship between social support and health. *American Journal of Epidemiology, 117* (5), 521–537.

Cassel, J. (1976). The contribution of the social environment to host resistance. *American Journal of Epidemiology, 104,* 107–123.

Cassel, J. (1972). Health consequences of population density and crowding. In R. Gutman (Ed.), *People and buildings.* New York: Basic Books.

Christenson, W. N., & Hinkle, L. E., Jr. (1961). Differences in illness and prognostic signs in two groups of young men. *Journal of the American Medical Association, 177,* 247–253.

Cobb, S. (1976). Social support as a moderator of life stress. *Psychosomatic Medicine, 38,* 300–314.

Cohen, S., & McKay, G. (1984). Social support, stress and the buffer hypothesis. In A. Baum, S. Taylor, & J. E. Singer (Eds.), *Handbook of psychology and health* (Vol. IV). Hillsdale, NJ: Erlbaum.

Colligan, M. J., Pennebaker, J. W., & Murphy, L. R. (Eds.). (1982). *Mass psychogenic illness: A social psychological analysis.* Hillsdale, NJ: Erlbaum.

Festinger, L., Schachter, S., & Back, K. (1950). *Social pressures in informal groups.* New York: Harper & Row.

Gans, H. (1962). *The urban villagers.* New York: Free Press.

Holahan, C. J., & Moos, R. H. (1981). Social support and psychological distress: A longitudinal analysis. *Journal of Abnormal Psychology, 49,* 365–370.

Holmes, T. H. (1956). Multidiscipline studies of tuberculosis. In P. J. Sparer (Ed.), *Personality, stress and tuberculosis.* International University Press.

Ingersoll, B., & Depner, C. (1980, September). *Support networks of middle-aged and older adults.* Presented at the meeting of the American Psychological Association, Montreal, Canada.

Lindheim, R., & Syme, S. L. (1983). Environments, people, and health. *Annual Review of Public Health, 4,* 1335–1359.

McFarlane, A. H., Neale, K. A., & Norman, G. (1981). Methodological issues in developing a scale to measure social support. *Schizophrenic Bulletin, 7,* 90–100.

Miller, P. M., & Ingham, J. G. (1976). Friends, confidants, and symptoms. *Social Psychiatry, 11,* 51–58.

Mishler, E. G., & Scotch, N. A. (1963). Sociocultural factors in the epidemiology of schizophrenia. A review. *Psychiatry, 26,* 315–351.

Newman, O. (1972). *Defensible space.* New York: Macmillan.

Patterson, M. L. (1976). An arousal model of interpersonal intimacy. *Psychological Review, 83,* 235–245.

Schachter, S. (1959). *The psychology of affiliation.* Stanford, CA: Stanford University Press.

Singer, J. E., Baum, C. S., Baum, A., & Thew, B. D. (1982). Mass psychogenic illness: The case for social comparison. In M. J. Colligan, J. W. Pennebaker, & L. R. Murphy (Eds.), *Mass psychogenic illness: A social psychological analysis.* Hillsdale, NJ: Erlbaum.

Stephens, R. C., Blau, Z. S., & Oser, G. T. (1978). Aging, social support systems, and social policy. *Journal of Gerontological Social Work, 1,* 33–45.

Tillman, W. A., & Hobbs, G. E. (1979). Social background of accident-free and accident repeaters. *American Journal of Psychiatry, 106,* 321–333.

Yancey, W. C. (1972). Architecture, interaction, and social control: The case of a large scale housing project. In J. F. Wohlwill & D. H. Carson (Eds.), *Environment and the social sciences: perspectives and applications.* Washington, DC: American Psychological Association, 1972.

CHAPTER 17

Policy Implications of Research on Social Support and Health*

Charles A. Kiesler

Introduction

This volume documents a wide variety of research and thought brought to bear on the general relationship of social support and health, both physical and mental. This chapter evaluates the policy implications of this work and outlines the research issues necessary for policy implementation. As I shall show, the current data are inadequate for even preliminary policy analysis, and even the most consistent findings in the literature do not lend themselves to conclusions at a level appropriate for immediate policy implementation.

The Policy Perspective and Issues

In this chapter I will stress top-down policy analysis, taking a national policy perspective that attempts to assess the following questions: What is the national problem for policy analysis? What is known scientifically that

*I thank Amy Sibulkin and the editors for helpful comments on an earlier version of this chapter.

347

can be applied to the problem? Can what is known be applied (that is, which specific legislative, regulatory, or value consensus actions could be taken)? What otherwise attractive policy alternatives need more research (that is, which policy questions still need to be answered)?

The general policy issues here relate to health and mental health. (Following the general usage in this book, I will use the WHO definition of health to include both health and mental health). Specifically, the policy issues rest on a potential and presumably positive relationship of social support to health. My very preliminary analysis of these issues led to the following nine policy questions. They do not provide an exhaustive list of policy issues, but do serve to open the discussion of the potential of the existing data base for public policy.

1. The first policy question is whether social support reduces (buffers) the impact of stress in ways that can be objectively measured and are socially desired. The buffering hypothesis implies an interaction between social support and stress in which social support lessens the negative impact of stress. If that is the proper scientific conclusion, then social support efforts in public policy should be directed toward groups under, or expected to be under, great stress. Is that the correct conclusion? Alternatively, does social support have only a positive main effect irrespective of level of stress? For example, does increased social support lead to fewer physical symptoms, less use of physical health resources (thereby decreasing the national medical bill), less incidence of specific costly national problems such as alcoholism and absenteeism, increased productivity in the workplace, less frequent mental hospitalization, or longer life?

Phrased in the terms of inferential statistics, does increased social support produce a positive main effect independently of level of stress? Further, does degree of social support interact with level of stress so that negative effects of high stress are reduced by increased social support? Only the latter represents the buffering hypothesis. It is important in this chapter that the reader keep the distinction between the buffering hypothesis and the hypothetical main effect for social support carefully in mind.

2. If the empirical data are consistent with the buffering hypothesis and/or a main effect for social support, is the effect causal? That is, can social support of individuals be increased, thereby increasing valued outcomes and decreasing undesirable ones across the board? A subsidiary part of this question is whether the methods of increasing social support are cost-effective, given the outcomes.

3. How does social support and its related guises such as self-help groups

relate to the effects now produced by professionals?[1] That is, does social support provided through, for example, a self-help group have an ameliorative effect on health and mental health problems similar to that provided by professionals? If it does have an effect, is the effect independent of professional services, or does the impact of social support and professional services interact in some way?

4. Can social support or self-help groups substitute for professional services? Can their effects be enhanced in some way by a more active involvement by professionals?

5. If social support reduces risk, what are the ways open to the public to increase social support to a very large population? For example, could reduced health and mental health insurance premiums for a group less at risk (presumably those high in social support) produce an effective incentive for individuals to increase their social support?

6. What are the demographic (race, age, and sex) differences in the amount and type of social support available and used? Obviously some groups are more at risk than others, but does a specific type and amount of social support vary in its availability, attractiveness, and effect for different groups? If so, which public policy alternatives would be fair and equitable across groups?

7. Does the current style of service provision facilitate or interfere with increasing social support and its impact on physical and mental health? That is, most health and mental health services are now delivered by private practitioners, with third-party payment; the professional essentially waits in a central place for a patient with a problem to come to him or her. Do some of the potential effects of social support relate to this essentially reactive style of service provision? If so, would more direct effects come through changing the method of service provision? In other words, are any effects of social support direct, or do they depend on a cold, reactive form of service provision? If the latter, would they still be observed in other forms of service delivery such as that involved in holistic health? That is, should public policy concentrate on increasing social support or changing methods or style of service delivery?

[1]It could easily be argued that mental health professionals routinely provide social support for their clients. However, that point is not germane to what follows in this chapter. From the policy perspective there is now a de facto system of mental and physical health care in place. My discussion assumes that as a given, and asks what is known about social support that would add to or substitute for the current de facto system. Investigators wishing to ask scientific questions about the effect of social support would certainly include potential effects by professionals. For policy questions, the defacto system is a given and questions are about effects at the margin.

8. Does social support have similar effects for both physical and mental health? What are the potential savings to be realized by enhancing social support?

These are actually very preliminary policy questions. Most, however, cannot be answered with the current data. Space limitations prohibit a literature review, but I will selectively choose some current data in order to consider some of these policy questions.

Public Policy and the Buffering Hypothesis

The most interesting aspect of the social support literature for public policy is probably the buffering hypothesis—that is, the hypothesis that social support acts as a buffer to reduce the potentially negative effects of stress and perhaps other negative environmental events. Although this is the most interesting hypothesis for public policy, it actually has the weakest empirical base in the social support literature, at least regarding policy issues. Let us consider for a moment why the buffering hypothesis should be so interesting for policy, and what the requirements for policy use are that the data (and theory) must meet.

If the buffering hypothesis were a valid representation of reality, then very useful public policy could be built. We could identify wide varieties of stress in the environment currently having negative effects, which society as a whole would wish to reduce. We could apply reliable methods of enhancing the social support of these groups at risk, thereby reducing the consequent negative effects, enhancing public satisfaction, and reducing public cost. This is a somewhat overly simplified description of public policy, but it is a useful pedagogical method for considering public policy alternatives.

To consider such public policies, policymakers should be able to: (1) identify reliably those varieties of stress consistently producing negative effects for subpopulations that could be described in detail and inexpensively identified; (2) describe methods of enhancing social support that are reasonably inexpensive and can easily be applied to very large populations at risk (e.g., new mothers, the widowed, or the unemployed); and (3) state precisely what the ameliorative effects are, the proportion of the population at risk they will be observed in, the relative cost-effectiveness of the policy, and the risks of negative unintended consequences of the policy.

The current state of the scientific literature on the buffering hypothesis does not allow us to be confident about meeting any of these requirements for policy implementation. Indeed, there is some controversy in the literature concerning the reliability (and/or validity) of the effect. Some investigators and reviewers have been quite positive (e.g., Broadhead *et al.*, 1983; Gottlieb, Chapter 15, this volume; Greenblatt, Becerra, Serafetinides, 1982; Leavy, 1983), whereas others have been fairly negative (e.g., Husaini, 1982; Wallston, Alagna, DeVellis, & DeVellis, in press).

The preceding discussion sounds like a critical and negative review of the scientific literature related to the buffering hypothesis. It is not. The reader must make an important distinction between the current scientific state of a field and its readiness for use in public policy. The buffering hypothesis is alive in scientific discussions and some progress is being made. For example, Cohen and McKay (1984), in a theoretically oriented article, positively reviewed the literature but pointed clearly to the need for a multidimensional view of the independent, dependent, and mediating variables involved in this line of research. I agree that research is progressing, but merely assert here that it is far from the point of easy adaptation for public policy use.

If the question is whether public policymakers can generally increase social support and thereby ameliorate the effects of stressful life events in the environment, the answer is clearly no. Even though some data are consistent with that hypothesis, the general array of data is sufficiently inconsistent (some even in the opposite direction) that a consistent public policy could not be considered.

Even if the data were consistent on the buffering hypothesis there would still be some problems in using this information for public policy. The data on the buffering hypothesis tend to be correlational in nature. It is instructive to consider alternative public policy programs as if they were independent variables in national experiments. Such a view raises special issues. For example, suppose there were a consistent correlation in the literature showing that people with high degrees of social support were less distressed by a negative life event than those with somewhat less support. This correlation could easily exist in the population without necessarily implying that an artificially or experimentally induced increase in social support would produce a consequent increase in the defense against negative life events. Thus, it is conceivable to consider arrays of data which would strongly support the buffering hypothesis, but which would not support any particular and direct public action capitalizing on the data. A somewhat different way of phrasing this issue is to say that policymakers could extrapolate from correlational research if they knew precisely why the correlation obtained. Because this is not known, further research is necessary prior to use of the correlation in policymaking.

Is There a Main Effect for Social Support?

Even though the interaction between social support and stress as demanded by the buffering hypothesis does not seem to hold consistently enough in the literature, the main effect for social support is still of interest in policy considerations. If increased social support consistently leads to decreased psychiatric and physical symptoms, then viable public alternatives could be considered. However, even here the data base is largely correlational in nature and, except under special circumstances (described later), experimental variations of social support probably would not consistently produce decreased physical or psychiatric symptoms. An example considered in some detail is the intriguing work of Berkman and Syme (1979). Berkman and Syme capitalized on a 1965 stratified systematic sample survey of Alameda County, California, housing units. In 1974 they collected mortality data for the intervening 9-year period. The various social support indexes had very powerful effects on subsequent mortality (controlling for initial health). For example, in the three age groups studied (30–49, 50–59, and 60–69 years) the proportion of married male respondents dying was approximately half that of the nonmarried. For both men and women, variables such as the degree of contact with friends and relatives and being a member of a church or another group independently had significant effects on mortality rates. House, Robbins, and Metzner (1982) reported similar effects for men in a 9–12-year follow-up of 2754 adults in the Tecumseh Community Health Study. "After adjustments for age and a variety of risk factors for mortality, men reporting a higher level of social relationships and activities in 1967–69 were significantly less likely to die during the follow-up period" (p. 123). In this case, however, even though the trends for women were similar they were much less significant.

Do these data have general policy implications that could be easily implemented? Perhaps, but closer inspection of the data suggests that the policy implications are somewhat limited. For example, House *et al.* broke down their data according to the degree of social relationships and contacts. The data are not uniform across the degrees and context of relationships. It appears from the data that, particularly for men, risk of mortality increased only at the extremely low levels of social relationships and contacts. Increasing social relationships and contacts beyond that minimum level did not lead to decreased mortality. Further, although the women generally had less incidence of mortality and more social contacts, they also did not show any decreased risk of mortality across a wide range of social relationships and contacts. It appears that the general result of decreased mortality through social relationships is specific to a group of men who have very few and very low quality social contacts and relationships. Consequently, a general public policy that enhances or increases the degree of social support for people in general would not be expected to decrease the risk of mortality throughout the population. Rather, it could be expected to decrease the risk of mortality only in a small segment of the population for one of the sexes. Further, given the usual methods of increasing social support, this subgroup of men would probably be least likely to make use of them.

Would Increased Social Support Decrease Psychiatric Symptomatology?

The relationship between social support and psychiatric symptomatology provides an example of some of the difficulties in extrapolating from current data to public policy. The hypothetical data depicted in Figure 17.1 are similar to those found by House *et al.* (1982): A negative relationship exists between social support and negative outcome, but the effects occur only for those very low in social support. Variations in social support beyond that minimal level do not have an effect on negative outcomes.

A budding policymaker might look at such data and conclude simply that a policy was needed specifically targeted to the population at risk, those very low in social support. Would that be reasonable? It can be argued that it is not reasonable to jump to a targeted public policy based on data such as those in Figure 17.1. The implied policy would run a substantial risk of either being ineffective or having negative consequences.

The same argument can be made irrespective of whether Figure 17.1 is based on prospective or cross-sectional data; the relationship of social sup-

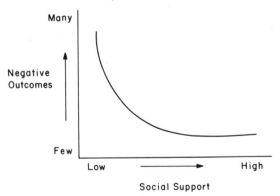

Figure 17.1. Hypothetical relationship in which such negative effects as psychiatric symptoms occur only at extremely low levels of social support.

port to psychiatric symptomatology can still be used as an example. The potential targeted group at risk is composed of people (generally males) with few or no social relationships. The implied public policy is to increase their social support in order to decrease their psychiatric symptomatology.

Generally it has been found in cross-sectional studies that people with little or no social support or social integration show more psychiatric symptomatology (e.g., Caplan, 1981; Gottlieb, 1981; Leavy, 1983). Would increased social support for these people in fact decrease their psychiatric symptomatology? Not necessarily. For example, an alternative explanation of those data is that people who show or will show severe psychiatric symptomatology are socially incompetent. They are people who can neither initiate or maintain the kinds of social relationships that public policy might consider increasing. Henderson, Byrne, Duncan-Jones, Scott, and Adcock (1980) carried out a study of the point prevalence of nine nonpsychotic psychiatric disorders in a systematic sample in Canberra ($N = 756$). They found that both attachment (affectionately close relationships) and social integration (more diffuse relationships) were negatively associated with neurosis. A lack of social relationships and social ties may indeed lead to psychiatric symptomatology, but it is also possible, even likely, that the same variables that produce the psychiatric symptomatology are the ones that lead to incompetence and inadequacy in initiating and maintaining close attachments and relationships. More colloquially, if these unfortunate people know how to have a friend, they would already have one.

The general point is related to causality, of course, but specifically the level of causality that directly affects potential public policy alternatives. If a lack of social support does not in some direct way *cause* (or otherwise directly influence) neurosis and other psychiatric symptoms, then increasing the level of social support may not have any effect on the psychiatric symptomatology.

The implied public policy may not have the intended positive effect on the targeted group. Further, under certain circumstances, it is conceivable that such increases artificially produced by outside forces could have a negative effect. For example, Tolsdorf (1976), while studying the coping and social support systems of schizophrenics, found that schizophrenic patients were not only reluctant to seek healthy relationships with relatives, they were also very hostile towards the relatives. This sort of hostility toward presumably close others appears to be general in schizophrenic populations. However, one obvious method of increasing social support is to increase contact with the immediate family. For this population, such a technique could produce a decided increase in psychiatric symptomatology and a consequent increase in the probability that some individuals would have to be hospitalized.

Figure 17.2 illustrates this possible consequence. It shows a social sup-

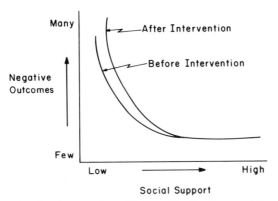

Figure 17.2. Results of a hypothetical intervention for the population described in Figure 17.1. Initial point of after-intervention curve is to the right of and higher than the initial point of the before-intervention curve.

port intervention producing a negative effect for those with initially little or no social support. After intervention those with no prior support showed even greater negative outcome (e.g., psychiatric symptomatology). At other levels of initial support, the hypothetical intervention produces no effect.

Figures 17.1 and 17.2 illustrate the need to be cautious when considering a special campaign or intervention with a specific subpopulation. For example, in considering the House *et al.* data it was suggested that the main effects found were concentrated in a group with little or no prior social support. One variation of such a conclusion is represented by Figure 17.1. A first reaction might be to concentrate the enhancement of social support specifically at that subpopulation. How good an idea that is depends on the answers to some other questions. In essence, it is necessary to know why the relationship in Figure 1 obtains in order to say (theoretically) why, and which type of, increased social support should lead to decreased negative outcomes. Otherwise, one unintended possible outcome suggested by these data on psychiatric symptomatology is that depicted in Figure 17.2. There, the effect of increased support, hypothetically at least, would lead to increased negative outcomes—quite opposite to what was planned by the policymaker.

The general point is that a lack of social support may not necessarily cause an increase in variable x (e.g., psychiatric symptomatology or morbidity), but rather the same variable that causes the lack of social support also is the cause of the other symptomatology. The area of psychiatric symptomatology is even more complicated, because the type of social support and when it appears must be considered. For example, Pattison, Llamas, and Hurd (1979) found that the mentally ill listed only about half as many people they were close to as did the nonmentally ill and also that the array of people they mentioned was much more homogeneous than that of the non-mentally ill. Others have found that a homogeneous social support network is best for handling a crisis in mental health but a more heterogeneous one works better in recovery (see Greenblatt *et al.*, 1982). The potentially positive and negative interactive effects are fairly clear, albeit complicated, for treatment.

Social Support and Active Treatment

I have reviewed the literature on treatment alternatives to mental hospitalization for seriously disturbed patients (Kiesler, 1982). More recently, in my reading of the literature on social support, I have been surprised to see the data on alternative treatments cited as evidence for the beneficial effects of social support. My own view is that alternative care is not evidence for the impact of social support and that, further, to interpret it as such is potentially seriously misleading. Let me explain why.

It is true that various forms of treatment alternatives to mental hospitalization depend heavily on social integration and support. Test and Stein (1976), for example, have repeatedly demonstrated that their Training in Community Living (TCL) program is an effective alternative to psychiatric hospitalization, even for chronically impaired patients. In this program treatment includes very direct and supportive instruction in the areas of employment and family interaction, interpersonal skills, leisure time skills, and various aspects of daily living. The site of treatment is usually where the patient is, whether it is at home, at work, or in leisure pursuits. The basic premise is to assume that the patient is deficient in skills for ordinary life and to attempt to train the patient directly in those skills within the environment in which the skills are used. Whether this is social support or active treatment or both, it clearly does work (see Kiesler, 1982, for a review of similar alternative treatment methodologies involving random assignment to condition).

The work of Test and Stein (and others) is germane to the criticism raised earlier that the correlation between the degree of social support and psychiatric symptomatology might well depend on the social incompetence of a subgroup of the population. The TCL program is designed less to increase the social support of the patient than it is to train the patient directly to be better able to relate to others and maintain social relationships (and hence social support). For the same theoretical reasons that this program does work, a direct increase of social support per se would not necessarily decrease psychiatric symptomatology (because the individual would still be incapable of maintaining the relationships).

The same point could be made regarding other alternative treatment modalities. For example, the work of Fairweather (1964) in treating schizophrenics is often cited in reviews of social support literature. Fairweather's lodge has been demonstrated to be effective and involves patients living together in the community. In the process of learning how to function effectively together, the patients theoretically become more interdependent, attend to and become more responsible for their own behavior, and learn the little things that allow functioning in day-to-day life. These are straightforward implications of Fairweather's theoretical understanding of schizophrenia. To call it social support as well, I would argue, adds little or nothing and, as a result of clouding the theoretical issues somewhat, may well impede scientific progress toward understanding the nature of schizophrenia.

These various forms of alternative care involve social support but they are not tests of it. Issues of both theoretical specificity and scientific generality underlie this discussion. By considering a highly technical form of psychiatric treatment to be an instance of social support, scientific advances in alternative care may well be retarded (by trivializing its complexities) and further understanding of the underlying mechanisms of social support may be inhibited (by needlessly confusing it with something it is not). Alternative initial assumptions of which is more general or complicated (alternative care versus social support) will inevitably lead to different scientific (and policy) directions. It is argued here that social support is involved in effective alternative psychiatric care, but alternative care is not a demonstration of the effectiveness of social support.

Social Support and Stressful Life Events

This section inspects the policy implications of the research literature on the use of social support in ameliorating the effects of particular stressful life events. The social support in these cases is time-bound and very specific to the particular life problem. These include effects such as that of widowhood, or of premature birth on mothers.

In general the notion of using social support concepts in developing intervention techniques to reduce the negative impact of time-bound life-stress events, is intuitively compelling. However, the actual literature on the subject is less compelling. Gottlieb (Chapter 15, this volume) has reviewed the literature and found few studies with minimal scientific criteria, such as random assignment to condition, a control condition (preferably also alternative treatment conditions), some theoretical statement of why (and which) effects should occur, and measurement specific to both the problem and society's goals. From a public health perspective, evidence of impact on more critical variables, such as reduced incidence of disease, lower medical costs, and reduced morbidity is desirable.

Some of the studies Gottlieb reviewed can be inspected with an eye to their public policy implications. A good study is that of Berkowitz, Kuipers, Eberlien-Frief, and Leff (1981), who effectively lowered the expressed emotion in families of schizophrenics. As expected on theoretical grounds, more patients in the treatment condition were well at follow-up than in the control. This is a study with some clear public policy implications. The outcome is important (percentage of patients well) and the results seem well grounded theoretically. A decent study with less clear policy implications is a study of widow's bereavement. Vachon, Lyall, Rogers, Freedman-Letofsky, and Freeman (1980) used a control and an experimental group consisting of a support group and one-to-one counseling (by another widow). They found the experimental treatment speeded adaptation. However, although desirable, speeding adaptation may not be sufficient impact for this technique to warrant broad adaptation. What does speeding adaptation mean and what is it worth in policy terms? Does it lead to increased productivity or reduced medical costs, for example? This study is reasonable but the policy implications are ambiguous.

Other studies seem to confuse the ultimate goals of an intervention with subgoals. For example, Minde, Schosenberg, Marton, Thompson, Ripley, and Burns (1980) reported successful intervention with parents of premature children, but did not measure the effects on the children themselves. If there is a public problem here, it is with the child, not the parent. Avoiding physical and psychological problems of premature children is very worthwhile and that is the public policy goal; behavior change of parents is only a subgoal. McGuire and Gottlieb (1979), in a study described as primary prevention, successfully intervened with parents of a first child. The kinds of effects reported show that physician time was certainly saved, but the child was not tested. The public policy question is what has been prevented? That same question could be applied to a study of D'Augelli, Vallance, Danish, Young, and Gerdes (1981) of a project to train community helpers. The treatment succeeded in changing the attitudes of the helpers somewhat, but there is no evidence that the potential recipients of the help benefited. In all of these studies the dependent variable is of interest, but cannot be regarded by itself as a valued public goal.

With some other referenced studies, the outcomes are as expected but the theoretical precision regarding social support is not clear. For example, Barrett (1978) studied the effectiveness of widows' therapy groups in facilitating change. In addition to a waiting-list control group, she had a self-help group, a confidant group, and a women's consciousness-raising group as variations to reduce the stress of recent widowhood. It is interesting that the most positive effect was produced by the women's consciousness-raising group. And, although all conditions produced higher self-esteem and significant improvements in ratings of future health, it is possible that the consciousness-raising group included more direct attempts to raise self-esteem, more direct training in handling awkward life situations, and more applause for assertiveness. On the other hand, the self-help group and the confidant group seem more typical implementations of what might be considered social support, but they were less effective. Put a different way, if assertiveness and self-esteem are the critical variables, perhaps they would have greater impact if enhanced directly rather than indirectly through social support (the extreme hypothetical case might be a computer course for assertiveness training). In any event, theoretical understanding of this study (and similar others) is rather limited and caution must be used about concluding that social support produced the effect.

These various studies are representative of this general area and are not unreasonable on scientific grounds. However, they are ambiguous with respect to public policy. On intuitive grounds, this area shows great promise. With respect to theory and data, however, the policy surface has barely been scratched.

In general, it might be expected that the more specific the life-stress problem and the greater the uncertainty of professional treatment (regarding such variables as information received or the feasibility of treatment), the greater the impact of social support interventions. These interventions have much going for them on theoretical grounds: the perceived similarity of the participants, the sense of sharing, information received and given, the knowledge that one's problem is not unique, distraction from a constant negative emotional state (e.g., depression or anger), and so forth. There are a host of such variables strongly implying that social support should have an effect. However, the most effective future interventions will depend on some theoretical understanding to maximize impact.

Information, Information Seeking, and Social Support

Naturally, the public policy implications of the social support literature depend on what is included in the definition of social support. That is obvious. Less obvious is that subtle but important distortions in potential public policies can be produced as well. Possible distortions can be seen when specific forms of psychiatric care (alternatives to mental hospitalization) are considered to be demonstrations of the policy implementation of the social support literature. (It was argued earlier that they were not). Another instance is the general area of the relationship of information and information seeking to physical and mental health.

The goal of this section is to separate on a theoretical level the effects of information per se from social support in general. This is done for two reasons: to provide a better theoretical understanding of these issues and to consider alternative implementations of public policy. For example, if the informational aspects of social support themselves both are critical (theoretically) and have an impact, public information campaigns (television and the like) may be more effective than any effort to increase social support more generally.

Let us first consider the more general areas of information, information gathering, and their relationship to physical and mental health in ways that may be independent of people per se (i.e., the "social" in social support).

The lack of effective communications is an important problem in the delivery of physical health services. Physicians do not effectively communicate to patients what their problem is, how routine or simple it is, how many others suffer similar complaints, what the medical regimen is, how the drug or other regimen will serve or ameliorate the complaint, how long it will take, or what the prognosis is. This leads to patients not following needed regimens, inappropriately using home remedies, worrying to the point of extreme psychiatric distress, or consulting another physician. Indeed, some have calculated the U.S. national cost of patients not following medical regimens alone to be about $30 billion per year (see Sackette & Haynes, 1976). Many, perhaps all, of these problems rest on a need for information.

At the same time, information needs are importantly related to psychiatric symptomatology as well. The patient is concerned with "What is wrong with me?" and specifically "Is my problem unique? Am I crazy?" The answers to the latter questions can often easily be given by a trained mental health professional ("the problem is common and can be solved"). It is not an unusual sequence for a person seeking psychiatric help to have gone through repeated consultations with various medical specialists, only to be told by each, "There is nothing wrong with you" or "It's all in your head" (or, perhaps worse, to be treated with inappropriate regimens).

This sequence probably accounts for some findings commonly observed in the literature. One is a characteristic peaking of medical use prior to mental health care (Kessler, Steinwachs, & Hankin, 1982; Tessler, Mechanic, & Diamond, 1976), and a second finding is a significant savings due to decreased physical health care following mental health intervention (Jones & Vischi, 1980). The latter is typically referred to as medical offset.

Simple information and information seeking are thus importantly related to both physical and mental health. Indeed, I have urged elsewhere (Kiesler, 1983) that the medical offset effects of psychotherapy could as easily be due to the reactive and uncommunicative forms of physical health care as to the effectiveness of psychotherapy per se.

The principal public health issues should include improving physicians' communications, sensitizing them to mental health problems, and involving mental health expertise more at the level of the primary physician. More and better quality information would have a significant impact on mental and physical health, the services associated with them, and their costs.

How does this relate to social support? It relates very clearly if information better delivered directly through public health campaigns and more effective professional communications are instead to be seen as potentially delivered indirectly through means of social support. For example, the provision of information was seen as psychological support by Cobb (1976) and as a subcategory of appraisal support by Pinneau (1975) (see Cohen & McKay, 1984, for further discussion of such definitional issues).

Cognitive information and public policy methods of enhancing it must be carefully distinguished from social support per se. Increased social support should typically increase information (and the exchange of information) regarding such things as health issues and practices, proper diet, and what to do in emergencies. Each could have a positive impact on health. However, friends give incorrect information as well as correct. Consequently, the policy analyst (as well as the therapist) should consider whether the information might be more effectively delivered independent of social support. Further, if information alone has a positive effect on physical and mental health, those effects should not be confused by concluding that they were due to social support. By conceptually beginning with a discussion of social support and working down to its presumed subcategories, such as information, investigators can easily draw rather distorted conclusions about the effects of social support and their implications for public policy.

Conclusions

This discussion has only scratched the surface of the relationship, real and potential, of public policy and research on social support and health. From the bottom-up view, this is an exciting scientific area. Clearly, progress is occurring briskly within each domain of investigation, and the number of such domains is also increasing at a rapid rate. A justifiable sense of intellectual excitement in the journals and at scientific meetings can be seen.

However, investigators adopting a top-down perspective and inspecting the demonstrated linkages to public policy with a critical eye will be struck immediately by the distance yet to go before useful policy implementation can be achieved. This concluding section will look at some overall research needs and point to some areas of particular promise.

One consistent methodological need regards the type of dependent measures. If a study is to be relevant to public policy, it must measure something of interest to public policymakers. For example, attitudes of parents, by and large, are not of interest to policymakers; enhanced health of children is. The substantial majority of studies in social support and health do not measure variables directly related to health policy. Indeed there is surprisingly little discussion in this literature of what current health policy is. Outcomes such as reduced system costs, lowered incidence of disease, reduced morbidity, less use of (and charges to) the physical health system, reduced insurance costs, and the like are of considerable national interest. Enhanced policy use of these data demands detailed attention to the selection of dependent variables.

Given a more appropriate selection of dependent variables, discussion can better be provoked regarding the cost-effectiveness and cost-benefit of social support interventions. Because U.S. national health policy is driven by an uneasy combination of medicine and health economics, data on cost-effectiveness are probably critical to consideration of policy changes.

Cost-effectiveness issues can probably best be explicated if research designs become more complicated. The number of true experiments in this area is not large, but in these few the design is typically an intervention versus a control condition. It is appropriate to detail in advance which specific goals are meant to be achieved by the intervention and then consider alternative techniques for teaching those goals. By including alternative intervention strategies in the same experimental design, conclusions are much more precise and the implications for public policy much clearer. Further, the isolated effects of one intervention technique should not be confused with the ease of implementation of the technique in a large population. Several techniques assessed in the same experimental design may assist in assessing potential ease of implementation. However, most work is not experimental in nature. It is typically very difficult to extrapolate from correlational work to public policy. Specifically, it is not clear in much of the work on the main effect of social support and in the buffering hypothesis that any positive effects would accrue as a result of increasing social support. That is the basic empirical question (for policy) in this field and it remains unresolved. If such effects could be reliably demonstrated, the reason why must be asked. That is the basic theoretical question of the field and it is largely untouched. Both questions need some specific answers before the policy implications become clear. Social support and health as a field of scientific inquiry is progressing very nicely, but the need for thoughtful policy-oriented research is very apparent. I emphasize that the two types of research are complementary, and one does not substitute for the other. Consequently, although I argue for policy research, I do not urge it at the expense of basic or applied research. Both are greatly needed.

References

Barrett, C. J. (1978). Effectiveness of widows' groups in facilitating change. *Journal of Consulting and Clinical Psychology, 46,* 20–31.

Berkman, L. F., & Syme, S. L. (1979). Special networks, host resistance and mortality: A nine-year follow-up study of Alameda County residents. *American Journal of Epidemiology, 109,* 186–204.

Berkowitz, R., Kuipers, L., Eberlien-Frief, R., & Leff, J. (1981). Lowering expressed emotions in relatives of schizophrenics. In M. Goldstein (Ed.), *New directions for mental health services: New developments in interventions with families of schizophrenics* (Vol. 12). San Francisco, Jossey-Bass.

Broadhead, W. E., Kaplan, B. H., James, S. A., Wagner, E. H., Schoenbach, B. J., Grimson, R., Heyden, S., Tibblin, G., & Gehlbach, S. H. (1983). The epidemiological evidence for a relationship between social support and health. *American Journal of Epidemiology, 117,* 521–537.

Caplan, G. (1981). Mastery of stress: Psychosocial aspects. *American Journal of Psychiatry, 138,* 413–420.

Cobb, S. (1976). Social support as a moderator of life stress. *Psychosomatic Medicine, 38,* 300–314.

Cohen, S., & McKay, G. (1984). Social support, stress and the buffering hypothesis: A theoretical analysis. In A. Baum, J. E. Singer & S. E. Taylor (Eds.), *Handbook of psychology and health* (Vol. 4). Hillsdale, NJ: Erlbaum.

D'Augelli, A. R., Vallance, T. R., Danish, S. J., Young, C. E., & Gerdes, J. L. (1981). The community helpers project: A description of a prevention strategy for rural communities. *Journal of Prevention, 1,* 209–224.

Fairweather, G. W. (1964). *Social psychology in treating mental illness.* New York: Wiley.

Gottlieb, B. H. (Ed.). (1981). *Social networks and social support.* Beverly Hills, CA: Sage.

Greenblatt, M., Becerra, R. M., & Serafetinides, E. A. (1982). Social networks and mental health: An overview. *American Journal of Psychiatry, 139,* 977–984.

Henderson, S., Byrne, D. G., Duncan-Jones, P., Scott, R., & Adcock, S. (1980). Social relationships, adversity and neurosis: A study of associations in a general population sample. *British Journal of Psychiatry, 136,* 574–583.

House, J. B., Robbins, C., & Metzner, E. L. (1982). The association of social relationships and activities with mortality: Prospective evidence from the Tecumseh community health study. *American Journal of Epidemiology, 116,* 123–140.

Husaini, B. A. (1982). Stress and psychiatric symptoms: Personality and social support as buffers: Special Editor's Comments. *Journal of Community Psychology, 10,* 291–292.

Jones, K., & Vischi, T. (1980). Impact of alcohol, drug abuse, and mental health treatment on medical care utilization: Review of research literature. *Medical Care,* (Suppl. 17, 12).

Kessler, L. G., Steinwachs, D. M., & Hankin, J. R. (1982). Episodes of psychiatric care and medical utilization. *Medical Care, 20,* 1209–1221.

Kiesler, C. A. (1982). Mental hospitals and alternative care: Non-institutionalization as potential public policy for mental patients. *American Psychologist, 37,* 349–360.

Kiesler, C. A. (1983). Psychology and mental health policy. In M. Hersen, A. E. Kazdin, & A. S. Bellack (Eds.), *The clinical psychology handbook.* New York: Pergamon Press.

Kiesler, C. A. (in press). Prevention and public policy. In J. C. Rosen & L. J. Solomon (Eds.), *Prevention in health psychology.* Hanover, NH: University Press of New England.

Leavy, R. L. (1983). Social support and psychological disorder: A review. *Journal of Community Psychology, 11,* 3–21.

McGuire, J. C., & Gottlieb, B. H. (1979). Social support groups among new parents: An experimental study in primary prevention. *Journal of Child Clinical Psychology, 8,* 111–116.

Minde, K., Schosenberg, N., Marton, P., Thompson, J., Ripley, J., & Burns, S. (1980). Self-help groups in a premature nursery—A controlled evaluation. *Journal of Pediatrics, 96,* 933–940.

Pattison, E. M., Llamas, R., & Hurd, G. (1979). Social network mediation of anxiety. *Psychiatric Annals, 9,* 56–67.

Pinneau, S. R., Jr. (1975). Effects of social support on psychological and physiological strains. (Unpublished Doctoral Dissertation, University of Michigan). *Dissertation Abstracts International, 32.*

Sackett, D. L., & Haynes, R. B. (Eds). (1976). *Compliance with therapeutic regimens.* Baltimore, MD: The Johns Hopkins University Press.

Tessler, R., Mechanic, D., & Diamond, M. (1976). The effect of psychological distress on physician utilization: A prospective study. *Journal of Health and Social Behavior, 17,* 353–364.

Test, M. A., & Stein, L. I. (1976). Practical guidelines for the community treatment of markedly impaired patients. *Community Mental Health Journal, 12,* 72–82.

Tolsdorf, C. C. (1976). Social networks, support, and coping: An exploratory study. *Family Process, 15,* 407–417.

Vachon, M., Lyall, W., Rogers, J., Freedman-Letofsky, K., & Freeman, S. (1980). A controlled study of a self-help intervention for widows. *American Journal of Psychiatry, 137,* 1380–1384.

Wallston, B. S., Alagna, S. W., DeVellis, B. M., & DeVellis, R. F. (in press). Social support and physical health. *Health Psychology.*

Author Index

Numbers in italics refer to the pages on which the complete references are cited.

A

Abbey, A., 293, 296, *299*
Abeles, R. P., 200, *212*
Abramis, D. A., 293, *299*
Abrams, N., 165, *172*
Aday, L., 37, *39*
Adcock, S., *21*, 77, *80*, 354, *363*
Adelberg, T., 35, 36, *40*
Ader, R., 167, *169*, 258, *259*
Aiello, J., 341, *344*
Ainlay, S. L., 13, *20*, 37, *39*
Ainsworth, M. D., 155, 156, 158, 162, *169*
Alagna, S. W., 15, *22*, 84, *108*, 281, 284, *302*, 351, *364*
Aldous, J., 141, *147*
Aldrich, C. K., 210, *212*
Alexander, E. S., 287, *300*, 316, *325*
Allen, C., 152, *173*
Allen, N., 165, *172*
Als, H., 154, 155, *170*
Altman, I., 63, *78*
Amenson, C. S., 66, 72, *81*
Anderson, R., 37, *39*
Andrews, F. M., 293, *299*
Andrews, G., 178, 179, *192*, 222, 228, 234, *238*, 271, *276*
Aneshensel, C. S., 118, *123*, 178, 179, *192*, 223, 228, 233, 234, *238*, 271, 275, *276*
Antonovsky, A., 163, *169*, 201, *212*, 241, 258, *259*
Antonucci, T. C., 7, 13, *20*, *22*, 52, *60*, 69, 75, *78*, 84, 94, 96, 99, 102, 104, *105*, *107*, 135, 141, *145*, 289, *300*
Aponte, H. J., 153, 166, *169*
Argyle, M., 62, 71, *78*
Arling, G., 138, *145*
Aronowitz, E., 316, *323*

Aronson, G., 187, *195*
Asher, S. J., 66, *79*, 188, *192*
Atchley, R., 206, 208, *212*

B

Babchuck, N., 135, 136, *146*
Back, K., 330, 331, 332, 333, 339, *345*
Baker, L. H., 319, *323*
Baldassare, M., 139, *146*
Bandura, A., 65, *78*
Banfield, E. C., 58, *59*
Barker, C. B., 63, 68, 70, 74, *78*, *79*
Barnard, K. E., 158, *169*
Barner, J., 30, *39*
Barrera, Jr., M., 13, *20*, 37, *39*
Barrera, M., 95, *105*, 289, 291, *298*
Barrett, C. J., 310, *323*, 358, *363*
Barron, N., 318, *326*
Bartrop, R. W., 259, *259*
Basham, R. B., 95, *108*
Baum, A., 97, *106*, 330, 336, 337, 339, 341, 342, *344*, *345*
Baum, C. S., 339, 341, *344*, *345*
Beard, J. H., 321, *323*
Beautrais, A. L., 165, *169*
Bebbington, P., 121, *124*
Becerra, R. M., 351, 356, *363*
Becker, J., 293, *300*
Beckwith, L., 158, *169*
Bedeian, A. G., 118, *124*
Bee, H. L., 158, *169*
Bell, R. A., 222, 228, *238*
Bell, R. Q., 157, *169*
Bell, W., 242, *259*
Belle, D., 54, *59*, 93, *105*, 177, 186, 187, 188, *192*, 296, *298*

365

Subject Index